THE SECRET HISTORY
1660–182

Secret history, with its claim to expose secrets of state and the sexual intrigues of monarchs and ministers, alarmed and thrilled readers across Europe and America from the mid-seventeenth to the mid-nineteenth century. Scholars have recognised for some time the important position that the genre occupies within the literary and political culture of the Enlightenment. Of interest to students of British, French, and American literature as well as political and intellectual history, this new volume of essays demonstrates for the first time the extent of secret history's interaction with different literary traditions, including epic poetry, Restoration drama, periodicals, and slave narratives. It reveals secret history's impact on authors, readers, and the book trade in England, France, and America throughout the long eighteenth century. In doing so, it offers a case study for approaching questions of genre at moments when political and cultural shifts put strain on traditional generic categories.

REBECCA BULLARD is a Lecturer in English Literature at the University of Reading. Dr Bullard is the author of *The Politics of Disclosure, 1674–1725: Secret History Narratives* (2009) and editor of *The Fair Penitent* and *The Ambitious Step-mother* for *The Plays and Poems of Nicholas Rowe* (2017).

RACHEL CARNELL is a Professor of English at Cleveland State University, Ohio. Professor Carnell is the author of *Partisan Politics, Narrative Realism and the Rise of the British Novel* (2006), *A Political Biography of Delarivier Manley* (2008), and co-editor of the five-volume *Selected Works of Delarivier Manley* (2005).

THE SECRET HISTORY IN LITERATURE, 1660–1820

EDITED BY
REBECCA BULLARD
AND
RACHEL CARNELL

CAMBRIDGE
UNIVERSITY PRESS

University Printing House, Cambridge CB2 8BS, United Kingdom

One Liberty Plaza, 20th Floor, New York, NY 10006, USA

477 Williamstown Road, Port Melbourne, VIC 3207, Australia

314–321, 3rd Floor, Plot 3, Splendor Forum, Jasola District Centre, New Delhi - 110025, India

79 Anson Road, #06-04/06, Singapore 079906

Cambridge University Press is part of the University of Cambridge.

It furthers the University's mission by disseminating knowledge in the pursuit of education, learning and research at the highest international levels of excellence.

www.cambridge.org
Information on this title: www.cambridge.org/9781316604908
DOI: 10.1017/9781316584132

© Rebecca Bullard and Rachel Carnell 2017

This publication is in copyright. Subject to statutory exception and to the provisions of relevant collective licensing agreements, no reproduction of any part may take place without the written permission of Cambridge University Press.

First published 2017
First paperback edition 2019

A catalogue record for this publication is available from the British Library

ISBN 978-1-107-15046-1 Hardback
ISBN 978-1-316-60490-8 Paperback

Cambridge University Press has no responsibility for the persistence or accuracy of URLs for external or third-party internet websites referred to in this publication, and does not guarantee that any content on such websites is, or will remain, accurate or appropriate.

Contents

List of Figures	*page* vii
Notes on Contributors	viii
Acknowledgements	xii

	Introduction: Reconsidering Secret History Rebecca Bullard	1

PART I   SEVENTEENTH-CENTURY ENGLAND

1	*Paradise Lost* as a Secret History Michael McKeon	17
2	Secret History and Seventeenth-Century Historiography Martine W. Brownley	33
3	Secret History and Restoration Drama Erin M. Keating	46
4	Secret History and Allegory David A. Brewer	60
5	Secret History and Amatory Fiction Claudine van Hensbergen	74
6	Secret History and Spy Narratives Slaney Chadwick Ross	87

PART II   EIGHTEENTH-CENTURY BRITAIN

7	Secret History, Parody, and Satire Melinda Alliker Rabb	103
8	Secret History and It-Narrative Rivka Swenson	117

9	Secret History, Oriental Tale, and Fairy Tale *Ros Ballaster*	134
10	Secret History and the Periodical *Nicola Parsons*	147
11	Secret History and Censorship *Eve Tavor Bannet*	160
12	Secret History and Anecdote *April London*	174
13	Secret History in the Romantic Period *Miranda Burgess*	188

PART III FRANCE AND AMERICA

14	Secret History in Pre-Revolutionary France *Allison Stedman*	205
15	Secret History in Late Eighteenth- and Early Nineteenth-Century France *Antoinette Sol*	216
16	Secret History in British North America and the Early Republic *Kevin Joel Berland*	229
17	Secret History in the Early Nineteenth-Century Americas *Gretchen J. Woertendyke*	242
	Epilogue: Secret History at the Start of the Twenty-First Century *Rachel Carnell*	256

Select Bibliography — 265
Index — 277

Figures

1 *Paradise Lost. A Poem in Twelve Books. The Author John Milton. The Third Edition. Revised and Augmented by the same Author* (London: Printed by S. Simmons, 1678). Osborn pb9. The James Marshall and Marie-Louise Osborn Collection, Beinecke Rare Book and Manuscript Library, Yale University. *page 63*
2 *Absalom and Achitophel. A Poem. The Third Edition; Augmented and Revised* (London: Printed for J.T. and Sold by W. Davis, 1682). PR 3416.A2 1682b. The Rare Books and Manuscripts Library, The Ohio State University. 70
3 *Absalom and Achitpohel. A Poem. The Second Edition; Augmented and Revised* (London: Printed for J.T. and Sold by W. Davis, 1681). PR 3418.A2 1681A. Special Collections Research Center, University of Chicago Library. 71
4 *Carlo, the Roscius of Drury Lane Theatre*. Hand-coloured aquatint, depicting the famous scene from *The Caravan*. The full print (width: 20.3 cm., height: 30.4 cm.) includes lines of verse below the image. Published in London (26 January 1804) by Laurie and Whittle. © Victoria and Albert Museum, London. 128

Notes on Contributors

ROS BALLASTER is Professor of Eighteenth-Century Studies in the Faculty of English, Mansfield College, University of Oxford. She has published widely in the field of eighteenth-century literature (including *Seductive Forms: Women's Amatory Fiction 1684–1740* (1992) and *Fabulous Orients: Fictions of the East in England 1662–1785* (2005)) and has particular research interests in women's writing, the novel, oriental fiction, and the interaction of prose fiction and the theatre. She has edited works by Delarivier Manley and Jane Austen.

EVE TAVOR BANNET is George Lynn Cross Professor of English and Women's and Gender Studies at the University of Oklahoma. Her monographs include *The Domestic Revolution: Enlightenment Feminisms and the Novel* (2000), *Empire of Letters: Letter Manuals and Transatlantic Correspondence 1688–1820* (2005) and *Transatlantic Stories and the History of Reading: Migrating Fictions 1720–1810* (2011). Previous essays on secret history include 'The Narrator as Invisible Spy' (2014) and 'Secret History: or Telling Tales Inside and Outside the Secretorie' (2006).

KEVIN JOEL BERLAND, Professor Emeritus of English and Comparative Literature at Pennsylvania State University, recently published a new edition of *The Dividing Line Histories of William Byrd II of Westover* (2013). He has published widely on various topics, including British and Early American literature, Socrates in the eighteenth century, physiognomy, and newspaper ballads. He is the founder and moderator of C18-L, the international, interdisciplinary online forum.

DAVID A. BREWER is Associate Professor of English at The Ohio State University and the author of *The Afterlife of Character, 1726–1825* (2005). He is currently completing a book on the uses to which authorial names were put in the eighteenth-century Anglophone world. His essay here is part of a new project devoted to rethinking the relationship between fictionality and reference in eighteenth-century literature, theatre, and visual art.

MARTINE W. BROWNLEY, Goodrich C. White Professor of English, is the Director of Emory's Bill and Carol Fox Center for Humanistic Inquiry. She has written or edited *Reconsidering Biography* (2011), *Clarendon and the Rhetoric of Historical Form* (1985), *Deferrals of Domain: Contemporary Women Novelists and the State* (2000), *Women and Autobiography* (1999), and various articles.

REBECCA BULLARD, Lecturer in English Literature at the University of Reading, UK, is author of *The Politics of Disclosure: 1674–1725: Secret History Narratives* (2009), and co-editor, with John McTague, of Volume 1 of *The Plays and Poems of Nicholas Rowe* Routledge (2017). Her research explores the intersections between literature, politics, book history, and gender during the seventeenth and eighteenth centuries.

MIRANDA BURGESS teaches English at the University of British Columbia. She is the author of *British Fiction and the Production of Social Order, 1740–1830* (2000) and essays on British and Irish Romantic topics such as Wordsworth, Austen, Scott, Owenson, Mary Shelley, nationalisms, mobilities, media, and form. Her current project explores ideas and forms of transport in medicine, technology, and Romantic poetics.

RACHEL CARNELL, Professor of English at Cleveland State University, is the author of *Partisan Politics, Narrative Realism, and the Rise of the British Novel* (2006) and of *A Political Biography of Delarivier Manley* (2008). She is the co-editor of the five-volume *Selected Works of Delarivier Manley* (2005) and the author of articles on Aphra Behn, Samuel Richardson, Eliza Haywood, Charlotte Lennox, Jane Austen, Anne Bronte, as well as several articles on secret history.

ERIN M. KEATING is Assistant Professor in the Department of English, Film, and Theatre at the University of Manitoba. Her research, which brings together Restoration theatre, secret history and affect theory, has been published in *Restoration* and the *Journal for Early Modern Cultural Studies*.

APRIL LONDON is Emeritus Professor of English at the University of Ottawa. She is currently Editor of *The Cambridge Guide to the Eighteenth-Century English Novel, 1660–1820*. In addition to numerous articles on eighteenth–century topics, she is the author of *Women and Property in the Eighteenth–Century Novel* (1999), *Literary History Writing, 1770–1820* (2010), and *The Cambridge Introduction to the Eighteenth–Century Novel* (2012).

MICHAEL MCKEON is Board of Governors Distinguished Professor of Literature at Rutgers University, New Brunswick. He is the author of *Politics and Poetry in Restoration England* (1975), *The Origins of the English Novel, 1660–1740* (1987) and *The Secret History of Domesticity* (2005), as well as fifty essays and articles. He is also the editor of *Theory of the Novel, A Historical Approach* (2000).

NICOLA PARSONS is Senior Lecturer in Eighteenth-Century Literature at the University of Sydney. Her first book, *Reading Gossip in Early Eighteenth-Century England* (2009), focuses on the secret history and the novel, considering texts by Delarivier Manley, Richard Steele, Daniel Defoe, and Jane Barker. She has published essays on the early novel, on Queen Anne's letters, Elizabeth Singer and John Dunton.

MELINDA ALLIKER RABB is Professor of English at Brown University and author of *Satire and Secrecy in English Literature 1650–1750* (2007). She has published on eighteenth-century writers including Swift, Pope, Defoe, Fielding, Sterne, Johnson, Richardson, Manley, Godwin, and on topics such as gender, material culture, and cognitive literary studies.

SLANEY CHADWICK ROSS teaches at CUNY Staten Island and Fordham University. She is completing a study on spy narratives and secret histories in the long eighteenth century.

ANTOINETTE SOL is Professor of French at the University of Texas at Arlington. She recently published three editions in the L'Harmattan series 'Autrement mêmes' in collaboration with Sarah Davies Cordova. They are currently working on a fourth project which will appear in 2017.

ALLISON STEDMAN is Associate Professor of French at the University of North Carolina at Charlotte. She has published articles on early modern French literary portraits, psalm paraphrases, novels and fairy tales, as well as on pedagogical strategies for teaching French and Italian literature and culture at the university level. With Perry Gethner, she is the co-editor and translator of *A Trip to the Country* by Henriette-Julie de Castelnau, Comtesse de Murat (2011). She is also the author of *Rococo Fiction in France 1600–1715: Seditious Frivolity* (2013; paperback 2014) and of a modern French edition of Murat's 1699 experimental novel, *Voyage de campagne* (2014).

RIVKA SWENSON is Associate Professor of English at Virginia Commonwealth University. Her first book, *Essential Scots and the Idea of Unionism in Anglo-Scottish Literature, 1603–1827* (2016), was published by Bucknell University Press in the series 'Transits: Literature, Thought & Culture 1650–1850'. Other recent work includes essays in *The Oxford Handbook of British Poetry, 1660–1800*, *The Cambridge Companion to British Women's Writing, 1660–1789*, and *The Cambridge Companion to 'Robinson Crusoe'*. She has recently co-edited, with Manushag N. Powell, a special issue of *The Eighteenth Century: Theory and Interpretation* ('Sensational Subjects'), and is co-editing, with John Richetti, an edition of Daniel Defoe's *The Farther Adventures of Robinson Crusoe*. She also co-edited *Imagining Selves: Essays in Honor of Patricia Meyer Spacks* (2009).

CLAUDINE VAN HENSBERGEN is Senior Lecturer in Eighteenth-Century Literature at Northumbria University, Newcastle-upon-Tyne. Claudine is a volume editor (Vol. 3, The Late Plays) of *The Plays and Poetry of Nicholas Rowe* (2017) and has co-edited two special journal issues on 'Queen Anne and British Culture, 1702–1714' (2014) and the eighteenth-century letter (2011). Claudine has published on wider research interests including Aphra Behn, Rochester and miscellany culture and public sculpture and is currently preparing a monograph on the courtesan in the literary marketplace.

GRETCHEN J. WOERTENDYKE is an Associate Professor and McCausland Faculty Fellow of English at the University of South Carolina. Her research and teaching focus on eighteenth- and nineteenth-century US literature, hemispheric studies, and theories of the novel. In addition to essays in collections on Haiti in the early US and the slave narrative before Frederick Douglass, she has published in *Early American Literature*, *Narrative*, and *Atlantic Studies*. Her book *Hemispheric Regionalism: Romance and the Geography of Genre* was published in 2016. She is currently working on a book titled *A History of Secrecy in the New World*.

Acknowledgements

We are grateful for the enthusiasm about secret history that was generated at roundtables in 2015 at conferences hosted by the American and the Canadian Societies for Eighteenth-Century Studies. Travel funding from Cleveland State University and the University of Reading enabled the editors to attend these conferences and make plans for the current volume. Many thanks to Paula Backscheider for her suggestion that we put together a volume of essays and to Kathy King for her encouragement. A Cleveland State University Faculty Scholarship Initiative grant in 2015 enabled further collaboration on this project. Thanks are also due to Erin Keating and the Alternate Histories Research Cluster at the University of Manitoba's Institute for the Humanities for inviting Rachel Carnell to deliver a lecture that touched on the ideas in the Epilogue; the discussion following that lecture in January 2016 was tremendously productive.

Both editors gratefully acknowledge Martine Watson Brownley's mentorship (and patience with us) as well as April London's expert editorial advice and prompt response to all queries. Thanks are due to Daniela La Penna and Sara Pozzato who helped with the cover image for this volume.

Chapter 1 first appeared, in very different extended version, in *Milton in the Long Restoration* (2016). We thank Oxford University Press for permission to reprint the small amount of overlapping material.

The editors would also like to thank Alison and Greg Lupton and Paddy, Clem, Louis, and Connie Bullard for their enthusiasm, support, and good humour along the way.

Introduction
Reconsidering Secret History
Rebecca Bullard

In 1674, a small octavo volume became the first work published in English to bear the title 'secret history'. *The Secret History of the Court of the Emperor Justinian* was an English translation of a French translation (*Histoire secrète de Procope de Césarée* (Paris, 1669), trans. Leonor de Mauger) of a Latin translation (*Arcana historia* (Lyon, 1623), trans. Nicolò Alemanni) of a Greek text: *Anekdota*, meaning 'unpublished [things]', by the sixth-century Byzantine historian, Procopius of Caesarea. Commentators across Europe expressed an immediate interest in this new form of history writing. In 1685, the French historian Antoine Varillas attempted to define it according to the model presented by Procopius and in contrast with orthodox neoclassical history. The orthodox historian, according to Varillas, 'considers almost ever Men in Publick', whereas the secret historian 'only examines 'em in private':

> Th'one thinks he has perform'd his duty, when he draws them such as they were in the Army, or in the tumult of Cities, and th'other endeavours by all means to get open their Closet-door; th'one sees them in Ceremony, and th'other in Conversation; th'one fixes principally upon their Actions, and th'other wou'd be a Witness of their inward Life, and assist at the most private hours of their Leisure: In a word, the one has barely Command and Authority for Object, and the other makes his Main of what occurs in Secret and Solitude.[1]

Secret history peers into secret spaces and allows its readers to see their rulers (and, later in the eighteenth century, a broader social range of subjects) in a metaphorical and literal state of undress. A kind of printed gossip, it soon became a target for critics, who attacked both its ethical and literary credentials.[2] The sustained popularity of secret history over the course of more than a century provoked critics who condemned these 'immodest Productions' as 'abusive Forgeries', *'Foolish Toys'*, and 'Libels'.[3]

It may have been easy to attack secret history on grounds of bad taste and bad faith but, as the essays in this volume show, the genre is nevertheless a complex historical form that demonstrates, over the course of a century, sustained and serious political engagement and a sophisticated awareness of its own rhetorical and literary characteristics. Secret historians from Procopius onward acknowledge that their revelations might 'seem neither credible nor probable', condemning them to be read as 'narrator[s] of myth' rather than writers of history.[4] But they also expose the failings of neoclassical 'perfect history', which prudishly and mistakenly prioritises the battlefield over the bedchamber in detailing the causes behind historical events.[5] They suggest that the 'secret springs' behind the visible events of history are part of a complex machine – that each revelation is 'a Wheel within a Wheel' which potentially exposes still more closely concealed secrets.[6] Writers including Aphra Behn, Delarivier Manley, Daniel Defoe, and Eliza Haywood (to name just a few of the better-known secret historians) elicit a range of responses – prurience, scepticism, fear, and outrage among them – as they re-plot familiar narratives of the past, often along partisan lines.

This volume of essays explores the relationships between secret history and other literary genres in Britain, and it sketches out the contours of secret history as it developed in France and America over the course of the long eighteenth century. This introduction to the volume delineates the genre at the moment of its emergence in Western literary culture during the later seventeenth century. It examines secret history's classical inheritance, its engagement with other kinds of contemporary polemical literature, and its connections with the European romance tradition. By outlining the key features of this form – still relatively unfamiliar, even within eighteenth-century studies – it helps to illuminate the ways in which writers within and outside the secret history tradition engaged with its literary conventions and political associations, which are the subject of the essays that follow.

Secret History from the Classical to Neoclassical Era

Written some time in the mid-sixth century, *Anekdota* offers a scurrilous reinterpretation of the characters and actions that were the subject of Procopius's earlier *History of the Wars of the Emperor Justinian*. While the *History of the Wars* highlights the personal and strategic prowess of the empire's leaders, *Anekdota* peers into cellars, closets, and bedchambers to reveal the personal and political weakness and corruption of the Emperor

Justinian and his General Belisarius. Both men, the secret history claims, committed outrages against their subjects while under the control of wives (the Empress Theodora and Antonina, respectively) who exercised tyrannical power through a combination of sexual and magical force. Procopius highlights *Anekdota*'s supplementary status by repeatedly referring readers back to his published texts, while insisting that, in those earlier narratives, 'it was not possible, as long as the actors were still alive, for … things to be recorded in the way they should have been', and that 'in the case of many of the events described in the previous narrative I was compelled to conceal the causes which led up to them'.[7] By keeping his *History* in view throughout *Anekdota*, Procopius emphasises the lasting power of historians to shape public interpretations of events – a power that they wield even over tyrannical, but transitory, rulers. 'For', as *Anekdota* puts it, 'what man of later times would have learned of the licentious life of Semiramis or of the madness of Sardanapalus and of Nero, if the records of these things had not been left behind by the writers of their times?'[8]

Yet at odds with this apparently powerful revelatory impulse is Procopius's decision to suppress his text at the moment when it was written because 'neither was it possible to elude the vigilance of multitudes of spies, nor, if detected, to escape a most cruel death'.[9] Indeed, so effective was Procopius's suppression that *Anekdota* remained unpublished, a 'secret' text, until it turned up in the Vatican library in the early seventeenth century. Early commentators noted a crux in the title of Nicolò Alemanni's 1623 Latin translation, which turned Procopius's Greek title, *Anekdota*, 'unpublished [things]', into *Arcana historia*, or secret history. Does the adjective 'secret' refer to Procopius's text, as well as to the events revealed in it?[10] In what sense can any published information really be described as a 'secret', since the act of publication itself necessarily undermines any claim to secrecy?[11] The model that Procopius bequeathed to later secret historians is a complex one. It suggests that secret history, apparently a genre designed to disclose secret intelligence, in fact involves acts of both revelation and concealment. The tradition of *roman à clef*, in which the identities of public figures are concealed under assumed names, offers just one instance of the ways in which later secret historians engage with a tension also evident in their ancient forebear.[12]

Responses to *Anekdota* in early modern Europe were as ambivalent as Procopius's text itself. Many commentators were outraged both by the Greek original and by Alemanni's Latin translation, condemning them in literary terms as low satire or gossip rather than history, and in moral terms as an affront to decency.[13] Not all commentators or translators emphasised this text's shocking characteristics. Several attempted to incorporate *Anekdota* into a neoclassical canon, publishing it in prestigious versions licensed by the state censor, and highlighting its continuity with the work of Roman historians including Plutarch and Suetonius.[14] Procopius's example may have disconcerted some early modern secret historians – even Antoine Varillas, his greatest champion, follows Procopius only 'seeing I cannot find any other Guide' to the genre – but it provided an important classical precedent for this apparently new historiographical tradition.[15]

The majority of writers who reworked *Anekdota*, however, saw it not as an antiquarian object of interest, but as a potent weapon in a literary campaign against the twin threats of 'popery and arbitrary government'.[16] In the wake of the Revolution of 1688–89 that brought William and Mary to the English throne, Whig supporters of the Revolution and a smaller and more clandestine group of writers in France used the genre to attack the regimes of James II, James's (dead) brother Charles II, and his (living and powerful) ally Louis XIV. Secret history became a means of asserting the end of one political era – that of the would-be absolutist Stuart kings – and the beginning of a new one under the mixed monarchy of William and Mary.[17] By exposing Stuart secrets, secret historians 'let all the World judg of the Furberies and Tyranny of those Times, and the Integrity, Sincerity, and Sweetness of Their Present Majesties Reign'.[18] Against the secrecy and silence of arbitrary power, secret history pits the publicity and populism of print.

Of course, secret history was not the only form of seventeenth-century polemical literature to demonstrate an ideological commitment to print. Fuelled by 'discoveries' of plots and counterplots, writers of all political persuasions participated in a public sphere characterised as much by suspicion and fear as by the rational exchange of opinions and ideas.[19] Polemicists opposed to a perceived threat of arbitrary government had discovered the propaganda value of publishing the secrets of those in power long before the first vernacular translations of Procopius. During the English civil wars and interregnum, the King's putative correspondence was made available for public inspection in texts such as *The Kings Cabinet Opened* (1645), which offered its readers 'certain packets of secret letters & papers, written with the Kings own hand, and taken in his cabinet at Nasby-Field, June 14. 1645' containing 'many Mysteries of State', and *Cabala, Mysteries of State* (1654), in which readers could find 'LETTERS of the great MINISTERS of K. James and K. Charles WHEREIN Much of the publique Manage of Affaires is related'.[20] When the secret historian

Introduction: Reconsidering Secret History

David Jones reflected in 1697 that '*there is a very engaging part naturally couched under such a method of bringing* State-Arcana's *to light, by way of* Letters, *which, in the very Notion of them carry something of Secrecy*' he was situating his own epistolary text within a seventeenth-century tradition of published opposition to a perceived threat of arbitrary rule.[21]

At the same time as they merged with and participated in an already well-established English polemical tradition, however, secret historians also drew on the more exotic set of literary conventions that constitute early modern romance. French *histoires amoureuses* and *histoires galantes*, which reveal noble characters in a state of undress, 'veiling' them only in Italianate or oriental pseudonyms, are very close relatives of *histoire secrète*.[22] Indeed, whether or not they were meant as reflections on particular characters in public life, many romances were read *à clef*, while others, published with an accompanying key, demanded this kind of referential reading practice that connects them with *anecdota*. Romance shares with secret history an emphasis on the importance of love as a controlling passion in public as well as private affairs, an interest in the private motivations behind public actions, and a commitment to exploring the most secret space of all: the interior world and the hidden passions and motivations of individual agents.[23] Whether they offer us a glimpse into private life through letters (as do the first two parts of Aphra Behn's *Love-Letters between a Nobleman and his Sister* (1684, 1685, 1687)) or through omniscient narration (as, for instance, in *The Secret History of Queen Zarah and the Zarazians* (1705)), romance-inspired secret history exploits the pleasures involved in putting minds as well as bodies on display. The opportunity to glimpse into private affairs – of rulers and of lovers – was politically effective because it aroused an affective as much as an intellectual response.

As the always-plural synonym for secret history suggests, *anecdota* embody multiplicity. In part, this is because secrets have a gossip-like tendency to grow and spread; secret historians uncover 'wheels within wheels' and new discoveries supplement one another. *Anecdota* are also plural, however, because, like so many other characteristically eighteenth-century genres, secret history is a mixed form, created by and through competing influences and impulses.[24] Alongside and in relationship with other eighteenth-century prose genres, including the fairy tale, the oriental tale, and the realist novel, secret history engaged in extended dialogue with the classical past, a wide range of European literary traditions (including traditions that seek inspiration outside Europe's borders), and domestic political contexts. From the classical exemplar of Procopius (a writer from

Caesarea working as an official in Byzantium) onwards, secret history displays the kind of hybridity and polyvocalism that Srinivas Aravamudan associates with Enlightenment Orientalism.[25]

And yet in spite (or perhaps because) of its hybridity, secret history's early modern commentators sought to delineate this genre for their readers. Several practitioners of the genre offer prefatory discourses on secret history as both a radical and neoclassical form of historiography: the self-styled 'Anecdoto-grapher', Antoine Varillas in his *Anekdota heterouiaka, or, The Secret History of the Medicis* (1686) as well as his translator, Ferrand Spence; the anonymous author of *The Secret History of the Reigns of K. Charles II and K. James II* (1690); David Jones, who edited the letters of a spy to create *The Secret History of White-hall* (1697); and John, Baron Somers in his *Secret History of the Lives and Reigns of all the Kings and Queens of England* (1702).[26] Perhaps the most incisive analyses of the genre, however, come from its detractors. Early assaults, like *The Blatant Beast Muzzl'd* (1691) – an anonymous invective against *The Secret History of the Reign of K. Charles II and K. James II* in particular, but by extension secret history in general – outline the form the better to undermine it. The characteristics of Enlightenment secret history that these commentators – both negative and positive – highlight might be summarised as follows:

- Secret histories make a claim, whether or not substantiated, to reveal secrets – hidden facts, concealed motives, and the mysterious operations of government – that will supplement and change their readers' perception of the recent past.
- They are iconoclastic, both towards those in positions of power, and towards orthodox or official historiography.
- They privilege the perspectives of marginalised and conventionally unreliable groups and individuals, including women (especially courtesans), spies and servants (especially treacherous ones), objects such as shoes and pennies and non-human animals like dogs, both as subjects and also as sources of intelligence.
- They often exhibit a high degree of self-consciousness towards the concept of secrecy, and the ethical and epistemological implications of claiming to reveal secrets.
- They manifest a deep interest in fragmentary forms of documentation – letters, incomplete manuscripts; anecdotes (in the later eighteenth-century sense of notable story, as well as the earlier sense of previously concealed information) – and a keen awareness of the implications of different forms of mediation: oral, manuscript, and print.

- They exist in proximity to and in relationship with non-literary, including non-written, forms of discourse such as news, partisan polemic, gossip, and scandal, as well as to recognisable literary genres including history writing and romance.

Secret history's most distinctive features make a number of demands of their readers, the most consistent of these being the demand that we keep more than one object in view as we read. Secret history asks us to compare the version of events that we think we know with the new one that it offers. It requires us to interpret romance names and to understand that an exotic island, a distant land or a fairy kingdom represents familiar territory such as France or England. It asks us to recognise the relationship between secret history and other genres and to collate the familiar with the strange. Secret history solicits what we might think of as 'transverse' reading practices. These texts ask us to read *across* boundaries: between texts, literary traditions, cultures, and geographical territories. They require us to treat secret history as a genre that has a set of recognisable and distinctive conventions and characteristics, but also to recognise that those conventions and characteristics generate close relationships between secret history and other, related species of discourse. Like many genres that developed during this period, then, secret history responds better to a 'both/and' approach to generic characteristics than to an approach that seeks to impose rigid boundaries around its representative formal features.

The Aims of this Volume

The past twenty-five years have witnessed a growing recognition of both the sophistication and complexity of secret history, and also of its importance to eighteenth-century political, intellectual, and literary culture. A number of recent publications, including brilliantly concise essays by Eve Tavor Bannet and Peter Burke, delineate the genre, emphasising its distinctive characteristics and making a bid for its coherence as a recognisable form of Enlightenment historiography.[27] Some studies situate secret history within the frenzied partisan struggles of the late seventeenth and early eighteenth centuries, highlighting its importance to liberal or Whig writers and its appropriation by their conservative or Tory opponents.[28] Others explore secret history's longer trajectory, as a form that both predates and survives the particularly fraught political atmosphere that prevailed from the late 1670s until the late 1710s. According to Michael McKeon, for instance, secret history both facilitates and indexes the emergence of separate domains of public and private over the course of the early modern period and the eighteenth century – a process of separation that, for McKeon, characterises modernity itself.[29] Secret history's literary and political characteristics continue to have resonance well beyond the particular political moment that first engendered the form.

As a genre that straddles and interrogates the boundary between fictional and historical modes of writing, secret history has been particularly important within analyses of both the early novel and eighteenth-century history writing.[30] Research in these overlapping areas highlights the peculiar challenges that secret history poses to its near relatives, including realist fiction and neoclassical history. Like Tacitean historiography, secret history explores the motives of those in power and the mechanisms of government. Unlike its more respectable counterpart, however, it identifies those motives in sexual desire and the mechanisms of government in backstairs intrigue, and consequently accords significant political power to female agents.[31] The exploration of hidden motives, intimate physical spaces and female agents connects secret history to simultaneous developments in 'realist' fiction, but at the same time it retained a strong interest in the fantastic and the exotic and in monarchs and ministers as well as their mistresses and servants. Some recent analyses of the form contend that secret history was 'erased' and 'overwritten' by realist fiction over the course of the eighteenth century; others emphasise its ongoing resonance as an alternative tradition that implicitly and sometimes explicitly challenges the domestic or national novel.[32] Scholarly debates, as well as the primary texts themselves, reveal the power of secret history to resist and disrupt neat taxonomical categories and critical shorthands – ancients v. moderns, realism v. romance, the rise of the novel, and so on. Just as secret history directed its iconoclastic energy against orthodox or public history in the late seventeenth century, so research on secret history today challenges some of the teleological assumptions, critical categories and norms that can structure our consideration of eighteenth-century literary culture.

The essays in this volume adopt a range of critical approaches to their central subject. Taken together, they reveal the ways in which secret history moves through and across wide tracts of generic, cultural, and also territorial terrain over the course of the eighteenth century. Part I focuses on the period during which secret history emerged in England, up to and including the 1690s when, following the Williamite revolution, secret histories of the Stuart and Bourbon courts proliferated rapidly. This section investigates the relationships between secret history and other genres – including close relatives, such as spy narratives and amatory fiction and also more culturally distant forms, such as heroic poetry and Restoration drama. Part II addresses eighteenth-century Britain when, as the febrile political and literary culture that had fostered secret history gradually cooled, the conventions of secret history began to be deployed inventively in different partisan and also non-partisan contexts. Even as it became less strongly rooted in polemical discourse, the fact that this genre privileges the voices and perspectives of marginalised groups and individuals gave secret history an inherently subversive political bent. Its self-conscious interest in peering into postbags and closets, in anecdotes (in the sense of both secret intelligence and personal stories), and in narration 'from below' enable it to cross-fertilise with other traditions – adapting and hybridising even as it remains a visible form in its own right. Part III explores the ways in which secret history travelled across geographical terrain by focusing on two countries – France and America – with a tradition of producing secret history that was both related to and distinct from that of the British Isles. These essays reveal that secret history's partisan and literary characteristics developed through an international network of texts and ideas, even as they responded to national and domestic concerns and priorities.

The essays in this volume suggest that, although secret history interacted with many generic traditions over the course of the eighteenth century, the nature of those interactions varied considerably one from another as writers responded to secret history's characteristics in a range of ways. Essays by Nicola Parsons on periodicals and Claudine van Hensbergen on amatory fiction, for instance, emphasise secret history's interest in sex and scandal as well as its self-conscious approach to the temporality of revealing secrets. Parsons demonstrates that the absorption of tropes from secret history in periodicals sexualised the serial nature of this kind of publication, while van Hensbergen argues that Aphra Behn deliberately sought to distance political secret history from amatory fiction during the first two parts of the serially-published *Love-letters between a Nobleman and his Sister* in order to 'stag[e] their subsequent collision in the work's final volume' (77). Secret history's association with sexuality could be used, it seems, to generate new kinds of reading pleasure based on novelty and revelation but also – as Erin Keating's essay on Restoration drama demonstrates – to create an impression of affective intimacy between celebrities and their audiences. These essays suggest, then, that since early readers of secret history responded to this genre's key tropes in complex and varied ways, we too should recognise and respond to their nuances in our analysis of this tradition and its legacy.

The complexity of secret history becomes apparent not only in its relationships with other genres but also, as many essays in this collection demonstrate, in its self-conscious approach towards its own conventions and characteristics. Several essays, including those by April London and Allison Stedman, reflect on evolving responses to and uses of anecdote (a synonym for secret history at the start of the century, a stand-alone human interest story by its end) as a flexible narratological tool that allows authors to engage with secret history even as they address apparently domestic or orthodox historical concerns. Others focus on the attention that secret history directs towards its own narrating subjects – spies in the case of Slaney Chadwick Ross's essay, coins and dogs in Rivka Swenson's. Secret history in this vein asks its readers to consider the ethical, epistemological, and phenomenological implications of making a claim to reveal secrets – often to the extent that it knowingly challenges the reliability of its own revelations. In an essay that situates this genre within the broader tradition of history writing in early modern England, Martine Brownley argues that secret history's sceptical, self-reflexive tendency is its hallmark: 'the primary authority that secret history destabilized', she asserts, 'was its own' (41). It is surely significant that the double-voiced parodies of secret history which form the focus of Melinda Rabb's essay in this collection externalise many of the self-conscious tendencies that secret histories themselves exhibit.

Because of its complex relationship with other genres and its self-conscious approach towards its own generic characteristics, secret history trained its readers in new forms of textual engagement. Many of the essays in this collection take as their subject the transverse reading practices that secret history encourages. Michael McKeon, for instance, reads across different generic traditions – secret history, heroic poetry, sacred scripture – to suggest that even texts not usually designated *anecdota* (like *Paradise Lost*) nonetheless elicit methods of reading that are also associated with this genre, while David Brewer pays attention to tensions between allegorical designations and their 'secret' extra-textual referents. Brewer's essay, as well as those by Eve Tavor Bannet and Ros Ballaster, draws attention to the difficulties and dangers that, as contemporaries were well aware, attends any attempt to read for secrets. Bannet and Ballaster suggest two quite different ways in which secret historians and their readers responded to these difficulties. Bannet (like Keating in her essay in this volume) highlights the affective closeness and reliance on a shared common sense that secret historians attempted to develop with

Introduction: Reconsidering Secret History 11

their readers; Ballaster, however, argues that secret history inculcates in its readers a form of radical scepticism as it reveals the 'fantasmatic basis of all [political] power' (135). These essays, along with the earlier work of Nicola Parsons, Erin Keating, and Kate Loveman, demonstrate the multiplicity of ways in which a secret history contributed to the history of eighteenth-century reading.[33]

Secret history may have been fostered by the particular political and cultural conditions of late seventeenth- and early eighteenth-century England, but the essays in this volume demonstrate that it was remodelled in a much wider range of geographical and cultural contexts than a narrow focus on this partisan one would reveal. Ros Ballaster and Miranda Burgess show that writers of secret history in England adapted the form in response to the very different prevailing political conditions of, respectively, the mid-eighteenth century and the turn of the nineteenth. The final set of essays in the volume, by Allison Stedman, Antoinette Sol, Kevin Joel Berland, and Gretchen Woertendyke, explore secret history's intervention in political cultures outside the British Isles. Stedman and Sol trace the political uses of the form both in the *ancien régime* and in revolutionary France. Berland and Woertendyke uncover the secret history of this genre in eighteenth and nineteenth-century America. These essays explore the interaction of secret history with a range of genres from history, romance, and *libelles* in France to journalism, novels, and slave narratives in America. They offer a glimpse of the ways in which secret history mediates both domestic and international literary and political networks over a century of revolution.

As Rachel Carnell's epilogue to this volume points out, secret history continues to thrive in the twenty-first century, taking on new forms in the electronic public sphere. By returning to the moment of its emergence in British, French, and American culture, we hope that this collection of essays helps to uncover previously overlooked aspects of our literary and political past. As it re-evaluates secret history over the course of the long eighteenth century, it aims to reveal 'the Secret Springs and real Causes from whence so many strange and various Effects', not to mention texts, 'have proceeded'.[34] But, like good secret historians, we know that any claim to reveal previously hidden information is liable to open up further revelations, and we acknowledge that, in this field of studies, 'many secret Histories are yet behind untold, which it were very useful to have made known' – even that 'there are yet several large Fields that are not mentioned, or entred into'.[35]

Notes

1. Antoine Varillas, *Anekdota Heterouiaka. Or, The Secret History of the House of Medicis*, trans. Ferrand Spence (London, 1686), a4v–a5r.
2. Attacks began to appear immediately after the first, Latin translation. They include Thomas Ryves, *Imperatoris Iustiniani defensio aduersus Alemannum* (Londini [London], 1626); René Rapin, *Instructions for History, with a Character of the Most Considerable Historians Ancient and Modern*, trans. J. Davies (London, 1680), 54–5; and N. N., *The Blatant Beast Muzzl'd: or, Reflexions on a Late Libel, entituled, The Secret History of the Reigns of K. Charles II and K. James II* ([London], 1691).
3. N. N., *Blatant Beast Muzzl'd*, A7v–A8r, A9r.
4. Procopius, *Anecdota or Secret History*, trans. H. B. Dewing (London: Heinemann, 1935), 5.
5. As Varillas puts it, 'there's no kind of Slavery greater, for an Anecdoto-grapher, than to be ty'd to tell the truth in all its Circumstances, ev'n when he handles the nicest matters' (*Anekdota Heterouiaka*, a2v). On 'perfect history', see Robert Mayer, *History and the Early English Novel: Matters of Fact from Bacon to Defoe* (Cambridge: Cambridge University Press, 1997), 22, 26.
6. Daniel Defoe, *The Secret History of the October Club; From its Original to this Time*, 3 parts (London, 1711), 1:56.
7. Procopius, *Anecdota*, 3.
8. Procopius, *Anecdota*, 7.
9. Procopius, *Anecdota*, 3.
10. François de la Mothe le Vayer suggests that 'the title *Anecdotes* shows that this is a secret work and that its author did not want [his name] to be revealed' ['Le nom d'*Anecdotes* monstre que c'est un travail secret, & que son Auteur ne vouloit pas estre divulgué'] (*Oeuvres*, 2 vols. (Paris, 1662), 1:356).
11. When Ferrand Spence worries that 'some will, perhaps, carp at me, for calling my Traduction a Secret History, whereas the Original had already made the matter Publick' (*Anekdota Heterouiaka*, A7v) he points towards the difficulty of calling any information that has already reached the public domain a secret. See also Ros Ballaster's essay, below 134–46.
12. For more on the ways in which *roman à clef* negotiates both revelation and concealment, see David Brewer's essay, below 60–73.
13. See Ryves, *Imperatoris Iustiniani defensio*, 9–10, and Rapin, *Instructions for History*, 54–5.
14. The French translation by Leonor de Mauger is published alongside the rest of Procopius's output, 'avec Privilège' (*Histoire secrète de Procopie de Césarée* (Paris, 1669)). Antoine Varillas insists that the secret historian 'cannot dispence himself from any of the Rules that *Aristotle, Cicero, Plutarch* and other the Masters of th'Art have so judiciously prescrib'd for Publick History' (*Anekdota Heterouiaka*, a1v). The author of *The Secret History of the Reigns of K. Charles II. and K. James II* ([London], 1690) implicitly compares himself to Suetonius in the Preface to this work (A2r). Ferrand Spence affirms that

Introduction: Reconsidering Secret History 13

Varillas is a neoclassical author who 'has the Gravity of *Livy*, the Politeness of *Salust*, the Policy of *Tacitus*' (Varillas, *Ankedota Heterouiaka*, A5v).
15 Varillas, *Anekdota Heterouiaka*, a1v.
16 Annabel Patterson, *Early Modern Liberalism* (Cambridge: Cambridge University Press, 1997), 153–281.
17 Rebecca Bullard, *The Politics of Disclosure: Secret History Narratives, 1674–1725* (London: Pickering & Chatto, 2009), 45–62.
18 *Secret History of the Reigns of K. Charles II. and K. James II*, A2v.
19 Rachel Weil, *A Plague of Informers: Conspiracy and Political Trust in William III's England* (New Haven: Yale University Press, 2013); Mark Knights, *Representation and Misrepresentation in Later Stuart Britain: Partisanship and Political Culture* (Oxford: Oxford University Press, 2005).
20 *The Kings Cabinet opened: or, certain packets of secret letters & papers, written with the Kings own Hand, and taken in his Cabinet at Nasby-Field, 14 June 1645* (London, 1645), title page; *Cabala, Mysteries of State* (London, 1654), title page.
21 Jones, *Secret History of White-Hall*, A6r.
22 Texts in this vein include, most famously, Roger de Bussy-Rabutin's *Histoire amoureuse des Gaules* (Liège, 1665), but also Claude Vanel, *Galanteries des rois de France* (Bruxelle [Brussels], 1694), Charlotte Caumont de la Force, *Anecdote galante et secrète de la duchesse de Bar* (Amsterdam, 1709), and Anthony Hamilton, *Mémoires de la vie du comte de Grammont* (Cologne, 1713).
23 On the persistence of romance in seventeenth- and eighteenth-century literary culture, see Michael McKeon, *The Origins of the Eighteenth-Century Novel, 1600–1740* (Baltimore: Johns Hopkins University Press, 1987) and Ros Ballaster, *Seductive Forms: Women's Amatory Fiction from 1684–1740* (Oxford: Clarendon Press, 1992).
24 On mixed genres, see Michael McKeon, *The Secret History of Domesticity: Public, Private and the Division of Knowledge* (Baltimore: Johns Hopkins University Press, 2005), 388–435, and Kathryn R. King, 'Genre crossings', in *The Cambridge Companion to Women's Writing in Britain, 1660–1789*, ed. Catherine Ingrassia (Cambridge: Cambridge University Press, 2015), 86–100.
25 Srinivas Aravamudan, *Enlightenment Orientalism: Resisting the Rise of the Novel* (Chicago: University of Chicago Press, 2011), especially Chapter 5.
26 Varillas, *Anekdota Heterouiaka*, A3r–A8v, a1r–d4r; *Secret History of … K. Charles II and K. James II*, A2r–v; Jones, *Secret History of White-hall*, A3r–A8r; John Somers, *True Secret History of the Lives and Reigns of all the Kings and Queens of England* (London, 1702), A2r–A3v.
27 Eve Tavor Bannet, '"Secret History": Or, Talebearing Inside and Outside the Secretorie', in *The Uses of History in Early Modern England*, ed. Paulina Kewes (San Marino: Huntington Library, 2006), 367–88; Peter Burke, 'The Rise of "Secret History"', in *Changing Perceptions of the Public Sphere*, eds. Christian J. Emden and David Midgley (New York and Oxford: Berghahn Books, 2012), 57–72.

28 Patterson, *Early Modern Liberalism*, 153–281; Bullard, *Politics of Disclosure*; Parsons, *Reading Gossip*.
29 McKeon, *Secret History*, 469–659.
30 On secret history as a form of history writing, see Mayer, *History and the Early English Novel*, 94–112; Gallagher, *Historical Literatures*, 63–110; Rivka Swenson, 'History' in Ingrassia (ed.) *Cambridge Companion to Women's Writing*, 135–46; on secret history and the novel see Ballaster, *Seductive Forms*; McKeon, *Origins of the English Novel*, 54–61, and *Secret History of Domesticity*, 621–59; William Warner, *Licensing Entertainment: The Elevation of Novel Reading in Britain, 1684–1750* (Berkeley: University of California Press, 1998), 1–127; Rachel Carnell, 'Slipping from Secret History to Novel', *Eighteenth-Century Fiction* 28:1 (2015), 1–24. Analyses of secret history often situate this form outside familiar genres such as 'history' or 'the novel'. Alison Conway explores secret history as a form of courtesan narrative in *The Protestant Whore: Courtesan Narrative and Religious Controversy in England, 1680–1750* (Toronto: University of Toronto Press, 2010), 80–109, and Srinivas Aravamudan highlights secret history's relationship to other forms of Enlightenment Orientalism (*Enlightenment Orientalism*, 202–29).
31 Although he attacks secret history because of its emphasis on sexual motivation, René Rapin acknowledges that 'perfect history' (i.e., history that explains the motives behind and reasons for public actions, including Tacitean history) is designed to 'excite the Curiosity of men' by revealing 'secret Springs and Resorts' – an analysis that suggests the proximity of secret history and other forms of neoclassical perfect history (Rapin, *Instructions for History*, 59).
32 Warner, *Licensing Entertainment*, represents the former position, Ballaster, *Seductive Forms*, and Aravamudan, *Enlightenment Orientalism*, the latter.
33 Nicola Parsons, *Reading Gossip in Early Eighteenth-Century England* (Basingstoke and New York: Palgrave Macmillan, 2009); Erin Keating, 'In the Bedroom of the King: Affective Politics in the Restoration Secret History', *Journal for Early Modern Cultural Studies* 15:2 (2015), 58–82; Kate Loveman, *Reading Fictions, 1660–1740* (Aldershot: Ashgate, 2008), 109–26.
34 Somers, *True Secret History*, 1.
35 Daniel Defoe, *The Secret History of the White-Staff*, part 3 (London, 1715), 27, 80.

PART I

Seventeenth-Century England

I

Paradise Lost *as a Secret History*

Michael McKeon

Heroic Poetry

Milton and his contemporaries speak less often of 'epic' than they do of 'heroic poetry', a relatively recent synthesis that bespeaks a reflexive element of formal self-consciousness. The ease with which modernity attributes antithetical contents and forms to twelfth-century epic and romance was alien to medieval thinking.[1] Even when Renaissance scholars began to apply the formal standards of Aristotelian epic to romance and to find romance wanting, the result was not a definitive separation but rather the elaboration of the category 'heroic poetry' in which the best of epic and romance might stand together.[2] By the seventeenth century, readers were becoming increasingly preoccupied with a primarily content-based tension between romance and epic unstably schematized as one between personal love and public warfare. After the Restoration this heroic nexus was chronically suspect, its elements self-consciously distinguished although not yet fully separated. So the experimental work of heroic poetry was to confront the emergent, modern opposition between epic warfare and romance love with the more traditional, but increasingly archaic, view of them as unequal versions of each other. But the parodic recollection of the tradition was mandatory if the modern confrontation was to be achieved. Only when war and love are experimentally separated out from each other can their conjunction be perceived and criticized as a gross incompatibility rather than experienced more or less tacitly, as in tradition, as a unified whole.

In a more extended essay I have read *Paradise Lost* (1667, 1674) alongside several long narratives, published between 1663 and 1687, by Samuel Butler, John Bunyan, John Dryden and Aphra Behn.[3] None of these narratives are even broadly categorized as epics. Rather, like *Paradise Lost*, they show the influence of several experimental, mixed forms that flourished during the Restoration period – some of traditional standing, some emergent, some momentary and occasional. My concern in that essay is not to show Milton's influence on these other authors but to show their common formal enterprise, to disclose Milton working among his contemporaries. In keeping with the specific generic concern of this volume, I will concentrate my attention on *Paradise Lost* as a secret history, although I will attribute at least part of this form's appeal to the reconception it offers Milton of the dilemma set by another genre with which he experiments, heroic poetry. To sharpen the focus of my reading, but also to keep it within bounds I will limit my comparison of *Paradise Lost* to a single contemporary text: Behn's *Love-Letters Between a Nobleman and His Sister* (1684, 1685, 1687).

The entire narrative of *Paradise Lost* is what Christian theology calls an 'accommodation' of the spiritual realm to materiality, of divinity to humanity. Accommodation had been controversial from the Church Fathers onward. In his best-known statement Milton's position was straightforward and clear: 'our understanding cannot in this body found itselfe but on sensible things, nor arrive so cleerly to the knowledge of God and things invisible, as by orderly conning over the visible and inferior creature.'[4] Yet the texture of *Paradise Lost* is shot through with apprehensions that its bold accommodations are at best erroneous and at worst blasphemous.

Like *Paradise Lost*, *Love-Letters* is structured as a signifying relationship between one realm and another. Unlike *Paradise Lost*, its aim is to signify not spirit by 'sensible things' but political actuality by amatory romance.[5] In systematically alluding to contemporary politics, Behn – ten years after the twelve-book version of *Paradise Lost* was published – picks up chronologically where Dryden's *Absalom and Achitophel* (1681) leaves off, narrating the period from 1683 to 1685, in which Dryden's Absalom (James, Duke of Monmouth) continues to be a central figure. *Love-Letters* begins in epistolary mode but modulates to a third-person narration in which letters are plentifully embedded. Although not a poem, Behn's narrative is preoccupied with the hallmark question of heroic poetry: are war and love compatible? Political allegory aims both to conceal and to reveal, setting signifier and signified apart in the very act of semantic association. Soon after she begins Behn's narrator claims that '*'tis not my business here to mix the rough relation of a War with the soft affairs of Love …*' (10). But her insistence that the two are actually entailed in each other goes well beyond the merely structural logic of allegorical signification.

True, the amatory affairs and stock Italianate names give Behn's plot a perfunctorily 'low' romance flavor. But these fictions stand for players actually involved in the high politics that succeed the Exclusion Crisis and that eventuate in warfare between Monmouth and the king's forces. Nor are they really fictions: Behn's literal plot centers on the seduction of a lady by her brother-in-law, Philander, a figure for Lord Grey of Wark and a master of libertine opportunism, who as one of Monmouth's main supporters is also a master of protoliberal opportunism. Behn's romance is therefore a royalist argument about the Whig cause in the 1680s that allegorically characterizes Monmouth's Rebellion as the public equivalent of Petrarchan adultery, a hypocritical power grab masquerading as highminded devotion. Moreover as Behn's plot unfolds much of it directly represents this power grab in political and military terms. But the association of love and war goes even further than this, metaphorically and metonymically weaving into the local texture of events a reflexive interpenetration of high and low 'affairs'. As war is saturated by love, so love is saturated by war. Signifiers become signifieds and vice versa. And when, toward the end of *Love-Letters*, the narrator disingenuously repeats that 'it is not the Business of this little History to treat of War, but altogether Love' (426), we know to read this denial as equally an affirmation. *Love-Letters* is structured by this ambivalence, both affirming the incompatibility of war and love, epic and romance and affirming their inseparability.

Milton calls *Paradise Lost* heroic poetry; like Behn he considers both epic battle and romance love as possible generic models for his poem. At the beginning of Book 9 his narrator modulates his tone to tragic in anticipation of the Fall, disavowing at greater length than he has before the limitations entailed in the classical model that has guided him thus far. His is a

> Sad task, yet argument
> Not less but more Heroic than the wrath
> Of stern *Achilles* on his Foe pursu'd
> Thrice Fugitive about *Troy* Wall; or rage
> Of *Turnus* for *Lavinia* disespous'd,
> Or *Neptune's* ire or *Juno's*, that so long
> Perplex'd the *Greek* and *Cytherea's* Son[6]

But although 'this Subject for Heroic Song / Pleas'd me long choosing', chivalric romance no more than classical epic is 'that which justly gives Heroic name / To Person or to Poem' because it too treats of war, not love (9.25–6, 40–1). Like Behn, Milton conceives heroic poetry to include both epic and romance; but for him there need be no inquest into their compatibility because on the crucial issue they are the same. So, although the opening of the climactic Book 9 may create the expectation that Milton will now confirm the status of *Paradise Lost* as a heroic poem by showing its vacillation between the congruence and the disparity of these two forms, the familiar trope turns out to have been something of a decoy. Heroic poetry is not for Milton an experimental inquiry into the relation between the two great narrative genres of the past at the present moment of self-conscious stocktaking. It is an experiment in a new, superior enterprise, a parody of those older forms that aims to supersede the ambivalent duality of the heroic tradition by proposing the singular and self-consistent heroism of Christian love.

That we must wait until Book 4 to arrive in Eden and to encounter this representation only heightens its significance, as does Milton's enumeration of what Christian love is not: neither 'the bought smile / Of Harlots', nor the 'Court Amours, / Mixt Dance, or wanton Mask, or Midnight Ball' of romance, nor the metaphorical warfare of the Petrarchan 'Serenate' (4. 765–70). Christian love is 'wedded Love, mysterious Law': lawful sexual coupling, which is the 'true source / Of human offspring', the 'sole propriety / In Paradise of all things common else' (4. 750–2). During the Restoration, 'propriety' still can carry the connotation of 'property': conjugal monogamy is the bulwark against promiscuity. But the sanctity of marriage also legitimates the sexual pleasures gained through sensible things. To this end God made the 'blissful Bower' in Eden 'when he fram'd / All things to man's delightful use … ', and here Adam and Eve perform 'the Rites / Mysterious of connubial Love', 'And heav'nly Choirs the Hymenæn sung' (4. 690, 691–2, 711, 742–3). So the old tension between love and war is resolved by the unity of Christian love consecrated by heavenly love. But if Christian heroism thus supersedes the ambivalence of heroic poetry, it also preserves that essential tension within its own peculiar form, the ambivalence that inheres in the accommodation of heavenly spirit by what Milton calls the bodily matter of 'sensible things'. To accommodate spirit by matter is to justify the ways of God to men, a bold and risky enterprise in parody in which the entire narrative of *Paradise Lost* consists.

Contemporaries sometimes spoke of Christian accommodation as an act of domestication. Metaphorically speaking, 'to domesticate' is 'to naturalize' or 'to familiarize' the great, the noble, the public, the distant, the worldly, the strange, or the foreign by 'bringing it home' – through the medium of the little, the common, the private, the proximate, the local, the familiar, or the native. Probably the best-known accommodation in *Paradise Lost* that invites this metaphor occurs in Book 5 when

Eve 'entertain[s] our Angel guest' Raphael at 'Dinner' and the communication of spiritual knowledge is domesticated to a domestic setting (5. 308–512). The exchange, motivated by that setting, is about accommodation. Adam wonders if angels, creatures of spirit, can eat human food (5. 401–2). Raphael not only affirms that they can, but predicts that humans may come to eat angelic food, thematizing the formal act of knowledge-giving at the level of content. Prodded by Adam, Raphael conveys through the epistemological process of accommodation its ontological counterpart:

> Time may come, when Men
> With angels may participate, and find
> No inconvenient diet, nor too light fare;
> And from these corporal nutriments perhaps
> Your bodies may at last turn all to spirit (5. 493–7)

What Adam learns is not simply that there exists an analogy between spiritual knowing and domestic eating that accommodates the first through the second. He learns that the material process of eating is the means by which humans may in tract of time attain both the epistemological powers and the ontological condition of spiritual beings. A strikingly confident domestication of the invisible spirit by sensible things, this encounter also thematizes that formal act in the substance of Raphael's discourse, which ups the ante by suggesting the yet more remarkable notion that angelic spirit and human sense are continuous and ultimately coextensive. It is hard to imagine an accommodation of spirit by matter less ambivalent than this one.

But accommodation is sustained in our minds as an unsettled question. Adam will continue to ask Raphael 'to impart / Things above Earthly thought, which yet concern'd / Our knowing, as to highest wisdom seem'd', grateful for 'This friendly condescension to relate / Things else by me unsearchable' (7. 81–3; 8. 9–10). Raphael will continue on 'commission from above / … to answer thy desire / Of knowledge within bounds; beyond, abstain / To ask'. Hence 'if else thou seek'st / Aught, not surpassing human measure, say' (7. 118–21, 639–40). And as Adam has invoked Raphael, so Milton's narrator famously invokes the heavenly muse: 'Up led by thee / /Into the Heav'n of Heav'ns I have presum'd, / An Earthly Guest', and asks thence to be safely guided down 'Lest … on th' *Aleian* Field I fall / Erroneous' (7. 12–4, 17, 19–20). Neither angel nor narrator seems entirely confident about the bounds and measure of human knowledge. In fact, Raphael's response to Adam's desire to learn about the war in heaven later in this same book is surprisingly dubious:

> High matter thou injoin'st me, O prime of men,
> Sad task and hard, for how shall I relate
> To human sense th' invisible exploits
> Of warring Spirits[?] (5. 563–6)

But has not Raphael just been engaged in this very process of domestication on the metaphysics of food, as has the narrator himself by depicting this dinner scene – indeed, by narrating *Paradise Lost*? As if in acknowledgment, the problem immediately evaporates. '[Y]et for thy good', the angel continues, 'This is dispens't, and what surmounts the reach / Of human sense, I shall delineate so, / By lik'ning spiritual to corporal forms / as may express them best …' (5. 570–4).

This ambivalence is most forcibly expressed at the beginning of Book 9, when Milton's narrator recurs to the dinner scene, now troubled, as Raphael momentarily had seemed to be, by its accommodation of heaven to earth:

> No more of talk where God or Angel Guest
> With Man, as with his Friend, familiar us'd
> To sit indulgent, and with him partake
> Rural repast, permitting him the while
> Venial discourse unblam' d (9. 1–5)

Permission for that discourse is of course the province of Milton's narrator and the angel. But to call it venial might nonetheless seem to beg the question of who bears responsibility for it: the man whose mortal sin is foreknown but not yet committed, or the narrator whose bold project is to justify the ways of God to men? However we answer this question, Milton hereby draws attention to his formal method and its problematic ambivalence, once again thematizing it on the level of content and throwing its authority into question.

And there is a related obscurity. 'The Argument' to Book 5 prefaces its rural repast and dialogue with the information that 'God to render Man inexcusable' has sent Raphael 'to admonish [Adam] of his obedience, of his free estate, of his enemy near at hand; … and whatever else may avail *Adam* to know'. Having revealed to Adam his most breathtaking possibilities of advancement to an angelic state Raphael adds a proviso: 'If ye be found obedient' (5. 501). And Adam replies with gratitude for the knowledge that 'In contemplation of created things / By steps we may ascend to God' – but also with a question: 'But say, / What meant that caution join'd, *if ye be found / Obedient?*' (5. 511–4). Raphael briefly explains that true obedience depends on free will. He does not remind Adam that true freedom depends on knowing whatever may avail him to know – that is, knowledge sufficient to render man inexcusable of disobedience. But how is the sufficiency of knowledge to be assessed when spiritual knowledge is accommodated in material terms? This question is fundamental both to the ambivalence of accommodation and to the Fall, which turns on the tension, within the Christian heroism of love, between spirit and matter as expressed by the tension between divine and human love. To adumbrate if not to answer it Milton, having superseded heroic poetry, narrates the secret history of the Fall.

Secret History

Defending the regicide in 1649, Milton had criticized Charles I as an exemplar of 'how great mischief and dishonour hath befall'n to Nations under the Government of effeminate and Uxorious Magistrates. Who being themselves govern'd and overswaid at home under a Feminine usurpation, cannot be but farr short of spirit and authority without dores, to govern a whole Nation'. Milton uses 'effeminate' in the traditional sense of the word to characterize the gender ambivalence not of the man who is excessively like a woman (as in the word's modern meaning) but of the man who excessively likes women.[7] In *Paradise Lost,* he returns to the topic of the male ruler besotted and unmanned by his devotion to his ambitious consort, a topic whose deep roots are commonly traced to the *Anekdota* of Procopius of Caesarea (c. CE 550). His title means literally 'unpublished things', but it came to be translated as 'secret history', a form devoted to making public what never appears in the official histories: the low scandals of people in high places – in this case the Emperor Justinian and his Empress Theodora.[8] Shakespeare's *Antony and Cleopatra* (written 1606–07) and Dryden's reconception of it in *All for Love* (1673) are the two great English enactments of the Procopian theme. Over the course of the Restoration and much of the eighteenth century, the secret history enjoyed great popularity as a narrative device for exhuming scandals of various kinds, but the original, Procopian kind was as compelling as any. How does the ambivalence of masculine and feminine stereotypes in Procopius's secret history engage the ambivalent relationships – epic and romance, war and love – that preoccupy heroic poetry? How does Milton's disclosure of the tension between divine and human love within the Christian heroism of love supersede yet preserve that engagement?

For Milton in 1649 the ruler in question was Charles I. For Behn in 1685 it is Cesario (Monmouth), the leader of the rebellion against Charles's younger brother, who in Part 3 of *Love-Letters* falls hard for Hermione (Lady Henrietta Wentworth). Charles's bastard son, Monmouth was the dashing and deeply charismatic embodiment of cavalier gallantry, intrepid valor and libertine nerve. Denied what to many seemed his birthright, during the Popish Plot he became the people's cultural hero and alternative heir. But by the end of Behn's romance Cesario has come to the end of the line, desperate for recognition and, once enthralled by love, cursed by the confusion of amatory with political ambition. An associate fears he has been 'perfectly effeminated into soft Woman' by Hermione's '*Grace so Masculine*', and in his climactic and doomed rebellion against his uncle he fights bravely enough, but 'Love, that coward of the Mind, ... had unman'd his great Soul' to such a degree that he forgoes the noble Roman expedient of falling on his sword: '[E]ven on the Scaffold ... he set himself to justify his Passion to *Hermione*, endeavouring to render the Life he had led with her, Innocent and Blameless in the sight of Heaven'.[9]

The genre of the secret history presupposes a revelatory difference between the official history and history from below. To read *Paradise Lost* as a secret history requires that we understand Genesis, authored by God, to be the official history of the Fall, and there Adam's act of disobedience is scarcely motivated at all: on receiving the apple from Eve he eats it. Like Behn's, Milton's account supplements the official history with knowledge gained through his narrator's third-person detachment and his character's self-consciousness, and this greatly augments our understanding of Adam's part in the Fall.

When we first hear of Eve and Adam's relationship in Book 4, the narrator affirms her 'absolute' 'subjection' to him (4. 301, 308; see 295–311). But in Book 8, Adam recounts to Raphael how, having named the animals, he doubted that their (in God's words) 'low subjection' to him was an appropriate model for this human relationship; God, agreeing, makes Eve from Adam's own body, 'Thy likeness, thy fit help, thy other self' (8. 345, 450). Once he sees Eve, now a sensible thing, Adam is more than pleased with God's creation: 'I now see / Bone of my Bone, Flesh of my Flesh, my Self / Before me ...' (8. 494–6). And once he has made sexual love to Eve, 'so absolute she seems ..., Seems wisest, virtuousest, discreetest, best; / All higher knowledge in her presence falls / Degraded ... ' In Eden, Adam's bodily senses have given him much delight in many objects, which nonetheless 'works in the mind no change'; 'but here / Far otherwise, transported I behold, / Transported touch'. There is 'an awe / About her, as a guard Angelic plac't', Adam tells Raphael, who discerns in him a felt 'subjection' to Eve (8. 525, 528–30, 547, 550–2, 558–9, 570). Consequently, the angel instructs Adam in the workings of the *scala amoris*, whose rungs lead us upward, from passion for sensible things to rational and heavenly love. But whereas this lesson recalls Raphael's earlier account of the *scala alimentorum* in Book 5, there is a crucial difference. In the realm of nourishment, the continuity between the pleasures of sensible things and those of the spirit is confirmed by nothing less than the sight of Raphael eating human food. But when Adam asks if angelic and heavenly love, to which humans also may aspire, partakes of the sensible pleasures of 'immediate touch', the angel's reply is obscure: 'Whatever pure thou in the body enjoy'st / we enjoy / In eminence, and obstacle find none / Of membrane, joint, or limb, exclusive bars: / ... nor restrain'd conveyance need / As Flesh to mix with Flesh ...' (8. 622–5, 628–9). The terms of Adam's impending choice – what may avail him to know – are left doubtful.

If Milton's secret history of the Fall confers on Adam a 'feminine' sensitivity to his love for Eve, it also gives Eve a prudent 'masculine' tenacity in pursuit of external goals. Her wish to 'divide our labours' bespeaks both an industrious economy and an autonomy of choice that 'domestic Adam' equates perhaps too easily with studying 'household good' (9. 214, 233, 318).[10] Once Eve eats the apple, she wonders that it has been 'let hang, as to no end / Created; but henceforth my early care, / ... / Shall tend thee ... ' (9. 798–9, 801). And in this sentiment, she recalls Satan's remark about the unproductivity of 'The Gods': '[T]his fair Earth I see, / Warm'd by the Sun, producing every kind, / Them nothing ... ' (9. 720–2). Eve's unwonted masculine prudence even borders on a 'feminist' self-interest that incidentally evokes the discourse of God and Adam concerning her place in the hierarchy. Eve's new knowledge, she speculates, might 'add what wants / In Female Sex ... / And render me more equal, and perhaps, / ... sometime / Superior ... ' (9. 821–3, 824–5). So Adam is disclosed by Milton's narrator as the besotted hero of a secret history. At the moment of the Fall

> [H]e scrupl'd not to eat
> Against his better knowledge, not deceiv'd,
> But fondly overcome with Female charm. (9. 997–9)

And after the Fall Adam is confirmed in this role by God himself:

> Was shee thy God, that her thou didst obey
> Before his voice, or was shee made thy guide,
> Superior, or but equal, that to her
> Thou didst resign thy Manhood, and the Place
> Wherein God set thee above her ... [?] (10. 145–9)

Our access to Adam's inwardness, through both first- and third-person narration, alters the official history's absolute emphasis on Adam's Fall as an act of disobedience to God by emphasizing his absolute physical devotion to Eve. Not that Milton's secret history challenges the fact or the consequences of Adam's disobedience. But it parodies that curt official story by giving the Fall a psycho-subjective intention. When Raphael reproaches Adam for his seeming subjection to Eve, he replies: 'I to thee disclose / What inward thence I feel, not therefore foil'd' (8. 607–8). 'Subjection' unfolds to express not simply a one-dimensional subordination to authority but a state of multi-intentional subjecthood in relation to other subjects. This is an ultimate effect of accommodation.

True, the condition of materiality subordinates human love to the transcendent spirituality of divine love. But in providing the only medium through which the spirit can be known, materiality also provides the multiple vehicles of sensible relation that diversify and subtilize, beyond hierarchy, what it means to be subjected. Reading *Paradise Lost* as a secret history also deepens our sense of it in the tradition of the heroic poem, an unstable synthesis designed to elevate the growing tension between epic war and romance love to a high level of generic self-consciousness. *Paradise Lost* preserves, but then stabilizes and supersedes, that tension through its self-conscious claim to the status of a Christian epic and its affirmation of a transcendent Christian love. But Milton's synthesis in turn generates its own instability, reproducing and preserving that tension as one between divine love and the sensible things of human love. Its source is the Procopian secret history, whose generic aim is to challenge from below the official history of hierarchy by disclosing its perversely inverted gender relations. This aim is well served by the effeminate weakness Milton finds in Charles I and Behn finds in the Duke of Monmouth. But in *Paradise Lost* Adam's choice of human love – his choice to fall with Eve – transvalues and supersedes those gender relations. Milton's secret history of the Fall is that as an act of disobedience it was motivated not by a will to higher knowledge or power but by a desire to retain the lower capacities of subjectivity and sensible things.

The Novel

Like his contemporaries Butler, Bunyan, Dryden, and Behn, Milton self-consciously aimed to represent his subject parabolically, signifying with brilliant indirection what he thought was not susceptible to more direct description and narration. These authors had varied motives – rhetorical, political, theological – for their indirection, but they also shared in the complex indeterminacy characteristic of a historical context that seemed more than most to require innovative methods of understanding, not least because English people were for the first time learning to conceive innovation itself in positive terms. The genre of the novel also emerged at this time; its earliest experiments, parodic in form and content, bear an arresting relation to what these authors' texts, represented in this argument by Behn's *Love-Letters*, were variously attempting to do.

Formally speaking they have much in common. The 'antiromance' movement, generated by the auto-parodic Renaissance *romanzo* and the followers of *Don Quixote*, fueled the Restoration and early eighteenth-century outcry against 'romance', which attained not only the generic but also the broadly epistemological status of a lie, an impossible or trivial ideal, or a gross error. For Milton, the dubious compound of romance and epic of which heroic poetry consists expressed the incapacity but indispensability of traditional forms, and ultimately of all material things, to accommodate the truth of divine spirit. The positive standard by which the early novel condemned romance – the empirical and quantitative measures of truth championed by the permanent revolution of the new philosophy – might for a moment seem almost the opposite of Milton's, and for the better part of the century they were most commonly identified in narrative with the generic tag 'history' or 'true history'. But Milton's materialism is implicated in his theology, and in other respects he shared fully in the proto-scientific skepticism of the proto-novelists. Moreover by the 1740s, the naïve empiricism of the early novel's claim to historicity was being supplanted by an epistemology of aesthetic realism that bears comparison with Milton's heterodox practice of accommodation.[11] The difference lies in the ontology of what is being futilely represented – on the one hand, the invisible and inaccessible realm of the spirit, on the other hand, the pristine presence of the object, unavailable to the inevitable partiality of the subject. What is shared is the sophisticated skepticism of suspended disbelief in both representations, whose formal hallmark is textual reflexivity, the self-conscious thematizing of formal experimentation, our subliminal awareness of domestication always at work.

What the novel does not share with *Paradise Lost* and the texts I have compared it to is the ladder of domestication, whether accommodation or allegory, that is entailed in narrative signification, whereby what is signified by the signifier exists on a separate and higher level of reality. At least this is the theory. What makes this time and these texts distinctive, however, is the tendency of the two, ontologically separate levels to bleed into each other; or to put this differently, the uncertainty that signification across two discrete realms is semantically required. All of these texts are distinctive in the way they shake the ladder of signification by promoting a less strictly differential interchange between the two levels of signifier and signified. This is perhaps most obviously so in the case of Christian accommodation, in which the materiality of the signifier has absolute authority in representing the invisible signified. In political allegory, this absolute difference between the two levels is absent. But in Behn's *Love-Letters* we're in no doubt on the rules for reading the manifestly uneven relationship between the discrete realms of low signifier and high signified. Yet as the masquerade becomes sophisticated and habituated, its semantic force and interest are increasingly located in the realm of the signifier itself. The high-low differential remains constant, but the hermeneutic key to characterization shifts from the macro-level of the allegorical mode, in which character is disclosed as a correspondence to public exteriority and actual particularity, to the micro-level, on which it is the personal space of character in all its intimate interiority and virtual particularity that claims our attention. Epistolary form gives way to third-person narration as the sheer documentary secrecy of letters comes to feel less expressive than the secrecy of the motives that lie behind and beneath them. The secrets of political history become less compelling, less revelatory than the secrets of the personal – the casuistical and psychological – case history. Yet the political reference of the narrative is preserved even as it is superseded.

What does *Paradise Lost* share with the nascent novel genre regarding the crucial conflict, on matters of amatory choice, between the authority of the father and the desires of youth? By the end of the seventeenth century, both the ideology and the institution of estate settlement were in dispute. In *Love-Letters*, marriage among the nobility and gentry is conceived exclusively as a means of settling and perpetuating the family estate. In the eighteenth century, love has become an acknowledged motive even for the elite, and the most insistent thematic pattern in the early novel genre is the conflict between these two models of marriage. The first is the 'arranged' or 'forced' marriage (or marriage 'of convenience'), engineered by the parents and dominated by the consanguineal interests of patrilineal inheritance. The cornerstone of patrilineal inheritance was the rule of male primogeniture, whose purpose was to ensure the integrity of the family estate by passing it in perpetuity to the firstborn sons in the paternal line. The second model is marriage for love, motivated by the free choice of the couple and representative of the emergent, conjugal paradigm of the family.

In *Paradise Lost*, Milton is committed to the accommodation of an immaterial and invisible world by means of familiar sensible things. What might this look like in novelistic terms, when the ladder of signification is thought no longer to be necessary? In the summary novelization of *Paradise Lost* that follows and brings this essay to a close, I indicate by quotation marks where significant words actually figure in the relevant passages of Milton's poem.

Milton tells the story of a wealthy landowner Lord G___, patriarch of the most ancient and noble family in the kingdom and father of two sons. The eldest son, Jesus, being the first-born, is 'heir' (5. 720) to his father's vast estate. Adam, Lord G___'s 'youngest son' (3. 151), is a mild and unassuming gentleman. G___ himself is an old-fashioned landholder who believes in the time-honored principle that the only real estate is land, uncorrupted by innovative agricultural technologies and the diabolical craft of financial instruments. Like many of his generation, G___ associates such practices with the ungodly Puritans and, together with his eldest son, who is Justice of the Peace for the County of_____ and a pattern of militant 'Manhood' (3. 314), has recently played a central role in enforcing the laws against nonconformists so as to 'root them out' (6. 855) of all government posts and clerical livings. Lord G___ is no Lord in the sacred sense of the term. Nonetheless, the godlike power to confer perpetuity does reside in his authority to ensure the continuity of the patriline through arranged marriages based on consanguineal family values. By the rule of primogeniture, G___'s ambitions for the perpetuation of family honor and property have been exclusively focused on his worldly son Jesus. But he also loves his more contemplative and retiring son Adam, and when an old friend who has settled in the 'New World' urges his Lordship to purchase a plantation there – one that's proved so lushly productive of 'wanton growth' that it requires no more than energetic maintenance – G___ decides to settle Adam in the colonies (4. 629). The untimely death of the plantation's owner has left a young widow, Eve, from whom G___ buys the plantation and between whom and Adam he arranges an opportune marriage. No need to look further into Eve's situation: she is innocent and ignorant and will be pleased to serve as Adam's docile and humble helpmeet. If his son feels he's been exiled from the family estate, Lord G___ will reward his success by welcoming them both back home. But in G___'s disdain for looking further (his pride in his powers of foreknowledge is legendary) he ensures his ignorance of the fact that along with her husband's wealth the widow Eve has inherited the rebellious spirit of her father, a parliamentarian general during the late civil wars.

In Adam Eve finds a gentle and thoughtful spirit, a true instance of 'manly grace' unlike the men of power she's accustomed to, and they delight in endless conversation (4. 490). On only one topic do they discover a seed of disagreement. Before Adam's arrival, Eve had devoted much thought to how her plantation Eden might be developed by the latest techniques of agrarian improvement, perhaps on the model of Paradise, Eden's central 'enclosure green' (4. 133). However Lord G___ has just sent one of his estate factors, Raphael, to require that the plantation be maintained, not improved. Even Paradise, which had been planted with exotic species and enclosed for future horticultural experiment, is subject to this prohibition in the case of one tree in particular. Because the unique botanical properties of that tree hold mysteries that, if mastered, might revolutionize knowledge of artificial propagation and reproduction, Lord G___ insists that even its harvesting be forbidden.

Adam recognizes in this prohibition his father's atavistic antipathy toward what G___ regards as one more 'devilish machination' of modernity (6. 504), but he's inclined to obey the old man if only to avoid conflict. However 'advent'rous *Eve*' (9. 921), lacking her husband's pious subservience to patriarchal authority – as she puts it to Adam, he 'is *thy* Law, *thou* mine' (4. 637) – is powerfully self-reliant. Lord G___, unable to reconcile this quality with the stereotypical weakness of a woman, displaces it from Eve to the all-purpose figment of his superstition that he calls Satan and personifies as an alien and malevolent enemy. Eve bridles at G___'s prohibition, which recalls the arbitrary royal absolutism she was raised by her own father to abhor, secretly resolving to oppose it. Echoing Adam's own earlier advocacy of strenuous horticultural 'reform', Eve reminds him that 'the work under our labor grows, / Luxurious by restraint' (9. 208–9; see 4. 623–33), adding the basic axiom of economic productivity: 'Let us divide our labors' (9. 214). Adam fears that, if left alone, Eve will be led by her enthusiasm rather than her reason, and he cautions against division. But Eve, cannily echoing her father-in-law, argues against a cloistered female virtue always under male protection.

Eve is well trained in the Puritan discipline of casuistry, and once alone she debates within herself the case of conscience that pits the ethics and consequences of defying her husband and father-in-law against those of abandoning the promise of the wonderful tree, and she resolves to take a cutting of it. Adam is shocked at Eve's '[b]old deed' and at the 'peril great provok't' by it; but he too ponders the choice now before him (9. 921, 922). Lord G___will demand that he abandon his wife and return home to a life of obedient ease on the family estate. But the crisis has educated Adam in what he really wants. To return will be to exchange the vitally present and sensible pleasures of conjugal union for a deadening devotion to the family lineage, to a past and future in which he has no share. When Adam first arrived in the New World he experienced his rustication as a devastating privation, an exile from the value-generating presence of his father and the family estate. But in his time with Eve, Adam has come to experience his privation as instead the positive privacy of life with a self-reflective equal. So he resolves to push away the domesticating ladder of dependence.

Looking backward, Milton's generic experiment turns on the tension, within love, between its divine and human fulfilments. Looking forward, it turns on the tension, within marriage, between those arranged to suit parental interests and those motivated by the love between their children. G___, enraged, disinherits Adam and evicts both of them from the plantation. Domestic Adam and adventurous Eve make their way out into the welcoming wilderness of the New World, remembering to take with them the cutting of the plant they have come to call 'the tree of knowledge'. Soon Eve's application of that knowledge to the progressive improvement of AdEve Enterprises will have tripled its acreage and productivity, with the aid and at the expense of neighbouring settlers, slaves, and native Americans. Absolute monarchy will have been definitively superseded, and preserved, by absolute private property.[12]

Notes

1 See Michael McKeon, *The Origins of the English Novel, 1660–1740* (Baltimore: Johns Hopkins University Press, 1987, 2002), 35–9.
2 See Joel E. Spingarn, *Literary Criticism in the Renaissance*, 2nd edn (New York: Columbia University Press, 1912), 112–24; Bernard Weinberg, *A History of Literary Criticism in the Renaissance,* 2 vols. (Chicago: University of Chicago Press, 1961), vol. 2, ch. 19, 20; and Alban K. Forcione, *Cervantes, Aristotle and the Persiles* (Princeton: Princeton University Press, 1970), ch. 1, 2 (p. 23 on 'heroic poetry'). Colin Burrow's approach to the problem of how romance stands in relation to epic begins in antiquity and culminates in an illuminating consideration of *Paradise Lost* that shares many of this essay's broadest concerns. Colin Burrow, *Epic Romance: Homer to Milton* (Oxford: Clarendon Press, 1993).
3 '*Paradise Lost* in the Long Restoration, 1660–1742: The Parody of Form', in *Milton in the Long Restoration*, eds. Blair Hoxby and Ann Baynes Coiro (Oxford: Oxford University Press, 2016), 503–30.

4 John Milton, *Of Education. To Master Samuel Hartlib* (1644), Donald C. Dorian (ed.), vol. 2 (1959) of John Milton, *Complete Prose Works of John Milton,* 8 vols. (New Haven: Yale University Press, 1953–1982), 2: 368–9. Hereafter cited as *CPW*.
5 [Aphra Behn], *Love-Letters Between a Nobleman and his Sister*, ed. Janet Todd (Harmondsworth: Penguin, 1996). For a full reading of *Love-Letters* see Michael McKeon, *The Secret History of Domesticity: Public, Private, and the Division of Knowledge* (Baltimore: Johns Hopkins University Press, 2005), ch. 11.
6 See John Milton, *Paradise Lost, A Poem in Twelve Books* (1674), 2 vols. Ed. Thomas Newton, 3rd edn (London, 1754), 9.3–9. Further citations will appear parenthetically in the text.
7 Milton, *Eikonoklastes*, in *CPW*, 3, 421. On 'effeminate' see McKeon, *Secret History*, 581.
8 The *Anekdota* was first translated into English in 1674 from an earlier French translation, then reissued in 1682. On Procopius and the seventeenth-century English secret history see McKeon, *Secret History*, ch. 10. Of course Milton would not have required either translation, but the proximity of their dates to the publication of *Paradise Lost* (and to those of *All for Love* and *Love-Letters*) may suggest a current interest in the *Anekdota*'s theme.
9 Behn, *Love-Letters*, 325, 434, 438.
10 Milton writes at a time when the traditionally flexible distinction between male outside and female inside work in the agrarian economy was becoming a more ossified division of labor. The division Eve proposes would go against that historical tendency but at the same time accord with a modernizing movement toward greater efficiency and productivity. See McKeon, *Secret History*, 170–7.
11 However Fielding's epistemological breakthrough in *Joseph Andrews* (1742) was inspired by that of Cervantes a century-and-a-half earlier; it was perfected in English as early as Milton's contemporary William Congreve's *Incognita; or, Love and Duty Reconcil'd …* (1692) (on which see McKeon, *Origins of the English Novel*, 61–3).
12 On this shift in 'absolutism' see McKeon, *Secret History*, ch. 1: 'The Devolution of Absolutism'.

2

Secret History and Seventeenth-Century Historiography

Martine W. Brownley

Complaints about the dearth of effective historical writing in England were ubiquitous among contemporary seventeenth- and early eighteenth-century commentators. Yet what historians of the period lacked in praiseworthy results, many of them made up in energy. A major source of their difficulties was the inadequacies of the forms they were using; in reaction, they actively experimented, seeking other structures to convey different kinds of understanding of the past. Their lack of success in historical writing itself has at times obscured their considerable achievements in related genres. After mid-century these ongoing historiographical experiments were generating a number of new hybrids, among which was secret history. Various historiographical conditions shaped its emergence, development, and fairly rapid demise as a form of English historical writing.

Seventeenth-century English historians inherited two primary genres: the chronicle, which was in decline, and the politic history, a humanist form that prospered as the dominant model.[1] Both proved troublesome legacies. By early in the century, the chronicle's accretive annalistic structure could no longer assimilate the mass of accumulating historical materials, even with sporadic literary upgrades.[2] Many chronicle materials also failed to satisfy the more stringent standards for historical evidence emerging over the century. Under pressure from Baconian proto-scientific approaches, new methods of antiquarian scholarship, and the resulting clashes that Michael McKeon has traced between 'naïve empiricism' and 'extreme skepticism', the genre lost some of its most popular elements, which had long been considered integral parts of history.[3] John Donne and others might dismiss the 'triviall houshold trash' that filled chronicles, but a considerable audience missed the colourful anecdotes, personal details about characters, and traditional moral lessons, which disappeared along with the legends, wonders, and miracles.[4]

As seventeenth-century English historiography began to break loose from the chronicle form, politic history offered the major formal alternative.⁵ Focused primarily on statecraft and war, it was written to provide practical political analyses of both for rulers and their counsellors. Politic history offered principles of selection and organization among rapidly proliferating historical materials, although at some cost in scope; most of these histories were limited to a single reign or event. Influenced directly by Machiavelli, Guiccardini, and later sixteenth- and early seventeenth-century Continental historians such as Famiano Strada, and Enrico Davila, politic historians also looked to classical historians, particularly Polybius, Thucydides, and above all, Tacitus. These writers offered analytical depth lacking in earlier English historiography. Like its models, politic history frequently dealt with darker aspects of state power unseen by the general public – some of the same kinds of concerns that secret history would later inflate to exploit.

Politic history similar to Continental and classical models flourished only briefly in England, roughly from the 1590s to the later 1630s.⁶ From the beginning, the genre showed considerable formal flexibility. A minor example is the style. Although Continental politic historians employed terse and epigrammatic Tacitean prose, aside from Sir Francis Bacon and Sir John Hayward, that style never took root in England. By the later 1630s, under the pressure of events, politic history began to mutate structurally. The genre turned out to be unstable in two directions; its historical content was vulnerable to different displacements, depending on the scope of the individual work and the proclivities of the writer. Politic history could easily expand to become discourse on political theory, with past events serving merely as examples in what were in essence treatises on governance. Thus, Arthur B. Ferguson describes Hayward's *Henrie IIII* and Bacon's *Henry VII* as 'basically treatises on the art of statecraft'.⁷ Alternatively, the politic model could narrow its scope to function simply as political propaganda. In both cases, the results blurred the distinctions between historical narrative and political and polemical discourse, while reducing the narrative space left in histories.

Although Thomas Hobbes in *Behemoth* and a few others employed history as a vehicle for political theory, the second option was far more common during the Restoration and early eighteenth century. As the civil wars, the Exclusion Crisis, the Glorious Revolution, and controversies over the succession created violent partisanship, the emphasis on politics in early politic history rapidly became simply an excuse for direct and indirect propaganda. D. W. Woolf has traced how the consensus in early Stuart historiography that 'history was and should be the least controversial of literary genres' shattered after 1640, resulting in works constructed in terms of 'controversy, dispute, and debate'.[8] Polemic eventually invaded even the most rudimentary historical writing. In 1649, for example, a brief epitome for popular consumption, *The Number and Names of All the Kings of England and Scotland*, highlighted on the title page 'how many of them came to untimely Ends'.[9]

Problems with polemic were, of course, particularly acute in accounts of more recent history, where the representation and interpretation of events directly involved current political concerns. Not coincidentally, the writing of such history was the major historiographical effort in England from the civil wars to the early eighteenth century, as historians reflected in their works the primacy of political imperatives in the life around them. Earlier seventeenth-century historians, mindful like Sir Walter Ralegh that 'who-so-ever in writing a moderne Historie, shall follow truth too neare the heeles, it may happily strike out his teeth', prudently restricted themselves to early periods.[10] Although later historians constantly cited Ralegh's remark, they found contemporary history too compelling to resist.

With its principles of selection and organization offering some control over a rapidly expanding historical field, early English politic history had generally exercised a positive influence on historical form. After 1640, however, the ubiquitous propaganda in its polemical derivatives led to serious narrative disruptions and distortions. Structuralist distinctions between story and discourse have been deconstructed in a number ways for more complex literary texts. But they still work fairly well for early modern historical writing, where elements of discourse, particularly authorial commentary or analysis, are more easily separable from those of story.

Originally the analytic discourse of politic history, which increased explanatory power and added causal connections, represented a significant historiographical advance over the chronicle. When later politic history devolved into polemic, in which the primary focus was not events but the promotion of partisan interpretations of events, the amount of discourse rose commensurately. As analysis predominated over narrative, the first casualty was usually story, which had been the bedrock of the best Tudor chronicles. Integrating narrative and discourse is usually difficult in any case, as Gérard Genette long ago pointed out, because narrative does not integrate discourse as easily as discourse receives narrative grafts. 'Narrative inserted into discourse is transformed into an element of discourse', Genette explained, while 'discourse inserted into narrative remains discourse'.[11]

Given this relative independence of discourse as a textual component and the high percentages of discourse in later politic histories, narrative became truncated, or in some cases almost completely elided. For example, although Sir William Dugdale actually fought on the Royalist side at Edgehill, his *Short View of the Late Troubles in England* (arguably mistitled at 650 folio pages) deliberately omits any description of the battle, and covers other military actions only in annual chronological lists.[12] Similarly, when Hobbes in *Behemoth* mentions the treatment of Charles I before his execution, he refers readers curious about the King's experiences 'to the chronicle itself'.[13] Using – and misusing – forms of later politic history, Restoration and early eighteenth-century historians were losing their stories.

Problems with discourse were exacerbated in later politic history when historians began to structure their works as rebuttals to other historians. As histories generated anti-histories in a particularly stifling form of intertextuality, the potential of historical writing as a dialogue with the past was lost in a dialogue with one specific opponent. Historical writing increasingly became discourse on discourse. Much of the discourse in early politic histories was comprised of analysis or reflections; later the discourse became predominantly straightforward polemical denunciation or invective. With the scope of politic history narrowing, such discourse simultaneously lessened its depth.

The long-term importance of politic history for English historiography is that many of the methods it introduced and the attitudes it fostered outlived the relatively restricted period of its initial form, and after mid-century continued to thrive in numerous derivatives well into the eighteenth century. Aside from antiquarian works, in terms of form much of Restoration and early eighteenth-century historiography can be viewed as the gradual deterioration of politic history into different polemical forms.

Secrets Omitted and Disseminated

From classical times to the Renaissance, it had been a commonplace that, as Cicero put it in his famous formulation, 'Nam quis nescit, primam esse historiae legem, ne quid falsi dicere audeat? Deinde ne quid veri non audeat?' ['For who does not know history's first law to be that an author must not dare to tell anything but the truth? And its second that he must make bold to tell the whole truth?'].[14] By the early seventeenth century, the second law was being widely ignored in English historical practice. Those who wrote history made it clear that they were deliberately omitting certain material from their works.[15]

Jacques Amyot, the influential French translator of Plutarch, wrote in 1559 that historians needed 'good judgement to discerne what is to be sayd, and what to be left unsayd', because their 'chiefe drift ought to be to serve the common weale'.[16] After Sir Thomas North's translation of Amyot in 1579, English historians and commentators began to echo this sentiment. Samuel Daniel promised in his history to 'deliver nothing but what is fit for the world to know'.[17] William Camden quoted with approval Dionysius of Halicarnassus's injunction that 'it is unlawfull, it is doubtfull and dangerous' to search out the 'hidden Meanings of Princes', and asserted in his own history of Elizabeth I: 'Things manifest and evident I have not concealed; Things doubtfull I have interpreted favourably; Things secret and abtruse [sic] I have not pried into.'[18]

Along with state secrets, the scandals of private life were a restricted area for historians. Prevailing views of decorum considered only the public roles of individuals appropriate for histories. Warning that the historian was 'prohibited from looking too curiously into other Peoples Concerns, to enter the Closets, lift up the Vails, and draw the Curtains that cover the Secrets of Families', Pierre Le Moyne emphasized that in the private sphere, the historian's 'Prerogative reaches not Secret things'.[19] Lingering commitments to history as a moral instructor also encouraged the omission of negative examples. If such historiographical lacunae protected the ruling class from scrutiny, it was also viewed as serving the larger interests of the nation. Richard Braithwaite cautioned in 1638 that there could be danger to the state in 'laying it open too much'.[20]

In some cases, prudence dictated historiographical omissions. Camden early in the seventeenth century indicated that he 'said but little' of the living, 'either in their Praise or Dispraise' (5). Almost a century later, Abel Boyer explained that he chose to write annals because the extended analyses of events and characters required in a history were 'not *safe*' to include about 'Men Living, and in Power'.[21] While fear protected the living, a complex of reasons centered on ideals of fairness and decorum kept the dead safe, including royalty. Daniel believed that 'there may (in a kind) be *Laesa Maiestas*, even against dead Princes' (A_4^r). Many of the authorial practices that whitewashed seventeenth-century biographies, resulting in lifeless portrayals and empty panegyrics, similarly marred historical writing.

It is important to note that even commentators who urged self-censorship on historians usually hedged their admonitions. For example, after writing that information undermining a state or ruler should be omitted, Braithwaite added the caveat: 'if it may stand with the body of the History' (85). Significantly, however, he places the clause in parentheses; the emphasis falls on the silencing. In practice, sizable areas of public and private life were generally inaccessible to historical representation.

Very slowly over the seventeenth century, restrictions on such material began for many reasons to crumble. The traditional moral aims of historical writing were increasingly ignored in practice. The dissemination of previously secret political documents by both sides in the civil wars and periodic lapses in press censorship both during and after the conflicts revealed more to the reading public about the actual workings of power than ever before, including disturbing revelations about the Stuarts themselves. John Rushworth wrote that 'howsoever all possible diligence may have been used to carry things in secret, and to act by colourable Pretences ... yet in these our days hath God brought great things to light, discovering many secrets and close contrivances, many private consultations and hidden designs, which otherwise probably, neither we nor our posterity should have ever known'.[22] The growth of journalism over the period both reflected and fed the desire for information. Even matters formerly private began to engage historians, as changing parameters of the public and private spheres altered views of decorum. William Nicolson pointed out that those 'entrusted with the Mysteries of Government have all their private Affairs so interwoven with the Publick, that they are not to be consider'd asunder'.[23]

Although restrictions on some historical representations gradually eased, the public's perception that the ruling class and those who served it would not write the historical truth remained widespread. Historians were often considered royal pawns; René Rapin in 1680 described 'most Historians' as 'ordinarily Court-Pensioners'.[24] As the historical focus shifted to contemporary events, Jean Le Clerc wrote that "tis almost impossible to write in any Government by public Order, and in consequence of a Pension, the Transactions that lately fell out, and at the same time to confine [oneself] religiously to the Truth'.[25] Finally, the positions of those who knew very much about the truth made their telling it unlikely. Lord Lonsdale concluded that "tis almost impossible to write a good Historie', since 'it cannot be performed without being the Repositorie off the Secrets off the Prince, from whom alone spring all the great Affairs that make up the matter off Historie, and if one were so, ... their obligation and dutie will prohibit the devulging them.'[26] The belief that official historians were the tools of those in power was specifically linked to the taste for secret history by John Cockburn. Noting the 'Prejudice against what is published by the Licence or Permission of Authority', he wrote that as a result the most curious readers showed 'a strong Inclination after *secret History*, and all *forbidden Books*, as if Truth were more surely to be found in them'.[27]

With the growing recognition of potential deficiencies in participants' accounts, by the Restoration an impasse of sorts was developing over the question of who should write history. Politic history had removed historical writing from chroniclers and compilers, who lacked access to salient facts – particularly secret ones – as well as literary abilities. Later, when those who possessed both were no longer trusted to write the truth, the amount of printed information available enabled more people to write history. As Grub Street scribblers sharpened their quills, the politic history originally composed by counsellors of kings was commandeered by hacks. Secret history was a primary beneficiary of this depreciated authorial status; contemporary commentators frequently associated the two.

Early politic history had been a genre for elite readers. As its scope narrowed to polemic and a new class of historians emerged, its targeted readership broadened. Remarks in prefaces indicate that later politic histories were aimed at a wider popular audience. James Tyrrell, for example, explained that he included political observations in his *General History of England* for 'such Readers, as not being conversant in State-Affairs, may perhaps not be able to make 'em themselves'.[28] Henry Care addressed his *History of the Damnable Popish Plot* to 'the *Common People*, who in their degree are not unconcerned to be faithfully informed of the Progress of this *Hellish Plot*'.[29] As Care's polemical language suggests, the political advice crafted for kings was rapidly becoming party lessons for a wider readership. By 1724 the notorious secret historian John Oldmixon was questioning 'whether any modern Historian ever thought of more than pleasing the Prince or Party for whom he wrote'.[30] Certainly Oldmixon himself never did.

Thus over the seventeenth century, trends in historical writing emphasized the need to discover, analyze, and publish state and private secrets. A public eager for such information was not very particular about the credentials of any writer who claimed to provide it. By the time of the Restoration, the title pages of histories played to such expectations. Few failed to promise things not published before or not available in other historians. Even the title page of the fourth edition of Sir Richard Baker's famously long-lived *Chronicle* proclaimed that its continuation to the Restoration was extracted from 'the *Journals* and *Memorials* of those imploy'd in the most Important and Secret *Transactions* of that time'.[31] All forms of historical writing adjusted to reflect the premium on previously inaccessible information.

'A Story Fit to Gain Credit': Secret History as Historical Writing

The deliberate omissions in early politic history created a range of opportunities for secret historians. Faced with interstices, they enthusiastically filled in the gaps with extravagant embellishments to please their markets. They retained a number of the characteristics of later politic history, while reacting against others. Secret history reflected the lessened scope of politic history, along with the present orientation and curtailed dialogic structures. It shared much of the vocabulary of politic history. Favourite expressions of secret historians, such as 'mysteries of state' and 'secret springs' actually recur throughout English historical writing of the period. Like later politic history, secret history was marked by extended discourse and the resulting problems with narrative coherence. Finally, secret history functioned as a powerful controversial weapon.[32]

In exposing the mysteries of state and boudoir, secret history restored materials that both early and later politic history tended to exclude, while brazenly violating decorum. Personal details about individuals, colourful anecdotes, and moral outrage over wicked examples – all popular features of the disappearing chronicle – reappeared, albeit in salacious, dissolute, and sometimes treasonable garb. Particularly appealing was its reinstatement of story; narrative as well as discourse conveyed its polemical attacks.

The contributions of secret history to English historiography cited by literary critics include its restoration of story and character details, its manipulations of narrative voice, and its rejection of decorum.[33] However, these features were shared by a number of other historical hybrids that developed during the Restoration. In 1658, the first work entitled 'memoirs' was published in England; towards the end of the century, writers produced versions of the 'life and times'; experimentation with biography and autobiography was vigorously sustained throughout the period. In diverse ways most of these genres sought to bring back narrative and personal elements, to test the limits of decorum, and to enlarge prevailing conceptions of the kinds of truths that histories should represent. In addition, because the ongoing conflicts over who should write history raised formal questions about the kinds of authority that historians should assume within their texts, experiments with narrative voice and perspective marked most of these forms.

Another contribution to English historiography credited to secret history is its destabilization both of official accounts and also of 'the very idea of authoritative historical knowledge'.[34] However, in an historiographical context created when politic history, itself an unstable genre, was fragmenting into even more unstable derivatives, most of which were polemical attacks on some kind of authority, such destabilization was widespread in historical writing, particularly after 1640. In fact, the primary authority that secret history destabilized was its own.

Most critics have noted the self-consciousness of secret historians; Rebecca Bullard has analyzed in detail how secret history's self-referentiality repeatedly undercuts the claims it makes.[35] This tendency is particularly clear in its deployment of historical material and conventions, where the vulnerability of its authority as historical writing is directly inscribed in the text. Standard sources are ostentatiously ignored. Oldmixon asserts that in writing his *Arcana Gallica*, he 'wou'd not so much as consult' François Eudes de Mézeray, because had he done so, he 'shou'd soon lose the Character of a Writer of *Anecdotes*, and deaden the Curiosity of the Publick'.[36] Witnesses are cited but not named and hearsay, regularly amplified by conjecture, disfigures many of the texts. The methods of secret historians frequently made their appropriations of historical conventions seem almost parodic.

Similarly, all forms of seventeenth-century politic history were marked by omissions, but secret history's lacunae were particularly damaging. Critics have emphasized the amount of documentary evidence that secret history includes.[37] Yet again and again, this documentation proves insufficient. Crucial evidence regularly turns out to have disappeared. As proof of Charles II's Catholicism, one secret historian cites a letter in Charles's 'own Hand, written in the Year 1652 to the Pope himself'. This letter 'once was printed in *Whitlocks Memoirs*; but upon the considerations of the danger that might ensue upon divulging it at that time to the World, [was] torn out before the publishing of the Book'.[38] The same historian never mentions Clarendon or Danby. Instead the reader gets Charles II's incest with his sister Minette and also with Castlemaine, identified as the daughter of Henrietta Maria and Henry Jermyn (49–50, 22). The major omission in secret history was too often historical fact.

Secret history depended on exaggeration, which can backfire. As Edward Gibbon pointed out in assessing Procopius, because the Byzantine historian's 'malevolent pencil' shows only Justinian's vices, 'a lover of truth will peruse with a suspicious eye the instructive anecdotes of Procopius'.[39] Secret histories displayed the imagination sorely lacking in many other contemporary histories, but the English fairly quickly recognized that imagination in these works was not employed in a historically appropriate way. Although secret history expanded the historical field, its own extensions of it soon proved unacceptable. Its existence as even a putatively historical form was brief, while some of the other hybrids of the period survived to exert long-term historiographical influence.

Because potentially important contributions to historiography could become liabilities in the hands of unscrupulous secret historians, not surprisingly the primary historiographical impact of the genre was a negative one. Secret history was a major contributor to the growing reaction in the later seventeenth and early eighteenth centuries against politic history as a genre, particularly against its later mutations. The analyses characteristic of politic history required moving beyond the extant evidence by using imagination, along with knowledge and experience, to create new interpretations. In later derivatives, the result was often overly elaborate discourse that was too subjective. Rushworth complained that in 'diving after the secret Reasons' for actions, 'Authors many times relate their own *Conceits*, rather than the *true Motives* which induced the Actors to such Resolutions' (6: 1). Thomas Hearne also warned against the disproportionate analyses that were disfiguring later politic history, warning that the historian 'must not be one of those over-curious Politicians ... who change all their Paths into Labyrinths by stuffing their Heads with Chimerical Notions'.[40] The reaction against authorial commentary represented by the documentary histories of Rushworth and John Nalson was another reflection of the widespread concern about the effectiveness of politic history as a form.

Contemporaries worried that fair and adequate representations of the past were becoming lost amid the blatant bias, the inflated and subjective discourse, and ultimately the fiction in some derivatives of politic history. In no contemporary form were the problems more obvious than in secret history. The scurrilous invectives that comprised much of its analytical discourse in effect functioned almost as caricatures of the analyses in earlier politic history. Politic history as it developed in England over the seventeenth century eventually became so mired in polemical discourse that it could no longer serve as a viable historiographical model. The flagrant distortions in later politic histories by secret historians offered particularly compelling examples showing why the form had become too corrupted to be sustainable.

In English historiography, the secret history can best be understood as a corrupted offshoot of seventeenth-century politic history – a generic dead end of sorts. Early commentators had traditionally compared history to the epic. As the chronicle fell into disrepute, it was often associated with romance. The changing scope of later politic histories is suggested by the tendency of commentators such as Rapin and Le Moyne in the 1680s and 1690s to compare them to gazettes (58; 118–19). Metaphorically, secret histories failed to reach even the gazette level. Instead, they were tarred with the romance associations that had been used to denigrate the later chronicles.[41] Typical was the comment that one secret history 'disgraces History by being nam'd such, having scarce as much Truth in it as is generally found in Romances'.[42] Most of all, secret histories were associated with novels. One secret historian admitted that part of his account was 'so Romantick, that it looks more like a Novel, than a Story fit to gain Credit'.[43] By 1724 Thomas Salmon described certain accounts as '*pure secret History*; or in other Words, perfect Novels'.[44] Of course, for exactly that reason, as many critics have shown, even as secret history proved a generic dead end for historians, its materials turned out to be recyclable by other writers. What the historians of the time cast aside, those who wrote early novels as well as satire were able to put to very good use.

Notes

1 Among historiographical overviews that include this period are D. W. Woolf, *The Idea of History in Early Stuart England* (Toronto: University of Toronto Press, 1990), and Woolf's 'From Hystories to the Historical', ed. P. Kewes, *The Uses of History* (San Marino: Huntington, 2006), 31–67; Philip Hickes, *Neoclassical History and English Culture* (New York: St. Martin's, 1996); F. J. Levy, *Tudor Historical Thought*, 1967 (Toronto: University of Toronto Press, 2004); Robert Mayer, *History and the Early English Novel* (Cambridge: Cambridge University Press, 1997); F. S. Fussner, *The Historical Revolution* (London: Routledge, 1962).
2 Woolf dates the chronicle's peak in the mid-1500s and its decline from the 1570s (*Reading History* [Cambridge: Cambridge University Press, 2000]), 47, 8. On chronicles, see Woolf, *Reading*, 11–78; Levy, 167–201; and Annabel M. Paterson, *Reading Holinshed's Chronicles* (Chicago: University of Chicago Press, 1994).
3 Michael McKeon, *Origins of the English Novel* (Baltimore: Johns Hopkins University Press, 1987).
4 John Donne, *Satyre IV, Satires, Epigrams, and Verse Letters*, ed. W. Milgate (Oxford: Oxford University Press, 1967), 17; line 98.
5 Examples include Sir John Hayward's history of Henry IV (1599), Samuel Daniel's *Collection of the History of England* (1618), Sir Francis Bacon's history

of Henry VII (1622), and William Camden's history of Elizabeth I (1615 and 1627 in Latin; English edition in 1630); on politic history, see Woolf, *Idea*, 77–169, and Levy, *Tudor*, 237–85.

6 Levy dates the end in 1640 (*Tudor*, 252); Woolf sees English historiography in 'a state of stagnation' by the mid-1630s (*Idea*, 246).

7 Arthur B. Ferguson, *Clio Unbound: Perception of the Social and Cultural Past in Renaissance England* (Durham: Duke University Press, 1979), 10.

8 Woolf, *Idea*, 264, xii.

9 John Taylor, *The Number and Names of All the Kings of England and Scotland* (London, 1649).

10 Sir Walter Ralegh, 'Preface', *The History of the World* (London, 1614), n.p.

11 Gérard Genette, *Figures of Literary Discourse*, trans. Alan Sheridan (New York: Columbia University Press, 1982), 141.

12 Sir William Dugdale, *Short View of the Late Troubles in England* (Oxford, 1681), 108.

13 Thomas Hobbes, *Behemoth or the Long Parliament*, ed. Ferdinand Tönnies, 2nd edn. (London: Cass, 1969), 154.

14 Marcus Tullius Cicero, *De Oratore*, ed. and trans. E. W. Sutton and H. Rackham (Cambridge: Harvard University Press, 1942), 242, 244; English translation 243, 245.

15 Eve Tavor Bannet in ' "Secret History": Or, Talebearing Inside and Outside the Secretorie' writes that a debate among secret historians regarding the importance of disseminating previously unpublished information about the powerful 'suggests that at least in some quarters, secret history emerged as a conscious response' to the lacunae in histories now viewed as 'more respectable' (383). The following section makes clear my agreement, without the qualification.

16 'Amiot to the Readers', Plutarch, *Lives of the Noble Grecians & Romanes*, 1559, trans. Thomas North (London, 1579), A$_3^r$.

17 Samuel Daniel, *First Part of the History of England* (London, 1613), A$_4^r$.

18 William Camden, *The History of the Most Renowned and Victorious Princess Elizabeth*, ed. W. T. MacCaffrey (Chicago: University of Chicago Press, 1970), 6, 5.

19 Pierre Le Moyne, *Of the Art Both of Writing and Judging of History* (London, 1695), 113.

20 Richard Braithwaite, *Survey of History* (London, 1638), 85.

21 Abel Boyer, 'To the Reader', *History of the Reign of Queen Anne* (London, 1703), n.p.

22 John Rushworth, *Historical Collections*, 8 vols. (London, 1721), n.p. This quotation was copied by a secret historian; see R. B., 'The Preface', *Secret History of the Four Last Monarchs* (London, 1691), n.p.

23 William Nicolson, *English Historical Library* (London, 1696), 156.

24 [René Rapin], *Instructions for History*, trans. J. Davies (London, 1680), 32.

25 John Le Clerc, *Parrhasiana* (London, 1700), 121.

26 John Lowther, Viscount Lonsdale, 'The Memoirs of the First Lord Lonsdale', ed. C. H. Firth, *EHR*, 30 (1915), 91–2.
27 John Cockburn, *Specimen of Some Free and Impartial Remarks* (London, 1724), 5, 6.
28 James Tyrrell, 'The Preface to the Reader', *The General History of England*, 5 vols. (London, 1704), 2: xxiii.
29 Henry Care, *History of the Damnable Popish Plot* (London, 1680), A₃ᵛ.
30 John Oldmixon, *The Critical History of England; Ecclesiastical and Civil*, 2 vols. (London, 1726), 2: 10.
31 Sir Richard Baker, *Chronicle of the Kings of England*, 4th edn. (London, 1665).
32 Rebecca Bullard's *The Politics of Disclosure* (London: Pickering & Chatto, 2009) is the major treatment; see also Noelle Gallagher, *Historical Literatures* (Manchester: Manchester University Press, 2012), 80–93; Melinda A. Rabb, *Satire and Secrecy* (Basingstoke and New York: Palgrave, 2007), 80–86; Michael McKeon, *The Secret History of Domesticity* (Baltimore: Johns Hopkins University Press, 2005), 469–73, 482–6, 492–9; Mayer, *History*, 97–8.
33 Gallagher's account is the most detailed, in *Historical*, 65–93.
34 Gallagher, *Historical*, 73, and see also 67, 71–6; Rabb, *Satire*, 68–72.
35 Bullard, *Politics*; Bannet, '"Secret History"', 370–1, 385; Gallagher, *Historical* 84; Rabb, *Satire*, 68–72.
36 John Oldmixon, 'The Preface', *Arcana Gallica: Or, the Secret History of France* (London, 1714), v.
37 Bannet, '"Secret History"', 384–5; Mayer, *History*, 99–101; Gallagher, *Historical*, 78–81.
38 *Secret History of the Reigns of K. Charles II and K. James II* ([London?], 1690), 11.
39 Edward Gibbon, *The History of the Decline and Fall of the Roman Empire*, ed. David Womersley, 3 vols. (New York: Allen Lane, 1994), 2: 586. See also Mayer, *History*, 97–8.
40 Thomas Hearne, *Ductor Historicus* (London, 1698), 110.
41 The romance comparison recalls French connections with English secret histories. McKeon writes that the French heroic romance 'exerted a profound influence on certain strains of the English secret history' (*Secret History*, 487); J. C. Major connects the *chronique scandaleuse* with 'the decadence of the heroic romance' in *The Role of Personal Memoirs in English Biography and Novel* (Philadelphia: University of Pennsylvania Press, 1935), 100.
42 N. N., *The Blatant Beast Muzzl'd: or, Reflexions on a Late Libel, entituled, The Secret History of the Reigns of K. Charles II and K. James II* ([London], 1691).
43 *Secret History of the Reigns of K. Charles II and K. James II.*, 205.
44 Thomas Salmon, *Impartial Examination of Bishop Burnet's History of His Own Time*, 2 vols. (London, 1724), 1: 616.

3

Secret History and Restoration Drama

Erin M. Keating

In 1693, celebrity actress Anne Bracegirdle narrowly avoided being abducted by Captain Richard Hill, an overzealous suitor who, having been rebuffed by the actress multiple times, decided to try force. In the course of the events, Bracegirdle's fellow actor William Mountfort was killed by Hill, who was convinced that the married actor was the real obstacle to his courtship of Bracegirdle. The incident and the subsequent trial of Hill's accomplice Charles Lord Mohun gave rise to a rash of popular print, including the published account of the trial that featured the testimony of Bracegirdle herself, a satirical elegy lamenting Mountfort's death and a prose secret history of the event published anonymously under the title of *The Player's Tragedy* (1693). Shortly after the incident, Thomas D'Urfey capitalised on the continuing interest in the scandal by writing a parallel plotline into *The Richmond Heiress* (1693), having Bracegirdle again be subjected to attempted abduction.

The London audience's eagerness for details of the abduction attempt was intimately bound with their desire for access to Bracegirdle herself, a desire heightened by her celebrity and her persona as the virgin actress. This interplay of desire, knowledge, performance and emotional connection, which significantly informs current critical understandings of the rise of celebrity culture throughout the eighteenth century, has been theorised in multiple ways, as 'it' by Joseph Roach, 'the interiority effect' by Felicity Nussbaum and 'betweenness' by Diana Solomon.[1] However, an affective intimacy based upon knowledge is not exclusive to celebrity; it is also an integral part of the secret histories that were popular during the later years of Charles II's reign, throughout the 1670s and early 80s.[2] It is this affective intimacy, rather than a shared interest in the political, that provides the strongest link between the secret history genre and the Restoration stage, which was often barred from presenting close representations of political figures within the playhouse. This chapter will demonstrate the connection between the secret history and celebrity genres during the Restoration as it is played out in and around the theatre, ultimately arguing that these genres began to separate out from one another in the 1690s, differentiating themselves through their changing affective techniques and engagement with the political, and ultimately taking part in the larger social and literary process of 'distinction to separation' which Michael McKeon argues is characteristic of the modern period.[3]

Secret history, as it was popularised in late seventeenth- and early eighteenth-century England, claims to tell the true, often sexually motivated, tales behind the political events of the present and recent past. This telling is complicated, however, by the 'teasing' nature of these narratives, which, as Rachel Carnell reminds us, are distinguished by tropes of 'simultaneous revelation and disguise'.[4] McKeon's capacious definition of secret history, which includes texts that openly declare themselves as such, as well as those 'that signal their secrecy through allegorical, amatory "romance" plots that sanction techniques of close reading to uncover their deepest public meaning', provides a useful generic umbrella under which to specify and further delineate the different forms of secret history that are used by writers working in a variety of larger genres.[5] Despite their varied techniques and genre affiliations, all secret histories are characterised by a strong connection to their moment of authorship and reception and to the particular events they purport to represent. They are also, as Rebecca Bullard argues, intimately connected to official historiography in that they offer 'an alternative vision of the recent political past, which deliberately chafes against official accounts and orthodox historical methods'.[6] While this proximity to the event is fruitful for prose secret histories, which are often anonymous, hidden under false imprints and distanced from their audience through the use of diversionary prefaces and multiple frames of narrative and translation, it is problematic for stage representations that are denied the same anonymous screens. Even if a playwright maintains his/her anonymity, the embodiment, locatedness and witnessing that are necessary elements of performance prevent the artful disconnection between text and event created by the secret history text.

There are numerous instances of what Robert Hume terms 'parallel plays' being subjected to pre-performance or early performance censorship during the Restoration because of their connections with particular ministers or controversies of the day.[7] Some of these plays, like Sir Robert Howard and George Villiers, Duke of Buckingham's *The Country Gentleman* (1669), were barred from performance entirely.[8] Others were pulled from the stage, like Nahum Tate's *Richard II* (1680), which after being refused a licence was performed under the title *The Sicilian Usurper*, an act of defiance that temporarily caused the closure of the theatre.[9] Other political plays, such as Thomas Shadwell's *The Lancashire Witches* (1682), required extensive cuts before they were considered suitable for performance.[10] That is not to say that plays with political implications and resonances were not performed on the Restoration stage. As Susan Staves argues in her analysis of political drama during the Restoration, many of the plays performed throughout Charles II's reign reflected either directly or indirectly on the political climate of the times; from the allusive critical dramas of the 1660s to plays that directly commented on the political crises between 1676 and 1682, the London theatres were filled with topical, political performances.[11] However, while these plays alluded to particular individuals and events, they did not feature the sustained parallel narratives that characterised the prose secret histories of the 1670s. Rather, plays like Thomas Otway's *Venice Preserv'd* (1682) relied on self-contained satirical portraits, such as the famous Nicky-Nacky scenes directed at Anthony Ashley Cooper, Earl of Shaftesbury, along with indirect allusions and imperfect parallel plotting to avoid the censor's eye.

Even with these strategies of obfuscation, plays representing incidents that adhered too closely to known ministerial or aristocratic figures could be barred from performance, as was the case in Buckingham's direct satire of Sir William Coventry in *The Country Gentleman*. Even staunchly royalist writers like John Dryden and Aphra Behn could fall afoul of the censors. Dryden and Nathanial Lee's *The Duke of Guise* (1682) was briefly suppressed for its critical representation of James Scott, Duke of Monmouth, who, despite his role in the Exclusion Crisis, was still a favourite of his father. Mary Lee, Lady Slingsby, and Aphra Behn were both arrested after Lee performed an epilogue, written by Behn, for the anonymous *Romulus and Hersilia, or, the Sabine War* (1682), which also was considered to reflect too closely on Monmouth. In the politically sensitive environment immediately after the Exclusion Crisis, the arrests aptly demonstrate the implication of the individual actor or actress performing political speech upon the stage; far from being an 'empty vessel for the playwright's words [...] Lady Slingsby was held legally responsible for the words she uttered onstage, as could be any performers of paratexts'.[12] Not merely subject to legal repercussions for their performances, actors and authors could be threatened or even set upon physically for controversial, satirical performances. Edward Kynaston's impersonation of Sir Charles Sedley in William Cavendish, Duke of Newcastle's *The Heiress* (1669) led to the actor being 'exceedingly dry-beaten with sticks [...] and forced to keep his bed'.[13] Hume and Love attribute the suppression of *The Country*

Gentleman less to the offending satire and more to the potential physical violence threatened by the challenge sent to Buckingham from Coventry. Rather than put up with the threatened violence between his ministers, Charles suppressed the offending play.[14] Thus, in stark contrast to the many screens offered to the secret history authors in print, the stage fully exposed its performances to the critical eyes of both the London public and the censors.

The stage had to take far more care with its connection to the contemporary political scene than the print secret histories because it was limited in its ability to clearly depict Charles II or his inner court circle in a way that could be conceived of as critical. This is in stark contrast to the alignment between narrative and contemporary individuals that can be seen in prose secret histories during the 1670s and 80s. Sébastien Brémond's *Hattigé, ou les Amours du Roy de Tamaran* (1676, first English translation 1680), for instance, clearly centres on Charles II and his attempts to please both his leading mistress and leading minister at the time the secret history is set – Barbara Palmer, Duchess of Cleveland, and Buckingham. The anonymous *Homaïs, ou La Reine de Tunis* (translated into English in 1681) takes this specificity further, providing details of the initial introduction of Charles II to his future mistress Louise de Kéroualle, Duchess of Portsmouth, at Dover in 1670.[15]

Given all of the problems introduced by performance and the censorship of the stage, it can seem that the secret history modes being explored and popularised in print had little impact on the Restoration theatre. However, the secret history mode is not defined solely through its content or form: a key part of McKeon's definition cited earlier is 'plots that sanction techniques of close reading'.[16] The secret history's reception practices, which were social, sceptical, and affective, are a defining element of the genre. While McKeon does not focus his own analysis of early secret histories on these reading practices, Kate Loveman's work on literary hoaxes in Restoration London has begun to fill this gap with its emphasis on sceptical reading – a social reading practice that required readers 'to look beneath a writer's professed design to discern a hidden agenda … commonly a controversial biographical, political or religious interpretation of the text'.[17] It is on the level of reception – particularly socially affective reception – that the stage meets the secret history page in Restoration London.

The creation of a bond of affective intimacy between the reader and the subject of a secret history was a key element of the secret history genre during the Restoration; it was also being used to shape the emerging fan culture surrounding celebrity actresses like Nell Gwyn and, a decade later, Anne Bracegirdle. Early celebrity in England has been theorised effectively by Roach in his study *It*, where he emphasises the ability of celebrity to project a quality of 'public intimacy' (3) that creates an illusory connection, based on an illusion of availability on the part of the public figure for his/her audience.

Nussbaum refines this illusion, arguing that the celebrity actresses of the eighteenth century created 'an interiority effect' cultivated alongside their public personas. This provided an illusion of interior depth 'to which celebrity could attach itself' (20) but which was just as much a construction as the characters the women played upon the stage. The actors' and actresses' mobilisation of their public personas and nurturing of their celebrity status came to fruition during the eighteenth century with the rise of actress and actor memoirs and the growth of the popular press. This provided a vast range of venues in which to address the public for these later theatre celebrities.[18] In the early days of celebrity culture, the theatre writers, like the early writers of secret history, were still experimenting with different ways of activating the intimacy between the players and their audience. By investigating these early attempts to mobilise audience affect specifically directed towards the secret history subjects and the players on the stage, we can see the complex exchanges taking place between writers, performers and audiences. This investigation provides a nuanced picture of the negotiations taking place between the audience's desire for access, whether it be to their monarch or to the 'queen' on the stage before them, and the writers' attempts to provide the illusion of access while maintaining the boundaries, both affective and epistemic, between the audience and the subjects of their desire.

In the 1670s and again in 1695 after the veteran actors split from the United Company and set up their own theatre in Lincoln's Inn Fields, the competition between the stages was a popular topic for prologues and epilogues. Most of these paratexts treat the topic generally, broadly enticing the audience to take the side of the company that they are currently patronising. However, a few go further, addressing specific moments within the rivalry, playing to theatre-goers whose frequent attendance and attention to current events would allow them to recognise the digs at the rival company, thus using audience knowledge affectively to, at least temporarily, create a bond of feeling between the performers and their audience. The comedian James Nokes of the Duke's Company initiated a series of these topical paratexts when he ridiculed French fashion during a performance of John Caryll's *Sir Salamon Single* for the English and French nobility at Dover in May 1670. Equipped with a sword and belt belonging to the Duke of Monmouth and dressed in a ludicrously short coat that referenced and exaggerated French fashion, Nokes turned his character of Sir Arthur Addle into a caricature of the French members of the audience. Prompter John Downes reports that Nokes' display 'put the King and Court to an Excessive Laughter; at which the *French* look'd very Shaggrin, to see themselves Ap'd by such a Buffoon'.[19] Using his body to carry the visual joke, Nokes astutely played on his royal audience's pleasure in seeing the specific satire involved in this type of performance, a notion strengthened by the other play chosen by the court to be performed at Dover, Thomas Shadwell's *The Sullen Lovers*. As Samuel Pepys reports in his diary, Shadwell's play caused a great deal of amusement at court in its portrayal of Sir Robert Howard as Sir Positive At-All. The recognition of the direct satire led Pepys to revise his original opinion of the play as 'tedious'; writing after seeing it a third time, Pepys reports: 'I for that reason like it, I find, the better too'.[20] Seemingly, the recognition of direct satire was enough to create audience interest and enjoyment in a play that might otherwise be found lacking. In showcasing Shadwell's play at Dover, Charles clearly demonstrated the court's desire not merely to tolerate but even to encourage moments of direct theatrical engagement with members of the court, but only when the targets were irritant ministers or foreign delegations.

The success of Nokes' Dover performance was repeated a number of times back in London, presumably catering to eager audiences who had heard reports of the joke and wanted to experience it for themselves. The prologue to Dryden's *The Conquest of Granada*, performed by Nell Gwyn by early January 1671, directly references this repetition and the origin of the jest: 'This jeast was first of t'other houses making, / And, five times try'd, has never fail'd of taking'.[21] Perhaps motivated by professional jealousy at not being chosen to accompany the court to Dover, the King's Company co-opts Nokes' joke for themselves a few months later, bringing out their most popular actress (and royal mistress) Gwyn, dressed in a 'broad-brim'd hat, and a wastbelt' (2: 381), to capture both the joke and the audience and to sway them to their side. Gwyn, who had been giving birth to her second son by Charles II at the time of the Dover meeting, uses the prologue to bodily re-assert her celebrity and her position as the king's entertainer, both in the theatre and in the bedroom. While criticising Nokes – and by extension the entire Duke's company – for repeatedly resorting to such a cheap tactic to get a laugh, Gwyn's performance draws on her public persona as beloved comedian and acknowledged royal mistress to appropriate the comedic performance for herself:

> This is that hat whose very sight did win yee
> To laugh and clap, as though the Devil were in yee.
> As then, for *Nokes*, so now, I hope, you'l be
> So dull, to laugh, once more, for love of me. (2: 381)

Re-directing the laughter from Nokes' joke to the audience's love for their favourite actress, Gwyn both criticises the low comedy of the original while elevating it through her personal popularity and her public persona. It is referenced at least twice more over the ensuing weeks, demonstrating its ability to speak to an audience familiar with the running joke.[22] The jest, which begins as a politically tinged caricature of the French, is transformed through its repetition in the London playhouses into a competition for audience affection and loyalty. Played out through the bodies of Gwyn and Nokes, the jest capitalises on the personal popularity both of these players and their perceived ability to link the London audiences to the actors themselves and, through its link to the Dover performance, to Charles II and his court.

By the 1690s, the celebrity performed by the leading actors and actresses is less about their links to the court and more about audience interest in the celebrities themselves. A group of paratexts that demonstrate this interest references the rivalry between the two competing theatre companies, Christopher Rich's company at Drury Lane and the newly formed company at Lincoln's Inn Fields under the leadership of Thomas Betterton, Elizabeth Barry and Anne Bracegirdle. When the veteran actors split from Rich's company, both playhouses marked the occasion with paratexts directly commenting on the supposed issues behind the actors' revolt.[23] However, the paratext that is most akin to secret history is a prologue spoken by Bracegirdle and, according to Pierre Danchin, printed separately in order to be available for the opening performance of the new company, thus serving as advertisement, secret history and performance.

Bracegirdle's prologue seems to provide the inside story on the motivation for the split, while also revealing how the players were able to get their licence for a new company. Playing on the prevailing political sentiments of the times, Bracegirdle raises the spectre of a tyrannical, absolute monarchy, which as Bullard argues was a favourite target of secret history writers during the 1690s and aligns the players with supporters of the 1688 revolution: 'A Free-born Player loaths to be compell'd / Our Rulers Tyraniz'd, and We Rebell'd' (5: 180).[24] Implicitly comparing the theatrical strife with the Glorious Revolution, Bracegirdle aligns the actors with the audience, augmenting the social cohesion created by the event of performance.

However, Bracegirdle's prologue quickly turns away from the political to the sex behind the politics. Addressing hypothetical questions about the actors' ability to attain a royal patent, Bracegirdle implies that she was the bribe that smoothed the way for the rest of the company: 'But you perhaps, wou'd have me here confess / How we obtain'd the Favour; – Can't you guess? ... By Brib'ry, errant Brib'ry, let me dye:' (5: 180–1).

Bracegirdle follows the familiar pun on 'dye' with a long passage of sexual innuendo and cheeky self-reference ending with the lines 'The Young Men kiss'd me, and the Old I kiss'd, / And luringly, I led them as I list' (5: 181). Throughout her career, Bracegirdle maintained a reputation as the virgin actress, despite performing highly suggestive prologues and epilogues and a variety of sexually experienced roles. As Solomon has argued, the tension between Bracegirdle's celebrity virgin persona and her performance of paratexts that seemed to offer an 'interiority effect' of a sexually experienced and in-control woman was one of the very conditions that made her such a star, the paradox between virgin / seductress being essential to her own 'it' factor. In the case of this secret history prologue, Bracegirdle, on the one hand, brings together politics with the hidden sexual motives that the genre always implies lie underneath the public decisions while, on the other hand, she plays on and strengthens her personal celebrity by, in Solomon's words, 'creating a titillatingly blurry boundary between her roles and her persona'.[25]

Bracegirdle's ability to perform multiple personas that appeared to provide differing levels of access for her fans heightened those fans' increasing desire for yet more of the 'real' celebrity. This desire for access clashes with the changes going on within the secret history genre after 1688. As Bullard argues, the secret history of this period conforms to one of two modes – texts either distance their readers from the absolute monarchs of the past, in the process creating a shared feeling of political allegiance among their Whig audience, or they destabilise the very idea of an allegiance based on secret knowledge by creating 'an arena in which no one can be sure of the extent or the accuracy of his or her knowledge', thereby complicating the view of secret history as always affectively creating a group of insiders based on privileged information.[26] The separation of the secret history and celebrity genres during the 1690s was driven by divergent motivations within changing political culture and the growth of fan culture in London. *The Player's Tragedy* which, as mentioned at the opening of this chapter, depicts the attempted abduction of Bracegirdle and the death of Mountfort, is a particularly interesting and, I argue, important prose secret history in that it exposes the limitations of that genre as celebrity fiction. Furthermore, it marks the divergence of the separate genres of the secret history and celebrity narratives during the last decade of the seventeenth century through its use of distancing techniques and its destabilisation of assumed audience knowledge with respect to its central subject, Bracegirdle.

As a secret history about the stage, *The Player's Tragedy* promises its readers access to Bracegirdle and, in particular, to the details surrounding the tragic death of Mountfort after the failed abduction attempt. Instead of this promised access, however, the anonymous author tantalises the reader (and his main character, Montano) with glimpses of Bracegirdle in the theatre and on the stage but keeps her at a distance through his use of disguise and layered narratives. Like the secret histories of the 1670s whose methods were so useful in early celebrity paratexts, *The Player's Tragedy* seems to promise the affective intimacy hungered for by fan culture; however, in reality, the text both emphasises the disconnection between the reader and its subject, Bracegirdle, and undermines the knowledge that Montano claims to be acting upon in his interactions with the actress. This is more like secret histories from the 1690s which either distance the reader from their villainised subject or destabilise the very idea of secure knowledge. In *The Player's Tragedy* this distancing leaves an uncomfortable void at the centre of the narrative layers and raises questions about who exactly is being villainised by the text.

The narrative of *The Player's Tragedy* focuses on Hill (called Montano in the story) and his pursuit of Bracegirdle (who is given the name of Bracilla). The convoluted plot includes Montano's description of his courtship and Bracilla's refusals, which result in a bawd offering to intercede on his behalf with Bracilla for the right amount of money. Coromella, the bawd, outlines further conditions for the encounter, one of which is that it must take place in total darkness. Though Montano enjoys his seeming possession of Bracilla for a while, he eventually discovers that he has been duped and that he has been having an affair with an entirely different woman, who is given her own back-story in a lengthy, interpolated tale. After this, Montano attempts to abduct Bracilla and, failing that, kills Monfredo (Mountfort) and immediately flees the country.

Rather than attempting to create the affective bond that is characteristic of early secret history and, as I have shown, of the creation of celebrity during the Restoration, *The Player's Tragedy* presents Bracilla as unattainable for Montano, and for the reader, while the events that created the scandal – the attempted abduction, duel and their aftermath – are literally kept to the outskirts of the text, occupying only the final few paragraphs of the narrative. This distancing effect begins immediately with a narrative description of Bracilla's 'insensible' nature and 'cold indifference' to 'those Miseries her Eyes daily caused to all that beheld her'.[27] It is further emphasised by the mediation of our access to Bracilla solely through Montano's self-serving and self-aggrandising narrative of the progress of his amours. While he insists on reading all of her rebukes as 'words of course, and what Women will say at the beginning of an Intrigue' (25), it is clear to the reader that Montano's relationship with Bracilla is even more a product of his imagination than is an audience member's perceived connection with the real actress behind the character upon the stage. The strength of Montano's imagined connection to Bracilla is given form in the narrative through the activities of the bawd and the body of the woman at the centre of the interpolated tale, Clelia, who impersonates Bracilla in a series of sexual encounters with Montano. Although the cheat is eventually discovered, it is sustained for a significant part of the text, during which Montano gazes upon the real Bracilla from a distance at the playhouse and holds the feigned Bracilla in her private chambers at night. The Bracilla that Montano enjoys and believes to be in his possession is an unseen creation of his imagination, who is only linked to the public actress through his desire and belief.

Thus, in *The Player's Tragedy*, readers are given a woman playing an actress, an actress playing roles in the theatre, a hero who conflates both the woman and the roles with the actress herself (exemplifying the public reputation given to the actress by her audience), and the actress behind the scenes who is both withheld from the reader and who, when she is allowed to speak, pushes against the hero's conflation of her self with her roles on stage. The text exaggerates the detached nature of an actress's social reputation, actually embodying this reputation in another woman, Clelia, thus exposing the Restoration audience's tendency to reify the actress's public reputation. As the *Count de la Lune*, an associate of Montano's, describes her, an actress is one 'whose Reputation, as well as Person is exposed for the Pleasure, and Diversion of the Audience' (10).

Despite seemingly contributing to this audience appropriation, and thus belonging with the many satires of the players popular throughout the Restoration, *The Player's Tragedy* manages simultaneously to attack and to uphold Bracegirdle's public reputation for chastity. Bracilla herself never takes part in the amorous encounters represented in the text; rather, it is Clelia impersonating Bracilla. Thus, the reader can imagine the mistress behind the virtuous persona while separating the actual woman on stage from the one in the bedroom; in effect, the story uses another woman's body to literalise the 'betweeness' created by the celebrity actress/character/persona for her audience. Yet by literally separating the bodies of the actress on stage and the 'actress' possessed by the eager fan, Montano, the text exposes and negates the pleasurable illusion of the intimate connection between fan and celebrity upon which the genre of celebrity fiction relies.

In shifting from the affectively connective secret histories of the 1670s to the distancing, destabilising secret histories of the 1690s, the genre realigns its connectivity from the subjects of the text to an implied community of readers constructed in opposition to the villainised subjects. Despite the community of London theatregoers that is available to be harnessed by a secret history of the stage, *The Player's Tragedy* does not encourage this type of audience cohesion. Rather, the text distances itself from its readers through its satirical depiction of Montano, which mocks the naiveté and ignorance of theatre audiences who mistake the emotions and behaviours that they see on stage with reality. Montano's ignorance, his conflation of Bracilla's stage characters and her private self, is revealed by his conviction that Bracilla must be capable of loving him because 'so much of it … appear[s] in [her] bare personating a Lover' (13). Yet Bracilla scorns Montano's declarations of love, declaring "tis pity you shou'd fling it away, and a thousand fine sayings to boot on me, since I vow Sir, I'm as deaf to that, as the People to Virtue in distress' (14). Satirising the prevailing tastes of her theatre audiences who relished her performances in plays like Nicholas Brady's *The Rape* (1692), the character here evokes Bracegirdle's performances and reputation, while scorning her audience and, in effect, interrupting the illusion of intimacy and preventing an impulse to community by shaming the text's own readership, who presumably would be those same audiences enjoying Bracegirdle represent destroyed virtue night after night on the London stage.

I have spent so much time on a fairly unknown and, by all appearances, unsuccessful secret history because its failure is uniquely revealing of the changes going on in both the secret history and celebrity genres during the 1690s. While those genres were experimenting with similar affective techniques in both their prose and dramatic forms throughout the Restoration period, they began to emerge as separate genres by the end of that period as writers adapted their techniques to the changing political and theatrical climates. While Kristina Straub has pointed to a continued connection between secret history and celebrity fiction later in the eighteenth century, this connection has become superficial – reduced to the mere assertion of private secrets made public and disconnected from the political and historiographical discourses that were once an integral part of the developing genre of celebrity discourse.[28] This is not to say that eighteenth-century celebrity memoirs did not reflect on and participate in their contemporary political landscapes; however, this connection is no longer a defining element of the genre by the middle of the eighteenth century. What bringing together the Restoration stage and the secret history reveals is the complex negotiations that were taking place within the realms of the political, theatrical, literary and social during the late seventeenth century and the ways that this interplay of affect and trope developed and differentiated into separate genres with the growth of expanded audiences and changing political climates.

Notes

1 Complementary in their theorisations of celebrity and their analyses of Restoration and eighteenth-century theatre, Roach, Nussbaum and Solomon all offer nuanced accounts of the ways that celebrity culture and the actors and actresses themselves manipulated their public personas to heighten audience desire and engagement while maintaining a degree of control over audience access to their private selves. See Joseph Roach, *It* (Ann Arbor: University of Michigan Press, 2007), 8; Felicity Nussbaum, *Rival Queens: Actresses, Performance, and the Eighteenth-Century British Theatre* (Philadelphia: University of Pennsylvania Press, 2010), 20–1; and Diana Solomon, *Prologues and Epilogues of the Restoration Theater: Gender and Comedy, Performance and Print* (Newark: University of Delaware Press, 2013), 18–19.
2 See Erin Keating, 'In the Bedroom of the King: Affective Politics in the Restoration Secret History', *Journal for Early Modern Cultural Studies*, 15 (2015), 58–82.
3 Michael McKeon, *The Secret History of Domesticity: Public, Private, and the Division of Knowledge* (Baltimore: Johns Hopkins University Press, 2005), xx.
4 Rachel Carnell, 'Eliza Haywood and the Narratological Tropes of Secret History', *Journal for Early Modern Cultural Studies*, 14 (2014), 115.
5 McKeon, *Secret History*, 471.
6 Rebecca Bullard, *The Politics of Disclosure, 1674–1725: Secret History Narratives, Political and Popular Culture in the Early Modern Period* (London: Pickering & Chatto, 2009), 18.
7 Robert D. Hume, *The Development of English Drama in the Late Seventeenth Century* (Oxford: Clarendon Press, 1976), 220.
8 Sir Robert Howard and George Villiers, Duke of Buckingham, 'The Country Gentleman', in *Plays, Poems, and Miscellaneous Writings Associated with George*

58 ERIN M. KEATING

Villiers Second Duke of Buckingham, eds. Robert D. Hume and Harold Love, 2 vols. (Oxford: Oxford University Press, 2007), 1: 231–58. See Hume and Harold Love's introduction to the play for details of the events leading to its suppression.
9 See Hume, *Development of English Drama*, 222.
10 Thomas Shadwell, *The Lancashire Witches* (London, 1682). Shadwell complains in his preface that the Master of the Revels, responding to rumours about the play being 'full of dangerous reflections' (A2r), expunged whole sections of dialogue, which Shadwell restored and italicised in the print edition.
11 Susan Staves, *Players' Scepters: Fictions of Authority in the Restoration* (Lincoln: University of Nebraska Press, 1979). See in particular 51–88.
12 Solomon, *Prologues and Epilogues*, 39–40.
13 Samuel Pepys, *The Diary of Samuel Pepys*, eds. Robert Latham and William Matthews, 11 vols. (Berkeley: University of California Press, 1971, 2000) 9: 435.
14 Hume and Love, *Buckingham*, 235.
15 Both the dating and authorship of *Homaïs* remain uncertain, as the name provided on the first English translation, Sebastien Grenadine, is almost certainly a pseudonym. Edwin Grobe, in an unpublished dissertation, compellingly argues for Brémond's authorship but further research is required for a definitive attribution. Edwin Paul Grobe, 'Sébastien Bremond: His Life and His Works', unpublished PhD thesis, Indiana University (1954), 69–73.
16 McKeon, *Secret History*, 471.
17 Kate Loveman, *Reading Fictions, 1660–1740: Deception in English Literary and Political Culture* (Aldershot: Ashgate, 2008), 20.
18 There has been a great deal of strong critical work on celebrity memoirs and the roles of actors and actresses in Restoration and eighteenth-century England. In addition to Roach, Nussbaum and Solomon, see Kristina Straub, *Sexual Suspects: Eighteenth-Century Players and Sexual Ideology* (Princeton: Princeton University Press, 1992); Elizabeth Howe, *The First English Actresses: Women and Drama 1660–1700* (Cambridge: Cambridge University Press, 1992); Gilli Bush-Bailey *Treading the Bawds: Actresses and Playwrights on the Late-Stuart Stage* (Manchester: Manchester University Press, 2006) and Helen E. M. Brooks, *Actresses, Gender, and the Eighteenth-Century Stage: Playing Women* (Basingstoke and New York: Palgrave Macmillan, 2015).
19 John Downes, *Roscius Anglicanus, or an Historical Review of the Stage* (London, 1708), 29.
20 Pepys, *Diary*, 9: 183, 186.
21 Danchin, Pierre (ed.), *The Prologues and Epilogues of the Restoration 1660–1700*, 6 vols. (Nancy, France: Publications Université Nancy II, 1981), 2: 381.
22 See Danchin, *Prologues and Epilogues*, 2: 399, 402.
23 See Danchin, *Prologues and Epilogues*, 5: 176, 182.

24 Bullard, *Politics of Disclosure*, 47.
25 Solomon, *Prologues and Epilogues*, 161.
26 Bullard, *Politics of Disclosure*, 57.
27 *The Player's Tragedy. Or, Fatal Love, A New Novel* (London, 1693), 4.
28 See Straub, *Sexual Suspects* (111).

4

Secret History and Allegory

David A. Brewer

When it comes to political allegory, otherwise sophisticated scholars of the late seventeenth century often grow curiously incurious. Especially in the classroom, but also while annotating and arguing, we tend to treat the relationship between allegorical figures and their supposed referents in parallel poems, like *Absalom and Achitophel*, as more-or-less straightforward equations. So, our notes tell us, we tell our students that David 'is really' Charles II, that Absalom 'is standing in for' the Duke of Monmouth, that when Dryden refers to Achitophel 'he really means' the Earl of Shaftesbury, and so on. If there is an obvious discrepancy between the biblical figures and those of the Exclusion Crisis, it is either hailed as evidence of Dryden's rhetorical genius (e.g., his talent for converting what might seem a liability – Charles's brood of illegitimate children – into an asset), dismissed as a local clumsiness of no great import, or cordoned off as an antiquarian puzzle to be solved with a report from the archives. Any evidence from the period of how the allegory was read – say, annotated copies of the poem or published keys – tends to be dispatched with the same alacrity. If a contemporary identification of a figure seems correct, it is treated as a simple confirmation of our annotations. If it seems implausible (say, a key's equation of Corah in *Absalom and Achitophel* with Stephen College, 'the Protestant Joiner', rather than Titus Oates), it is dismissed either as a laughable mistake or, at best, a reminder that late seventeenth- and early eighteenth-century readers were working with imperfect information.[1]

As my tone probably suggests, I think we need to do better if we are ever going to do justice to the complexity of either Dryden's work and its numerous imitators (what Alan Roper calls 'Absalom's Issue') or the reading practices of the late seventeenth and early eighteenth centuries, when what Catherine Gallagher once termed the 'desire to open every book to some extra-textual reality, to read everything double' dominated political and literary culture to a degree that we have still not fully grasped.[2] These are big issues and this essay is but a first stab at articulating an alternative way of approaching the problem. Put simply, I would like to propose that the discrepancies and competing marginal identifications that we have pushed aside as outliers and exceptions are, in fact, completely typical. Not necessarily typical in the statistical sense (although Roper's examination of 149 copies of *Absalom and Achitophel* turned up far more varieties of reference than our editions ever acknowledge), but typical in the Shklovskiian sense of *Tristram Shandy* being 'the most typical novel in world literature'.[3] That is, typical in that they lay bare the type and so allow us to see how even the most seemingly straightforward equations between an allegorical figure and its putative referent are shot through with discrepancies, departures from the supposed parallel, details that do not correspond, and so on. The fact that we can readily attach Charles's name to David and Absalom's name to Monmouth, but are still uncertain of the 1681 counterpart to Agag (for whose 'murther' Corah called) is not evidence of a difference in kind, but only of degree.[4]

Coming to terms with this will not only help us better grasp the workings of parallel poems such as *Absalom and Achitophel* (and their cousins in prose, such as *The Fugitive Statesman*), it will also help illuminate the affinities between parallel poems and other forms of partisan writing in the period, including secret history. Now secret history might seem to operate by rather different rules and in some senses it did. Secret histories present themselves as revisionary supplements to the official account, those that show 'what really happened'. As such, they can go in any number of directions, although they tend to resort to explanations of illicit sexuality and corruption at the behest of foreign powers.

Parallel poems, however, would seem bound by their use of typology. Their explanations are not, one would think, revelations of new facts or discoveries of hitherto unsuspected villainy, but predictions of how present crises will resolve: as it was in scripture, so it will be again. In strict formal terms, then, secret histories and parallel poems would appear to work by rather different logics toward rather different ends. As such, it might seem perverse to devote a chapter to exploring their affinity.

However, literary forms never work in a vacuum. Rather, they are necessarily caught up in and often distorted by the reading practices of the age in which they are operating. In the practices with which we are concerned (which hit their most fevered pitch in the years of the Exclusion Crisis –the heyday of parallel poems) almost any reference, no matter how apparently removed it was from the present moment, could be allegorised into the partisan revelations that we now think of as key to secret history. Put another way, if we conceive of secret history in formal or narratological terms, then it makes sense that its closest affinities would be with some of the varieties of prose fiction that we retrospectively call 'the novel'.[5] However, if we think of secret history not so much as a fixed genre but as an activity or event (and remember Stanley Eveling's dictum that 'an object is just a slow event'), then the form's place in the literary system becomes quite radically realigned.[6] In a world in which the young Francis Atterbury could casually presume that Moloch's frown and 'look denounc[ing]/Desperate revenge' in *Paradise Lost* was 'probably ye Picture of some great man', all literature was potentially allegorical and all allegory a potential revelation of secrets (see Figure 1). Indeed, I would contend that the self-proclaimed secret histories that emerge after the Revolution are in some ways but a codification of the breathless probing, comparing and speculative plunging down rabbit holes that characterised the reading practices of the previous decade and whose operations we can perhaps best see at work in parallel poems such as *Absalom and Achitophel* and the uses to which readers put them. Not all secret histories are allegories, but the partisan allegorising of the late 1670s and early 1680s was a necessary precondition for the emergence of what we would now describe as secret history.

Enough preliminaries. The basic problem, as Samuel Johnson recognised, is that 'allegories drawn to great length will always break; Charles could not run continually parallel with David'.[7] No matter how apt the comparison, sooner or later there will be some aspect of what is being allegorised that will not line up; it will be true for one side of the putative equation, but not the other. Some of Dryden's contemporaries tried to dismiss this as a problem. For example, *Some Memoirs: or, A Sober Essay for a Just Vindication of the Right Honourable the Earl of Shaftesbury* (1681) argued that a comparison 'must not … be accounted ridiculous, because it cannot *in omnibus Quadrare*, or have an happy Hit in ev'ry punctilio … There is never a *congruity*, either in Civil or sacred History, which will not well enough admit of some Disparity … there is no Type in the Law propounded for its likeness to the Anti-type, but it contains in it some unlikeness thereunto in some circumstantial Adjuncts … there's no *Parable* or *Similitude* in the Gospel … which hath not still some Dissimilitude'. Even Plutarch, 'Famous for Paralels', was 'oft put hard to it to make an happy Hit in all particulars'.[8] Similarly, *A Loyal Congratulation to the Right Honourable, Anthony, Earl of Shaftesbury* (1681) counselled its addressee to 'let them with their Poetick Malice swell, / Falsely apply the Story, known so well, / Of *Absalom*, and of *Achitophel*', which, in its condemnation of false application, suggests the possibility that there could be true.[9] But a

Book II. **Paradise Lost.** 31

On this side nothing; and by proof we feel
Our power sufficient to disturb his Heav'n,
And with perpetual inrodes to Allarme,
Though inaccessible, his fatal Throne:
Which if not Victory is yet Revenge.
  He ended frowning, and his look denounc'd
Desperate revenge, and Battel dangerous
To less then Gods. On th' other side up rose
Belial, in act more graceful and humane;
A fairer person lost not Heav'n; he seemd   110.
For dignity compos'd and high exploit:
But all was false and hollow; though his Tongue
Dropt Manna, and could make the worse appear
The better reason, to perplex and dash
Maturest Counsels: for his thoughts were low;
To vice industrious, but to Nobler deeds
Timerous and slothful: yet he pleas'd the ear,
And with perswasive accent thus began.
  I should be much for open Warr, O Peers,
As not behind in hate; if what was urg'd   120.
Main reason to perswade immediate Warr,
Did not disswade me most, and seem to cast
Ominous conjecture on the whole success:
When he who most excells in fact of Arms,
In what he counsels and in what excels
Mistrustful, grounds his courage on despair
And utter dissolution, as the scope
Of all his aim, after some dire revenge.
First, what Revenge? the Towrs of Heav'n are fill'd
With Armed watch, that render all access   130.
Impregnable; oft on the bordering Deep
Encamp thir Legions, or with obscure wing
Scout farr and wide into the Realm of night,
Scorning surprize. Or could we break our way

Figure 1. Francis Atterbury's presumption that *Paradise Lost* was best read à clef. Courtesy of the James Marshall and Marie-Louise Osborn Collection, Beinecke Rare Book and Manuscript Library, Yale University (Osborn pb 9).

more clear-eyed view of the problem can be found in the assessment of the genre offered a decade later in *Rabshakeh Vapulans* (1691). The author asks plaintively 'But in good earnest wou'd you have me look / Each Verse or Chapter in the *Pentateuch*, / And hunt for *Paralells* in every Book? / Murder *Chronology*', 'And right or wrong make out the *Paralell*'.¹⁰

The problems that arise from the inevitability of the allegory breaking are only compounded when there are multiple figures involved. One side of the equation will almost always involve figures who have no clear counterparts on the other side. These supernumeraries either need to be excluded to maintain the parallel (which then misrepresents that side of the equation) or have counterparts invented or foisted in from elsewhere, which creates a whole new set of complications. Consider just two examples from *Absalom and Achitophel*. The portrait of the second Duke of Buckingham as Zimri is rhetorically devastating (indeed, it has come to be the first and often the only thing people know about Buckingham): 'Stiff in Opinions, always in the wrong; / Was every thing by starts, and nothing long: / But, in the course of one revolving Moon / Was Chymist, Fidler, States-Man, and Buffoon.'¹¹ But there is no Zimri in 2 Samuel 13–18 (the passage in scripture in which we get Absalom's rebellion against David). Dryden has taken the name either from Numbers 25:6–18, in which Zimri, a Jewish prince, and his Midianitish mistress, Cozbi, were caught *in flagrante* and slaughtered by a priest in order to atone for Israel's 'whoredom with the daughters of Moab' and so stop a plague that was threatening the nation, or from 1 Kings 16:9–20, in which Zimri, 'captain of half of his [King Elah]'s chariots', murdered his monarch's entire house and ruled Israel for seven days until, besieged by another military leader, he committed suicide by setting fire to the palace. The first Zimri is from the time of Moses (more than 400 years before David and Absalom); the second is from several generations after David. Neither offers a wholly sustainable parallel with Buckingham. Buckingham did have an affair with the Countess of Shrewsbury (and killed her husband in a duel), but adultery is not the same as miscegenation, the affair began after the plague had already come through, and Buckingham was still very much alive in 1681, despite his transgressions. Similarly, Buckingham might have been scheming against his king (insofar as the Tories thought that Opposition was, by definition, incipient treason) but he certainly had not slaughtered the Stuarts or set fire to Whitehall. Christopher Nesse mocked what he called Dryden's '*Cento Talmud*' for these disparities in *A Key (with the Whip)* (1682), asking 'which of th'two *Zimri*'s *He*'s, thou canst not tell. / Not *Cozbi*'s Rogue *he* is, nor *Ela*'s Traitor,/ Neither of these agree in mode or matter': '*He* [the first Zimri] was *Young*, *this* [Buckingham] *old*, / *He* hug'd *Outlandish*, *this* true *English Mold*: / A Foreign Whore, and a Domestick Wife, / Differs *them* much in *Law* as well as *Life*'.[12] Much the same point was made by Elkanah Settle in *Absalom Senior*, who, tongue in cheek, begged pardon for 'clapping but about a score of years extraordinary on the back of my *Absolom*' and pled the precedent set by Dryden's poem, 'where we see him bring in a *Zimri* into the Court of *David*, who in the Scripture-story dyed by the Hand of *Phineas* in the days of *Moses*'.[13]

A similar anachronism and incongruity haunt the case of Corah, whom most keys and marginal annotations identify as Titus Oates, the principal witness (and inventor) of the Popish Plot. The scriptural Korah – in Numbers 16 – led a rebellion against Moses and Aaron (again, centuries before David), alleging that they had illegitimately elevated themselves 'above the congregation of the Lord', 'all' of whom were 'holy'. In order to prove that his authority was divinely established, Moses predicted that Korah, his followers and all their goods would be swallowed up by the earth, and so they were.

Oates's accusations, on the other hand, were primarily against secular figures and (to the Tories' chagrin) no chasm had opened its mouth for him. Again, Nesse pounced on the disparity, declaring 'thy Type' 'Jars with th' Antitype, / They suit in nothing, save both *Levites* be / A *Rebel That*, but *Loyal This* all see': 'Twixt thy two *Corahs* in the *Act* or *End*, / Vast difference in *both* thou maist attend: / How can thy Jingles jump in any one / Of *Corahs Acts* (Ramm'd with Rebellion) / With this brave *Doctors* brisk Discovery/Of the Rude Romish-Rebel's Treachery'.[14] But even from a perspective more sceptical of the Popish Plot than that of the ardently Whiggish Nesse, one would be hard pressed to sustain the Corah/Oates parallel beyond a broad sense of both men being vaguely clerical rabble-rousers.

To complicate matters still further, the relationships *between* figures on one side are rarely completely parallel to those on the other. So, for example, early on in *Absalom and Achitophel*, David's lack of a legitimate heir is blamed on his Queen, Michal, 'a Soyl ungratefull to the Tiller's care'.[15] The keys all agree that Michal stands in for Catherine of Braganza, Charles II's wife, who, like the scriptural Michal in 2 Samuel 6:16–23, 'had no child unto the day of her death'. But Michal's barrenness was the result of her reproaching David for leaping and dancing before the ark and serving food to the 'whole multitude of Israel', thereby debasing himself 'in the eyes of the handmaids of his servants'. Catherine, by contrast, was extraordinarily long-suffering and seems to have gone out of her way to avoid criticism of her husband's conduct. Still more striking is the fact that Michal was the daughter of Saul, who elsewhere in *Absalom and Achitophel* apparently corresponds to Oliver Cromwell. Not only was Catherine Portuguese, rather than from Cambridgeshire, but a Cromwell–Stuart alliance would have been pretty much unthinkable at any point in the Restoration.

The problem I am outlining is not simply one of recent history failing to correspond to the scriptural account of Absalom's rebellion. Scripture, in turn, frequently did not foreshadow recent history. So, for example, Achitophel insists that David's generosity is a mark of his weakness: 'Let him give on till he can give no more, / The Thrifty Sanhedrin shall keep him poor: / And every Sheckle which he can receive, / Shall cost him a Limb of his Prerogative.'[16] As a description of Charles's financial negotiations with Parliament, this seems reasonably apt. But the biblical David's funds were not dependent on grants from the Sanhedrin (which was, in any case, merely a judicial body) and figuring constraints on the prerogative as a kind of pruning conjures up the royal oak, a tree with which David had no connection, although – unfortunately for the parallel – Absalom inadvertently caught his neck in one, leaving him vulnerable to summary execution by Joab. Similarly, Shimei (the supposed counterpart to Slingsby Bethel, the jury-packing Whig Sheriff of London) is ironically praised for his frugality, as evidenced by his cool kitchen: 'For Towns once burnt, such Magistrates require / As dare not tempt Gods Providence by fire.'[17] However, the burning of Jerusalem still lay centuries in the future. Traces of the Great Fire, on the other hand, could be seen in London on a daily basis.

I could go on (and detail, say, how one of the key events defining the scriptural Absalom – his murder of Amnon for raping his half-sister – does not correspond to anything in Monmouth's life), but I suspect the pattern is clear. Again and again, what are presented as parallels do not line up; what are offered as congruous end up being different shapes. My point in all this is not to disparage Dryden, who handles the comparisons better than many of his contemporaries (Samuel Pordage's *Azaria and Hushai* is one long orgy of anachronism) but rather to insist that the very project is an impossible one. Johnson was right: extended allegories 'will always break'. They will break all the more once readers get involved, as they necessarily had to if these parallel poems were to have any chance of swaying the public in such a politically charged age. As Roper's survey of annotated copies reveals at a macro-level, and a dip into my own institution's holdings confirms at a micro-level, the equations between the personages of Davidic Israel and those of Exclusion-era Britain were not only fraught within the text of the poem, but also involved far more competing candidates than the straightforward translations of our annotations like to admit.

Consider only 'wise *Issachar*', the 'wealthy western friend' who supplied 'hospitable treats' on Absalom's 'Progress' 'from East to West'.[18] A copy at the Clark identifies him as 'M[r] Teke', a copy at the Huntington as 'S[r] W[m]: Coven', a copy at Ohio State 'Tho: Thyn', and another copy at Ohio State just 'T:T:'. Copies at the University of Chicago and at the John Rylands Library insist on Lord Grey (who is himself a bit of floating referent: he is tied to 'no fewer than five' of Dryden's personages in various copies of the poem).[19] Indeed, another Clark copy, Roper's own personal copy, and a copy at All Souls College, Oxford even map out the Issacharian alternatives: 'either S[r] Willm Courtney or Speak in Dorsetshire', 'Esq[er] Thinne or … will Courtney', 'M[r] Thinn or M[r] Speak [or] S[r] W[m] Courtney'.[20] So we have at least five, possibly six or seven candidates (depending on whether one presumes Teke and Speak are the same person and that T.T. is Thomas Thynne) to serve as the counterpart to a single figure from scripture. It is entirely possible that other, still unsurveyed copies offer yet more possibilities: Monmouth was hosted by at least eight Whig magnates on his western progress in the summer of 1680. Similarly, depending on which copy one is looking at, Bathsheba, in whose 'Embraces' David has grown 'old', is either the Duchess of Portsmouth or the Duchess of Cleveland (and, who knows, perhaps in other, yet unsurveyed copies, Nell Gwyn or the Duchess of Mazarin: after all, an early eighteenth-century key hedged its bets with 'D. *Portsmouth*, or any other Concubine').[21] Given all this, it may be telling that the (wholly insincere) *A Panegyric on the Author of Absolom and Achitophel* refers to the figures of the poem as plural: 'no wonder then so Feelingly he tells / Of *Corahs, Shimeis*, and *Achitophells*.'[22]

Of course, the referents become still more varied once we bring in the various replies to *Absalom and Achitophel*. In *Absalom Senior*, for example, Settle reworks the story for Whiggish ends, making the rebellious Absalom and his evil councillor Achitophel into clear stand-ins for the Duke of York (the future James II) and the Earl of Halifax, respectively, while the King's faithful servant Barzillai has become a lightly disguised version of Shaftesbury.[23] Similarly, in *Azaria and Hushai*, the opportunistic Shimei is transformed into Dryden himself.

My point in rehearsing all this, though, is not simply to point out the sheer variety of referents, but to suggest how, in conjunction with the disparities and incongruities we have already explored, that variety can shed light on the kinship between these parallel poems and other forms shaped by the reading practices of the period, most notably secret history. Given the constraints of an essay, we will focus on a single example, but similar problems and opportunities crop up throughout the poem and its imitators. Let us return to Bathsheba. As we just saw, there are at least two referents for her given in the surviving annotated copies: the Duchess of Portsmouth (see Figure 2) and the Duchess of Cleveland (see Figure 3). There is also a quite striking disparity between the scriptural Bathsheba and either of Charles's mistresses: namely, that by the time of Absalom's rebellion, Bathsheba had become David's wife. Here is where this kind of allegory's affinities with secret history start to come into view. If Bathsheba is supposed to stand in for Louise de Kéroualle, the Duchess of Portsmouth, does that mean that she and Charles were secretly married (after all, they had had a mock-wedding back in 1671)? If so, that would further confirm Whig fears that Charles was in thrall to the French. If Bathsheba is supposed to stand in for Barbara Palmer, the Duchess of Cleveland, does that mean that *she* and Charles were secretly married? If so, that would corroborate Whig fears of Catholic influence at court. Either way, there would be a legitimate heir (five, in Palmer's case) who would supplant the Duke of York in the line of succession. Either way, additional significance might attach to the Popish Plot or the incessant rumours of an impending French invasion. These were not idle questions for readers of the early 1680s. Nor were they impertinent. Just a year before *Absalom and Achitophel*, Charles had to issue a public declaration denying 'a most false and scandalous Report, of a Marriage ... made between Us, and one Mrs. *Walters*, ... Mother of the present Duke of *Monmouth*', which would 'bring into Question, the clear undoubted Right of Our True and Lawful Heirs, and Successors to the Crown'.[24] There is no reason to think that Dryden was trying to hint at any of this. But his intentions are beside the point. The mere fact of the overt disparity between Bathsheba and Portsmouth or Cleveland sets up a structure that, given the reading practices of the time, elicited speculation about what the parallel and its apparent gaps revealed and how far the royal mistresses' plotting in the service of Popery and arbitrary government 'really' extended. Which is to say, allegory's propensity to break and so open up questions along these lines transforms it into something akin to secret history, whose central claim is, as Rebecca Bullard notes, always one of disclosing 'previously undiscovered intelligence', 'supplement[ing] and undermin[ing] public versions of history'.[25] Or, as Michael McKeon puts it elsewhere in this volume, secret history 'presupposes a revelatory difference between the official history and history from below'.[26] By virtue of containing what a newsletter termed 'lively characters ... under Jewish names', *Absalom and Achitophel* and its progeny encouraged a kind of reading in which the 'official history' of the overt, unambiguous parts of the allegory risked being sidelined in favour of the more intriguing and compelling – because apparently more 'secret' – hints and whispers offered up by the disparities and incongruities and failures to completely map.[27] Secret history as a recognisable and regularly produced form may not have emerged until after the Revolution, but the hunger for scandalous revelations that it fed was well established a decade prior.

In closing, I would like to briefly consider another of allegory's affinities, one that might illuminate how both parallel poems and secret histories worked in the late seventeenth-century world. In the collection long known as the 'Buckingham commonplace book' – though it seems doubtful that any of the work contained in it is actually by Buckingham – there are some verses addressed 'To Dryden' that complain 'As witchs images of wax invent / To torture those theyr bid to represent. / And as the true live substance do's decay / Whilst that slight Idol melts in flames away / Such and no lesser witchcraft wounds my name / So thy ill made resemblance wasts my fame'.[28] So, either for Buckingham or someone ventriloquising him, the portrait of Zimri was a kind of volt sorcery – what I grew up calling a voodoo doll: a representation that could affect and afflict its supposed original. This, I would like to propose, is not too far afield from the effigies of the Pope that were burned at the close of huge processions in London – and smaller ones in Scotland and the provinces – throughout the 1670s and early 1680s, including on the 1681 anniversary of Queen Elizabeth's accession (in a nice coincidence, this was the day Narcissus Luttrell acquired his copy of *Absalom and Achitophel* and so, most likely, its date of initial publication). One Whig estimated that the Pope burning of 1679 attracted 'near Two Hundred Thousand People', which, if correct, meant it was witnessed by between one-third and one-half of the entire population of the metropolis.[29] Obviously no one present thought the actual Bishop of Rome was getting a taste of his own medicine. But I would wager that the vast majority of those in attendance wished him ill and hoped that their ritual destruction of his effigy would somehow contribute to his fall. So too, I would like to propose, the denizens of *Absalom and Achitophel* and other parallel poems are by no means of a piece with the actual Charles, Monmouth, Shaftesbury, et al. Nor is, say, the 'James II' of a secret history one and the same with the actual monarch of that name. But here again, I suspect, the public hoped that their manipulation of a representation could have powerful consequences on the conduct,

[19]

Th' admiring Croud are dazled with surprize,
And on his goodly person feed their Eyes:
His joy conceal'd, he sets himself to show;
On each side bowing popularly low:
His looks, his gestures, and his words he frames,
And with familiar ease repeats their Names.
Thus form'd by Nature, furnish'd out with Arts,
He glides unfelt into their secret hearts;
Then, with a kind compassionating look,
And sighs, bespeaking pity e're he spoke:
Few words he said; but easie those and fit:
More slow than Hybla drops, and far more sweet.

I mourn, my Country-men, your lost Estate;
Though far unable to prevent your Fate:
Behold a banish'd man, for your dear Cause
Expos'd a Prey to Arbitrary Laws!
Yet oh! that I alone coud be undone,
Cut off from Empire, and no more a Son!
Now all your Liberties a Spoil are made;
Ægypt and *Tyrus* intercept your Trade,
And *Jebusites* your Sacred Rites invade.
My Father, whom with Reverence yet I name,
Charm'd into Ease, is careless of his Fame:
And brib'd with petty sums of Foreign Gold,
Is grown in *Bathsheba*'s Embraces old: *Duches Portsmouth*
Exalts his Enemies, his Friends destroys:
And all his pow'r against himself imploys.
He gives, and let him give my right away:
But why should he his own, and yours betray?
He onely, he can make the Nation bleed,
And he alone from my revenge is freed.
Take then my tears (with that he wip'd his Eyes)
'Tis all the Aid my present pow'r supplies:
No Court-Informer can these Arms accuse;
These Arms may Sons against their Fathers use;
And, 'tis my wish, the next Successor's Reign
May make no other *Israelite* complain.

D 2   Youth,

Figure 2. Bathsheba as the Duchess of Portsmouth.
Courtesy of the Rare Books and Manuscripts Library of The Ohio State University Libraries (PR 3416.A2 1682b).

[19]
Th' admiring Croud are dazled with surprize,
And on his goodly person feed their eyes:
His joy conceal'd, he sets himself to show;
On each side bowing popularly low:
His looks, his gestures, and his words he frames,
And with familiar ease repeats their Names.
Thus, form'd by Nature, furnish'd out with Arts,
He glides unfelt into their secret hearts:
Then, with a kind compassionating look,
And sighs, bespeaking pity e'r he spoke,
Few words he said; but easie those and fit:
More flow than Hybla drops, and far more sweet.

   I mourn, my Country-men, your lost Estate;
Though far unable to prevent your Fate:
Behold a Banish'd man, for your dear cause
Expos'd a prey to Arbitrary Laws!
Yet oh! that I alone coud be be undone,
Cut off from Empire, and no more a Son!
Now all your Liberties a spoil are made;
Ægypt and *Tyrus* intercept your Trade,
And *Jebusites* your Sacred Rites invade.
My Father, whom with reverence yet I name,
Charm'd into Ease, is careless of his Fame:
And, brib'd with petty sums of Foreign Gold,
Is grown in *Bathsheba*'s Embraces old:
Exalts his Enemies, his Friends destroys:
And all his pow'r against himself imploys.
He gives, and let him give my right away:
But why should he his own, and yours betray?
He onely, he can make the Nation bleed,
And he alone from my revenge is freed.
Take then my tears (with that he wip'd his Eyes)
'Tis all the Aid my present pow'r supplies:
No Court-Informer can these Arms accuse:
These Arms may Sons against their Fathers use;
And it's my wish, the next Successor's Reign
May make no other *Israelite* complain.

Figure 3. Bathsheba as the Duchess of Cleveland.
Courtesy of the Special Collections Research Center, University of Chicago
(PR 3418 A2 1681a).

perhaps even the lives, of the subjects of that representation: one commentator suggested that Dryden's muse 'in effect' took it 'upon her to hasten' Shaftesbury to 'the Hangman's Ax'.[30] Allegories may be doomed to break, but I submit that, once you start looking, their shards, and the unexpected directions in which they point, often end up being the most interesting thing about them.

Notes

1. [John Dryden], *Absalom and Achitophel. A Poem* (London, [1708?]), 1.
2. Alan Roper, 'Absalom's Issue: Parallel Poems in the Restoration', *Studies in Philology* 99:3 (2002), 268–94; Catherine Gallagher, *Nobody's Story: The Vanishing Acts of Women Writers in the Marketplace, 1670–1820* (Berkeley: University of California Press, 1994), 124. The single best account of these reading practices remains Steven N. Zwicker, *Lines of Authority: Politics and English Literary Culture, 1649–1689* (Ithaca: Cornell University Press, 1993).
3. Alan Roper, 'Who's Who in *Absalom and Achitophel*?', *Huntington Library Quarterly* 63:1 (2000), 93–138; Victor Shlovsky, 'Sterne's Tristram Shandy: Stylistic Commentary' in *Russian Formalist Criticism: Four Essays*, trans. Lee T. Lemon and Marion J. Reis (Lincoln: University of Nebraska Press, 1965), 57.
4. John Dryden, 'Absalom and Achitophel. A Poem' in *Poems, 1681–1684*, ed. H. T. Swedenberg, Jr., *The Works of John Dryden*, 20 vols. (Berkeley: University of California Press, 1972–1990), 2: 25.
5. See, for example, Rachel Carnell, 'Slipping from Secret History to Novel', *Eighteenth-Century Fiction* 28:1 (2015), 1–24.
6. Eveling's pronouncement seems to have never been committed to print. See Barbara Kirshenblatt-Gimblett, 'The Museum as Catalyst', keynote address to Museums 2000: Confirmation or Challenge, 19 n 28. Available at: www.nyu.edu/classes/bkg/web/vadstena.pdf.
7. Samuel Johnson, 'Dryden' in *The Lives of the Most Eminent English Poets; with Critical Observations on their Works*, ed. Roger Lonsdale, 4 vols. (Oxford: Clarendon Press, 2006), 2: 136.
8. *Some Memoirs: or, A Sober Essay for a Just Vindication of the Right Honourable the Earl of Shaftesbury. Containing the most Material Remarques and the Principal Passages of his Publick Life, Most Memorably Transacted Hitherto* (London, 1681), 7.
9. *A Loyal Congratulation to the Right Honourable Anthony, Earl of Shaftesbury: Upon the Disappointment of his, the King and Kingdoms Enemies, by the Loyal Grand Juries Finding the Bill against Him Ignoramus* (London, 1681), 1. For surveys of the dozens of prior applications of David and Achitophel to seventeenth-century politics, see Richard F. Jones, 'The Originality of *Absalom and Achitophel*', *Modern Language Notes* 46:4 (1931), 211–18; Dryden, 'Absalom and Achitophel', 230–32; and John Dryden, *The Poems of John Dryden*, ed. Paul Hammond, 5 vols. (London: Longman, 1995), 1: 446–8.

10 *Rabshakeh Vapulans: or, An Answer to the Tribe of Levi; in Vindication of the Clergy. A Poem. With a Preface, Reflecting on the Wit and Civility of that Famous Poem, and some late Pamphlets of the same Nature* (London 1691), 11–12.
11 Dryden, 'Absalom and Achitophel', 21.
12 [Christopher Nesse], *A Key (With the Whip) to Open the Mystery & Iniquity of the Poem Call'd Absalom & Achitophel: Shewing its Scurrilous Reflections upon both King and Kingdom* (London, 1682), 28.
13 [Elkanah Settle], *Absalom Senior: or, Achitophel Transpros'd. A Poem* (London, 1682), A2v.
14 [Nesse], *A Key*, 34–5.
15 Dryden, 'Absalom and Achitophel', 5.
16 Dryden, 'Absalom and Achitophel', 17.
17 Dryden, 'Absalom and Achitophel', 24.
18 Dryden, 'Absalom and Achitophel', 27.
19 Roper, 'Who's Who', 107–8, 102. The Ohio State copies are PR 3416.A2 1681 c.2 and PR 3416.A2 1681.
20 Roper, 'Who's Who', 108.
21 Dryden, 'Absalom and Achitophel', 26; Roper, 'Who's Who', 108–9; [Dryden], *Absalom and Achitophel*, 1.
22 *A Panegyrick on the Author of Absolom and Achitophel, Occasioned by his Former Writing of an Elegy in Praise of Oliver Cromwel, Lately Reprinted* (London, 1681), 2. Cf. [Nesse], *A Key*: 'Thus art thou *lame* in both thy Parallels, / Thy *Absoloms*, and thy *Achitophels*' (27).
23 There are alternative counterparts as well to Hushai, Caleb, Jonah, Nadab, Shimei, Corah, Amiel, Jotham and Adriel.
24 *The London Gazette*, 7–10 June 1680.
25 Rebecca Bullard, *The Politics of Disclosure, 1674–1725: Secret History Narratives* (London: Pickering & Chatto, 2009), 3, 20.
26 Michael McKeon, '*Paradise Lost* as a Secret History', in this volume (17–32).
27 Historical Manuscripts Commission, *Tenth Report, Appendix, Part IV: The Manuscripts of the Earl of Westmoreland, Captain Stewart, Lord Stafford, Lord Muncaster, and Others* (London: His Majesty's Stationery Office, 1906), 174.
28 *Plays, Poems, and Miscellaneous Writings associated with George Villiers, Second Duke of Buckingham*, ed. Robert D. Hume and Harold Love, 2 vols. (Oxford: Oxford University Press, 2007), 2: 253.
29 *Domestick Intelligence, or News both from City and Country. Published to Prevent False Reports*, No. 40, 21 November 1679.
30 *Poetical Reflections on a Late Poem Entituled, Absalom and Achitophel. By a Person of Honour* (London, 1681), B1v.

5

Secret History and Amatory Fiction

Claudine van Hensbergen

Just hours before consummating a much-anticipated affair with her brother-in-law, the heroine of Aphra Behn's epistolary novel, *Love-Letters between a Nobleman and his Sister* (1684–7), writes to her lover and compares herself unfavourably to a rival mistress, his 'graver business of State':

> does not *Silvia* ly neglected and unregarded in your thoughts? hudled up confusedly with your graver business of State, and almost lost in the ambitious crowd? … but you must espouse a fatal cause too, more pernicious than that Matrimony, and more destructive to my repose: oh give me leave to reason with you, and since you have been pleas'd to trust and afflict me with the secret; which honest as I am I will never betray yet, yet give me leave to urge the danger of it to you, and consequently to me, if you pursue it.[1]

As Silvia's letter reveals, her chief reservations about their (by contemporary standards) incestuous affair do not spring from Philander's marriage to her sister but from his political engagement with 'a fatal cause'. This had an all-too-real parallel in the Whig conspiracies of contemporary England. For in the three volumes of *Love-Letters*, Behn was responding to current scandal, using her novel as a means of exposing the sexual debauchery of the aristocracy and capitalising upon unfolding political events. The work documented a publicly reported case in which Ford, Lord Grey (Philander), was put on trial in 1683 on charges of seducing his sister-in-law, Lady Henrietta Berkeley (Silvia). Grey was found innocent, having married Henrietta to his own servant, yet the couple continued to invite political interest since Grey, a prominent Whig, was subsequently involved in the Rye House Plot (1683), fleeing to the Continent with Henrietta upon its failure, and returning to England in 1685 as one of the leaders in Monmouth's failed rebellion.[2]

Of all Behn's writing, *Love-Letters* harbours the clearest characteristics of secret history, a genre which claimed to expose the true workings of the State and the corrupt nature of those in power. Whilst critics have analysed aspects of its political content, and others have labelled and understood *Love-Letters* as a secret history, the work is most widely discussed both in relation to the tradition of amatory fiction and to its formative role within the development of the English novel.[3] The recent critical interest in analysing secret history as a genre in its own right has seen Rebecca Bullard challenge the basis upon which *Love-Letters* may be claimed as such.[4] Conceding that it engages 'in a variety of ways with ideas about secrecy', Bullard suggests that the work does 'not reveal the combination of self-consciousness towards the rhetorical act of disclosure and the deployment of this self-consciousness to a partisan end that characterise the Whig tradition of secret history'.[5] As both a Tory and highly partisan writer, Behn was unlikely to engage with the emerging genre of secret history in an altogether similar way to contemporary Whig writers. Indeed, Bullard herself demonstrates that Behn's successors in the 'fair triumvirate', Delarivier Manley and Eliza Haywood, purposefully adapt and redeploy Whig approaches to secret history and in so doing turn it to specifically Tory ends.[6] Taken together, the work of these three women writers suggests that a key thread of secret history lies in its engagement with amatory fiction, with this constituting a specific Tory variation of the genre whose origins predated the highpoint of the genre in the 1690s.

Behn perceived the possibility of adapting secret history to her own purposes as early as the mid-1680s, with her composition of *Love-Letters* constituting a highly partisan interjection in the genre's development. Melinda Zook's extensive research has emphasised the political nature of Behn's work; more recently, Rachel Adcock has explored the ways in which Behn's drama of the 1680s mimics the voices of Whig ideology for Tory ends.[7] It seems entirely plausible that Behn's reconfiguration of Whig characteristics in her drama was a strategy likewise deployed in the amatory fictions she wrote as she turned from dramatic to prose writing. Taking *Love-Letters* as a case study, the present essay invites increased scrutiny of Behn's engagement with secret history in a work more often read as amatory fiction. In exploring this idea, I do not wish to suggest that Behn herself conceived of secret history or amatory fiction as clearly defined genres; the attempt to impose such an understanding was a later phenomenon and, as the present volume's existence illustrates, the exact parameters of these genres remains under investigation. I therefore use the labels 'secret history' and 'amatory fiction' as broadly representative of two sets of literary characteristics around which Behn purposefully structured *Love-Letters*, at a time when she could not yet know the future trajectories that would channel them into more established genres.[8]

Competing Plots: Amatory Fiction Versus Secret History

In the first volume of *Love-Letters*, Philander's political plots, his 'graver business of State', repeatedly disrupt the amatory plots of the lovers as they attempt to consummate their relationship. Silvia's earlier cited complaint is one reiterated throughout much of volume one in the lovers' correspondence. Affairs of state hover in the margins of the pages of *Love-Letters*, fleetingly referenced but serving as a threatening presence that can, and does, thwart amorous encounters. This creates a structural competition, one of push and pull, between love and politics. As Toni Bowers has argued, '[d]espite the narrator's claims to the contrary, in fact, this is to a large extent a novel *about* the rebellion of Cesario/Monmouth, precisely because that story is at once relegated to the margin, "almost out of frame but everywhere glimpsed as part of the frame"'.[9] Whilst relatively little textual space is given over to a consideration of political affairs in the first two volumes of the novel, Behn creates the anticipation, mirroring that of the lovers themselves, that political events may take over at any point: that Behn's amatory fiction may transform into a secret history.

In his exploration of the erotic in Behn's novel, William B. Warner acknowledges '[t]he double provenance of *Love Letters* – as a polemical intervention within a political crisis, and as translation onto the English market of a well-developed species of Continental novel'.[10] Yet, like other critics, Warner does not conceptualise this division as one between two genres.[11] Francis F. Steen has understood the narrative's vacillation between these poles almost as a failure of the work:

> Behn vacillates between identifying her protagonists with real political agents and embedding them within a fictive world with an autonomous dynamic. Her strongest claim to loyalty lies in her persistent attempt to map the sentiment of love, the internal battle of erotic affection, onto the public struggle for power.[12]

There is a reason Behn's persistent attempt is not satisfactorily achieved: in volumes one and two Behn is not attempting to bridge these divisions, but purposefully draws them apart.[13] The incompatibility of Philander's dual pursuits in love and politics provides a model for understanding *Love-Letters* as a novel that frames the competing claims of two distinct genres for the attention of Behn's readers. The narrative movement between the concerns of amatory fiction and secret history could be seen as a natural, and chance, product of Behn's pen; as an experimental writer operating in late seventeenth-century London, she must have unconsciously absorbed ideas from an expanding and diversifying literary marketplace. However, certain markers in *Love-Letters* suggest that Behn was just as self-conscious in her engagement with secret history as she was with amatory fiction, purposefully leaving the parameters of each genre distinct, prior to staging their subsequent collision in the work's final volume.

From the outset of the novel, Philander conceives of himself as torn between two physical realms: his and Silvia's pastoral idyll of love at Belfont (the Berkeley family seat of Durdans, near Epsom), and the Whig cabal then based in London:

> 'tis true I move about this unregarded world, appear every day in the great Senate House at Clubs, Caballs, and private consultations (for *Silvia* knows all the business of my Soul, even its politicks of State as well as Love) I say I appear indeed, and give my Voice in publick business, but oh my Heart more kindly is imploy'd, that and my thoughts are *Silvia*'s! (20).
>
> Say fond Love whither wilt thou lead me? thou hast brought me from the noysey hurry's of the Town, to charming solitude; from Crowded Cabals, where mighty things are resolving to loanly Groves, to thy own abodes, where thou dwell'st, gay and pleas'd. (34–35)

Silvia also conceives of these two realms in opposition to one another; Philander's attention to and presence within one demands his removal from the other.[14] She cautions: 'you cannot intend Love and Ambition, *Silvia* and *Cesario* at once: No, perswade me not, the Title to one or t'other must be laid down *Silvia* or *Cesario* must be abandon'd' (43). In Silvia's formulation, Cesario (James, Duke of Monmouth) stands for politics, Silvia for love: this is an equation which runs throughout Behn's novel as Philander moves between these poles, the closets of Silvia and Cesario. Silvia's caution here is part of an extended passage (38–43), by far the longest of its kind in volumes one and two in the attention it pays to Philander's political activities. As noted, the world of the cabal is here invoked at length as a marker of Silvia's anxieties and her fears about where Philander's political plots may lead. Yet Behn's decision to include this lengthy passage relatively early in volume one can also be read as an authorial attempt to establish the conflicting spheres of romance and politics in the novel. The amatory adventures of the protagonists are allowed to dominate the first two volumes, with the two spheres colliding, to tragic effect, in volume three. In the novel's final installment, the secret history of Philander's political activities, previously a consideration relegated to the margins of his and Silvia's seduction narrative, shifts into greater focus. For the first time in the novel, the reader is placed in the same geographical locale (Brussels) as the Whig cabal and enters into an unfolding frame of political action, encountering partisan players including Cesario, Tomaso (the Earl of Shaftesbury), and Fergusano (Robert Ferguson, Shaftesbury's secretary). Whereas, in volumes one and two, Behn repeatedly draws our attention to political plotting without following through with detailed explications, the reader is now placed within the political plot, privy to the activities of the Whig conspirators. The genre of secret history thus comes to dominate the reading experience of the novel. So many of the 'secrets' referenced, but not explained, in the earlier volumes are now laid bare.

Reading Philander: Libertine Hero or Political Traitor?

In engaging with two competing generic modes in *Love-Letters*, Behn invites two alternative, albeit not exclusive, models for reading the novel: reading for love and reading for politics. In the first, Philander is the novel's libertine hero, the man who seduces Silvia, and inviting her to step beyond the confines of social rules and expectations and indulge herself in a pastoral world where desire trumps all. Yet in the second case, Philander represents the novel's traitorous villain, a man who outwardly aligns himself with Whig interests to mask his individual Machiavellian ambition. Accessing Philander's private correspondence with his mistress, Behn's reader exposes his true, inward, sentiments about Cesario's right to the throne: 'oh *Silvia*! when Three Kingdoms shall ly unpossest, and be expos'd, as it were, amongst the raffling Crowd, who knows but the chance may be mine […] if the strongest Sword may do't, (as that must do't) why not mine still? […] *Cesario* has no more right to it than *Philander*' (45). In a reading of the novel as Tory secret history, Behn here characterises Philander as a perversion of Whig principles of constitutional government; Philander advocates rule by the sword, and manipulates Cesario to serve his own political ends. Ironically, it is Silvia who most clearly articulates this dual reading of her lover, reading him simultaneously as her amatory hero and a false political traitor, governed by an ambition which she prophecies will lead to his destruction:

> I have a fatal prophetick fear, that gives a check to my soft pursuit, and tells me thy unhappy ingagement in this League, this accursed Association, will one day undo us both, and part for ever thee and thy unlucky *Silvia* […] my Soul does presage an unfortunate event from this dire ingagement; nor can your false Reasoning, your fancy'd advantages reconcile it to my honest, good natur'd heart, and surely the design is inconsistent with Love,

for two such mighty contradictions and enemies as Love and ambition, or revenge, can never sure abide in one Soul together, at least Love can but share *Philander*'s Heart, when blood and revenge (which he means Glory) Rivals it, and has possibly the greatest part in it. (38–39)

Philander's 'false' political reasoning stands in opposition to Silvia's 'good natur'd' Tory heart; that which he interprets as partisan 'Glory' she translates into 'blood and revenge'. The latter, she acknowledges, 'has possibly the greatest part' in Philander's heart, a guess which proves well-founded as the novel progresses. Thus, Silvia makes both an amatory and a political reading of Philander: she reads him as a secret history (as a Tory reading of Whig deception), which conflicts, but does not eclipse her reading of him as the hero of her romantic desires.

Silvia here provides a model for Behn's readers. For the means by which we choose to read Philander is, in turn, key to how we choose to interpret the novel. Critics have tried to 'fix' Philander's character, to establish a single reading of him (and in so doing infer that Behn intended such a thing). Melinda Zook has suggested that '*Love-letters* charts a transformation in Behn's politics from a strident royalism to an increasingly tolerant view of the opposition', and

> [T]hough Whig politics are chided (and punished) in the novel as sins against 'our good, our gracious monarch', transgressions against custom by the novel's Whig-cavalier, Philander, are never condemned. Philander eloquently convinces his sister-in-law, Sylvia, that they should love freely and not be frightened by artificial conventions such as marriage or that which calls their passion 'incest'.[15]

Toni Bowers offers a different interpretation of Philander's heroism, reading *Love-Letters* as a critique of corrupt Whig ideology:

> As Behn's narrative pivots between Philander's involvement in Cesario's revolt and his many cynically waged sexual conquests … much is made of the consonance of Philander's disregard for authority, his sexual deceit, and his capacity for treason. Philander's every enterprise is a version of the same faithless spirit; an exclusion-era Whig partisan, he is exactly the kind of person who *would* elope with his wife's sister and betray his sovereign.[16]

Zook's interpretation of Philander's character is based upon a reading of the work in which he is the libertine hero of an amatory fiction; Bowers' configuration is one that prioritises a political reading of the work in which Philander's partisan activities are exposed through secret history. This critical ability to read Philander's characterisation in opposing, yet equally supportable, ways reflects an intentional effect of the novel's dual engagement with both genres.

These dichotomous readings of Philander epitomise the 'doubleness' at the heart of the text. This is a novel in which Philander's romantic liaisons are recorded and celebrated to incite the curiosity of Behn's readers, yet it also warns against excessive liberalism and domestic corruption. Behn invites a dual reading of Philander as early as the dedication to the first volume of *Love-Letters*. Dedicating the work to the Tory libertine, Sir Thomas Condon, Behn suggests he is an apt recipient due to his similitude with her 'hero': 'Sir, I would fain think that in the Character of *Philander* there is a great Resemblance of your self as to his Person, and that Part of his Soul that was possess'd with Love' (5). Yet Behn's initial claims to the bi-partisan appeal of Philander, couched upon his similarity to a prominent Tory (Condon), are tempered in an ensuing clause which affirms the political difference of these men:

> He was a *French* Whig, 'tis true, and a most apparent Traitor, and there, I confess, the Comparison fails extreamly; for sure no Man was ever so incorrigible, so harden'd in Toryism as your self, so fearless, so bold, so resolute, and confirm'd in Loyalty; in the height of all Dangers and Threatenings, and in the blessed Age of Swearing, and the hopeful Reign of Evidences, you undaunted held forth for the Royal Cause … a thousand instances, a History I cou'd write of your discourses and acts of Loyalty; but that even your Enemies allow, and I will spare it here. (5)

Behn extends this comparison of Condon's celebrated Toryism versus Philander's implicitly condemned Whiggism across several pages, drawing attention to the partisan nature of literature and acknowledging the tendency to read along party lines. Yet even in this act she allows for the possibility of bi-partisan praise, noting that Condon's 'Enemies allow' his value, just as Condon may be encouraged through Silvia's example to admire Philander:

> Perhaps you'll be out of humour, and cry, why the Devil did'st thou dedicate the Letters of a Whigg to me, but to make you amends, Sir, pray take notice *Silvia* is true Tory in every part, if but to love a Whigg be not crime enough in your opinion to pall your appetite, and for which even her youth and beauty cannot make an attonement. (6)

Thus, whilst Behn appears to set up *Love-Letters* as a text with bi-partisan appeal, dedicated to a Tory yet featuring a prominent Whig as its hero, she simultaneously raises the idea of literature's partisan agenda. The novel functions at the surface diegetic level as an amatory fiction appealing to a broad spectrum of readers, but implicated in this is a further reading of the work as highly partisan secret history.

Wizards and Whig History

As we have seen, from the outset of *Love-Letters* Behn establishes competing amatory and political ways of reading the work. Yet it is only in the novel's final volume that these narrative strands collide. Here, amatory adventures are almost entirely subsumed within, and elided by, the novel's political events, culminating with Cesario's failed rebellion and subsequent execution. In this volume, the true nature of Philander's partisan treachery is exposed most clearly through his association with his fellow cabalists, notably Tomaso, Hermione (Monmouth's mistress, Henrietta Wentworth), and the '*High-land Wizard*' (402) Fergusano. Behn leaves us in no doubt about how these characters are to be read: each of them is corrupt and self-serving in their respective dealings with, and encouragement of, Cesario, who serves as a touchstone by which Behn measures political rectitude.[17] Here, then, Behn switches to a model of narrative construction proximate to secret history; her main subject is the detailing of recent Whig plots and the exposure of their perpetrators as corrupt villains whose seditious activities claim the life of a tragic prince, who has unwittingly become the figurehead of a cause he does not fully espouse.

In her recent analysis of *Hattigé* (1680) and *The Perplex'd Prince* (1682), Erin Keating suggests that Bullard's 'interest in post-1688 texts leaves untouched the rich field of secret history written during the Stuart Restoration and particularly those which relied more on their relationship to romance fiction rather than historiography'.[18] Yet in volume three of *Love-Letters*, Behn articulates the concerns of secret history through an engagement with romance whilst simultaneously engaging with issues of historiography. Albert J. Rivero has usefully drawn attention to the importance of one particular episode, which in addressing issues of historiography, constitutes the novel's most explicit engagement with secret history and the partisan print tradition from which it emerged. In this episode, Cesario is taken to Fergusano's house and conducted to a grotto at the end of the garden where he is shown '*the Adamantin Book … where all the Destinies of Princes are Hieroglifick'd*' (404).[19] Here, accompanied by his German confederate, the wizard carries out an incantation in which the rock moves to reveal an apparition of an apartment in which various scenes, suggestive of Cesario's future glories as king, are enacted.[20] This scene, invoking the allegory of Plato's cave, is reminiscent of a device used in Behn's farce *The Emperor of the Moon* (1687), written that same year: here Doctor Baliardo is tricked into allowing his daughter and niece to marry their chosen suitors after viewing, down his telescope, a tableau they have orchestrated in which he believes he is being visited by the Emperor of the Moon. Whilst Baliardo's deception is justified by the romantic motives of its perpetrators, Fergusano's deception of Cesario is founded on corrupt and malicious intent. The partisan writer in Behn seems to despise Fergusano more than any of the Whig targets here in view. Brilljard closes his account of the grotto scene in condemning the wizard as:

> the most subtle and insinuating of all his Non-conforming Race, and the most malignant of all our Party, and sainted by 'em for the most pious, and industrious Labourer in the *Cause*; all that he says is Oracle to the Crowd, and all he say's Authentick; and 'tis he alone the great Engin, that sets the great Work a turning. (409)

Whig ideology is shown here to be founded upon an illusion projected against the wall of a dark and dingy cave. Brilljard voices a Whig insider perspective of Fergusano, one that unwittingly exposes the corrupt and insidious nature of the true manager of the party's cause. His words reveal the disjunction between *how* Fergusano is seen by the Party and *what* he really is. In explicating the reality behind the management of the Whig plot to overthrow James II, Brilljard lays bare the total corruption underpinning their cause, where publicly invisible operators, like Fergusano, govern the publicly visible figurehead of Cesario.

Rivero has argued that the grotto scene in *Love-Letters* most powerfully sets out Behn's 'double conception' of history. This reveals her purposeful engagement with a core facet of secret history: the genre's self-referential acknowledgement that there are competing historical narratives to be told: 'Fergusano's magical representations of reality remind us of – and compete with – Behn's own 'historical' representations. Both Behn and Fergusano know the various ways in which allegories of history can be deployed to serve political purposes.'[21] Indeed, Fergusano's future scenes – his fictional version of Cesario's future history – are proven incorrect by the reality of a failed rebellion that in the world has already taken place of the reader. Rivero conceives of the grotto scene as one in which Behn writes secret history from the perspective of the victor, explicating the foundation of a Whig conspiracy whose wider outcome is known:

> What we have here, in short, is an exposition of the complex relations between historical facts – Monmouth's invasion, capture, and

execution – and, depending on the political party of the historian, their various narrative representations ... Behn knows that historical events can be distorted in historical narratives ... Behn confirms the authenticity of her representation of historical events by reference to the outcome of those events. Her reading of history must be correct because the Monmouth rebellion failed.[22]

Whilst this places Behn in a proximate position to those Whig writers of secret history in whose hands the genre would soon flourish – and whose own readings of history were borne out by the fact that the Glorious Revolution had (by 1688) occurred – she is making a wider point here about the writing of history and the reliability of the hands in which that pen is held. Robert Ferguson was a more pertinent source for Behn's wizard than Rivero proposes. As Melinda Zook has outlined, Ferguson was a prominent and prolific propagandist operating at the forefront of the early Whig campaign.[23] The author of numerous pamphlets printed between the years 1680–1689, Ferguson sought to promote Whig interpretations of recent historical events such as the Black Box affair, the Popish Plot, the alleged murder of the Earl of Essex, and the Glorious Revolution. By inserting a scene in which Fergusano lays his '*Adamantin Book*' before Cesario, Behn was surely invoking and actively undermining the partisan 'histories' written by Ferguson. High on this list of publications, Behn may have had in mind Monmouth's Declaration, a document which justified his rebellion by accusing James II of poisoning his brother in order to usurp the throne.[24] The declaration was penned by Ferguson, who ventriloquised Monmouth's voice in the work, just as Fergusano becomes Cesario's puppet-master in *Love-Letters*. In the grotto scene, Behn turns the claims of Monmouth's Declaration upon itself, holding up a mirror to show where the real '*Arbitrary Power*' lies, thereby exposing the true 'continued conspiracy against the ... rights of the *Nation*'.[25] *Love-Letters* thus embodies an active and highly partisan attempt to reinscribe Ferguson's published histories by undermining their validity and exposing them as the tricks of a corrupt operator, 'the great Engin' of a (seemingly) doomed political cause.

It may be argued that, in the course of its composition, *Love-Letters* naturally developed its engagement with the genre of secret history. As the Rye House Plot gave way to Monmouth's Rebellion, Behn increasingly saw the potential, both partisan and literary, of tapping into these sensational political events. A closer reading of the work suggests that Behn envisaged her novel as one that purposefully invoked the generic characteristics of secret history from the outset. As early as volume one,

Philander conceives of his life as a story (and history) that will be told: 'I am sensible that when my story's told (and this happy one of my Love shall make up the greatest part of my History)' (44). Whilst he envisages that story to be, overwhelmingly, an amatory one, he gestures simultaneously to its competing partisan story as 'that secret that so concern'd my Life' (44). In writing these words, Philander claims that the true marker of his love for the Tory Silvia is demonstrated by the position he has granted her as his 'dear Councellor' (44); one privy to all the secrets of his plots and, by implication, those of the entire Whig cabal. Behn's decision to write *Love-Letters* in the epistolary mode was a masterstroke, as it enabled her to reveal Philander's secrets within the context of his amatory story; in the process of reading a correspondence between two lovers, the reader is exposed to partisan secrets intended for Silvia's eyes only, and thereby finds a secret history between the covers of Behn's amatory fiction.

Love-Letters foreshadows the types of adaptive and politically responsive uses of secret history that Bullard shows Manley and Haywood were soon to employ in their subsequent *roman à clefs*. Behn provided a model of how Tory purposes could be served through the adaptation of what was, by the 1710s, a genre more clearly defined through its alignment with Whig objectives and ideology. Certainly the work was still being widely read as the seventeenth century gave way to the eighteenth, with new editions of *Love-Letters* printed long after it had lost its immediate political topicality. As Kate Loveman notes, *Love-Letters* was 'one of the most reprinted novels of the early eighteenth-century, with eight editions by 1735'.[26] Its influence on subsequent secret histories, as well as amatory fictions, should not be underestimated despite Behn's own self-deprecating posturing. As Rivero notes, Behn herself often refuted her position as a partisan writer, and 'when she most vehemently protests that she is merely concerned with romance, reminding her readers that she is writing "amatory fiction" ... she is most fully engaged in refashioning History and scoring her most telling political points'.[27] Similarly, Rachel Carnell has reflected that '[w]hat is striking is how frequently Behn's innovations in formal structure appear to have a political motivation or foundation'.[28] *Love-Letters* stands as a perfect illustration of these views, with this ground-breaking prose fiction born out of an engagement between two emerging forms: one amatory, one partisan. Here, in the world of Silvia and Philander, Behn was pushing the boundaries of genre far beyond their previous confines, experimenting with cutting-edge generic developments by structuring her narrative as one in which amatory fiction competed with secret history, only for them to collide in the work's final volume. In doing so they formed something greater than their component parts: the English novel.

Notes

1. Aphra Behn, *Love-Letters between a Nobleman and his Sister*, ed. Janet Todd, *The Works of Aphra Behn*, 7 vols. (London: William Pickering, 1993), 2: 38–9.
2. For a detailed historical overview of the Grey-Berkeley scandal and the accompanying legal trial see Toni Bowers, *Force or Fraud: British Seduction Stories and the Problem of Resistance 1660–1760* (Oxford: Oxford University Press, 2011), 103–14.
3. A notable exception to this is Michael McKeon, who analyses *Love-Letters* primarily as a secret history rather than as an amatory fiction; see Michael McKeon, *The Secret History of Domesticity: Public, Private, and the Division of Knowledge* (Baltimore: Johns Hopkins University Press, 2005), 506–46. See also his '*Paradise Lost* as a Secret History' in this volume, 17–32.
4. Rebecca Bullard, *The Politics of Disclosure, 1674–1725: Secret History Narratives* (London: Pickering & Chatto, 2009). Bullard develops Annabel Patterson's earlier work on secret history. Patterson argued for the existence of two types of secret history. Like Behn's novel, one used pseudonyms to lightly disguise the court and society figures whose lives it mocked; see Patterson, *Early Modern Liberalism*, 183–184.
5. Bullard, *Politics of Disclosure*, 22–3.
6. Bullard, *Politics of Disclosure*, 85–110, 161–81.
7. Rachel Adcock, "'Jack Presbyter in his Proper Habit': Subverting Whig Rhetoric in Aphra Behn's *The Roundheads* (1682)', *Women's Writing*, 22:1 (2015), 51.
8. Rachel Carnell has cautioned that imposing modern understandings of generic categories onto works of the period is problematic, reflecting that '[I]n works from the 1720s Haywood sometimes used both "secret history" and "novel" on the same title page'; see Carnell, 'Eliza Haywood and the Narratological Tropes of Secret History', *Journal for Early Modern Cultural Studies*, 14:4 (2014), 104.
9. See Bowers, *Force or Fraud*, 133.
10. William B. Warner, *Licensing Entertainment: The Elevation of Novel Reading in Britain, 1684–1750* (Berkeley: University of California Press, 1998), 52.
11. Alternatively, Bowers has read this structural division as reflective of the changing political situation: 'Shifts in the succession struggle, and in the viability of Tory ideology between the early 1680s and the middle years of the decade, help to explain the much-noted structural differences between the novel's parts'; see Bowers, *Force or Fraud*, 116.
12. Francis F. Steen, 'The Politics of Love: Propaganda and Structural Learning in Aphra Behn's *Love-Letters between a Nobleman and His Sister*', *Poetics Today*, 23:1 (2002), 112.
13. Warner accepts this structural incoherence, conceptualising it as a result of the novel's serial publication; see Werner, *Licensing Entertainment*, 64.

14 McKeon has noted the competitive claims of Philander's political and amatory concerns; see McKeon, *The Secret History of Domesticity* (509, 511).
15 Melinda Zook, 'Contextualizing Aphra Behn: Plays, Politics, and Party, 1679–1689' in *Women Writers and the Early Modern British Political Tradition*, ed. Hilda L. Smith (Cambridge: Cambridge University Press, 1998), 88, 84.
16 Bowers, *Force or Fraud*, 115–116. This is a view also advocated by Ros Ballaster in *Seductive Forms: Women's Amatory Fiction from 1684 to 1740* (Oxford: Clarendon Press, 1992), 107.
17 Bowers convincingly argues that Behn projects Monmouth as 'an object of pity' in the novel; see Bowers, 'Behn's Monmouth: Sedition, Seduction, and Tory Ideology in the 1680s', *Studies in Eighteenth-Century Culture*, 38 (2009), 30.
18 Erin Keating, 'In the Bedroom of the King: Affective Politics in the Restoration Secret History', *Journal for Early Modern Cultural Studies*, 15:2 (2015), 76 n7.
19 Albert J. Rivero, '"Hieroglifick'd" History in Aphra Behn's *Love-Letters between a Nobleman and his Sister, Studies in the Novel*"', 30:2 (1998), 126–38.
20 Scholars have yet to determine the identity of the '*German* Conjurer' (398) who arrives in Brussels with Fergusano.
21 Rivero, 'Hieroglifick'd History', 132.
22 Rivero, 'Hieroglifick'd History', 134.
23 For an account of Ferguson's activities and an overview of his political writings see Melinda S. Zook, 'Turncoats and Double Agents in Restoration and Revolutionary England': The Case of Robert Ferguson, the Plotter', *Eighteenth-Century Studies*, 42:3 (Spring, 2009), 363–4.
24 Monmouth's Declaration has received little scholarly attention despite being 'the only surviving manifesto of radical Whig proposals from the early 1680s': see Zook, *Radical Whig and Conspiratorial Politics in Late Stuart England* (Pennsylvania State University Press, 1999), 131.
25 *The Declaration of James Duke of Monmouth* [London, 1685], 2.
26 Kate Loveman, *Reading Fictions: Deception in English Literary and Political Culture* (Aldershot: Ashgate, 2008), 113.
27 Rivero, 'Hieroglifick'd History', 134–5.
28 Rachel Carnell, *Partisan Politics, Narrative Realism, and the Rise of the British Novel* (Basingstoke and New York: Palgrave Macmillan, 2006), 46.

6

Secret History and Spy Narratives

Slaney Chadwick Ross

Eighteenth-century secret histories flourished in tandem with narratives by and about spies. There are so many similarities between secret histories and spy narratives that it is less useful to consider them as separate genres entirely than to think of the two as interwoven: the secret history frequently uses the figure of a well-placed spy as the lens for its salacious projections.[1] To briefly delineate a few of the rhetorical similarities between the two genres: both have narrators who present themselves as well-connected, yet overlooked, insiders; both claim to be presenting fresh information about past events (the secret, in many secret histories, is that there is no secret); both portray the political world as a conspiratorial network or networks. As Rebecca Bullard has observed, both 'undermine received or official accounts of the recent past by exposing the seamy side of public life' by exposing the mess that intrigue leaves behind, including emotional and financial trauma; and both rail against the totalitarian nature of arbitrary government. In so doing, their 'historiographical weakness' becomes their central narrative strength.[2] Both spies and secret historians claim to have access to information that other people do not have, and to read a secret history or a spy narrative is to gain the same privileged information and access to power that the writer possesses.

This chapter explores a wide range of spy narratives in the eighteenth century as they relate to, overlap with, and draw inspiration from secret histories. Spies narrate a number of early secret histories; additionally, they surface as the perambulating urban protagonist of periodicals such as Edward Ward's *The London Spy*, and, eventually, as narrators (and sometimes protagonists) of amatory fictions. Including spy narratives in the study of secret histories allows us to understand the way in which both genres employ both narrators and characters who are spies in order to re-centre historical narrative on the individual, and on the unknowable psychology of the self. The novel's interest in watching and listening, and in revelations of secrets, in many respects answers to secret histories and other surveillance fictions of the late seventeenth and early eighteenth century.

Spy narratives share some of the generic qualities of secret histories identified by Melinda Alliker Rabb, particularly in that they 'claim the authority to reimagine respectable and important events or people' and, in so doing, 'have the effect of undermining the certainty of authority, and constructing new identities'.[3] One of the main points of comparison between spy narratives and secret histories is narrative voice: early spy narratives are generally first-person accounts, while secret histories include first- and third-person narratives, and even appear as allegorical *romans à clef*. Writers in both genres, however, claim unique and total access to the information they present and are thus distinguished from another popular narrative construction of the early eighteenth century, that of the Spectator who, as Eve Tavor Bannet has argued, 'could only guess at truths to which the spy gained access'.[4] The spy John Ker, for instance, makes a claim familiar to readers of secret histories when he supposes 'that some people will be pleased with what they find here, because many things are discovered, which have hitherto been secrets; or rather which few people ever knew but my self, and consequently I am forced to be an author, whether I will or no'.[5] As the century progresses, the spy figure is continually represented as a political informer, but while the spy and the writer are not separate entities in earlier spy narratives, later examples of the genre show a distinction between the two. This is also true of secret histories. The title character from Eliza Haywood's *Invisible Spy*, for instance, requires anonymity in order to perform her enchanted surveillance, unlike earlier spy narrators who hunger for recognition and recompense. At the same time, the Invisible Spy deploys the fantastical elements of an invisibility cloak and magical tablets, which recall the ways that early spy narrators portrayed the abilities of intelligence gatherers as almost supernatural. The Spy is concerned to appear properly reticent about relaying scandalous gossip: 'the secrets of families, and characters of persons, shall always be sacred with me'; yet at the same time, she sees herself as a powerful agent of justice: 'I am enabled by this precious gift to set both things and persons in their proper colours.'[6]

Spy Narratives and the Novel

Spy narratives can also help us understand the relationship between the secret history and the development of the novel. As Rachel Carnell has noted, 'by the mid-eighteenth century, many novelists had borrowed narratological tropes of secret history even as secret histories themselves remained a more obviously politicized genre'.[7] This is confirmed at the end of the eighteenth century when the novel was well-established as a genre and numerous secret histories were circulated in response to the French Revolution.[8] In the late seventeenth century, however, narratives by and about spies were a form of historiographical life writing, which allowed both writer and reader to respond to the tumultuous century; thus, these spies inform their readers about moments of historical upheaval such as the Civil Wars, Glorious Revolution, and Jacobite rebellions.[9] This trope allows readers to take up subject positions at the centre of these events – a strategy that would be repeated by early novelists. For instance, Giovanni Paolo Marana's fictional *Turkish Spy* (1687–1694) is an inspirational text for both secret historians and spy chroniclers. Marana's fictional account bears a great deal of similarity to accounts by real-life spies such as Joseph Bampfield, John Ker, and John Macky, who act as secret historians in transmitting illicit information about powerful people. As Carnell points out, these narratorial perspectives are already familiar to readers of the novel – so familiar, in fact, that the secret history as a genre has been marginalized or ignored until fairly recently.[10]

If early spy narrators claimed authority over their witnessing of historical events, secret historians took up this mantle of authority and often extended the imaginative embellishments found in spy narratives. Secret historians fashion themselves as spies, often through remarkably imaginative means, and they also tend to include characters in their tales who bear hallmarks of the spy figure. These figures appear to have extra-human command of information: in *The Turkish Spy*, Cardinal Richelieu's extensive spy network gives him the appearance and authority of a magician whose preternatural knowledge seemingly allows him to conform time and space to his desires, with rather serious implications for English politics.[11] In several of his pamphlets, secret historian John Dunton endows himself with a supernatural ability to gain knowledge by fashioning himself as a ghost who writes from beyond the grave, having been (figuratively) killed for his commitment to broadcasting the truth or 'calling a spade a spade'.[12] Much later, in Sophia Lee's *The Recess* (1783–1785), Queen Elizabeth is represented as an expert in surveillance, employing a number of all-seeing spies among her court in an effort to control and contain political threats, although at the same time she is most concerned with spying into the hearts of the novel's protagonists.

Elizabeth is recognizable as a tyrannical protagonist akin to Richelieu in Marana's account (right down to her 'keen eye' capable of a 'killing look'): she is powerful but ultimately flat in comparison to Lee's more fully fleshed original heroines, Ellinor and Matilda, who resemble other persecuted heroines of late eighteenth-century gothic fiction.[13] *The Recess* revises and repeats the early Whig secret history's critique of corrupt, absolutist structures of power, but does so under the generic heading of both gothic novel and secret history; in this respect the novel encapsulates a century of transmission between spy narrative and secret history.

Divided Subjectivities

Like secret histories, then, spy narratives were highly informed by narratives of the East, mediated through the figure of the outsider spy who has finagled his way into the inner circles of a foreign government. Spying in Western Europe as a profession emerged out of a systematic network of diplomats and agents who operated at a distant remove from their employers.[14] It is helpful to think of bureaucracy as a mechanism of power that also distances people from the source of power; thus, if a bureaucratic state usually consists of a series of systems and rules designed to control and regulate power and information between the people and the government, it also necessitates decentralization and depersonalization that both spies and secret historians use to their advantage. One way that this bureaucracy is represented in early spy narratives is through contact with other cultures. The origins of the spy narrative in Western literature are situated in the cultural and political contact of the Ottoman Empire with Western powers. The definitive spy figure of this period is Mahmut, the narrator of Marana's *Turkish Spy*, which was published in French and Italian from 1684 to 1686, and in English, as *Letters Writ By A Turkish Spy*, in eight volumes from 1687 to 1694. The narrator's one-sided correspondence with figures throughout Europe and the Ottoman Empire offers a commentary on European and Ottoman politics from 1637 to 1682, a treatise on various religions, a series of philosophical discourses, and an personal account of the toll taken by the various masks he must wear to treat with members of the Ottoman bureaucracy and French nobility. As Ros Ballaster and Srinivas Aravamudan have both convincingly argued, oriental tales deeply influenced British narrative form in the eighteenth century and beyond. The informant narrator who 'puts the West on display to his correspondents "back home"' is a key feature of the oriental tale which also reverberates throughout the tradition of secret histories and spy narratives.[15] Aravamudan notes that 'The portrait of a spy under an assumed identity visualizes self-revelation alongside imposture' that is, the spy is at once both himself and someone else.[16] This subject position can be at once exhilarating and enervating, as the stress of performing multiple identities takes its toll among many early spy narrators, exemplified in the case of *The Turkish Spy*.

Mahmut's position as a spy is remarkably precarious; his work is quite dangerous, and his writing reflects his constant fear of discovery. At the beginning of the second volume, for instance, he imagines he is constantly being watched: 'When I sit in my chamber, and hear any discoursing in the house, I imagine 'tis about me; when I go along the streets, if any man fastens his eyes on me, he arrests me with fear and apprehension' (II: 2). According to Ballaster, this paranoia is a side-effect of Mahmut's work as spy: the very act of creating this type of narrative 'draw[s] European readers into the fictionalized psyches of fearful, paranoid, and subjugated "representatives" of the subjects of [the oriental] empire' (148). Mahmut's paranoia and self-reflection, as well as his practical concerns about the nature of his work, bleed into late seventeenth-century spy narratives by spies and writers who took on spy eidolons.[17] As Ottoman rule waned in the mid-seventeenth century, Ballaster contends, 'the idea of the "spy" lost its political and incendiary associations and became attached to the more general sense of the "informant", an observer who by virtue of his (and it is always his) distance from the culture he occupies is able to provide a defamiliarized sense of its absurdity' (42). Edward Ward's urban spy fiction, *The London Spy* (1698–1700), for instance, is in many respects a send-up of Marana's contemplative – yet often deeply paranoid – reflections on Louis XIV's Paris.[18]

Yet late eighteenth-century readers, coming retrospectively to Marana's account, would have known that none of the schemes for Ottoman dominance over Europe had come to pass; this, perhaps, made his position even more attractive: readers often enjoy the imaginative exercise that comes from briefly seeking identification with defeat and loss.[19] In fact, many spy narrators echo Mahmut's position as a pillar of a lost cause. The Royalist army officer Joseph Bampfield, who worked as intelligence agent on behalf of both Charles I and Cromwell, is one example of a spy who takes up Mahmut's rhetoric of personal sacrifice. Bampfield was 'a fairly obscure West Country cavalier' who began his career delivering messages between Charles I and those members of the army who were still willing to negotiate with him.[20] Later, he was entrusted with smuggling the Duke of York out of England. After Charles's execution, he travelled throughout Europe ostensibly in the service of Cromwell's intelligence ministers, thus acquiring the reputation of a turncoat. Despite Bampfield's years of service to the Stuart court, King Charles II refused to allow him back into England at the Restoration. He became involved with Dutch intelligence services until his employer's death forced him into early retirement. Financially bereft and emotionally traumatized, he wrote an account of his services as a last attempt to regain favour. His *Apology* was published in 1685, two years before the English publication of the *Turkish Spy* only it is hardly coincidental that Mahmut and Bampfield both record moments of extreme paranoia and existential angst brought on by their precarious professional lives. Towards the end of his narrative, Bampfield is both bitter and unsurprised that rumours of his past as a turncoat continue to plague him: ' … I did then, as I do now, think that if the very trees could have had the discoursive faculty, they would have been employed to my disadvantage, which made me as much as was decently possible … avoid the speaking with all mankind'.[21] Of course, as many of those involved in the Rye House Plot in 1685 had fled to Holland, and there was a warrant out for his arrest, he was quite right to be alarmed.[22]

John Ker's account, in contrast, illustrates how some spies took up a position opposite Mahmut's and Bampfield's paranoia: he displays a remarkable sense of grandiosity and self-importance in the face of world events. Ker's narrative is not so much an evolution of the genre as a representation of the spy narrative's potential for extremes: flashes of supreme self-confidence are a hallmark of spy narratives. Ker joins a few other spy narrators of the Scottish Act of Union and subsequent Jacobite uprising in publishing several decades after the fact, and sometimes, as in the case of Ker's enemy Nathaniel Hooke, posthumously.[23] After acting as a double-agent during the failed Jacobite uprising of 1708 – Ker claims that his loyalty to the Hanoverian succession led him to persuade the Cameronians not to support James Francis Edward Stuart during his attempted landing in Scotland – he fled first to the court of the Holy Roman Emperor, where he became friends with Leibniz, and then briefly to the court of the Electress of Hanover.[24] In exchange for his intelligence services, he expected the Hanoverian courts to reward him upon George II's accession to the throne: initially, he hoped for governorship of Bermuda, and when that was denied, he concocted a scheme for a trading company between the West Indies and Antwerp (152). Despite his confidence, his expectations were disappointed and he died in debtors' prison in 1726.[25] Like Bampfield's, Ker's narrative seems to have been a final attempt to gain recognition for his services. If Ker's view of himself did not bear out in terms of rewards and recognition, in rewriting history from his own perspective and placing himself at the centre of such a monumental series of events, he plays upon the rhetorical tradition of the secret history as a narrative of the 'secret springs' behind historical events.[26]

Dangerous Liaisons

Well-rewarded spies rarely needed to justify themselves through narrative. An exception, however, is John Macky, who uses his *Memoirs of the Secret Services of John Macky* (1733), to lay claim to thwarting the Jacobites' attempted invasion of Scotland in 1708. Like Ker, he claims he single-handedly circumvented the incursion by providing advanced warning to the Ministry.[27] Macky's publication of *Memoirs* is another example of a practical link between secret histories and spy narratives; it is an attempt to capitalize on the success of the first volume of Gilbert Burnet's *History of His Own Time* (1724–1734).[28] In this account, Robert Mayer notes that Burnet acts as 'a typical secret historian in that he wrote as an insider', reminding us that he goes so far as to include his correspondence with Queen Mary.[29] This is a move typical of spy narrators seeking to prove their credentials; in doing so, of course, they also aligned themselves with the fictional epistolary form. Macky also makes a point of following Burnet in delivering scandalous information about the courts of King William and Queen Anne that he claims that Burnet intends to deliver in subsequent volumes of his *History*. Macky thus writes such gossip into the historical narrative, centralizing it and undercutting official narratives.

Macky is anxious to align himself with the Hanoverian empire, and conspicuously claims that he performed the bulk of his secret services on behalf of Sophia, Electress of Hanover, with whom he allegedly corresponded (xxxiv–xxxvii). Because of his declared commitment to the Electress, Macky's gossip about the court of King William is coded as valuable intelligence intended to acquaint her with the characters she will soon govern. Of course, the Electress had been dead for almost twenty years by the time *Memoirs* was published, so the volume required a bit of rebranding: Macky dedicates his work to the Prince of Wales, who also heads the list of subscribers to the second volume of Burnet's *History* (1734). Macky's dedication skips over George I and George II, and, in consequence, his historical retelling of the attempted Jacobite invasions and the unwelcoming air of the exiled court of James II at St. Germain is done in service of the younger generation of the Hanoverian dynasty. Macky's history is thus interwoven with the 'increasingly mythologized and romantic treatments of Prince Frederick', whose love affairs, it should be noted, were documented in the secret histories of the 1730s.[30]

Macky's construction of himself as a man of the world, a sophisticated informer on matters at court and abroad, is illustrative of the way in which the spy, like the secret historian (and his gentlemanly counterpart, Mr Spectator) knows how to adapt himself to his surroundings, to move through the world freely. However, Edward Ward's adept perambulator, the London Spy, whose gritty moxie stands in contrast to Mr Spectator's urbanity and civic pride, highlights the gulf between spectator and spy. While the London Spy does not involve himself in private affairs to the extent that Haywood's Invisible Spy would do, the London Spy 'use[s] sardonic humour to push back against both civic boosterism and those Londoners who piously scorned the pleasures of taverns and brothels'.[31] During a visit to Bedlam, for example, he uses a madman as a self-implicating mouthpiece, proclaiming 'truth is persecuted everywhere abroad, and flies hither for sanctuary, where she sits safe as a knave in a church, or as a whore in a nunnery. I can use her as I please, and that's more than you dare do'.[32] The salacious edge to his accounts of pubs and prostitutes was probably designed to titillate a reading public eager for confirmation – and details – of such malfeasance.

This figure of the spy as a romantic agent is also evident in John Dunton's *Athenian Spy* (1704) narratives, in which members of the Athenian Society write to a circle of their female counterparts in hopes of convincing them to embark upon 'platonick courtship' – that is, 'the marriage of our minds', unions of the soul, not the body.[33] The project goes as well as one might expect. However, Barbara Benedict crucially points out that in the process of 'exposing romantic hypocrisy', Dunton 'assert[ed] the materiality of romance and the legitimacy of female inquiry'.[34] This issue of materiality – even of practicality – in romance draws attention to the sharp contrast between the high ideals and lofty language of love and the stark realities of lust, courtship, and marriage. Dunton's lovers undergo a process of disillusionment similar to that of (real and fictional) spies, as the ideological underpinnings of their work can rarely withstand the pressures of daily life, and most turn to publishing as a way to vent their spleens or earn back some of the money expended on their intelligence services.

The space for 'female inquiry' that Dunton's periodicals open is continued in amatory surveillance narratives of the early eighteenth century and is particularly exemplified in the works of Eliza Haywood. *The Invisible Spy*, for instance, features a narrator whose deliberate veiling of her identity stands in opposition to earlier spy narrators who yearn to be recognized.[35] As Carnell notes, 'Haywood not only takes pride in her narrator's identity being difficult to pin down, but she actively discourages her readers from seeking any more information'.[36] In refusing the reader clues about her narrator's identity and thus also keeping the reader guessing about her own political stances, Haywood draws on the secret history's critique of the historiographical process by demonstrating her narrator's ability to withhold information and to refuse to endorse a particular ideology or loyalty.[37] Christopher Loar suggests, for example, that Haywood's *Eovaii* (1736) and *The Invisible Spy* (1755), codify the self-surveillance strategies that earlier secret histories worked to inculcate.[38] Haywood's midcentury Invisible Spy thus shares the Restoration spy's chameleon-like ability to appeal – if not always successfully – to readers of various political inclinations.

Haywood's spy narratives, obsessed as they are with conspiracy and intrigue also demonstrate a link between plots and plotting in eighteenth-century narratives. Even the paranoid and the dispossessed find something in spying to enjoy, and it is this private delight in intrigue, combined with a steady search for recognition – and even justice – that leads to both amatory and urban spy fictions of the early eighteenth century. The erotic charge of amatory narrative is heightened by the secrecy and haste endemic to surveillance narratives. If, as Barbara Fuchs notes, 'Through the lens of nostalgia, the past can pose a significant challenge to the present', spies such as Bampfield, Smith, and Ker used their narratives as a way to seek atonement for the sins of their past, attempting to conjure up a sense of nostalgia in their readers for the heady days in which they formed mistaken allegiances, unfaithful allies, or unwise political connections.[39] They make a case for having acted in good faith in the past in order to ask for justice in the present.

These rhetorical strategies can tell us something broader about the implications of secret histories and spy narratives, which generally claim to be revealing secrets that will shock society to its core, change the reader's perspective, and potentially even destabilize the government. In practical terms, they did no such thing. However, narratives of secrecy tend to generate counter-narratives and, thus, the form constantly speaks back to itself. According to Bullard, 'the motif of revelation is fecund, having the power to generate endless, competing accounts of the past'.[40] Therefore, in the early decades of the eighteenth century, the secret historian and the spy became deeply associated with the romantic form in its dependence on secrecy and delay. These narratives of conspiracy share a commonality with the romance genre in their recurrent setting out and continuously futile searching for return and completion. The continuous presence of conspiracy, whether real or imagined, makes it impossible for a spy or secret historian to move forward or back, to resolve or fully revolve.

Notes

1. See Robert Mayer, *History and the Early English Novel: Matters of Fact from Bacon to Defoe* (Cambridge: Cambridge University Press, 1997). While I follow Mayer's contention that secret historians' tendency to stake out a space within historiographical discourse in considering the early origins of the secret history as a counterfactual political narrative related by an insider (100), I do not distinguish, however, between political secret histories and amatory secret histories; I see both as embedded in political discourse. See also Eve Tavor Bannet, '"Secret history": or, Talebearing Inside and Outside the Secretorie', *Huntington Library Quarterly* 68:1–2 (2005), 375–96. As Bannet notes, the secret history, by nature, 'straddles modern disciplines' (376).
2. Rebecca Bullard, *The Politics of Disclosure, 1674–1725: Secret History Narratives* (London: Pickering & Chatto, 2009), 1, 13.
3. Melinda Alliker Rabb, *Satire and Secrecy in English Literature from 1650 to 1750* (Basingstoke and New York: Palgrave Macmillan, 2007), 69, 71.
4. Eve Tavor Bannet, 'The Narrator as Invisible Spy', *Journal for Early Modern Cultural Studies* 14:4 (2014), 155.
5. John Ker, *The Memoirs of John Ker of Kersland in North Britain Esq. Containing His Secret Transactions and Negotiations in Scotland, England, the Courts of Vienna, Hanover, and Other Foreign Parts* (London, 1726), ix.
6. Eliza Haywood, *The Invisible Spy*, 2 vols., 2nd edn (London, 1759), 14.
7. Rachel Carnell, 'Slipping from Secret History to Novel', *Eighteenth-Century Fiction* 28:1 (2015), 5.
8. See, for example, François Xavier Pagès's *Secret History of the French Revolution* (London, 1797), Camille Desmoulins, *The History of the Brissotins* (London, 1794), Madame du Barry's *Genuine Memoirs of the Countess Dubarre* (London, 1780), and *History of the Revolution of the 18th Fructidor* (London, 1800).
9. See Susan Wiseman, *Conspiracy and Virtue: Women, Writing, and Politics in Seventeenth-Century England* (Oxford: Oxford University Press, 2006), 313–59. According to Wiseman, 'Relying on the truth-claims of the narrator, the memoir – as secret history, fiction, and history – was central to the construction of the Restoration political world, and especially to the shaping of that world's understanding of the English Civil War' (316).
10. Carnell, 'Slipping from Secret History to Novel', 6.
11. Giovanni Paolo Marana, *Letters Writ by a Turkish Spy*, ed. Robert Midgley, 8 vols. (Dublin, 1736), I: 109.
12. John Dunton, *The Art of Living Incognito* (London, 1700).
13. Sophia Lee, *The Recess; Or, a Tale of Other Times*, ed. April Alliston (Lexington: University Press of Kentucky, 2000), 157, 170.

14 See Geoffrey Smith, *Royalist Agents, Conspirators, and Spies: Their Role in the British Civil Wars, 1640–1660* (Farnham: Ashgate, 2011), and Alan Marshall, *Intelligence and Espionage in the Reign of Charles II, 1660–1685* (Cambridge: Cambridge University Press, 1994), as well as John Michael Archer, *Sovereignty and Intelligence: Spying and Court Culture in the English Renaissance* (Stanford: Stanford University Press, 1993) and Lois Potter, *Secret Rites and Secret Writing: Royalist Literature 1641–1660* (Cambridge: Cambridge University Press, 1989).

15 Ros Ballaster, *Fabulous Orients: Fictions of the East in England, 1662–1785* (Oxford: Oxford University Press, 2005), 149.

16 Srinivas Aravamudan, *Enlightenment Orientalism: Resisting the Rise of the Novel* (Chicago: University of Chicago Press, 2012), 45.

17 Rabb also raises an important point about how secret histories and satires create in the reader '[a] compulsion to find meanings everywhere, to perceive secret plots and conspiracies, to merge feelings of narcissism and persecution, and to regard patriarchal masculinity (and sexuality identity) with anxiety'; that is, the texts operate under the 'enabling interpretive strategy' of paranoia (178).

18 Edward Ward, *The London Spy*, 2 vols., 4th edn (London, 1709).

19 As Murray Pittock has shown in *The Invention of Scotland: The Stuart Myth and the Scottish Identity, 1638 to the Present* (New York: Routledge, 1991), Jacobitism was certainly romanticized in the late eighteenth century, after the credible threat had passed. Also, see Juliet Shields' *Sentimental Literature and Anglo-Scottish Identity, 1745–1820* (Cambridge: Cambridge University Press, 2010).

20 Smith, *Royalist Agents, Conspirators, and Spies*, 95.

21 Joseph Bampfield, *Colonel Joseph Bampfield's Apology*, ed. and Introduction, John Loftis and Paul H. Hardacre (Lewisburg: Bucknell University Press, 1993), 93.

22 Loftis and Hardacre, Introduction, 26. Bampfield's reputation was certainly not improved by his bigamous relationship with the unsuspecting Lady Anne Halkett (*ODNB*). However, Loftis and Hardacre, in their Introduction to Bampfield's *Apology*, note that 'A reading of his reports printed in the *Thurloe State Papers* should convince us that Thurloe and Thomas Scot were truthful in saying, not long before the Restoration, that their "best intelligence came from Bampfield" (22).

23 Another spy who wrote for posterity rather than revenge or vindication, Hooke was a contemporary of Ker's in Scotland during the Act of Union. He notably became a French citizen after performing services at the court of Louis XIV and was thus none the worse for wear after the failed uprising of 1708. See Nathaniel Hooke, *The Secret History of Colonel Hooke's Negotiations in Scotland, in Favour of the Pretender; in 1707* (Dublin, 1760).

24 John Ker, *The Memoirs of John Ker of Kersland in North Britain Esq. Containing His Secret Transactions and Negotiations in Scotland, England, the Courts of Vienna, Hanover, and Other Foreign Parts*, 3 vols. (London, 1726), 1: 59, 77, 83.

25 Hugh Douglas, 'Ker, John, of Kersland (1673–1726)', *Oxford Dictionary of National Biography* (Oxford University Press, 2004; online edn, May 2008).

26 Bullard, *Politics of Disclosure*, 21.
27 John Macky, *Memoirs of the Secret Services of John Macky, Esq … Also, The True Secret History of the Rise, Promotions, &c. of the English and Scots Nobility; Officers, Civil, Military, Naval, and Other Persons of Distinction, from the Revolution* (London, 1733), xv–xvi. Although Ker and Macky do not acknowledge one another, their narratives suggest that they were in contact with Lord Sunderland during this period (Ker 74; Macky xv–xvi).
28 Gilbert Burnet, *Bishop Burnet's History of His Own Time*, vol. II. (London, 1734).
29 Mayer, *History and the Early English Novel*, 102. Mayer also notes that Burnet's *History of His Own Time* 'invites us to read it as a work of fiction'. Many of the examples he gives are familiar from spy narratives, especially Burnet's portrayal of himself as a wise and important man of influence at court: 'Burnet presents himself as a confidant of kings, and it all sounds a little too good to be true' (104). This is also the case with regard to Macky's and Ker's accounts and follows from early spy accounts that represent figures such as Richelieu and even Cromwell as endowed with preternatural knowledge of state intelligence.
30 Paula Backscheider, Lacy Marschalk, and Mallory Anne Porch, 'The Empty Decade? English Fiction in the 1730s', *Eighteenth-Century Fiction* 26:3 (2014), 400, 391–2.
31 See Christopher Loar, *Political Magic: British Fictions of Savagery and Sovereignty, 1650–1750* (New York: Fordham University Press, 2014), 2–3. Loar notes that the urban spy figure made prominent in popular periodicals arises out of an impulse towards a self-policing citizenry just as England's government shifted from monarchy to bureaucratized state (181). Additionally, see Richard Squibbs, *Urban Enlightenment and the Eighteenth-Century Periodical Essay* (Basingstoke and New York: Palgrave Macmillan, 2014). Squibbs quite rightly situates Ward's characters within the sixteenth-century tradition of character writings that portray London as 'dark, coarse, greasy and more than vaguely threatening'; the figure of the London Spy is both tour guide and bawdy commentator, the spy unleashed from bureaucratic oversight (52).
32 Ward, *London Spy*, 1: 65.
33 John Dunton, *The Athenian Spy: Discovering the Secret Letters Which Were Sent to the Athenian Society by the Most Ingenious Ladies of the Three Kingdoms* (London, 1704), 3, 29.
34 Barbara Benedict, 'The Curious Genre: Female Enquiry in Amatory Fiction', *Studies in the Novel* 30:2 (1998), 195.
35 Manley's *roman à clef* secret history, *The New Atalantis* (1709), looms large here: *The New Atalantis* is a framed surveillance narratives which channels the revelations of its secrets in allegory through the figures of Astrea and Mrs Nightwork, and their supernatural abilities to see and hear everything, which draws together the all-seeing power of the sovereign with the literal figure of the work of surveillance, the lowly, but well-connected, spy. See *The New Atalantis*, ed. Rosalind Ballaster (New York: Penguin Classics, 1992).

36 Rachel Carnell, 'Eliza Haywood and the Narratological Tropes of Secret History', *Journal for Early Modern Cultural Studies* 14:4 (2014), 118.
37 Carnell, 'Eliza Haywood', 102–3.
38 Loar, *Political Magic* 182.
39 Barbara Fuchs, *Romance* (New York: Routledge, 2004), 7.
40 Bullard, *Politics of Disclosure*, 20.

PART II

Eighteenth-Century Britain

7

Secret History, Parody, and Satire
Melinda Alliker Rabb

Parody is one of literature's backhanded compliments. In order to become the object of parody, a work, writer or a mode of representation needs to have achieved a degree of recognition, even stature – like the epic, the pastoral, Miltonic blank verse, and the Horatian ode, which inspired memorable eighteenth-century parodies. Margaret Rose observes, 'history proves that only parodies of well-known … works survive', and even when the original text no longer is read, 'parody itself keeps its target alive to at least some extent by quoting or imitating something of it within itself'.[1]

If most secret histories had disappeared in published form after 1750, they remained visible (even if not recognized immediately by later readers) as parodies embedded in a variety of more canonical texts that share cultural anxieties about knowledge, power, and desire. Parody's irreverent deployment of the satirical, comic, exaggerated or inappropriate aligns well with secret history's challenges to official normative versions of people and events. This essay investigates the legacy of secret history in three representative permutations: the promise to uncover hidden 'springs' that explain but destabilize the past; the concepts of revelation and identity conveyed through the device of the accompanying 'key'; and the gendered fictions through which political (and personal) issues of liberty, authority, and succession are articulated.

Secret history's complex polemics engaging sex and politics took shape during the 1690s, largely as cautionary Whig documents warning readers of the dangers of arbitrary power lurking in the restored Stuart monarchy.[2] Beginning with the translation into English of Procopius' *Anekdota*, as *The Secret History of the Court of the Emperor Justinian* (1674), scandalous stories of corrupt libidinous rulers implied that the hard-won limitations on divine right secured by bloody civil wars and a 'glorious' revolution could still be at risk. But the strategy of attributing public power to private weaknesses did not remain strictly a Whig practice; it encouraged a readership eager for anecdotes in the original Latin sense of 'Secret, private, or hitherto unpublished narratives or details of history' (*OED*). Not only sovereign authority but also other power dynamics – befitting England's changing structures of governance, class, finance, and religion – could be shown to operate by hidden wheels within wheels.

In 1702, Baron John Somers claimed that 'so very fond are all English Men, of knowing what has been kept as a Secret, that no Secret History was ever yet publish'd, but has met with a kind Reception'.[3] Most early Whig 'secret histories' and 'memoirs' and 'anecdotes', including Somers' own, are no longer read by any but dedicated scholars. And yet such work was kept alive through the creative transmutations of parody. The most famous example of such parodic reinvention, Delarivier Manley's Tory *The New Atalantis* (1709), fulfils John Dryden's definition of parody: Whig secret histories are 'turned into another sense than their author[s] had intended them'.[4] Manley pushes secret history's characteristics to new extremes for new purposes. Threatened abuses of power include a broad spectrum of public figures. Scandalous sex is more transgressive and fantastically imagined. Gender is more self-consciously constructed, and women play even more prominent roles. The high-flown rhetoric of *histoire galante* and the creative name-substitutions of *roman à clef* conjoin in episodes in which identifiable people engage in petty acts of cruelty and misbehavior. If her work brilliantly repurposed a Whig original, it became a source of further parodic invention, so that when even the *Atalantis* went out of print, readers could still experience its defining features on the pages of other books.

Parodying Conventions of Secret History

The *Atalantis* offers a critically useful paradigm. Its conflation of sex and politics, its obsession with illicit physical desire, ambiguous agency, conspiracy, and corrupt social, legal, and economic relationships, popularized conventions for revealing these problems in scenes of seduction and near-rape. Here is one familiar cluster of details that become what Rose calls distinguishing 'preformed material' (52): warm weather, nudity, bathing, voyeurism, and physical assault:

> The beautiful Diana ... passed her down into the gardens. She had nothing on but a petticoat ... It was the evening of an excessive hot day. ... A canal run by ... [T]he dazzling lustre of her bosom stood revealed, her polished limbs all careless and extended ... Rodriguez ... stole close to the unthinking fair ... throwing himself at length beside her ... Her surprise caused her to shriek aloud.[5]

Diana and Rodriguez are among several couples who re-enact scenarios of vulnerability and aggression in the *Atalantis*. Jonathan Swift, who possessed a copy of Manley's narrative, reworks this 'preformed material' when describing Gulliver's ravishment by an amorous Yahoo:

> [T]he Weather exceeding hot, I entreated him to let me bathe in the River … I immediately stripped myself stark naked, and went down softly into the Stream; It happened that a young Female Yahoo … saw the whole Proceeding; and inflamed by Desire … embraced me after a most fulsome Manner; I roared as loud as I could.

Parallel phrases are striking: 'excessive hot day' / 'the weather exceeding hot'; 'the canal' / 'the river'; 'her bosom stood revealed' / 'I stripped myself stark naked'; 'throwing himself … beside her' / 'embraced … in a most fulsome manner'; 'shriek aloud' / 'roared as Loud'. Such intertextuality supports the view that Swift self-consciously parodies Manley.

What Mikhail Bakhtin describes as parody's 'vari-directional double-voiced discourse' (198) is well suited to Swift's unresolved ironies in the fourth voyage because it 'pull[s] in different directions'.[6] Parody, 'unlike forms of satire or burlesque which do not make their target a significant part of themselves, is ambivalently dependent upon the object of its criticism for its own reception … This ambivalence may entail not only a mixture of criticism and sympathy for the parodied text, but also the creative expansion of it into something new'.[7] If Gulliver's fourth voyage finally reveals the truth – 'For now I could no longer deny, that I was a real Yahoo, in every Limb and Feature' – the moment of discovery occurs through the conventions of secret history. Gulliver and the Yahoo perform a grotesque version of the erotic encounters typical of such texts. The 'secret springs' of humanity are revealed by uncovering a naked Yahoo driven by reckless desire. Gulliver tries to conceal his identity from his Houyhnhnm Master through the subterfuge of clothing. But eventually, 'the Secret Springs … will be seen naked, and Discover'd'.[8]

Gulliver's Travels is punctuated with scandalous contending versions of the past: the contradictory accounts of English history told to the King of Brobdingnag and Gulliver's Houyhnhnm Master, as well as in the revelations about 'great' figures from the past in Glubdubdrib. Swift had collaborated with Manley during the Tory ministry, in political pamphlets contradicting Defoe's *Secret History of the October Club* (1711) and *Secret History of the White Staff* (1714–15). He also, along with fellow Scriblerians, engaged in a second feature of secret history that would prove conducive to parody: the explanatory key.

Parodying 'Keys'/'Keys' as parody

The earliest English texts called 'keys' predate secret histories. They were straightforward practical manuals that instruct and explain pragmatically, not polemically, like William Potter's *The Key of Wealth; Or, a New Way for Improving of Trade* (1650) or *The Distiller of London: with the Clavis to unlock the deepest secrets of that mysterious art* (1668). But by 1690 partisan discourses give rise to supplementary 'keys' designed to unlock publications that wilfully obfuscate identities or events. Keys claim an authority that would provide grounds for further parody. Assertions about the mechanical operations of opening truth become occasions for irony.

While these texts often were imposed on a primary text by a second author, some shared the same author as the original. Manley's narratives had keys that she probably provided. Double columns listing fictitious names alongside corresponding real ones become part of the self-conscious apparatus of secret history. Formats varied from lists to detailed commentary to full-blown essay. Keys 'unlocked' capital letters followed by discrete dashes (the D – of M – – is the Duke of Marlborough) and libel-avoiding code names (Hilaria is Abigail Masham). Swift's *Tale* and *Travels* elicited keys written by others, as did George Villier's *The Rehearsal* (1672), John Dryden's *Absalom and Achitophel* (1681), Samuel Garth's *The Dispensary* (1699), Anthony Hamilton's *Memoirs of the Life of Count de Grammont* (1714), Eliza Haywood's *Secret History of the Present Intrigues of the Court of Caramania* (1726), Pope's *Dunciad* (1728) and the Scriblerian *Three Hours After Marriage* (1717). The apparent simplicity of the key in which A equals B or which urges a single indisputable interpretation is in tension with the complexity of the narrative it ostensibly clarifies. This discrepancy between hidden and revealed meaning enables what Bakhtin calls parody's ability to exert 'a counterforce against the author's intentions', to activate dual-planed dialogue 'with an orientation toward someone else's discourse' (198–9).

When keys become a part of the experience of secret history, they lose objectivity. Code names that insinuate personal qualities (like Count Fortunatus) thinly disguise public figures (John Churchill amassed a fortune under Queen Anne). One history of political corruption (Justinian's court or Biblical King David's reign) really means another (Charles II's). Dryden's *Absalom and Achitophel* substitutes Old Testament stories of adultery and seduction in the Book of Samuel as a way of revealing the secret springs of Monmouth's Rebellion. The poem prompted two keys: Christopher Ness's *A Key (with the Whip) to Open the Mysteries and Iniquity of the Poem Called, Absalom and Achitophel* and *Absalon's IX Worthies, or, A Key to the Late Book or Poem Entituled A.B. & A.C.* Both assert certain knowledge of people (Absalom is Monmouth; Achitophel is Shaftesbury and so on) and political scandals (Charles II fathered bastards; Shaftesbury seduced Monmouth to rebellion, and so on). But sometimes keys have the opposite effect. They show that proper names are not stable signs, that identity can be manipulated, and that authority may not be reliable. Henry Cary mocks Edmund Curll, 'that wonderful Unriddler of Mysteries ... who has ... given such proofs of his Abilities in his many & most elaborate Keys to Gulliver's Travels, which Gulliver himself could never have found out'.[9]

The promise of stable meaning about inherently unstable power struggles made the key vulnerable to the repurposing of parody. In the gamesmanship of controlling knowledge, keys assert with confidence what parody calls into doubt. Mock-keys could be downright silly. *Pudding and Dumpling Burnt to Pot. Or, A Compleat Key to the Dissertation on Dumpling. Wherein All the Mystery of That Dark Treatise Is Brought to Light* (1727) alludes to Swift:

> The Master Key to this Mystery is the explication of Terms; for example, by Dumpling is meant a Place, or any other Reward or Encouragement ... A Dumpling Eater is a Dependent on the Court ... A Cook is a Minister of State. The Epicurean & Peripatetic Sects, are the two Parties of Whigg & Tory, who both are greedy enough of Dumpling. (15).

Readers familiar with the metaphorical exuberance of *A Tale of a Tub*, in which air (wind, inspiration, farting, belching, Aeolism, imagination) and clothing (Christianity, language, the universe) explain 'Things invisible' with disorienting ingenuity, will recognize the 'dumpling' key as parody of both style and content.

Alexander Pope supplemented two poems, *The Rape of the Lock* and the *Epistle to Burlington*, with mock-keys that parody secret history.[10] Although *The Rape of the Lock* is best known as mock-heroic, Pope added *A Key to the Lock. Or, a Treatise Proving ... the Dangerous Tendency of a Late Poem, Entituled, The Rape of the Lock, To Government and Religion*, a textual apparatus certainly not associated with epic conventions. Pope's allusion to Manley in the poem's final canto (V. 165) supports the idea that he has her in mind (along with Virgil, Shakespeare, Ovid, and others) and that the 'amorous causes' and 'dire offenses' concerning Arabella Fermor are partly conceived as tongue-in-cheek secret history. Read in such a context, scandal in which a desiring nobleman violates the body of an innocent young woman should conceal some political meaning. Indeed, *A Key to the Lock*, attributed to the fictional Dutch apothecary Esdras Barnivelt, claims that the poem's 'secret Designs' are a dangerous Jacobite attack on the Barrier Treaty. Manley (who wrote pamphlets about the Barrier Treaty, as did Swift) had self-consciously manipulated the relationship of key to primary text so that it both exposes and discloses, a feature that Pope parodies and exaggerates.

Many characters identified in the *Key to the Lock* are familiar from *The New Atalantis*; at the same time they also parody secret history's practice of encoded names. If in the *Atalantis*, James Butler, Second Duke of Ormond, could appear both as Prince Adario *and* as the Prince of Majorca, so Pope's Belinda, according to the *Key*, represents England, Queen Anne, *and* the Whore of Babylon. A key that proliferates inconsistency and contradiction is hardly a reliable mechanism of revelation. Pope further parodies interpretive authority when Barnivelt describes encounters with two gentleman at two different coffeehouses – one 'a Roman Catholick knight' at The Cocoa Tree and the other 'a Roman Catholick Lord' at Will's – both 'railing in like manner' at having been satirized as Sir Plume of clouded cane and vacant brain. The key adds a third identity to Sir Plume – Prince Eugene, leader of the forces of the Holy Roman Empire. Ridiculously farfetched claims continue. Belinda's bodkin is the British sceptre. Clarissa and Thalestris are code-names for Abigail Masham and Sarah Churchill; sylphs and gnomes are various Tory and Whig ministers of state. The sylph cut in twain stands for Lord Townsend who negotiated the Barrier Treaty. Shock the lapdog is Dr Sacheverell who (hinting at sex as politics) 'wakes England' with his tongue. An even more ludicrous conflation of the sexual and political is Belinda's identity as Albion/England because her swelling snowy breasts correspond to the protruding white cliffs of Dover.

Here parody re-purposes its target of secret history, since the same political issues of Stuart succession from 1709 remain pressing in 1715 when the key was published. Pope had good reason to deflect attention away from the real political concerns of Catholic families, to make their possible allegiances seem the outrageous overreaction of an unreliable Protestant apothecary. '[T]he use of parody may aim both at a comic effect and at the transmission of both complex and serious messages', because the process of adaptation both criticizes and renews the original.[11]

Pope never published his second parody, *A Master Key to Popery, or, A True and Perfect Key to Pope's Epistle to the Earl of Burlington*, written soon after publication of the *Epistle* (1731), transcribed to Lady Burlington but not printed until 1949.[12] Pope's motivation seems to have been widespread criticism of his satire on the Duke of Chandos in the character of Timon, whose estate epitomizes the wrongful use of riches. Pope turns the explanatory authority of the key into a mock-attack on himself as an irresponsible purveyor of scandal – a kind of ironic apology: 'The extent of this man's malice is beyond being confined to any One. Every thrust of his satyr, like the sword of a giant, transfixes four or five, and serves up spitted lords and gentleman with less ceremony than skewered larks at their own tables'.[13] The playful disclaimer of responsibility for a specific attack on Chandos draws on the same 'multiple identity' ruse that animates *A Key to the Lock*. The four-foot poet (the 'giant') is always referring to several people at once.

Why did Pope never publish this key? *A Master-Key* suggests that in 1732 he was still experimenting with repurposing secret history's multivalent discourse. The title is both a pun and an allusion; it promises revelation about the poet (Pope-ery) and Catholicism (Popery). But it also shares a title with a work (published four times between 1724 and 1727) that Pope may have known, Antonio Gavin's *A Master-Key to Popery. A Discovery of the most secret practices of the secular and regular Romish priests*.[14] This original *Master-Key to Popery* is an episodic secret history of priests, narrated by a former member of the Catholic clergy who has converted to Anglicanism. Instead of 'memoirs', a series of 'confessions' disclose scandalous behaviors that conflate sex and power in the manner of *The New Atalantis*. In addition to telling stories in which 'holy fathers' seduce young virgins, Gavin exposes the church's obsession 'To heap up riches (67) by gathering thousands of Masses every year' (233). In detailed passages about 'the rarities and riches of the church', he describes exorbitance that provides no spiritual comfort or moral guidance:

> the great Altar thirty foot high and ten broad, all of Marble-stone, ... The front of the Altar's table is made of solid Silver, the Frame gilt and adorn'd with precious Stones ... the rich Chalice set in Diamonds ... 33 silver Crosses ... 10 foot high, ... a Relick ... set in precious Stones and many of them set in Diamonds. Thirty thee sacerdotal Cloaks ... edg'd with Pearls, Emeralds, Rubies, and other rich Stones. Sixty six silver candlesticks four foot high. A large gold Possenet, ... Three hundred and eighty Bodies of Saints, on their rich gilt pedestals (228–229).

The *Epistle to Burlington*'s stated theme is 'the uses of riches', and at Timon's villa, 'heaps' of wealth provide no physical comfort or aesthetic guidance. Perhaps Pope, in his own *Master-Key to Popery*, sought a way to expose the gaudy wastefulness of a Protestant lord while proving, by his own artistry, that a Catholic poet can be the arbiter of use-value and can set the public standard of judgment. However, if Pope knew Gavin's work, both its volatility and the hostile political context in which Pope lived, may well have kept the *Key* hidden at Chatsworth.

Parody, Secret History, and Women

Another source of parody generated by recognizable conventions of secret history consists of the gendered fictions through which political (and personal) issues of liberty, authority, and succession are articulated. Anxiety over petticoat government is a fundamental concern from the 1690s on. In contrast to the staunchly patriarchal assumptions of public versions of English history and government like John Milton's political tracts and Robert Filmer's *Patriarcha*, secret histories insist that women can govern men through sexual love. The power of erotic desire animates Whig secret histories of the Stuart monarchs. The *Secret History of the Duchess of Portsmouth* (1690) bluntly observes: 'Thus what all the arts of the most refined politicks and rhetoric could never have been able to bring about … was done with ease and diligence by a woman's tongue and tail' (132). Charles is led 'so much to alienate his mind from his own interest, that he should be brought to act so absolutely contrary to his own Design' (127); he commits deeds 'which it was impossible he should ever have been brought to, while he was himself'; the 'Mistress over his Mind … might command him as absolutely as she pleased' (110); her sexuality attained 'the highest Ascendant … that all the Policy in the world was never able to remove' (126). Many other narratives reassert the force of the boudoir on the public sphere.

In *A Tale of a Tub* (Sect. IX), Swift offers a burlesque version of the same 'Ascendant' over the mind for another king who, after desire 'ascended to the brain', 'raised a mighty army, filled his coffers with infinite treasures, provided an invincible fleet, and all this without giving the least part of his design to his greatest ministers or his nearest favourites'. Again, the 'secret wheel' of political history is a 'female':

> What secret wheel, what hidden spring, could put into motion so wonderful an engine? It was afterwards discovered that the movement of this whole machine had been directed by an absent female, … the collected part of [king's] semen, raised and inflamed … ascended to the brain.[15]

Manley's *New Atalantis* offers a wider-ranging exploration of the force and liabilities of women and power. Three female figures (Intelligence,

Astrea, and Virtue) narrate episodes that rework the interplay of sex, gender, and authority. A Duke becomes obsessed with his ward Charlot, so that despite 'excellent principles … he must love her!' (34). Things end badly for Charlot (and other women in the *Atalantis*), but by way of contrast, in Utopia 'women only are capable of the crown' (191), and in the New Cabal, 'How wonderful! Is the uncommon happiness of the Cabal? They have wisely excluded that rapacious sex who [make] a prey of the honour of ladies' (154). Swift acknowledges (perhaps begrudgingly) the political effectiveness of Manley's amatory ironies: "'This little maid / Of Love shall always speak and write': / 'And I pronounce', the satyr said, / 'The World shall feel her scratch and bite" (*Corinna: A Ballad*, 9–12).

Anxieties associated with the subject of power and women persist in later parodies of secret history. The prior century's fear of arbitrary power is complicated by unresolved consequences of regicide, rebellion, and restoration that necessarily involve women, especially the stable perpetuation of political order through legitimate birth of heirs to throne and property. Here is another link to secret history's fixation on female bodies, the conduit through which order or disorder can issue. The anxiety over succession in secret histories – the difficulty of begetting legitimate offspring that so plagued the Stuarts (and Tudors before them) – may well contribute to the burgeoning vogue for marriage-plot narratives by 1740, thus establishing another link between secret history, parody, and the development of prose fiction into the novel.[16]

In Charlotte Lennox's novel *The Female Quixote, or the Adventures of Arabella* (1752), arbitrary government and sanctioned familial continuity are driving forces.[17] Arabella claims life-and-death power over men, but in the end she marries her cousin. Fantasies of female empowerment dictate the heroine's actions until the last few pages when she is 'cured' by the men who would govern her disruptive self-assurance. As the title's allusion to Cervantes indicates, the novel is multi-layered: a parody of a parody of romance. Lennox adds more self-reflexive strata. Romance in the *Female Quixote* is known only through bad translations of seventeenth-century writers like Madeline de Scudéry. The poor translations themselves verge on parodies of their French originals. Awkward phrases from her reading permeate Arabella's speech, and stilted language is parodied further by her maid Lucy. Arabella's 'All the Blood in his Body is too little to wash away his guilt, or to pacify my indignation' becomes Lucy's 'something about washing in blood, and you must keep out of her sight, and not appear before the nation' (350).

Both *Don Quixote* and *The Female Quixote* achieve parody not only by arousing the expectations of readers who recognize allusions to external texts, but also by depicting a crisis of representation for the naive reader/ protagonist within the text. The old knight is oblivious to the realities underlying stories of giants and enchanters; the young *ingénue* is oblivious to the political implications of *romans à clef*. Lennox significantly expands the scope of her parody to include secret history, a discourse that Cervantes could not have known. Indeed, Arabella's and Lucy's comical meta-parody about washing in blood mimics not Cervantes but passages such as the following from *The Secret History of the Duchess of Portsmouth*: 'this doubtless to any other Lover, would have made him violently to rush into the Chamber, with Sword in Hand, and have made the Delinquent wash with Blood, the stain laid upon his honour' (115). Rose calls such echoes 'the multiplicity of encodings and decodings' that evoke and transform 'the expectations of the external reader' (39).

Arabella's paranoid fantasies of plots and conspiracies parody both Don Quixote *and* secret history. In quixotic fictions, parody reaches past a specific technique to the 'general mode of the work itself'; the reading of other works 'provides a textual background' that can 'be used for "meta-fictional" reflections on the writing of [an author's] fiction or on the writing of fiction in general'.[18] Lennox shares the general mode of self-conscious texts that claim to be merely translating or retelling: the manuscript of Amadis de Gaul (*Don Quixote*) or the recollections of Charlemagne's secretary Eginardus (*Memoirs of Europe*) or 'old Stories that all the World had long since reported' or 'Records, Monuments, Memoirs, and Histories' of 'Events [that] happened about two thousand Years ago'.[19] But in ways unlike Cervantes, although similar to Manley, love explains everything in *The Female Quixote*. The language of amorous hyperbole that typifies Manley's blend of *histoire galante* and local secret history is often a more relevant source of parody than the more comic and sometimes earthy Spanish original (or the more aristocratic escapades of French romance).

Recent critical interest in *The Female Quixote* has made much of the heroine's fantasies of female power, and of her insistence that women can have histories. But the novel's repurposing of secret history has been overlooked. In romance, the force of love drives men to extreme measures of worship and abduction. But in secret history, desirable women can be dangerous manipulators. The Duchess of Portsmouth aims 'to make the prince so surely her own, that she might command him as absolutely as she pleased … to expose his weakness naked before her … she could do more with him in one night, than [state ministers] could do with all their just reasonings' (111, 126, 123). When Arabella, who like the Duchess is raised in the quiet countryside by a father who has left court, confidently commands men to live or suffer banishment, some residual anxiety over female power is palpable. Was Cleopatra an Egyptian princess (according to Arabella) or a scheming whore (according to Mr Selvin)?

Not medieval chivalry but history is ultimately what is at stake in determining Arabella's fate. Different ways of accounting for the past are tested. A chapter is titled 'Containing some historical Anecdotes, the Truth of which may possibly be doubted, as they are not to be found in any of the Historians' (264). The term 'Anecdote' (Johnson's definition is 'something yet untold; secret history') recalls Procopius's irreverent *Anekdota*. Arabella claims to know the 'secret springs and motives' (266) (the signal-phrase of secret history) not of Justinian but of another ruler, Pisistratus. His 'Design of enslaving his Country' was aroused by 'violent affection he conceived for the beautiful Cleorante' while she, like Manley's nude wet objects of the desiring gaze, was performing naked ablutions at the baths of Thermopylae.

The character Mr Tinsel also parodies Manley, not Cervantes. In *The New Atalantis*, when the narrator Intelligence encounters an 'Assembly' of people at the Prado, she regales her companions with gossip, repeatedly voicing the injunction to 'see' or 'view' this lady or that nobleman before exposing hidden scandal: 'view that beautiful black lady' (99); 'See that dapper, squat gentleman' (100) or the 'gentleman ... so gay and coquet [whom] ... a certain military's wife has ... lavished with the prodigality of a new and true lover' (96) or the rich 'Chevalier [who] rose ... from the very dregs of people' (98). 'It is my duty to report ... whatever is new', Intelligence boasts (13). Mr. Tinsel similarly brags, 'my Intelligence is generally the earliest, and may always be depended on' (275). Lennox constructs a parallel episode in an 'Assembly-Room' (273) where Arabella's 'anecdotes unknown almost to any Body else' are one-upped by Mr Tinsel who, like Manley's narrator, resents other sources of insider-information. When Miss Glanville, like gossip-hungry Astrea, sees 'a tall Handsome Woman that had just enter'd [and] ask'd him ... to tell her History if he knew it' (275), he 'answer'd smiling, That the History of that Lady was yet a Secret'. What he reveals is straight out the *Atalantis*: 'That Lady was for many years the Mistress of a young military Nobleman' and the sordid details of her ruin follow. 'Observe', he says, 'Observe that gay, splendid Lady, I beseech you, Madam ... Would not one imagine ... this fine Lady was a Person of very exalted Rank, ... yet she is no other than the Daughter of an Inn Keeper at Spa' (276).

The vicissitudes of contradictory kinds of history ultimately stump Arabella during the conversation with the Doctor that leads to her so-called cure. How could the 'Memoirs and Histories' by French wits of the seventeenth century have access to 'Records and Monuments ... kept universally secret to Mankind' for 'about two Thousand years'? A fair question, and yet Procopius's secret *Anekdota* had to wait 1,100 years to come to light. In any case, a young woman's dreams of grandiose power are as much a parody of secret history as of an old man's delusions about puppet shows and windmills. Cervantes' aging knight, when disabused and facing death, is urged by his companions and family to retain his fantasies. However, the independent vitality of Lennox's marriageable protagonist ultimately is redirected in ways that limit her personal power and force her give over the idea that she is the secret spring or hidden wheel of anything.

Parody, Secret History, and Theory

From a theoretical perspective, secret history and parody share some important characteristics. Each mode of discourse has been associated independently with the rise of the novel but little has been said about their relationship to one another. Secret history is always a 'para' text – that is, a kind of writing that re-imagines a prior representation, that exists 'alongside' or 'parallel to' or 'against' an original that it resembles but replaces. For every secret history, there must be a public or alternate or official version of events and people. Both parody and secret history destabilize authority; both depend upon a degree of self-consciousness about their secondary status; both require decoding; both can convey an ambivalent mix of admiration and criticism toward their 'originals'. Both, however playful, can grapple with complex problems, and create 'text-worlds' that are capable of reshaping perceptions of the past. The implications of this process of 're-functioning' constitute a legacy of political and cultural work performed by what has been considered as an ephemeral marginalized form.

Notes

1 Margaret A. Rose, *Parody: Ancient, Modern, and Post-Modern* (Cambridge: Cambridge University Press, 1993), 47.
2 Rebecca Bullard, *The Politics of Disclosure, 1674–1725: Secret History Narratives* (London: Pickering & Chatto, 2009); Annabel Patterson, *Early Modern Liberalism* (Cambridge: Cambridge University Press, 1997).

3 Baron John Somers, *The True Secret History of the Lives and Reigns of all the Kings and Queens of England* ([London], 1702), 3.
4 John Dryden, 'A Discourse Concerning the Original and Progress of Satire' in *Of Dramatic Poesy and Other Critical Essays*, ed. George Watson, 2 vols. (London and New York: Dent; Dutton, 1962), 2: 103.
5 Delarivier Manley, *The New Atalantis*, ed. Ros Ballaster (London: Penguin, 1991), 245–6.
6 Mikhail Bakhtin, *Problems of Dostoevsky's Poetics*, ed. and trans. Carl Emerson (Manchester: University of Manchester Press, 1984), 194.
7 Rose, *Parody*, 55.
8 'The Arcanas of State, the Abstrucest Politicks will appear Unravel'd to your all Descerning Eyes. The Secret Springs, that set Party and Faction at work, will be seen naked and discover'd'. *Essays by the Original Inventor of the Band-Box Plot* (London, 1714), x.
9 *Pudding and Dumpling Burnt to Pot. Or, a Compleat Key to the Dissertation on Dumpling. Wherein all the mystery of that dark treatise is brought to light* (London, 1714), Preface, B1r.
10 *The Prose Works of Alexander Pope*, Volume 1, ed. Norman Ault (Oxford: Blackwell, 1936); Volume 2, ed. Rosemary Cowler (Hamden: Archon Books, 1986). See also *A Master-Key to Popery, or, A True and Perfect Key to Pope's Epistle to the Earl of Burlington*, transcribed to Lady Burlington and reprinted by John Butt in *Pope and His Contemporaries: Essays Presented to George Sherburn*, ed. James L. Clifford and Louis A. Landa (Oxford: Clarendon Press, 1949), 55.
11 Rose, *Parody*, 15.
12 Alexander Pope, *Epistles to Several Persons (Moral Essays)*, ed. F. W. Bateson (London: Methuen; New Haven: Yale University Press, 1951), Appendix C, 168–182.
13 Alexander Pope, *Epistles to Several Persons*, 180.
14 Antonio Gavin, *A Master-Key to Popery. Containing a Discovery of the Most Secret Practices of the Secular and Regular Romish Priests in the Auricular Confessions, etc.* (Dublin, 1724). Editions of 1725, 1726, and 1729 are published in London.
15 Jonathan Swift, *A Tale of a Tub and Other Works*, ed. Marcus Walsh (Cambridge: Cambridge University Press, 2010), 106.
16 The relationship between parody and the development of the novel is well known through the work of Victor Shklovsky and Mikhail Bakhtin. Both are interested in the quixotic paradigm. See Shklovsky, 'Sterne's *Tristram Shandy*: Stylistic Commentary' in *Russian Formalist Criticism: Four Essays*, ed. Lee T. Lemon and Marion J. Reis (Lincoln: University of Nebraska Press, 1965); *Theory of Prose*, trans. Benjamin Sher, with an introduction by Gerald L. Bruns (Chicago: University of Chicago Press, 1990); and Bakhtin, *Problems of Dostoevsky's Poetics*, trans. R. W. Rotsel (Ann Arbor: University of Michigan Press, 1973). The relationship between secret history and the novel has garnered more recent attention, for example, in Ros Ballaster, *Seductive Forms:*

Women's Amatory Fiction from 1684–1740 (Oxford: Clarendon Press, 1992) and William Warner, *Cultural Institutions of the Novel* (Durham: Duke University Press, 1996). Lennox's novel, in which parody and secret history converge, is an exemplary text for analysis.
17 Charlotte Lennox, *The Female Quixote*, ed. Margaret Dalziel (Oxford: Oxford University Press, 1989).
18 Rose, *Parody*, 5–6.
19 Manley, *Rivella*, 110; Lennox, *Female Quixote*, 375.

8

Secret History and It-Narrative

Rivka Swenson

If every *secret history* is not an *it-narrative* (a narrative about nonhuman perspective), arguably every it-narrative is a secret history, often explicitly so, that reveals privileged information thanks to its protagonist's undercover sentience. This essay engages the visible overlap of it-narrative and secret history in British literature during 'the second half of the eighteenth century and ... continuing ... in[to] the nineteenth century', when, as Mark Blackwell explains, 'it-fictions' rose in 'evident popularity', even as the secret history genre, illuminated recently by Rebecca Bullard, turned from the political-scandal mode generated by 'the partisan struggles' of the early 1700s.[1] At one end of the *it-narrative secret history* spectrum are non-it-centred narratives in which the *it* is a titular, otherwise absent, entryway into a mosaic of anecdotes about actual, fictive, and/or allegorical figures witnessed by *it*.[2] At the other end lies my subject: the increasingly popular *it-centred secret history*, wherein the secret history of the *it* is a primary focus, as in Charles Johnstone's *Chrysal; or the Adventures of a Guinea* (1760) and Elizabeth Fenwick's *The Life of Carlo, the Famous Dog of Drury-Lane Theatre* (1804).[3]

Non-animal protagonists of it-centred secret histories like *Chrysal* reveal secret sentience. Powerless physically, stable internally, these protagonists present uncanny counter-reflections of their outwardly empowered, internally unstable readers. As Jonathan Kramnick observes, '[f]or some writers, including Locke on occasion, [human] consciousness was something that bodies have and do. It was not a separate substance put into them', but, nevertheless, as he and Helen Thompson and others have described in theorizing the new materialism, there was little confidence in the existence of internally-derived consciousness.[4] *Chrysal* and its ilk thus emerge in a materially unstable world as a fantastical antidote to popular anxiety stoked by Lockean and Newtonian inflections of Democritus, Epicurus, Lucretius on the vulnerability of the sensitive human 'subject' who was not just *open to* but *produced by* external 'ideas' that inserted themselves into, impressed themselves upon, the brain's sensorium.[5] It-narrators, by contrast, held their own. But if the rise of it-narrative (or 'object-narrative', Lynn Festa's and Chloe Wigston Smith's apt term) re-energized secret history in the later eighteenth century with such durable-objective protagonists, a concomitant rise in animal it-narratives (dogs, ponies, cats, mice) ultimately overtook *Chrysal* et al. with a fresh, curious version of secret history.[6] We will see how Carlo and canine kind, for instance, rejected the fantasy of objective essence or essential objectivity, the fantasy (or nightmare) of bounded and anti-developmental consciousness, experienced by Chrysal and kind (for instance, Court, Shoe, Pandora's Box, Rupee, Atom, Pincushion, Quire, Ring). Carlo, like others such as Cato, Pompey, Bob, explores the paradox of so-called subjectivity as an organic, evolving, unknowable conversation between native qualities, environment, and what the hero perceives as choice.

Chrysal; or It-centred It-Narrative and the Secret History of Objectivity

Unlike their generic original in Procopius's *Anekdota*, not all secret histories (whether entitled as such, or not) reveal 'secrets'. As I have discussed elsewhere, the revelation of (faux or real) secrets per se is no generic baseline for English secret histories.[7] Likewise, we cannot assume it-narratives entail rich description or even intricate detail, or that they contribute as such to a literary progress from allegory, emblem, type, Platonic ideal, toward the particular, individual, Aristotelian nominal.[8] If it-centred secret history contributes to the rise of the novel or a larger cultural narrative, it does so some other way.[9] For instance, *Chrysal*, termed by Christopher Flint the 'most popular' example of the monetary subgenre, overtly eschews detail, self-consciously violating its own promise.[10] The secret in *Chrysal*, it seems, is the protagonist's essential identity, forever-gold against weak human mettle. Chrysal's masters (like other it-protagonists, Chrysal uses the term *master*) are ironically subjected *by* their experiences. Chrysal, by contrast, is essence, the truly objective spirit of gold, which is to say *it* remains unimpressed-upon, unchanged by climate, environment, experience, even as it influences those whose purview it enters.[11]

Anekdota found heirs in early eighteenth-century British scandal-politics but inheritors rejected its copious detail. This is true even of the English translation, *The Secret History of the Court of the Emperor Justinian* (1674), reissued as *The Debaucht Court; or, The Lives of the Emperor*

Justinian and his Empress Theodora the Comedian (1682).¹² Procopius depicts how in Theodora's youth she would 'stand naked' 'in the theatre', then 'spread herself out and lie face upwards', covered with 'barley grains on her private parts, and geese' would pick them up and eat.¹³ Procopius offers a taste of grain-like minutiae, poring over 'private parts', justifying his peeping by claiming Theodora wore her genitals on her sleeve, prima facie: 'she appeared to have her private parts not like other women in the place intended by nature, but in her face!'; although 'she brought three openings into service', she wished for a fourth.¹⁴ In English translation, however, she becomes merely a 'well-shaped' teen who performed onstage as a 'comedian'; she is still a 'Court[e]san' who 'prostituted herself indifferently', but there is explicitly no 'particular Narrative of all that happened' – no grain or openings, just a 'notion of her manners and inclinations'.¹⁵

It-centred secret histories are similarly fleshless. In *Secret History of an Old Shoe* (1734), 'historians do not tell whether [the Shoe] be of red or brown', and *Secret History of Pandora's Box* (1742) surprisingly deems detail 'extremely unjust'.¹⁶ *Chrysal*, too, disappoints. The sub-subtitle promises to '*exhibit* … Views of several striking Scenes, with Curious and interesting Anecdotes of … Persons … whose Hands it passed through'. We expect intimacy, but *Chrysal* thwarts, for instance, our 'curiosity to know the history of [a] young votary of Venus' (80). When its master 'give[s] loose to a joy' with 'the most celebrated courtesan of the age', the 'scene [is] too sensual for a spirit to describe' (122). Meanwhile, Chrysal's body is silently moved to the purse of 'the *compliant* fair': 'I shall not attempt to describe these mysteries' (121, 125). Later, when Chrysal gains a clerk for master, it can see 'into the whole mystery of justice' but declines, again, to 'reveal all the secrets', giving only 'general hints' (157): 'I have not entered minutely into the particulars of this horrid scene' but provided a 'slight sketch', 'general notion', 'outline' (2: 244). No body there.

Moreover, *Chrysal* scolds readers for wanting more. Mentioning a lavish banquet, it warns 'you must not expect a particular account or description'; '[a] few general hints must satisfy' (179). No sooner do we picture 'people, … eating … all the rarities of the season' than Chrysal stops our 'imagination' in its tracks, commanding in panic, 'stop! I see the very thought has an effect upon you, that favours too strongly of sensuality and delight' (179). Chrysal emphatically 'pass[es] over such a scene', obscuring even 'fragments of the feast', throwing no bones (179).

Why so stingy? And what, if anything, does Chrysal reveal to the alchemist who – hoping to learn nature's 'grand secret' (15) – composes

Chrysal's manuscript? Besides revealing its own secret sentience, Chrysal conveys that readers' soft brains are too impressionable to handle more. Impressed upon by external ideas intromitted into sensorium, impressed into service *of* those ideas, the self proves more malleable than the gold that sparks the self's desire. When Chrysal's body was mined in Peru and rose with 'pleasure' into 'light' (5), its essence 'entered into [the miner's] heart', where it expected to 'read the events of his life … deeply imprinted' (8). Instead, the heart was so filled with 'pain, with grief, and remorse, that I could scarce gain admission' (8). Next Chrysal 'mounted into the *censorium* [sic] of his brain, to learn from the spirit of consciousness, which you call SELF', what caused the self to leave the heart, 'as it is contrary to the fundamental rules of our order, ever to give up an heart of which we once get possession' [sic] (8, 9). Chrysal learns the miner's un-selfed heart is 'possessed by the love of gold' (8).

Recovery is impossible. His slate is un-blanked. His history, for which Chrysal searched at the heart's portal, is overwritten. Chrysal learns he was happy, before the love of gold impressed the 'SELF' or 'spirit' into administering the feedback loop (8, 9). Chrysal watches 'the spirit … running over a number of the *niches*, or impressions, on the fibres of the brain, some of which … she renewed with such force' and 'effaced others' (9). The spirit (referred to by Chrysal as 'she') elaborates,

> where we are, is the seat of memory; and these traces, which you see me running over thus, are the impressions made on the brain by a communication of the impressions made on the senses by external objects. – These first impressions are called *ideas*, which are lodged in this repository of the memory, in these marks, by running which over, I can raise the same *ideas*, when I please. (10)

The spirit conveys that 'touching these marks, on this material surface' (10), *makes* the miner, 'without doing which, a man would no longer continue the same person, for in this acquaintance, which is called *consciousness*, does all personal identity consist' (10–11).

But, although she speaks proudly, 'the work' she is 'engaged in' is hardly directed by her (11). The spirit follows the ('possessed') heart's dictates, which is to say: 'the love of gold' (8), engendered by 'impressions' or '*ideas*' that are 'made on the senses by external objects' (11). Banished from heart to sensorium (ironically desire's initial entry point), the doomed spirit neglects '[t]he traces of that happiness … which you see me pass over without renewing; by which means he forgets that he was ever happy', as does *she*, since '*his self*' is '*my self*' (11).

This privileged view of porous sensorium, soft heart, and externally directed spirit of consciousness appears contra the protagonist's essential objectivity. Chrysal is not the guinea ('*that* body ... torn from its peaceful bed 200 fathoms deep') with which it shares billing; no, Chrysal is the Spirit of Gold (5). The Spirit of Gold remains itself as it passes through 'three or four first stages', is 'purified from the mixtures of mineral dross' (39), is cast into 'the shape of a *doubloon*' (59), and is sent to 'the *Mint*' to become a guinea (78). The body is beside the point: 'I have often told you', Chrysal reminds us, 'sensuality is disagreeable to a spiritual being' (130). External changes, the only changes Chrysal undergoes, are irrelevant.

Other it-centred secret histories similarly depict human actions as produced by external forces. Helenus Scott's *Adventures of a Rupee* (1782) sees soft human brains: 'marked with impressions, like the figures on a celestial globe', they exhibit 'scratches made by objects which have been presented to the senses'.[17] Equally, Tobias Smollett's *History and Adventures of an Atom* (1769) sees in humans a 'weak brain', easily 'overwhelm[ed]'; impulses from without 'throng in like city-milliners to a Mile-end assembly'.[18] Atom's scribe, Nathaniel Peacock, 'haberdasher and author', reports, 'sitting alone in my study, ... I heard a shrill, small voice, seemingly proceeding from a chink of crevice in my own pericranium'.[19] Atom intones, 'I am an atom', and '[w]hat thou hearest is within thee – is part of thyself'.[20] When Atom commands, '[t]ake up the pen, ... and write what I shall unfold', terrified Peacock complies.[21] Atom, a hapless picaro transferred from body to body by kicks and sneezes, nonetheless powerfully influences from within, waving the feather in Peacock's pen, as it were, and inspiring fearful farting, too. Soft humans.

Correspondingly, Chrysal's essential objectivity is shared by a host of it-narrative secret history heroes, including but not limited to Smollett's Atom. Naturally, Atom is unassailable: '*Atomos* is a Greek word, signifying an indivisible particle'; atoms are 'constituent particles of matter, which can neither be annihilated, divided, nor impaired', 'component particles, that harden in rock, and flow in water; that ... steam from a dunghill'.[22] No wonder the human scribe is inspired to worry not about his narrative's coherency: the 'detached ... Parts' reflect 'the whole' of the '*Machine*'.[23] '[T]he integrity of an atom', 'the indivisible rotundity of an atom', is inherent.[24] Similarly, Scott's Rupee attests, 'every piece of gold contains in itself ... qualities ... known amongst mortals by the names of ductility, malleability, fusibility', *but* 'over these there is a superior spirit, to which they are all subordinate: this superior is myself, the Author of this History'.[25] Naturally, the hero of Mary Ann Kilner's *Adventures of a Pincushion* (1788) has no qualms about being 'stuck' by its mistress with 'all the [pins] she could find' (1780).²⁶ Likewise, the much-injured hero of 'Adventures of a Quire of Paper' (1779), a thistle that is transformed painfully to fabric to rag to paper, remains itself: 'my atoms', it says; and 'however divided', it says, 'I was ordained to be conscious, and feel as whole'.²⁷ Even the spirit of the ring melted down 'with other gold' in 'The Adventures of a Gold Ring' (1783), brought beyond 'the particles of *my individual self*', finds 'a new resurrection'.²⁸ Ditto Chrysal: soft humans 'are desirous to know how I could preserve my identity, when melted down with large quantities of the same metal', and so it explains (39), naturally, 'spirits' or essences have the 'power of expanding or contracting themselves into what dimensions they please'; moreover, 'life is not confined to any particular parts, as in the heart, or head, as in man, but is diffused through their whole bodies, so that any part, being separated from the rest, does not die, but … becomes a distinct spirit, … *ad infinitum*' (40). Such 'bodies can be infinitely divided, can regenerate' (40). Of course, Chrysal is unbothered by 'the addition of more matter' or the 'lessening' of 'my body': revision 'makes no alteration in my *sameness*' (40). Chrysal, uncanny specter of unchanging subjectivity and essential objectivity, is itself.

Carlo; or Canine It-Narrative and the Secret History of Carlo's Dilemma

The fantasy of non-phenomenological objectivity instantiated by *Chrysal* & co. was reified off the page by popular automata, as exemplified by Paul Philidor's 'MECHANICAL INVENTIONS'. Philidor's automatous rope-dancers, peacock, Cossack, and windmill, which became a permanent Lyceum exhibit in 1801 after touring through the 1790s, did their thing ad nauseam, while his 'INGENIOUS SELF-DEFENDING CHEST' made more pointed moves; unlike the miner's heart or haberdasher's pericranium, the 'INGENIOUS' genius of *this* place 'has always a Safe-guard against Depredators; for the concealed Battery of *Four Pieces of Artillery* … discharges itself when a Stranger tries to force open the Chest'.²⁹ But Philidor's automata carried on a fantasy-model of subjectivity-as-objectivity that it-centred secret history was leaving behind. Indeed, if it-narrative transformed secret history, animal protagonists transformed it-centred secret history. Increasingly (into and during the 1800s) animals, canines especially, served as heroes of it-centred secret histories. While animals were hardly new to narrative more generally, canine protagonists *à la* Fenwick's Carlo enabled a generative intersection of secret history and it-narrative while participating in the rise of children's literature and transformation of beast fable. *Carlo* and kind focus mostly on their protagonists; we do not tour a miner's sensorium, we hear animals' secret histories. Moreover, we see a turn from the fantasy of Chrysal et al., the fantasy (or nightmare) of intractable 'nature' and extreme objectivity. *Carlo*, uncanny in a different way than *Chrysal*, explores the hero's ability to develop, to transcend 'instinct', breed, species – but *Carlo*, informed by contemporary thought about human subjectivity, does not simply assert power-of-choice. Instead, *Carlo* radically reframes consciousness and personality as products of organic, ongoing, unknowable negotiation between nature (Carlo's supposed nature as Newfoundland dog), conscious choice, and the unpredictable effects of environment, experience.

In truth, Carlo cannot know, nor can we, why he saves a child, Vincent, from drowning, when Vincent falls overboard, but we can make an educated guess. What we know for *sure* is that Carlo, unbeknownst to all except Carlo and us, *intended* to ignore Vincent, who had been cruel to him and his master. As we shall see, thanks to Carlo's submerged-but-potent memory of his own mother's anguish (and his own?) when his puppy-siblings were cruelly drowned and he himself barely survived, he saves Vincent. Carlo acts, so he says, not out of compassion for Vincent, not in empathy for fifteen drowned siblings or even the puppy he once was, but out of sympathy for Vincent's keening father. And yet Carlo does not perceive how such sympathy is connected to his memories of mother/loss. We cannot be sure, either, but he begins his narrative by asserting, 'never can I forget the agony of my mother's howl when … I was torn from my mother's side' (5). Deidre Lynch reasonably observes that it-narratives 'play knowing objects against the humans who do not know their properties' histories',[30] a truism that makes Carlo's limited self-understanding of that history more striking. Indeed, Carlo's selective ignorance about the reasons for his crucial turn makes him seem, in my view, not unlike the hapless miner or haberdasher, all too human.[31]

Carlo was a real dog, famous for his 1803 Drury Lane debut in Frederick Reynolds's two-act afterpiece, *The Caravan; or, the Driver and his Dog*. The piece turns upon Carlo's heroism: he jumps into a contrived lake, saving little Julio after a villain orders him drowned. Reynolds calculated that 'the very novelty of real water on the stage, and … a dog to jump into it, from a high rock, for the purpose of saving a child', would succeed; he was right.[32] First, the water thrilled: a roiling 'tank of water between rollers, which rotated to give the effect of waves'.[33] But Carlo was the money-maker, 'hired from ... the proprietor of an *a-là-mode* beef shop', trained to leap from a rock and tow 'Julio', show after show.[34] Carlo was what contemporary Michael Kelly called '[t]he chief attraction', his plunge quickly earning Sheridan £350.[35] Due to 'the *eclat* [sic] with which the *principal performer* was received', on the second night the 'second title of *the Driver and his Dog*' was added: 'it is impossible to describe the sensations excited by ... this canine hero from Newfoundland'.[36] *The Sporting Magazine* noted 'the interchange of wit and humour in the public papers, by various writers, who have personated the dog'.[37] The visual record similarly bespeaks popularity: Carlo holding Sheridan aloft in an onstage lake (1803); Sheridan blowing bubbles to cheering crowds while Carlo sleeps (1805).[38] When *Caravan* toured Edinburgh (1811–12), it was introduced as 'the most successful piece ever known' for its unique '[t]heatrical enterprise'.[39]

But who was the canine thespian? How did he become the star? These questions underlie Fenwick's *Carlo*. The advertisement, like the 1806 preface, asks rhetorically, '[w]ho has not heard of Carlo, the renowned dog of Drury-Lane Theatre?'[40] 'These memoirs', with 'Portrait' and other plates, 'contain the history of Carlo, prior to his coming out as an actor', the advertisement says.[41] The so-called autobiography ends with Carlo's stardom after he makes good on his master's will that he can always leap for children: 'all said it never could be acted, as perhaps no dog could be found that might be depended on, always', but master insists, 'my Carlo will do it' (63). After all, Carlo has already saved two children (first a nice child, later nasty Vincent).

But there is more to the story. Unbeknownst to master, Carlo actually resisted saving Vincent, although he had recently 'plunged after' another child 'without a moment's delay' (37). Everyone assumed Carlo would act: 'Bring Carlo – he will save him!' (49). Instead, he 'was going to spring', but 'saw it was my cruel enemy Vincent, and turning away, I walked sullenly to the other side' (49). Carlo hesitates, he believes, because Vincent threw water in master Tom's face, and beat Carlo for defending him: 'resentment against him was so strong that I should have suffered him to perish' (49). But he yields at the sight of Vincent's father: 'pale as death, his hands clasped, his eyes uplifted, with quivering lips praying to heaven for the deliverance of his only son' (50). He concedes, '[m]y heart relented', and 'I leaped into the sea, and saved the boy' (50). In Carlo's own view, he cannot *be depended on, always*.

Yet there is more to it than Carlo knows. We see the limits of Carlo's consciousness when he identifies the sight of Vincent's father as the source for his turn but he never wonders why *this* should be more moving than the fact that he (a) witnessed the drowning deaths of his 'Sweet sisters' and 'darling brothers' and (b) almost drowned, too, and was laid with them all 'dead upon an ash-heap' (6). In a thoughtful essay, James P. Carson concludes that Carlo 'observes the power of choice in deciding not to perform a rescue, which would supposedly be instinctual for the Newfoundland'.[42] But it is no more guaranteed that Carlo did choose – either in denying or saving – than that he expressed his native personality *or* was influenced by experience. Whatever *Carlo* thinks about either his self-fashioning potential or his typological Newfoundland-ness, the influence of experience on behaviour remains almost as charmingly mysterious to him as it is to the humans – the three masters who unite to see Carlo in *Caravan* – who believe they too know his nature as dog, as Newfoundland, as Carlo.

The opening paragraphs convey Carlo's own assumptions about his personality; here is crucial information about his response to the ultimate crisis-of-Vincent that only Carlo and we know is the crisis, the resolution of which makes Carlo into a stage star and *Carlo*'s protagonist. First, Carlo positions himself within the Newfoundland aegis: 'I am descended both by my father's and mother's side, from the noble race of Newfoundland dogs' ([3]). Carlo defines Newfoundland-ness by describing mother: '[i]n resenting an insult, or defending the oppressed, she had all the courage of the fiercest of her species, yet, unprovoked, she was so gentle, she would not have hurt a worm' ([3]). Is this introduction as simple as it seems?[43] Man's best friend, fierce if provoked? No: Carlo's seemingly straightforward portrayal of Newfoundland-personality belies a hidden paradox revealed by his experience with Vincent. If a 'fine' specimen of 'the species' takes umbrage and protects the weak (3), what happens if the weak are the insulters?

Carlo suggests he chose: 'I was going to spring', then 'saw it was my cruel enemy' (49). But the crisis may turn on what we might call Carlo's Dilemma, a contest between two points of supposed nature: taking-umbrage-at-insult versus protecting-the-weak. We do know Carlo's grudges have no expiration date; for instance, one fellow caused 'excessive torment' by feeding Carlo mustard and snuff, and he declares: 'I never forgave him' (60). If, with Vincent, his 'heart relented', was this a choice or the primacy of protecting the weak over taking umbrage (50)? And/or are other factors involved in Carlo's dilemma?

Surely, the genesis of Vincent's salvation lies in the narrative's inaugural revelations, even if Carlo misses the connection. Precisely, Carlo introduces his memoir by sighing, 'never can I forget the agony of my mother's howl, when we were borne from the kennel where she was chained' (6). And yet he seems to forget, even though babyhood meant 'the kindest, best' mama, and siblings 'so warm, so snugly' (5). And although he has not 'beheld a family of such love and harmony … since [he] was torn from [his] mother's side', after he was saved from the old ashheap by young Edward he spendt only one night 'moaning softly for [his] mother' (5, 8). He tells us explicitly he cries no more. He thinks of her consciously only once, early on, in lean times with Edward. Carlo considers leaving, vowing sadly, 'never shall Carlo forget Edward'; ironically, in the same breath, 'I thought of my mother', rather, the 'meat that used to be brought to her kennel' (17). He 'resolve[s] to seek her out' (18). Alas, entering Cheapside, he is sidetracked by the Lord Mayor's Day Parade and '[h]am and veal' scents 'from every house' (19). The 'heaviest misfortune of my life', the distracted dog says later, was when he 'was separated for ever' not from mama, nor even Edward, but '[his] kind, affectionate [second] master, Tom' (52).

Neither mama nor her memory reappears, although the story's ending fulfils other fantasies of reunion, presenting a structural commonplace of limited recovery generic to many animal it-narratives. The canine hero of *Cato, or Interesting Adventures of A Dog of Sentiment* (1816), Carlo's heir, begins his story 'a few days after [his] birth', when he was 'comfortably asleep with [his] mother, brothers and sister', and proceeds to the drowning of siblings and traumatic separation from mother, and, although Cato is eventually reunited with his first loving master, his 'poor mother … had long paid the debt of nature'.[44] Cato's original, Carlo, similarly regains no mama but remains himself: 'ah! How [his] heart beat at the well known sound!' of his name, after being misaddressed as 'Lion, Tiger, Snap, Brush' (59); and when Edward returns and 'pronounced the name of Carlo', the latter 'instantly knew [him] to be Edward' (65). Tom, too, returns, and '[t]hree years had elapsed, … but I instantly knew him, as he came up the street' (65). Carlo spends the day with 'my three masters', they see him perform, and it is 'certainly the happiest day of my life' (66). *Never can I forget*, he says of his mother's woe when he and 'fifteen brothers and sisters' were taken (4), but he does forget.

Perhaps the strangest thing, though, is his total lack of empathy, considering his own near-drowning. Or does he feel more than he knows?

His secret history's inaugural revelations include the insistence that he 'will not grieve you by minutely describing' 'the sufferings of sixteen little wretches drowning', of which he himself was one (5). In his complexity – his grudges and limited self-awareness, his knowing and unknowing acts of traumatic repression – Carlo suggests an uncanny humanness.

Arguably, when Fenwick's Carlo saved the first child, he did what virtually anyone (Newfoundland/dog or not) would do, and the rest is all learning. Carlo learns to read (Edward unwittingly teaches him); does he not learn saving like he learns to ring monastery bells for food (57)? In his capacity to learn-for-reward, Carlo is heir to the dog-hero of Francis Coventry's *History of Pompey the Little* (1751); traded by humans for a watch, a pint of porter, and a pennyworth of oysters, Pompey does tricks best 'whenever he expected a new collar, or stood candidate for a riband with other dogs'.[45]

Carlo is also heir to the hero of *Dog of Knowledge; or, Memoirs of Bob the Spotted Terrier* (1801), who delights in learning and in the appearance (and perhaps reality) of exceeding what he calls his 'generic worth'.[46] Bob is 'paternally' descended from the 'ancient … family of the TERRIERS', a 'genuine aboriginal breed' that 'never changed their language nor their manners, in consequence of foreign conquest', but he is also half-beagle.[47] Unlike terrier-ancestors, he accepts 'change', adopts 'mild and conciliatory arts'.[48] 'Dancing in harlequin's jacket, fencing with a stick', Bob is not simply the 'spotted, smooth-haired terrier' his master intended. He takes a page and a half to 'unfold my figure and colours', exhibiting his own natural harlequin-hair: '[m]y neck was wholly white, and a peak of the same colour descended down my back, like a lady's handkerchief, on each side bounded with dark tan' while '[v]arious patches and lines of white and brindled tan diversified my sides'.[49] Bob, like Carlo, is complicated.

Amusingly, *if* Fenwick's Carlo – less a celebrity-culture one-off than a transformative version of intersecting prose traditions – has no intractable yen for saving children, real-life Carlo in Reynolds's *Caravan* initially showed no interest in hauling children from Drury Lane's 'lake'. Reynolds complained the water was more 'tractable and accommodating' than Carlo; only after numerous trials did Carlo make 'the desired leap'.[50] But real-life Carlo, like book-Carlo, did learn, gaining edible reward and nightly praise as *Caravan*-Carlo.

Still, published references to real-life Carlo emphasised the essential 'virtues of the Newfoundland breed', not his trained acting skill.[51] *Caravan* was, Reynolds underscored, a '*natural*' production.[52] An engraving

C A R L O,
THE ROSCIUS OF DRURY-LANE THEATRE.

Figure 4. *Carlo, the Roscius of Drury Lane Theatre*. Hand-coloured aquatint, depicting the famous scene from *The Caravan*. The full print (width: 20.3 cm., height: 30.4 cm.) includes lines of verse below the image. Published in London (26 January 1804) by Laurie and Whittle.
© Victoria and Albert Museum, London.

entitled *CARLO, The Roscius of Drury Lane Theatre* shows a majestic beast, black with shaggy white ruff, towing child through waves.[53] Carlo is '[n]o actor', unlike 'Garrick': 'Nature *herself* with Carlo takes the field'.[54] 'Was ever part so naturally play'd' when Carlo 'to his mother gave the babe she'd lost?'[55] He 'play[ed] the Dog', and 'Ne'er was he found imperfect in his part': 'His character was always GOT BY HEART'.[56] *Sporting Magazine* thanks this 'fine Newfoundland dog', as the 'momentous crisis' of the Marchioness's woe, when 'her child is precipitated from a rock into the foaming waves', is resolved.[57] While 'every bosom sympathizes with the pangs of maternal agony, the voice of the caravan driver is heard vociferating, "Carlo! Carlo!"'[58] Good dog, and a good thing, too, said a report on 'The New Performer' in *The Morning Chronicle*: '[t]he spectators in the gallery, who love *nature*, are delighted with the scene of *real water*. ' "None of your *made* stuff" '.[59] Carlo's other madcap antics – barking, peeing, howling, knocking over Marquis, roughing up Julio, refusing to share edible reward with master, and engaging in other unscripted hi-jinks while egged on by the audience's rewarding shouts of 'Carlo! Carlo!'[60] – were deemed evidence of naturalness.

Fenwick's *Carlo*, forged at the intersection of secret history, it-narrative, and children's beast fable, suggests the truth of personality is complicated and elusive. What is nature? What is choice? Whither climate, environment? Carlo's turn remains mysterious; he does not know how his heart goes from 'resent[ing]' to 'relent[ing]', and neither do we (49, 50). In thinking about the untraceable secret history of how memory and identity are co-produced in *Carlo* (an oddly existential offering for Tabart's young audience!) one is reminded less of obdurate it-ancestors like Chrysal than of *Chrysal*'s hapless miner whose brain, like ours, gets its groove on obscurely.

Notes

1 Mark Blackwell, 'Introduction: The It-Narrative and Eighteenth-Century Thing Theory', *The Secret Life of Things: Animals, Objects, and It-Narratives in Eighteenth-Century England*, ed. Blackwell (Lewisburg: Bucknell University Press, 2007), 9–18, 10. Rebecca Bullard, *The Politics of Disclosure, 1674–1725: Secret History Narratives* (London: Pickering and Chatto, 2009), 300; see Bullard's important work *in toto*. See also, among recent work on it-narratives: Jonathan Lamb, *The Things Things Say* (Princeton: Princeton University Press, 2011); Lynn Festa, 'The Moral Ends of Eighteenth- and Nineteenth-Century Object Narratives', *Secret Life of Things*, 309–28; Festa, *Sentimental Objects of Empire in Eighteenth-Century Britain and France* (Baltimore: Johns Hopkins University Press, 2006), 111–31; and Aileen Douglas, 'Britannia's Rule and the It-Narrator', *Secret Life of Things*, 147–61. See also, among recent work on secret history: Eve Tavor Bannet, '"Secret History": Or, Talebaring Inside and Outside the Secretorie', *The Uses of History in Early Modern England*, ed. Paulina Kewes (San Marino: Huntington Library, 2006), 367–88; Rachel Carnell, 'Slipping from Secret History to Novel', *Eighteenth-Century Fiction* 28:1 (2015): 1–24, and 'Eliza Haywood and the Narratological Tropes of Secret History', *Journal of Early Modern Cultural Studies* (2014): 101–21; Erin Keating, 'In the Bedroom of the King: Affective Politics in the Restoration Secret History', *Journal for Early Modern Cultural Studies* 15:2 (2015), 58–82; and Rivka Swenson, 'History', in *The Cambridge Companion*

to *Women's Writing in Britain, 1660–1789*, ed. Catherine Ingrassia (Cambridge: Cambridge University Press, 2015), 135–46.
2 For example: Daniel Defoe, *The Secret History of the White-Staff* (London, 1714–15) and *The Secret History of the Secret History of the White-Staff* (London, 1715); Nicholas Amhurst, *Terræ Filius: The Secret History of the University of Oxford* (London, 1721; 1726), ed. William E. Rivers (Cranbury: University of Delaware Press, 2004); Joseph Haslewood, *The Secret History of the Green Room* (London, 1790–93); John Roach, *The Authentic Memoirs of the Green Room* (London, 1806–14).
3 Charles Johnstone, *Chrysal; or the Adventures of a Guinea* (London, 1760). Elizabeth Fenwick, *The Life of Carlo, the Famous Dog of Drury Lane Theatre: with his Portrait, and other Copper Plates* (London, 1804; 1806), published by children's book publisher Benjamin Tabart; appeared minus the apparently unneeded preface as *The Life of the Famous Dog Carlo: with his Portrait, and other Copper Plates* (London, 1809). I quote from the 1809 edition unless quoting the preface.
4 Jonathan Kramnick, *Actions and Objects from Hobbes to Richardson* (Stanford: Stanford University Press, 2010), 10. See Helen Thompson, *Fictional Matter: Empiricism, Corpuscles, and the Novel* (Philadelphia: University of Pennsylvania Press, 2016).
5 See Thompson, *Fictional Matter*. See Swenson, 'Optics, Gender, and the Eighteenth-Century Gaze: Looking at Eliza Haywood's Anti-Pamela', *The Eighteenth-Century: Theory and Interpretation* 51.1–2 (2010): 27–43, and 'The Poet as Man of Feeling', in *The Oxford Handbook of British Poetry, 1660–1800*, ed. Jack Lynch (Oxford: Oxford University Press, 2016), 195–209.
6 On 'object narrative' rather than 'it narrative', see Festa, 'Moral Ends', 309–28; *Sentimental Objects*, 111–31; and Chloe Wigston Smith, *Women, Work, and Clothes in the Eighteenth-Century Novel* (Cambridge: Cambridge University Press, 2013), 73–9. See also Bill Brown's usage in *Other Things* (Chicago: University of Chicago Press, 2016). Volume 1 of *British It-Narratives, 1750–1830*, deals specifically with animal narratives. More broadly (beyond the space limitations of this essay), eighteenth-century animal studies is a burgeoning and important subfield of its own, as recent special issues attest. See for instance, Lucinda Cole, 'Human-Animal Studies', introduction, 'Animal, All too Animal', special issue, *The Eighteenth-Century: Theory and Interpretation* 52.1 [2011]: 1–11, and Glynis Ridley, 'Representing Animals', introduction, 'Animals in the Eighteenth Century', special issue, *British Journal for Eighteenth-Century Studies* 33.4 (2010), 431–6. For recent work that my enquiry resonates with in this essay's second half, see Tobias Menely's magisterial and moving *The Animal Claim: Sensibility and the Creaturely Voice* (Chicago: University of Chicago Press, 2015).
7 See Swenson, 'History', *Cambridge Companion*, 135–46.
8 See Cynthia Wall on the rise of detail and description, *The Prose of Things: Transformations of Description in the Eighteenth Century* (Chicago, University of Chicago Press, 2006). See, recently, Jenny Davidson, 'The 'Minute

Particular' in Life-Writing and the Novel', *Eighteenth-Century Studies*, 48.3 (2015): 263–81.
9 See Srinivas Aravamudan, *Enlightenment Orientalism: Resisting the Rise of the Novel* (Chicago and London: University of Chicago Press, 2012), 196–9.
10 Christopher Flint, 'Speaking Objects: The Circulation of Stories in Eighteenth-Century Prose Fiction', *Secret Life of Things*, 162–86, 174.
11 See Festa's insights on influential objects, *Sentimental Figures*, 122–3. For an interesting reading of things that differs from mine, see Crystal B. Lake, 'Feeling Things: The Novel Objectives of Sentimental Objects', *The Eighteenth Century: Theory and Interpretation* (54.2): 183–93.
12 Procopius, *The Secret History of the Court of the Emperor Justinian* (London, 1674); *The Debauch'd Court; or, The Lives of the Emperor Justinian and his Empress Theodora the Comedian* (London, 1682).
13 Procopius, *The Secret History*, trans. G. A. Williamson (London: Penguin, 1966), 84, 84–5, 85.
14 Procopius, *The Secret History*, 84.
15 Procopius, *The Secret History of the Court*, 47, 54.
16 *The Secret History of an Old Shoe* (London, 1734). *A Secret History of Pandora's Box* (London, 1742).
17 Helenus Scott, *The Adventures of a Rupee* (London, 1782), 126.
18 Tobias Smollett, *The History and Adventures of an Atom* (1769), ed. O. M. Brack (Athens, GA and London: University of Georgia Press, 2008), 57. See Swenson, *Essential Scots and the Idea of Unionism, 1603–1832* (Lewisburg: Bucknell University Press, 2016), 71–3, 97–8.
19 Smollett, *Atom*, [1]–2.
20 Smollett, *Atom*, 2–3.
21 Smollett, *Atom*, 5.
22 Smollett, *Atom*, 6, 3, 3.
23 Smollett, *Atom*, [ii].
24 Smollett, *Atom*, 16, 34.
25 Scott, *Rupee*, 9, 10.
26 Mary Ann Kilner, *The Adventures of a Pincushion: Designed Chiefly for the Use of Young Ladies* (London, 1780), 15.
27 'Adventures of a Quire of Paper', *London Magazine* 48 (August–October 1779): 355–8, 395–8, 448–52; 449, 357.
28 'The Adventures of a Gold Ring', *Rambler's Magazine* 1 (March–July 1783): 84–7, 128–30, 167–9, 207–9, 254–6; 256.
29 Lewis Walpole Library, *Scrapbook of advertisements, broadsides, poetry, newspapers*, Folio 66 748 Sc43, shelfmark Lwlpr29493, 72.
30 Deidre Shauna Lynch, *The Economy of Character: Novels, Market Culture, and the Business of Inner Meaning* (Chicago: University of Chicago Press, 2007), 99.
31 For a different reading, see James P. Carson: Carlo 'possesses greater than human sensitivity to the depth and reality of emotion'. Carson, 'The

Sentimental Animal', in *Reflections on Sentiment: Essays in Honor of George Starr*, ed. Alessa Johns (Newark: University of Delaware Press, 2015), 55–82, esp. 70–6; 76. Laura Brown writes that *Carlo* 'subscribe[s] to the … assumption … that the dog protagonist is endowed with special abilities that enable him to rival or even exceed … human-kind'. Brown, *Homeless Dogs and Melancholy Apes: Humans and Other Animals in the Modern Literary Imagination* (Ithaca and London: Cornell University Press, 2010), 134.
32 Frederick Reynolds, *The Life and Times of Frederick Reynolds*, 2 vols. (London, 1827), 2: 350–1.
33 BL, Drury Lane memoranda, unidentified clipping, February 1794, c. 120.h1.
34 Reynolds, *The Life and Times*, 2: 350–1. Michael Kelly, *Reminiscences of Michael Kelly, of the King's Theatre, and Theatre Royal Drury Lane* (London, 1826), 2: 192–3, 192.
35 Kelly, *Reminiscences*, 193. See also Reynolds, *The Life and Times*, 1: 194, 217, and 2: 350–1.
36 'Memoranda Dramatica, &c.', *The Monthly Mirror* (December 1803), 412.
37 'The Caravan, and the Dog Carlo', *The Sporting Magazine*, 23:135 (1803), 149.
38 James Sayers, *The Manager and his Dog* (London, 1803). James Gillray, *The Theatrical Bubble* (London, 1805)
39 James C. Dibdin, *The Annals of The Edinburgh Stage* (Edinburgh, 1888), 265.
40 *The Critical Review; or, Annals of Literature*, 3rd series (London, 1805), iv: 107.
41 *Critical Review*, iv: 107.
42 Carson, 'Sentimental', 76.
43 For Brown, such openings are parodic: '[m]any … dog protagonists … reproduce the trope of mock genealogy that links the experience of diversity to a parodic undercutting of ideas of established hierarchy' (*Homeless Dogs*, 134).
44 *Cato, or Interesting Adventures of A Dog of Sentiment* (London, 1816), 2, 2, 175.
45 Francis Coventry, *The History of Pompey the Little; or, the Life and Adventures of a Lap-Dog* (London, 1751), 166.
46 *The Dog of Knowledge; or, Memoirs of Bob the Spotted Terrier* (London, 1801), 6.
47 *Dog of Knowledge*, 4.
48 *Dog of Knowledge*, 65, 41.
49 *Dog of Knowledge*, 35, 8, 11, 12, 12.
50 Reynolds, *The Life and Times*, 2: 350–1.
51 Diana Donald, *Picturing Animals in Britain 1750–1850* (New Haven and London: Yale University Press, 2007), 136. Kelly is an exception: '[i]t was truly astonishing how the animal could have been so well trained to act his important character' (*Reminiscences*, 192).
52 Reynolds, *The Life and Times*, 1: 217.
53 *CARLO, The Roscius of Drury-Lane Theatre* (London, 1804). Engraving and verse.
54 *CARLO*, lines 1, 3, 4.
55 *CARLO*, lines 1, 4, 8, 13.
56 *CARLO*, lines 24, 27–8.

57 'The Caravan, and the Dog Carlo', 148.
58 'The Caravan, and the Dog Carlo', 148.
59 'The New Performer', *The Spirit of the Public Journals for 1804* (London, 1805), VIII: 45.
60 See for instance *Times*, London, 24 September 1804, 3, and 5 November 1804, 2.

9

Secret History, Oriental Tale, and Fairy Tale

Ros Ballaster

Realist technique in eighteenth-century fiction is, according to Rachel Carnell's persuasive account, the product of the partisanship of secret history: the competition to claim partisan versions of (political) subjecthood as universal means that fictional writing seeks methods of narration designed to 'convey an aura of reality and universal humanity to stories depicting particular people at particular times'.[1] Increasing particularity of narrative voice and description of character does not, however, preclude the continuing presence of the supernatural and the fantastic.[2] The fairy tale, the oriental tale, it-narrative, the animal fable, the imaginary voyage: these genres prosper throughout the century. Where the domestic novel depicts minds at odds with each other and promotes the disciplinary virtues of home, fantastic modes easily inhabit 'other' minds (of animals, of Eastern despots and harem women, of petticoats, needles, and coins) and travel continents in the flash of a fairy wing.

Is then the fantastic merely a primitive survivor in the face of modernity? Its resilience might be better accounted for by taking notice of the insight of psychoanalytic theory that the separation of real and fantasy is itself a consolatory fantasy. This essay proposes an uncanny relationship between secret history's claim to reveal secrets that are no secrets at all (a secret cannot be recognised as a secret unless it is already in some sense known) and Jacques Lacan's formulation, according to Slavoj Žižek, that 'fantasy' is a means of filling out a fundamental lack, of projecting the lack within the self onto an apparently 'full' Other: 'fantasy' is a screen masking a void. The social order is itself for Žižek a fantasy; to traverse the fantasy is a political act through which we come to experience the 'nothing' behind the fantasy, to know that it masks 'nothing'.[3]

To submit to the fantastic tale is to experience or traverse the fantasy: to recognise that fantasy is a screen for our own extrojected desire for absolute power.[4] The 'primary political purpose' of secret history, Rebecca Bullard reminds us, is to oppose 'arbitrary government'.[5] The act of printing lays bare or makes public the 'secret' machinations of power. However, the story is, surprisingly, never surprising: it is utterly familiar and predictable. The story of the seductive and corrupting effects of arbitrary power is a familiar one of temptation, fall, and resistance (whether from within or outside the magic circle of government). 'How', Rebecca Bullard asks, 'are we to interpret the motif of revelation in texts … which clearly contain little that might be described, in any ordinary sense of the term, as secret?' (10). One route may lie in Žižek's formulation of the need to 'traverse' fantasy, to travel through and with the fantastic narrative, precisely to expose the emptiness behind its apparent concealments. The supernatural elements of the oriental and the fairy tale are conjured in the secret historical versions of these genres precisely to be experienced and then dispelled leaving the newly wise subject to rule and regulate his or her own imaginative projections. Reader and protagonist learn alongside each other not the 'truth' of political power but rather the fantasmatic basis of all such power.

Oriental and fairy tales narrate the growth to moral responsibility of the ruler. A hugely influential and now neglected work in this tradition is that of François de Salignac Fénelon, the Archbishop of Cambrai's *Les aventures de Télémaque* composed for the seven-year-old duc de Bourgogne, grandson of Louis XIV in 1696, published in 1699 after Fénelon had been removed from his role as tutor, and translated into English in that same year.[6] Speaking truth to power, however juvenile that power may be (or perhaps precisely because of the despotism of youth) requires displacement into a world that is not immediately recognisable to the auditor: whether that of the animal fables, the oriental past or present, the world of fairy magic. Hence, the preface to *The Adventures of Telemachus* explains that:

> The Reason he had to involve his Instructions in Fable, will be obvious to all who shall consider that as he wrote for Princes, who seldom fail to reject all Precepts that are not guilded with Delight; so he lives under a Monarch that will not suffer open and undisguised Truth.[7]

Fénelon gives us the adventures of Ulysses' fiery, ambitious, amorous son who seeks news of his father as he travels across the Mediterranean in the company of a wise elderly guide named Mentor – known to the readers to be the goddess Minerva in disguise. Along the way, Telemachus is tested by sexual attraction, enslavement, and foreign wars; he encounters examples of good and bad government against which to measure his own future behaviour. The articulation of an opposition politics through the (disguised) 'romance' traditions of oriental tale, fairy tale and animal fable continues through the eighteenth century. I focus here on two periods of flourishing: first, the 1730s and those fictional works in sympathy with the patriot opposition to George II and the ministry of Robert Walpole which lionised Frederick Prince of Wales, then in his twenties; and second, the early 1760s and the fictional works composed in the period of the accession and early reign of Frederick's son, twenty-two year-old George III.[8] I consider the two translations by James Ralph and Eliza Stanley of Thémiseul de Saint-Hyacinthe's *History of Prince Titi* (1736); Eliza Haywood's *Adventures of Eovaai* (1736); John Hawkesworth's oriental tale, *Almoran and Hamet* (1761) and James Ridley's *Tales of the Genii* (1765).

Where the secret historical meets the oriental/fairy tale, a deeper kind of understanding of 'hidden' drives is achieved. The stated aim of arriving at a position of stable self-government is itself tried and revealed to be a fantasy. Intra- and extra-diegetic readers come to recognise that fantasy is not a means of avoiding reality but rather a means to cover up the fact that reality IS *lack*. Fantasy is the route to anagnorisis rather than a departure from it. There is no stable place of government in the self or state; introjecting that instability and owning it as a part of the self is the best opportunity for stability itself. The penultimate line of perhaps the best-known oriental tale of the period, Samuel Johnson's *Rasselas* (1759), points to this necessary process of introjection of the 'wishes' of fantasy. Rasselas and his party build future dreams of power but recognise: 'Of those wishes that they had formed they well knew that none could be obtained.'[9] This is not to repudiate the wish but to recognise that it is brought into being precisely to obscure, or keep secret, the void that was its origin. To 'know well' that 'nothing' is the object of traversing fantasy.

Fairy tales and oriental tales are preoccupied with the fantasy of the wish. A recurrent plot device is that of the wish brought to reality through supernatural agency; most often, of course, the wish is proved to disappoint when it is lived through. These tales teach their protagonists to contain their wishes and to recognise, as the wise tutor Omar puts it in Hawkesworth's *Almoran and Hamet*, that 'he that seeks to satisfy all his wishes, must be wretched; he only can be happy, by whom some are suppressed'.[10] The reader sees mirrored in the speculative futures passed through in the tale his or her own fantasies of power and is encouraged to follow the model of the young protagonist and subscribe to containing and delaying the desire to fulfil the wish. Here, the fairy and oriental tale interacts with the *speculum principis*, the mirror for princes: a form of narration which tells the 'secret history' of the potential future of a young ruler.[11] It is in this respect – rather than in the strictly generic terms of the 'fantastic'[12] – that the oriental/fairy tale traverses fantasy in and for and its reader. The princely addressee of Telemachus' adventures is told the story of potential futures he may live out depending on the choices he makes about his present: to suppress or enlarge upon the aspects of his character that unfit or fit him to rule. Here, too, the mirror for princes does not so much vary on the secret history as bring it to fulfilment: the secret history warns its readers of the dire outcomes of arbitrary power to avert its future grip on the state.

In the 1730s, the wish for political change is transformed into fantasy narratives that draw on the Telemachian plot. Patriot opposition imagines a promising future in the figure of the young Frederick Prince of Wales (1707–51), at odds both with his parents, George II and Queen Caroline, and with the Prime Minister, Robert Walpole. On 27 April 1736, Frederick, aged twenty-nine, married a seventeen-year-old princess, Augusta of Saxe-Gotha-Altenburg. In the same year, the oriental tale and the fairy tale were pressed into service of a wish-fulfilment account of the prospective heir's training in exile to become a Patriot prince. *L' Histoire de Prince* Titi. *A[legorie].R[oyale]* (1726) by the free thinker, modern, and satirist Thémiseul de Saint-Hyacinthe (his real name was Hyacinthe Cordonnier) enjoyed two separate translations into English. Christine Gerrard asserts that the French work was 'almost certainly' co-authored by Frederick himself.[13] The translation ascribed to the Patriot journalist James Ralph was entitled *The Memoirs and History of Prince Titi. Done from the French by a Person of Quality* (1736) and another penned by Eliza Stanley sought to capitalise on the translator's sex: *The History of Prince Titi. Translated by a Lady* (1736).[14] Comparison of the two translations reveals no variation in plot and some in style: Ralph's inclines more to the ornate than Stanley's. Stanley also appends 'An Essay upon Allegoric: Or, Characteristic Writing'; the essay concludes with a gesture to the 'keys' of secret history by indicating the '*Signification* of the Names made Use of in this History', but also repudiates that association by insisting the names indicate moral qualities rather than real persons. A final couplet asserts in the traditional misdirection of personal satire: 'If, to these Fairy-Figments, Claimants rise,/Welcome the Owners are to share the Prize' (xi).

The story concerns the lovely, generous, and innocent Prince Titi who is despised by his mean parents, Ginguet (weak, spiritless) and Tripasse (good housewife), who prefer his doltish younger brother, Triptillion. The royal allegory points to Frederick, George II, Queen Caroline and Frederick's younger brother, William, Duke of Cumberland. The prince's kindness to an old woman hurt by an equerry on a hunting expedition, enabled by the good offices of his page L'Eveille (liveliness), pays off when the old lady is revealed to be the good fairy Diamante (Stanley)/Diamantina (Ralph) in disguise. The fairy, like Minerva in Fénelon's tale, continues to protect her young charge providing L'Eveille with the helpful gift of invisibility (a familiar trope of the secret historian) so that he can gather information for his master about the court conspiracies against him. When Titi falls in love with a beautiful commoner girl named Bibi, who lives in quiet retirement in the countryside with her parents, the fairy uses her magic powers to enable the couple to adopt any animal form they choose to escape their pursuers until the time is ripe for Titi to claim his rightful place as king. Titi and Bibi nobly resist the temptation to sexual libertinism which they observe among the animal species they live with. They survive a number of close calls in their animal guises such as a vicious attack on Bibi when Bibi is in the guise of a sparrow by Queen Tripasse's diabolical cat. Titi, like Telemachus, proves himself not only through his military valour on behalf of other warring states he encounters in his travels but also through his patience and his deference to the supernatural power that guides him. Unlike Telemachus, however, he is not overly troubled by vanity and powerful passions. *Titi* has a lively charm and it wins admirers to the Patriot cause through a childlike playfulness not found in the often sternly masculine historiographical mythmaking of other Patriot writers such as David Mallet and Henry Brooke.[15]

Titi's story is a celebration of virtuous friendship in evident reference to the Patriot circle; it only criticises the false loyalty of venal ministers of state in passing. The story casts the weak King Ginguet and his spiteful Queen as the clear villains of the piece. By contrast, Eliza Haywood's less unambiguously Patriot satirical oriental fiction of the same year has the Prime Minister, Robert Walpole, clearly in its sights.[16] Here too, however, there is an interest in playing with the gendered disguises in *Telemachus*. The main protagonist of *The Adventures of Eovaai* is an orphaned Princess whose Eve-like curiosity leads her to open the case in which her father has enclosed a precious jewel with magical powers to protect her. The stone is snatched by a bird and Eovaai loses her powers of perception and good government. An evil magician, Ochihatou (Robert Walpole) from the neighbouring country, who keeps his king Oeros (George II) docile with the aid of an enchanted feather, courts Eovaai, aspiring both to her person and kingdom. Eovaai is almost duped, but a female genie Halafamai (another version of the Mentor figure) provides her with a small telescope which allows her to see through deceit. Eovaai (whose name we are told denotes 'The Delight of the Eyes' (55)) needs to see clearly the vices of others and to oversee her own passions if she is to be restored to power. Like Titi, she needs not only to act to resist but also to wait. After a series of abductions, near rapes, and Telemachian encounters with different forms of government among the states through which she wanders, Eovaai is only restored to her kingdom when she is saved from Ochihatou's final assault by the virtuous and heroic exiled Prince Adelhu, son to Oeros, who it transpires (in one of many pieces of shameless sexual symbolism) is the keeper of her lost jewel. Adelhu, as his initial suggests, is Adam to the protagonist's Eve, but he is also a version of Frederick, Prince of Wales; Eovaai is both Eve and England, the state restored to its original virtue by the intervention of its young Prince.

Eliza Haywood provides her Patriot romance with a complex frame narration; the tale is told by a young Chinese mandarin living in London from a work undertaken by a cabal of fifth-century Chinese literati at the bequest of a virtuous Emperor. It is studded with footnotes from members of the Cabal, a commentator named Hahehihotu and the Mandarin translator who is often keen to bring to his readers' attention the lapses in deference to liberty, autonomy and the capacity for female virtue indicated in these other voices. Haywood complicates the fairy tale here by alerting her readers to the play of voices all seeking to see their own wishes realised in the story they translate from one language and one culture to another.

By 1761, the oriental and fairy tale had a new 'prince' to educate and celebrate, Frederick's English born and raised son, George III, who acceded to the throne on his grandfather's death in October 1760. Magical powers of disguise and the dynamic between twinned protagonists are also important elements in John Hawkesworth's loyalist oriental tale, *Almoran and Hamet*. Hawkesworth originally wrote the story as a play to be staged by his friend, actor-manager David Garrick at Drury Lane, but the plan for production was abandoned due to the likely cost of the 'transformations and machinery'; Hawkesworth's widow, Mary, records in a letter to John Duncombe in December 1781 that her husband 'thought the sentiments peculiarly adapted for the use of a young monarch, and was tempted to give it in another garb to the public'.[17] Another of Hawkesworth's friends, John Stuart, Earl of Bute who had served as tutor to the young Prince George and became *de facto* Prime Minister on George's accession in late October 1760, obtained permission from the young king for the work to be dedicated to George. It was written and published a few months before his marriage to Princess Charlotte of Mecklenburg-Strelitz.

Hawkesworth was a man with a gift for friendship, who made the transition from Patriot opposition in the 1750s (when he wrote for the *Monthly Review* alongside James Ralph) to government loyalism as a Buteite Tory in the 1760s; *Almoran and Hamet* was the vehicle for that transition.[18] The tale is a thinly veiled allegory and compliment to George, whose character was close to that of the virtuous twin, Hamet: shy, devout and domestic. George's devotion to his counsellor friend and onetime tutor, Lord Bute, is evidently mirrored in Hamet's dependence on his loyal advisor Omar. By comparison, an evil genius steers the active, aggressive, and despotic twin, Almoran, to his downfall.

Almoran and Hamet concerns the conflict between two brothers whose father has left them in equal control of his kingdom. A genius provides the envious twin, Almoran, with the power to adopt the appearance of others; he uses this power to substitute for his brother in the courtship of a lovely commoner, Almeida, and to attempt to seize power from Hamet once the people have expressed a preference for him to be their single sovereign. Almoran's overreaching receives fit punishment. He pronounces the mystic words given to Hamet as a protective charm only to have a genius appear who announces that 'I have been appointed to perfect virtue, by adversity; and in the folly of her own projects, to entangle vice'.[19] Almoran is turned into stone leaving his worthy brother, his backbone strengthened from these experiences, to rule alone having assimilated the wise counsel of Omar. Fénelon's *Télémaque* was an obvious source and a work for which Hawkesworth clearly had a longstanding affection. His own translation of Fénelon's *Les aventures de Télémaque* was published by subscription, handsomely bound and illustrated, in 1768 and dedicated to Lord Shelburne, Secretary of State and cousin to Hawkesworth's patron's wife, Lady Caldwell.

Three years after the publication of *Almoran and Hamet*, James Ridley, an Oxford-educated chaplain who had returned after ill-health from chaplaincy in India to take up a quiet curacy in Essex found considerable success with his *Tales of the Genii*, published first in shilling parts and then as a whole in two volumes in London by J. Wilkie in 1764.[20] The debt to Fénelon was again evident in this series of nine tales supposedly translated by one Charles Morrell from a series of tales told him by a Persian imam called Horam whom he met at Fort St. George in Madras. Horam says he composed the tales to instruct Osmir, the five-year-old son of the Emperor Aurengzeb (reigned 1658–1707) in the path of virtue. He invents a frame to his tales in which two children, Patna and Coulor, are spirited by a female genie to a counsel of twenty-eight genii who sit on golden thrones; here the children receive instructive lessons through listening to tales about the importance of penetrating acts of disguise designed to tempt a variety of protagonists into acts of immorality. The tales are ornate and repetitive, but they take a sudden and decisive turn in the conclusion when the Protestant churchman pulls back the veil of his own disguise. The 'Muslim' tales are an entertaining means of conveying Christian values to his English readers. Ridley dedicated his work to George, Prince of Wales, who was only two years old on the work's first publication, with the hope that they would 'hereafter' meet with his 'approbation' (A2^v). The last of Ridley's tales returns the Telemachian paradigm to the more familiar practice of the secret history. Here, the wayward vizier Adhim is led by a virtuous Muslim named Mirglip to the friendly groves of the latter's retired father-in-law, Fincal. Fincal describes his happy band of like-minded morally incorruptible neighbours, many of them friends with whom he was educated. Adhim falls in love with Mirglip's sister-in-law Kaphira and the pair are protected by the genius of the groves, Nadam, from the machinations of Adhim's vicious vizier, Lemack, who has had the power to transform himself to look like Adhim conferred on him by an evil supernatural power named Falri. It transpires that this tale is itself a form of domestic 'secret history'. Annotations by the lawyer William Adams on his copy of the published work along with manuscript materials in the copy of the original first edition owned by one Elizabeth Ridley (an as-yet unidentified female relation) enabled scholars to identify the concealed identities of Ridley's circle of friends and the friends of his father, Gloseter Ridley, behind the anagrammatically 'oriental' names. Hence, 'Phesoj Ecneps' is Joseph Spence (1699–1768), author of *Polymetis* (1747), enthusiast for oriental gardens and natural genius; Gloseter Ridley is 'the Holy Dervise of Sumatra'; 'Mirglip' is an anagram of Pilgrim, identified by William Adams as 'guardian to the author's wife'. W. E. Buckley concluded in 1885 that 'they seem to have been a band of friends, a mutual admiration society, among whom James Ridley was the shining star'.[21]

Whatever the domestic secret historical referentiality of its last tale, and despite its vision of retired devout domestic harmony amongst friends, the *Tales of the Genii* alerts us to the unstable ethical claims of the fantastic tale to reform its intradiegetic protagonists. Ridley, having served himself in India, must have been acutely aware of the uncertain outcomes of the recent signing of a peace that brought an end to the Seven Years War between European powers. The 1763 Treaty of Paris left Britain struggling to assert its authority in its newly ceded territories of India and in Canada. Mirroring this uncertainty in the real world is the narrative acknowledgement that the closure of the oriental/fairy tale may not result in the moral reform of the intradiegetic reader. From their first introduction, we know that Horam's lessons have been 'unavailing' with their intended recipient:

> I conceived the purpose of disguising the true doctrines of morality, under the delightful allegories of romantic inchantment. Mine eye had seen the great varieties of nature, and the powers of my fancy could recall and realise the images. I was pleased with my own inventions, and hoped to find that virtue would steal into the breast, amidst the flowers of language and description.
>
> My lessons, though designed only for the young prince, were read and admired by the whole court. *Osmir* alone was displeased at them; his mind was not disposed to attention; he cursed the hours of his confinement; he read without benefit; he admired vice in all its deformity, and despised the lessons of virtue and goodness'. (xxvii)

Intradiegetic readers – the fictional readers of the frame tales, the young princes to whom works are dedicated and told – often remain stubbornly invested in retaining those powers, authorities, and vices that the tales are designed to suppress. What looks like conversion and transformation can often seem only like a new way of expressing an old vice. Hence, Eovaai's 'choice' of Adelhu is ironically represented as a means of rationalising a violent attraction: 'she determined to offer him her Crown and Person, *as she said*, to recompense him for herself and People, but *in reality* to gratify the Passion she was enflamed with for him' (158). Fénelon did not conclude his novel with an unambiguously autonomous hero no longer reliant on his Mentor/Minerva. Telemachus confides in Mentor his attraction to Antiope, daughter of Idomeneus, and his choice is approved because of the latter's capacity to maintain a diplomatic silence: 'she never speaks but when 'tis necessary' (129). Telemachus then encounters a melancholy man and fails to recognise that the man is his own father. Ulysses, like Telemachus' chosen bride, keeps his own counsel and Mentor/Minerva again advises the young prince that this is the best model to follow. Ulysses 'is the Wisest of all Men, his Heart is like a deep Well, there is no drawing any of his Secrets out of it' (166). Telemachus is, after all, a secret history, an instructional text about how to keep watch over one's own passions by carefully observing those of others. The 'great Business' of the ruler, according to Minerva, 'is to Converse with [men] in private; to draw from the bottom of their Souls all the secret Springs that lie conceal'd there; to handle 'em on every side, and sound their Maxims' (148).

To traverse the fantasy, to live through the fantastic speculative worlds of remote territories (oriental and fairy), is, then, to be returned 'home'. More often than not, the 'secret Springs' are revealed to be delusory fantasies rather than solid motives and intentions. We can turn to Samuel Johnson to celebrate the failure of disclosure, or what Žižek acknowledges as the problem that inheres in his own imagining of a politics informed by 'the idea that every act ultimately misfires, and that the proper ethical stance is heroically to accept this failure'.[22] Samuel Johnson turns the recurrent metaphor of the secret history – the 'secret Spring' – into the magical potion at the centre of his own fairy tale of 1766, *The Fountain*. He provided the story for a collection published to support a blind poet, Anna Williams, who lived with him and supervised his household from 1765 until her death in 1783.[23] The main protagonist is a girl, Floretta, who liberates a goldfinch from a lime twig and the threatening approach of a hawk. Unsurprisingly, the goldfinch is revealed to be a powerful fairy doomed to adopt bird form until she is the recipient of an act of unselfish kindness. In return, Floretta is provided by the fairy Lilinet with the opportunity to drink from two springs: one of joy and another of sorrow. The spring of joy brings to fruition Floretta's wishes: to be beautiful, to be rich, to be witty. But on each occasion she drinks too deep, finds herself the victim of others' envy, malice or opportunism and is obliged to take the antidote of the bitter spring of sorrow. Her last wish on drinking from the spring of joy is for immortality but even this she is obliged to reverse when she discovers old age brings ill-health and peevishness. The story concludes with the dying Lady Lilinet impressing a final kiss on Floretta's lips as she resigns herself to nature (141). Johnson concludes his story not with a sip from a secret spring or a moment of insight into hidden desire, past or future truths, but with an intimate gesture of union between tutelary power and pupil.

This is the familiar turn of eighteenth-century fiction: to sociable union as an alternative to competitive powers. In the end, the disguised tutor is a fantastic projection of the eager imagination's desire to see into its own future. However, it is necessary to traverse, to go through, the story to arrive at the capacity to introject the future store of wisdom required to govern both self and system. Like Floretta, the reader of the fairy tale is often left with a sour taste in the mouth only partially redeemed by the sweetness of that closing kiss. The cynical legacy of the secret history continues to trouble the apparent full (dis)closure of this fairy-tale education: disguise, diplomatic silence, and watchful observation may be the best means to survive the world of statecraft.

Notes

1 Rachel Carnell, *Partisan Politics, Narrative Realism, and the Rise of the British Novel*. (Basingstoke and New York: Palgrave Macmillan, 2006), 18.
2 For the most recent accounts of the persistence and prevalence of the fantastic mode as a feature of Enlightenment, rather than an outworn form, see Srinivas Aravamudan, *Enlightenment Orientalism: Resisting the Rise of the Novel* (Chicago: University of Chicago Press, 2012); David Sandner, *Critical Discourses of the Fantastic 1712–1831* (Farnham: Ashgate, 2011); Marina Warner, *Stranger Magic: Charmed States and the Arabian Nights* (London: Chatto and Windus, 2011) and Ros Ballaster, *Fabulous Orients: Fictions of the East 1662–1785* (Oxford: Oxford University Press, 2005).
3 Slavoj Žižek, 'Fantasy as a Political Category: A Lacanian Approach', *Journal for the Psychoanalysis of Culture and Society* 1:2 (Fall 1996), 77–85.
4 On extrajection, see Richard Koenigsberg, *The Fantasy of Oneness and the Struggle to Separate: Toward a Psychology of Culture* (Charlotte: Information Age Publishing, 2008): 'As the human being struggles to separate, to gain autonomy, to achieve freedom, he struggles to rid himself of the internalised object, which acts as a burden, a weight of oppression. He does so by *projecting* the internalised object onto objects in the externalised world, thus creating a certain "distance" between one's own ego and the object: to "extraject" the object is therefore to distance the object from the self: it is a mechanism toward autonomy' (24).
5 Rebecca Bullard, *The Politics of Disclosure, 1674–1725: Secret History Narratives* (London: Pickering & Chatto, 2009), 6.
6 See James Herbert Davis, Jr. *Fénelon* (Boston: Twayne, 1979) who reports at least sixteen French editions in 1699 and sixteen more between 1700 and 1712. At least sixteen translations in English appeared through the eighteenth century (108). Fénelon wrote a series of fables for the young prince when the latter was between eight and ten including animal and fairy stories and a series of 'Dialogues des morts' when the prince was ten of conversations between ancient and modern philosophers on literature, morals and politics. *Télémaque* was written for the prince in his adolescence. Jean de la Fontaine had, of course, in 1668 dedicated the first of his series of famous *Fables* on Aesopian principles to the six-year-old Dauphin, later to become the father of Fénelon's charge.
7 François de Salignac de la Mothe-Fénelon, *Les aventures de Télémaque* (La Haye [The Hague], 1699), A2r.
8 Fénelon's *Télémaque* was applied frequently to Walpole's ministry. Book 13, concerning a corrupt and fawning court favourite who ousts his rival, was translated separately by Charles Forman in 1730 as *Protesilaus, or the Character of an Evil Minister*.
9 Samuel Johnson, *The History of Rasselas, Prince of Abissinia*, ed. Paul Goring (London: Penguin, 2007), 112.

10 John Hawkesworth, Almoran and Hamet, in *Oriental Tales*, ed. Robert Mack (Oxford: Oxford University Press, 1992), 42.
11 See A.T. Gable, 'The Prince and the Mirror, Louis XIV, Fénelon, Royal Narcissim and the Legacy of Machiavelli', *Seventeenth-Century French Studies* 15 (1993), 243–68.
12 Tzvetan Todorov, *The Fantastic: A Structural Approach to a Literary Genre*, trans. Richard Howard (Ithaca: Cornell University Press, 1975) and Rosemary Jackson, *Fantasy: The Literature of Subversion* (London: Methuen, 1981). For Todorov, the fantastic genre involves the systematic inscription of a hesitation 'between a natural and supernatural explanation of the events described' (33). For Todorov then, both the oriental and fairy tale – in which commonly there is no hesitancy in accepting supernaturalism – fall outside the genre of the fantastic.
13 Christine Gerrard, *The Patriot Opposition to Walpole. Politics, Poetry, and National Myth, 1725–1742* (Oxford: Clarendon Press, 1994), 61.
14 Ralph's biographer, John B. Shipley, questions the ascription of the translation to Ralph in his 'James Ralph, Prince Titi, and the Black Box of Frederick, Prince of Wales', *Bulletin of the New York Public Library* 71 (1967), 143–57.
15 See Emrys Jones, '"Friendship like Mine/Throws All Respects behind It"': Male Companionship and the Cult of Frederick, Prince of Wales', *Studies in Eighteenth-Century Culture* 40 (2011), 157–178. For a fine reading of the Patriot references in Haywood's novel and an explicit linking of events and images to the Patriot circle at Stowe, the estate of Viscount Cobham, see Elizabeth Kubeck, 'The Key to Stowe: Toward a Patriot Reading of Eliza Haywood's *Eovaai*', in *Presenting Gender: Changing Sex in Early-Modern Culture*, ed. Chris Mounsey (London: Associated University Presses, 2001), 225–54. Kathryn R. King is more circumspect seeing the novel as 'a politically heterogenous work' drawing on Jacobite, royalist and Old Whig politics but also offering a 'feminist reworking of monarchical paternalism' (*A Political Biography of Eliza Haywood* (London: Pickering & Chatto, 2012), 93).
16 Eliza Haywood, *The Adventures of Eovaai, Princess of Ijaveo*, ed. Earla Wilputte (Peterborough: Broadview Press, 1999).
17 Quoted in John Lawrence Abbott, *John Hawkesworth: Eighteenth-Century Man of Letters* (Madison: University of Wisconsin Press, 1982), 113.
18 See Gabriel Glickman, 'Cultures and Coteries in Mid-century Toryism: Johnson in Oxford and London,' in *The Politics of Samuel Johnson*, ed. Jonathan Clark and Howard Erskine-Hill (Basingstoke and New York: Palgrave Macmillan, 2012), 57–89, especially 71–2.
19 John Hawkesworth, *Almoran and Hamet*, in *Oriental Tales*, ed. Robert Mack (Oxford: Oxford University Press, 1992), 112.
20 It had gone into seven editions by 1861 and was translated into French and German. References are to *The Tales of the Genii: or, the Delightful Lessons of Horam, the Son of Asnar*, 2 vols., 3rd edn (London, 1766).

21 See Wilfred Hargrave, *Notes and Queries* (1885) s6-XII (306): 367. doi: 10.1093/nq/s6-XII.306.367-d; W. E. Buckley and G.E.C., *Notes and Queries* (1886) s7-I (12): 230–1 230-d-230. doi: 10.1093/nq/s7-I.12.230-d.
22 Slavoj Žižek, 'Foreword to the Second Edition: Enjoyment within the Limits of Reason Alone' *For they know not what they do: Enjoyment as a political factor*, 2nd edn (London: New York, 1991), xii.
23 Anna Williams, *Miscellanies in Verse and Prose* (London, 1766), 111–41.

10

Secret History and the Periodical

Nicola Parsons

In the early eighteenth century, the secret history's distinctive blend of fiction, politics and gossip migrated from stand-alone publications to London's periodicals. Its influence on the periodical press is evident in the titles of foundational serial publications such as The *London Spy* (1698–1700) and the *Tatler* (1709–1711) that foreground an affiliation to the double discourse of concealment and disclosure that characterises the secret history. In other instances, the oppositional rhetoric of the secret history – that is, the desire to reveal the negotiations hidden and the characters screened by the official record – underwrites periodical participation in partisan debate.[1] A little-studied periodical from the 1720s, the *Tea-Table*, perhaps represents best the confluence of the secret history and the periodical evident in the early eighteenth century.[2] Published over thirty-six bi-weekly issues in 1724, the *Tea-Table* brings together the most recognisable tropes of the secret history with the equally distinctive tropes of the periodical press. This anonymously authored paper combines a title foregrounding the classic locus of periodical consumption, made iconic by the *Spectator*'s oft-quoted ambition to bring philosophy to dwell at tea tables and to become itself 'Part of the Tea Equipage', with the familiar commitment to principled disclosure that characterises secret histories.[3] The initial issue avows that 'we shall keep nobody's secrets but our own, and in their due time and season shall bring to light all the most private transactions of this town', while subsequent issues indicate that their public targets sometimes require the use of allegory as a form of truth-telling.[4] Here, the tea table becomes a striking figure for both the discursive space of the periodical and the dissemination of politically motivated secret history.

The convergence between secret histories and periodicals is understandable given their shared ideals linking the material form of print, publicity and transparency. The title given to Procopius's foundational secret history of Emperor Justinian's reign, *Anekdota* (literally, unpublished), not only foregrounds its supplementary relationship to his published, multi-volume history of the same reign, but places corresponding emphasis on the material form of the secret history.[5] This titular act makes the gesture of revelation, foundational to secret histories, identical with the act of publication. Printing is similarly integral to the rhetoric of eighteenth-century periodicals. It is evident in Mr Spectator's declaration in the first issue of his paper that he intends to 'print himself out', a statement that explicitly connects publication and knowledge. For these reasons, both the secret history and the periodical are central to arguments about the development of an eighteenth-century public sphere. The secret history, for example, is characterised by Eve Tavor Bannet as a 'coherent Enlightenment genre', while the work of Jürgen Habermas and Benedict Anderson respectively demonstrate the role periodicals played in the development of an active and engaged reading public.[6] However, this focus tends to overlook the complications presented by the equal commitment of secret histories and periodicals to secrecy and revelation, evident in the use of rhetorical figures and techniques of concealment in narrating events. Further, it does not attend sufficiently to the impulse to fragmentation present in both forms. This essay offers a different perspective on the secret history and the periodical by identifying connections between the distinctive tropes and particular narrative structure of the two eighteenth-century forms. Through an analysis of the *Review* (1704–11), the *Athenian Mercury* (1691–7), and *Harris's List of Covent Garden Ladies* (1760–95), this essay shows how the temporality of serial publication combines with the tropes of the secret history to produce new reading possibilities. In particular, it demonstrates the ways in which the periodical contributes to the materialisation of the secret, reifying a connection between secrecy and sexuality.

The *Review*: Fragmentation and Design

The secret history and the periodical share a complex, even dislocating, temporality. The anecdote is both central to the historiographic vision and narrative method of secret historians. As a category of historiography, it provides a means of radically supplementing the orderly, public narrative of history by cataloguing, in Ephraim Chambers' contemporary definition, 'things not yet known, or hitherto kept secret'.[7] As a narrative mode, it is a means of rejecting linearity, composing instead a fragmentary narrative that suggests associations between episodes but refuses to narrate connections.[8] Delarivier Manley's secret history of the Whig Junto, the *New Atalantis* (1709), exploits the possibilities of this method to the fullest, teeming with character and event and offering episodes that are often violently disconnected from each other.[9] The fact that secret historians from Procopius to Manley have such frequent recourse to the anecdotal method suggests their resistance to the ordering principles of history proper. Instead, their narratives invite multiple reading procedures, requiring readers to read non-telelogically.

Daniel Defoe's pioneering periodical the *Review* provides a compelling example of the confluence between the historiographic aspirations of the secret history, its miscellaneous structure and the periodical form. Begun in 1704 with the sponsorship of the Harley ministry, the *Review* commenced as a work of serial history; its ambition was to provide 'a compleat history of France' intended to impress upon readers the formidable threat that nation posed and reinvigorate waning public support for the War of Spanish Succession.[10] As the first issue makes plain, this narrative was envisioned as a counter history, as a means of correcting a 'Multitude of Unaccountable and Inconsistent Stories'. Indeed, in a procedural statement that chimes with those of secret historians, the *Review* contends it will 'pursue the Truth; find her out, when a Crowd of Lyes and Nonsense has almost smother'd her, and set her up, so as she may be both seen and heard'.[11] The historical design that actuates The *Review* and dictates its contents is kept continually in readers' view: frequent cross-references to elements of previous issues, along with the acknowledgment that a discussion of one topic must be concluded before another can commence, serve to remind readers that what they are reading is tightly controlled.[12] Readers, however, rarely kept the periodical's ever-unfolding design in mind when responding to single issues and, by the mid-point of the periodical's first year, the *Review* laments their evident expectation that:

> every Piece should be entire, and bear a reading by it self; If it must be so, I confess myself incapable; the Scheme is other ways laid, and a half Sheet of Paper can't do it. My Design in this History of the *French* Affairs, is as vast in Proportion, as theirs in Contriving; and as it requires time to finish it, it ought to have the Privilege of being view'd whole, before 'tis Condemn'd.[13]

The dissatisfaction Defoe recognises here on the part of his readers reflects the double temporality of periodicals, where each issue is a new and independent item at the same time as it exists within a recognisable series that stretches forward and backward.[14] Readers' corresponding desire for narratives that admit different reading practices, including the ability to forge their own connections between component parts, was satisfied by a supplementary section introduced in the periodical's second issue. This section – eventually titled 'Advice from the Scandal Club' – complicates both the temporality of the *Review* and its initial aspiration to produce a serial history of France.[15]

'Advice from the Scandal Club' initially aims to supplement the *Review* proper by identifying and remedying the factual and grammatical errors of newspaper writers in their reporting of events on the continent. However, this singular purpose only holds for a short time, as readers begin to write to the *Review* soliciting the Scandal Club's advice, and sometimes judgement, on matters as diverse as 'divinity, morality, love, state, war, trade, language, poetry, marriage, drunkenness, whoring, gaming, vowing and the like'.[16] In stark contrast to the evident control exerted over the *Review* proper, the periodical's new, supplementary section shifts in response to readers. In fact, in reflecting on its genesis in the preface to the first volume of collected issues, Defoe describes the section as 'casually and undesignedly annexed to our work'.[17] The sections themselves are structured to make a positive feature of their haphazard origins, showcasing the plenitude of correspondence the author complains of elsewhere.[18] No attempt is made to develop narrative connections between the letters and queries presented in these supplementary sections; instead, the questions sent in by readers or topics canvassed at their behest are showcased self-reflexively as miscellaneous. The sheer volume of material sent by readers is such that the Scandal Club sections begin to intrude on the main part of the paper – the thirty-fourth number, for example, notes that the extent of the Society's business obliges them to 'Intrench upon the Historical, which is otherwise the Principal part of this Design, and we are forced to break off sooner than usual, to take into consideration the many Letters laid before the Society this last Week' – before swelling to such an extent that it demands a monthly supplement.[19] The supplements, much like the 'Advice from the Scandal. Club' appended to the paper proper, stress the diversity and miscellaneity of their contents. Anecdotes butt up against each other, with readers implicitly invited to intuit connections between disparate materials.

Although the supplements named after the 'Scandal Club' ceased with that dated January 1705 (published four months late in May of that year), readers' desire for scandal – or, for parts they could treat as wholes – continues to shadow the *Review*. It found expression in two further changes to periodical's form: first, the publication of a second supplement, the *Little Review*, published in twenty-three numbers in mid-1705 on days the *Review* rested; then, the introduction of a section titled 'Miscellanea' that became a standing, if irregular, part of the periodical from January 1706. Both these supplementary sections appear designed to address a similar need: as reflected in the subtitle to the *Little Review*, 'an Inquisition of Scandal; consisting in Answers of Questions and Doubts, Remarks, Observation and Reflection'. The demand on behalf of readers to participate in the periodical and their desire for discrete narratives between which they can forge their own connections exerts pressure on the periodical's main design.

The *Athenian Mercury*: Curiosity and Secrecy

The capacity to elicit readerly curiosity is a hallmark of the secret history and the early eighteenth-century periodical alike. Historiographic secret histories, such as *The Secret History of the Court of the Emperor Justinian* (1674) or *The Secret History of White-Hall* (1697), implicitly encourage readers to adopt a critical view of the public record suggesting it is a narrative constructed to conceal private corruption. Later secret histories, most notably Delarivier Manley's *New Atalantis*, explicitly solicit readers' active involvement through the use of innuendo, allegory, and multiplying characters, encouraging them to collaborate with the narrative to activate the revelations it contains and construct a coherent narrative that can be brought to bear meaningfully on the recent past. As Ros Ballaster was the first to argue, the generic imperative of the secret history is to educate readers into more sophisticated (indeed, more sceptical) habits of reading.[20] Early periodicals capitalise on the hermeneutics of suspicion the secret history fostered, contributing to the development of a culture of curiosity and inquiry. Barbara Benedict has influentially described periodicals as 'formal embodiments of novelty', noting the discursive space they created for showcasing and satisfying questions and offering commentary on the most recent events.[21]

The *Athenian Mercury*, for example, often heralded as London's first periodical, enshrined readerly curiosity as its primary value. The subtitle given to the initial issues of the periodical – 'resolving weekly all the most *nice and curious questions* propos'd by the INGENIOUS' – foregrounds the Society's intention to develop a textual space that showcases and satisfies all manner of inquiry, while the first issue expresses their hope that readers will take advantage of the anonymity enabled by the penny post to counteract the 'shame or fear of appearing ridiculous by asking Questions'.[22] Similarly, the identity of the society who addresses readers' questions is carefully withheld. In contrast to later periodicals, which foreground the identities (be they positive or negative) of their fictional editors, the *Athenian Mercury* stresses the anonymity of its authors. The engraved emblem Dunton commissioned towards the end of the periodical's second year of publication makes a visual feature of that anonymity by depicting the society veiled, the meaning amplified by the poem below that notes 'behind the scenes sit mighty we / nor are we known nor will we be'.[23] This redoubled emphasis on anonymity indicates, as Rachel Scarborough King has recently highlighted, the centrality of privacy to the construction of the *Athenian Mercury*.[24] In offering opportunities for readers to submit queries anonymously and by withholding the identity of the Society who provide answers, the *Athenian Mercury* provides a forum wherein curiosity can be publicly satisfied at the same time that private identity is concealed.

Readers were quick to take advantage of the opportunities provided by this new forum and, much like the *Tatler* a decade later, the *Athenian Mercury* soon declared itself inundated by letters, begging respite from the 'CART-LOADS of Questions which … are likely to press us to death under their weight'.[25] These questions formed the substance of The *Athenian Mercury* over its seven-year run: issues are structured around the Society's responses to a series of queries – sometimes as many as fifteen – on topics as diverse as theology, romantic love, natural philosophy, and mathematics. The expression and satisfaction of curiosity was seemingly a straightforward matter, as questions met with published answers that drew on information already in the public domain. Although a correspondent complained in an early issue that the periodical's answers 'in effect tell the World nothing but what we all know already', Dunton made a virtue of the periodical's communal construction of knowledge, replying '*what one Man knows, another does not*, and diffusing knowledge is a sort of improving it'.[26] As this comment makes clear, although the periodical cultivates a culture of curiosity and inquiry, it does not appear to make a value of secrecy. However, Dunton tries to retrospectively invest the process of enquiry with secrecy in subsequent Athenian texts.

In the years that followed the demise of the *Athenian Mercury* in 1697, Dunton published a series of texts – seven in total – that sought to revive interest in his periodical. These subsequent publications not only recall the titles of his periodical but also return to and reprise much of its material. Taken together, they evidence a concerted effort to repackage the materials of the *Athenian Mercury* to better suit the tastes of its readers. The *Athenian Spy* and the serial publication *Athenae Redivivae: or The New Athenian Oracle*, both published in 1704, perhaps provide the clearest indications of what may have motivated this repackaging.[27] The former collects unpublished letters sent to the periodical by female querists; as the title page announces, the contents 'discover the *secret letters* which were sent to the Athenian Society by the most ingenious ladies of the three kingdoms, relating to the management of their affections'. The publication of letters occasioned by the periodical and yet concealed from view, hints at a hidden substratum to the knowledge solicited by published queries and collected together in the periodical's pages. This sense is taken up and amplified by *Athenae Redivivae*, which returns to queries sent to the original periodical but not answered, dividing the resulting material into three categories listed on the title page: the divine oracle (or directory for tender consciences), the philosophick and miscellaneous oracle, and the secret (or ladies) oracle.[28] The questions and answers gathered together under the heading 'the secret oracle' deal principally with sexual matters, including the generation of children, non-reproductive sexual practices, and marriage, forging a link between secrecy and sexuality. These texts, combined with Dunton's other attempts to revive Athenianism, suggest a concerted effort to move away from the straightforward exchange of curiosity and information originally staged in the periodical and invest the once-straightforward interaction with hitherto undisclosed layers of secrecy. The similar manner in which these texts return to and re-present the contents of Dunton's periodical and its relation to readers, combined with the coincidence of their publication in 1704, suggests a concerted effort on Dunton's behalf to reinterpret the meaning of Athenianism and to reinvest his question-and-answer periodical with an aura of secrecy.

Harris's List of Covent Garden Ladies: Secrecy, Sexuality and Consumption

In the mid-eighteenth century, the confluence of the secret history and the periodical took a particular turn. The 'Atalantis trope', a particular conjunction of secrecy, sexuality and miscellaneity, which had been appropriated, inhabited and renovated by many other authors since the publication of Manley's *succès de scandale* in 1709, became both newly visible and newly associated with serial publication.[29] It was adopted as the title of two serial publications in turn: first, for an annual collection of amorous stories that began with *The New Atalantis for the Year 1758*.[30] It was then taken up, in the same form, as a new subtitle for *Harris's List of Covent Garden Ladies*. *Harris's List* was one of the most enduring serial publications in eighteenth-century Britain, published annually for close to forty years.[31] It provided a catalogue of the prostitutes currently at work in London under thinly disguised names, together with their customary location and price, offering readers both a means to navigate the variety of pleasures available in the capital as well as an imaginative experience of those pleasures. The *List* was bound in such a way as to resemble annual lists of peers, members of the British parliament, and state office holders, such as the *Court and City Kalendar*, drawing a visual parallel between the anatomising of prostitutes and the cataloguing of public figures.[32] In revising the subtitle of the *List* from 'the Man of Pleasure's Kalendar' to 'the *New Atalantis*', those responsible for the text purposively associate its contents with the structure of secrecy, serial pleasure, and readerly involvement that characterised Manley's secret history. Indeed, the association stuck: readers were accustomed to refer to the annual List by its subtitle, a practice recorded by a French traveller to London who identifies this text 'with the title of the *New Atalantis*' as an index of the liberal attitude towards prostitution in the English capital.[33]

Harris's List of Covent Garden Ladies is an annual register of the women working in Covent Garden and surrounds. Each entry begins with a woman's name and location, the former almost always disemvowelled so as to increase the salacious allure. The editions of the *List* are organised according to different principles: the 1761 edition, for example, arranges 108 entries in alphabetical order followed by an appendix of a further fifty-five women, whose details 'came too late to be inserted alphabetically'. In contrast, the 216 entries in the 1765 edition follow no discernible order, but are prefaced by two tables of contents, one indexing the entries in alphabetical order, the other highlighting the 'new characters come to Hand' since the publication of the previous list.[34] The inclusion of the address at which individual women are to be found, along with occasional mention of the price they accustomed to charge for services rendered, makes the *List* a practical guide for gentlemen in search of physical pleasure. The *List's* practical benefits are foregrounded in the advertisement to the 1761 edition, which discourages readers from approaching the contents 'in the light of *romance* or *novel*, merely to draw the attention of the idly curious, … ; for we can assert that the facts herein contained have been most authentically proved to us'.[35] Tellingly, the *List* also solicits the active involvement of readers. On many occasions, the particular pleasure derived from an assignation with a specific woman is said to elude description, requiring readers to exercise their imagination in order to conjure the erotic pleasures suggested by the text.

In the 'tender preludes of bliss', Miss M-yne is said to be 'beyond description', the editors redoubling the point by emphasising that 'we cannot describe the joys of the emphatic squeeze, the grasp divine, or the imprinted kiss; this we leave to ******'.[36] On other occasions, readers are invited to contribute their own experiences with a particular woman that, once received, will be used to supplement subsequent editions. A striking example comes in the account of Miss Sm-th, whose notably wanton temper has attracted the explanatory attention of physicians. The narrators announce they are unable to determine the truth of the doctor's remarks, which identify a physical source of her temper, and invite readers to conduct their own examination of Miss Sm-th and submit their own opinions of this 'important affair'.[37]

However, the text has as much, if not more, to offer the reader who has no intention of experiencing those pleasures first hand. Unlike the *Wandering Whore*, a periodical that ran for five numbers in 1660 and is often cited as the model for *Harris's List*, which simply appended a list of women at work in Covent Garden to an English translation of Aretino's dialogues, *Harris's List* includes a short narrative account of the women it catalogues. These narratives sometimes encompass a physical description, sometimes an account of her entry into the trade, and at other times a selection of her particular adventures. Indeed, some entries appear to be designed purely to work on readers' imagination. The entry on Miss L – le begins with a very brief account of her appearance, before turning to 'a few anecdotes of this heroine' that trace the development of her amorous temperament and her first affair, begun in adolescence. Given that Miss L – le is now the kept mistress of an unnamed gentleman and is said to have 'not been as yet much in company, and affects to be little known', the entry seems designed to work solely on the erotic imagination of readers rather than be of use to a man canvassing options in advance of a night of pleasure.[38] In fact, there are points where textual pleasures are presented as equivalent to if not in excess of those of the flesh. On several occasions, the adventures of particular prostitutes are said to rival those found in episodic romances: the adventures of Kitty B-ckly, for example, 'would exceed a large volume', while a mere half of the intrigues of the two Miss Sh – ls would, were they to be enumerated, 'fill two pretty novels for Mr. Noble's Library'.[39] The narrator of the 1765 edition of the list makes explicit the interdependent relationship between prostitute and publisher, remarking in the course of describing Miss W-lk-nson that 'ladies of pleasure would do well to keep upon good terms with gentlemen that write, as the ladies are as much indebted for their fame to Poets, as even heroes themselves'.[40] This contributes to the intricate double structure of the text, which functions as both an imaginative experience of each woman it details and a practical guide. In much the same way as the secret history, then, *Harris's List* offers the imaginative experience of physical pleasure and also an account of the real woman that lies behind the text

The contents of the *List* are described on the title page as offering 'an exact description of the persons, tempers, and accomplishments' of ladies of pleasure and, accordingly, the majority of entries are devoted to describing each woman's distinctive characteristics and not to narrating her particular history or adventures. This dedication to description produces a particular kind of duration that frustrates narrative temporality by 'linger[ing] on objects and beings considered in their simultaneity, and … consider[ing] the processes themselves as spectacles'.[41] Description, then, combines with the atemporal narrative structure of the list or catalogue to produce the women it anatomises as objects to be recognised and pleasurably consumed.

Much like the title page of Dunton's *Athenæ Redivivæ*, where the advertised contents of 'The Secret (or Ladies) Oracle' include 'arcana naturæ' and 'love secrets', newspapers in 1782 arraigned *Harris's List* for detailing 'female secrets of a peculiar kind, which ought not to be exposed'.[42] The *List* showcases new relations between sexuality and secrecy, furthering the process evident earlier in the century whereby the secret is transformed into a serial, sexual form. *Harris's List* both demonstrates the ways that serialisation and sexualisation combine to produce static narratives that can be readily consumed, at the same time as its subtitle flags the origins of this discourse in the politically motivated secret history of the earlier eighteenth century. This trajectory anticipates, and perhaps contributes to the tendency in twentieth-century criticism to misread secret histories by women as mere romance.

Notes

1 The research informing this essay was supported by an Australian Research Council Discovery Grant. This is as true of the *Examiner* (1710–14) and the *Observator* (1702–10), which both adopt the distinctive vocabulary of the secret history identified by Rebecca Bullard in avowing dedication to discovering the 'secret springs' of public events, as it is of the *Craftsman* whose fictional editor identifies his 'chief business' in the first issue (5 Dec. 1726) as 'unravel[ling] the dark secrets of political craft'. Bullard, *The Politics of Disclosure, 1674–1725* (London: Pickering & Chatto, 2009), 17, 21.

2 At least three publications appeared with the title the *Tea Table* in quick succession: an anonymously authored periodical published by James Roberts; a multi-volume miscellany, compiled by Alan Ramsay; and a two-part prose

work authored by Eliza Haywood. I refer to the first of these publications. Manushag Powell is perhaps the only scholar to devote serious attention to the periodical entitled the *Tea-Table* Performing Authorship in Eighteenth-Century Periodicals (Lewisburg: Bucknell University Press, 2012), 44–5.
3 *Spectator*, 10 (12 Mar. 1711).
4 *Tea-Table*, 1 (21 Feb. 1724). The periodical advertises its use of allegory via a motto derived from Shaftesbury's *Characteristicks* (1711): 'If Men are forbid to speak their Minds seriously on certain Subjects, they will do it Ironically: if they find it really dangerous to speak at all upon such Subjects, they will then redouble their Disguise, involve themselves in Mysteriousness, and talk so as hardly to be understood, or at least not plainly interpreted by those who are dispos'd to do them a Mischief' (*Tea-Table*, 5 (6 Mar. 1724).
5 Bullard, *Politics of Disclosure*, 41.
6 Eve Tavor Bannet, '"Secret History": Or, Talebearing inside and Outside the Secretoire', *Huntington Library Quarterly* 68.1/2 (2005), 375. Annabel Patterson advances a similar argument in *Early Modern Liberalism* (Cambridge: Cambridge University Press, 1997), 183–231.
7 Ephraim Chambers, *Cyclopaedia: Or An Universal Dictionary of Arts and Sciences* (London, 1728), 87.
8 See Joel Fineman, 'The History of the Anecdote: Fiction and Fiction', in *The New Historicism*, ed. H. Aram Veeser (New York: Routledge, 1989), 49–76.
9 See Nicola Parsons, 'The Miscellaneous *New Atalantis*' in *New Perspectives on Delariver Manley*, eds. Aleksondra Hultquist and Elizabeth J. Mathews (New York: Routledge, 2017), 201–13
10 *Review*, 1.1 (19 Feb. 1704). J. A. Downie, 'Stating Facts Right about Defoe's *Review*', *Prose Studies: History, Theory, Criticism* 16, no. 1 (1993), 8–22.
11 *The Review*, 1.1 (19 Feb. 1704).
12 See, for example, *Review* 1.11 (11 Apr. 1704), 1.28 (10 Jun. 1704), 1.32 (24 Jun. 1704).
13 *Review*, 1.35 (4 Jul. 1704).
14 Margaret Beetham, *A Magazine of Her Own? Domesticity and Desire in the Women's Magazine, 1800–1914* (London: Routledge, 1996), 12; Uriel Heyd, *Reading Newspapers: Press and Public in Eighteenth-Century Britain and America* (Oxford: Voltaire Foundation, 2012), 82.
15 First titled 'Mercure Scandale: OR, ADVICE from the Scandalous Club: BEING, *A Weekly History of* Nonsense, Impertinence, Vice *and* Debauchery', the initial French is silently dropped from issue 17. The title is then abbreviated to 'Advice from the Scandal. Club', following letters from readers objecting to the implication that the club itself is scandalous. *The Review*, 35 (4 Jul. 1704) and 37 (11 Jul. 1704).
16 *A Supplementary Journal to the Advice from the Scandal Club* (Sep. 1704).
17 'Preface' to *Review*, vol. 1 (19 Feb. 1704–24 Feb. 1705), sig. A2r.
18 In the preface to the first volume, Defoe confesses that 'receiving or answering letters of Doubts, Difficulties, Cases and Questions … was the remotest thing

from my first Design of any thing in the World; and I could be heartily Glad, the Readers of this Paper would excuse me from it yet'. In spite of his professed reluctance to answer readers' letters, Defoe was able to turn these circumstances to an opportunity for personal profit by sending private responses for a fee. See *Review* 1.95 (30 Jan. 1705).

19 *Review*, 1.34 (1 Jul. 1704). The supplements appeared between September 1704 and January 1705.
20 Ros Ballaster, *Seductive Forms: Women's Amatory Fiction from 1684–1740* (Oxford: Clarendon Press, 1992), 131–6.
21 Barbara M. Benedict, *Curiosity: A Cultural History of Modern Inquiry* (University of Chicago Press, 2001), 93.
22 *Athenian Mercury*, 1.1 (17 Mar. 1690 o.s.).
23 Engraved by Fredrick Hendrik van Hove, the emblem first appeared in *The Young Student's Library* (London, 1692). Dunton highlights the importance of anonymity to the design of the periodical in *The Life and Errors of John Dunton* (London, 1705), 249.
24 Rachael Scarborough King, '"Interloping with my Question-Project": Debating Genre in John Dunton's and Daniel Defoe's Epistolary Periodicals', *Studies in Eighteenth-Century Culture*, 44 (2015), 128.
25 Preface, *Athenian Mercury*, vol. 4 (18 Aug.–17 Oct. 1691). Dunton maintained in his autobiography that the *Athenian Mercury* was 'immediately overloaded with LETTERS, and sometimes I have found several Hundreds for me at Mr. Smith's Coffee-House in Stocks-Market'. *The Life and Errors of John Dunton*, 256. Helen Berry includes these two examples in her discussion of readers' interaction with the periodical in *Gender, Society and Print Culture in Late-Stuart England: The Cultural World of the Athenian Mercury* (Aldershot: Ashgate, 2003), 36–56.
26 *Athenian Mercury*, 2.17 (21 Jul. 1691).
27 *Athenae Redivivæ: Or the New Athenian Oracle* was published serially in six parts in 1704. See Stephen Parks, *John Dunton and the English Book Trade: A Study of his Career with a Checklist of His Publications* (New York: Garland, 1976), 339–40.
28 *Athenæ Redivia: Or, the New Athenian Oracle*, 1.1 (1704), t.p.
29 Unlike other secret histories, the *New Atalantis* remained popular throughout the century, appearing among the 'romances and novels' available at metropolitan circulating libraries as late as 1797. See David Ogilvy & Son, *Catalogue of the London and Westminster Circulating Library* (London, 1797), 156.
30 Advertisements in other of H. Ranger's publications indicate these titles appeared annually between 1758 and 1763. Of these, only two editions survive: the 1758 edition recorded by the English Short Title Catalogue, and the 1760 edition held by Chawton House Library.
31 Janet Freeman has established that the first edition of *Harris's List* appeared in 1760, and that the 1757 edition sometimes cited by scholars is spurious. The last known copy of the 1760 edition entered a private collection in 1833,

making the 1761 edition held by the National Library of Scotland the earliest in public collections. 'Jack Harris and Honest Ranger: The Publication and Prosecution of *Harris's List of Covent-Garden Ladies, 1760–1795*', *The Library*, 7th ser., 13.4 (Dec. 2012), 455–6.
32 Freeman, 'Jack Harris and Honest Ranger', 446.
33 See Pierre Grosley's account of a 1765 visit to London in *A Tour to London: Or, New Observations on England and its Inhabitants*, trans. Thomas Nugent (London, 1772), 55.
34 *Harris's List of Covent Garden Ladies: Or, the New Atalantis for the year 1761* (London, 1761), 6; *Harris's List of Covent Garden Ladies: Or, the New Atalantis for the year 1765* (London, 1765), xiv–xxiii. This essay draws on the 1761, 1764 and 1765 editions of *Harris's List*. I am grateful to the National Library of Scotland and the Lewis Walpole Library at Yale University for generously making copies of the editions in their collection available to me.
35 *Harris's List*, 1761, vii–viii.
36 *Harris's List*, 1765, 2.
37 *Harris's List*, 1765, 123–4.
38 *Harris's List*, 1765, 42, 47.
39 *Harris's List*, 1765, 118; *Harris's List*, 1773, 9–10.
40 *Harris's List*, 1765, 76.
41 Gerard Genette, *Figures of Literary Discourse*, trans. Alan Sheridan (New York: Columbia University Press, 1982), 136.
42 *The General Advertiser, and Morning Intelligencer*, no. 1656, 28 Jan. 1782, and *Morning Herald, and Daily Advertiser*, no. 388, 26 Jan. 1782. Janet Freeman suggests this notice may have been part of a marketing campaign for the *List*, orchestrated by the publisher. See 'Jack Harris and 'Honest Ranger', 436–7.

11

Secret History and Censorship

Eve Tavor Bannet

First published anonymously in 1709, Shaftesbury's *Sensus Communis: An Essay on the Freedom of Wit and Humour in a Letter to a Friend* was one of many contemporary texts to disseminate knowledge of secret writing so that 'those who have ears to hear may hear'.[1] A thinker shaped by the seventeenth century who exerted considerable influence on the eighteenth, Shaftesbury wrote shrewdly as one for whom secret writing was what Robert Darnton calls 'a cultural system embedded in a social order' that ordinarily appeared in the everyday as 'part of the work-a-day world inhabited by writers, publishers and booksellers, and influential personages from the court and capital'.[2] However, Shaftesbury wrote this letter-essay as a practitioner of secret writing, who amused himself and his reader-friend/s by demonstrating as he went how 'sober raillery' (59) worked. His meaning is famously elusive as a result. As Philip Skelton complained in 1749, Shaftesbury 'asserts so sceptically or rather hypothetically, that neither his disciple, nor his adversary, knows well what to lay hold of;' or as Michael McKeon remarked in an endnote, 'Shaftesbury's raillery – his "seeming to be very different from what he really is" – can of course be found everywhere'.[3] Abhorring undecidability as nature abhors a vacuum, critics then and now have been at pains to extract firmly held convictions from Shaftesbury's Pyrrhonic play with assertions, genres and language in order to tell us 'what he really is' or what he really meant. The goal here is different. It is to allow *Sensus Communis* to guide us through 'Men, Manners, Opinions and Times', past and present, to striking features of the contemporary literary culture and social order that produced contrary effects – secret writing and revelatory rhetoric – and popularised enigmatical or esoteric 'fables' and 'histories', romances and novels. I begin with questions of language and form.

'If men are forbid to speak seriously on certain subjects', Shaftesbury observed in *Sensus Communis*, they will do it ironically. If they are forbid to speak at all upon such subjects, or if they find it really dangerous to do so, they will then redouble their disguise, involve themselves in mysteriousness and talk so as hardly to be understood, or at least not plainly interpreted, by those who are disposed to do them mischief. And thus raillery is brought more in fashion and runs into an extreme. It is the persecuting spirit has raised the bantering one. (34)

'Irony', 'banter' and 'raillery' are terms that Shaftesbury was using here to signify a variety of forms of secret writing. During the seventeenth and much of the eighteenth century, irony and banter were the erudite and cant signifiers, respectively, for words or texts that say one thing and mean another. Applying equally to prose and verse and to what we now distinguish as satire and fiction, both terms were also strongly identified with dissimulation, bamboozling and disguise.[4] This followed from irony's stock devices. In oratory and expository writing, these included blaming by appearing to praise, praising by appearing to blame and, Shaftesbury's favourite, assuming a mask of gravity in order to mock with a straight face.[5] 'Raillery' most often meant good-humoured ridicule, but masking one's true meaning for purposes of mockery or derision also made raillery, ridicule, satire, burlesque and irony 'loose and interchangeable terms' outside the rhetoric classroom – as they are in this text.[6] By association with Socrates, who disguised his wisdom by assuming the character of a diffident and unknowing man, and with Aesop who hid his political commentary in animal fables, irony's other stock devices took the form of 'mimicry' (34) – assuming or personating characters and 'mystifying' one's meaning in a fable or fiction. Norman Knox found that during this period 'Banter as deception was most often used to denote a verbal fiction of a sort offered with enough ostensible conviction to bamboozle an audience, temporarily at least'.[7] Shaftesbury took pains to include bamboozling fictions among the 'ironical' disguises to which he said writers were driven by 'the persecuting spirit': 'It may be necessary, as well now as heretofore, for wise men to speak in parables, and with a double meaning, that the enemy may be amused and they only 'who have ears to hear' may hear' (31). Or as Delarivier Manley put it: 'The Intrigues and Miscarriages of War and Peace are better many Times laid open and Satyriz'd in a *Romance*', for 'such disguis'd Discourses as these, promiscuously personating every Man and no Man, take their full Liberty to speak the Truth.'[8]

All fictions or satires may not have contained secret writing – veiled communication of 'seditious' attitudes and ideas, the questioning of political, moral or religious orthodoxies, the scandalous truth about what transpired behind closed doors, *arcana imperii* or state secrets, *scandalum magnatum* or libels upon the great, insinuation of a controversial sub-text. But secret writing always involved irony in Shaftesbury's sense. This is also where the 'persecutors' of literature sought it. William Prynne, Algernon Sidney, Daniel Defoe, Delarivier Manley, the printer and authors of *The Craftsman* and countless other writers and printers were arrested, charged or convicted in courts of law and at the Bar of the House of Commons because their accusers charged that their written or printed texts meant something other than what they said. *The British Journal* complained in 1722 that this involved 'strain[ing] their genuine signification to make [words or texts] intend Sedition'; and *The Craftsman* protested in 1730 that 'if we don't explain meanings in what the most "literal and common Acceptation" of them must import to every unprejudiced Understanding ... no writer can be safe in Writings of any kind; since the Wit of man has not yet been able to invent Words, that can possibly carry but *One Interpretation*'.[9] But this was disingenuous. For as Shaftesbury observed, ironical fictions and discourses dissembled 'in such a manner as to occasion no scandal or disturbance' by 'respect[ing] and honour[ing] conventions and societies of men' and trying not to 'offend the public ear' (36). As Perez Zagorin has shown, what Bacon called 'the enigmatical method' of concealing unorthodox beliefs and esoteric meanings in exoterically conformist texts had been widely practiced in England since the Reformation by imitating precedents familiar from the Ancients and the Church Fathers.[10] The trick, as Quintilian had said, was to 'speak as openly as you like ... against tyrants, as long as you can be understood differently'.[11] Outward conformity to received opinions and common literary forms ensured that writers could be understood differently, while placing the burden of interpretation squarely on readers or accusers – as rhetoricians bred on Quintilian explained:

> The way of distinguishing an *Irony* from the real sentiments of the speaker or writer, are by the accent, the air, the extravagance of the praise, the character of the person, the nature of the thing or the vein of the discourse: for if in any of these respects there is any disagreement from the *common sense* of the words, it plainly appears that one thing is spoken, and another is designed.[12]

It was up to readers to detect disagreements from the *sensus communis* – the 'common sense' of words, persons or things – by 'distinguishing an irony'. Irony or ridicule was first and foremost a test of truth in communication for readers considering a text's common sense to determine whether the speaker or writer meant what they were saying in its 'literal and common Acceptation', or whether their 'real sentiments' and true 'design' differed from that 'ironically'. Testing for 'ironical' double meanings was a way for readers to discover whether secret writing was present in a text. This is also why irony, banter or ridicule appeared so dangerous to what Shaftesbury called 'dogmatists', 'zealots', 'tyrants' and 'enthusiasts'. As he said, the problem was not so much what they pretended: that religion, the state and morality were under threat from writers who ridiculed them. It was that irony was a method of 'questioning received opinion and exposing the ridicule of things' (39) that readers could apply to any text.

Readers, who did not necessarily know *a priori* which texts were designed to be 'ironical', but did know that 'when a man maintains what is commonly believ'd, or professes what is publicly injoin'd, it is not always a sure rule that he speaks what he thinks', might find that dogmatical texts too could 'carry more than *One Interpretation*'.[13] Readers applying this manner of reading to the common sense (opinion, judgment (37)) of such texts might discover that 'certain modern zealots in their own controversial writings' were ridiculous – 'an executioner and a Merry Andrew acting their part on the same stage' (32) – or that 'nonsense' was 'the common sense of a great party among ourselves' (38) – or that some parties were endeavouring 'to make their private sense the public one' (38) where 'public' meant 'common' to 'the generality' of mankind (37). Readers might find that the common sense (received opinions and judgments) promoted by interested parties, and the commonly accepted sense of their words or texts, ran counter to 'the common good'. *Sensus Communis*, common sense, was the site where 'disagreements' between 'ironical' secret writers and their 'persecutors' occurred.

Censorship, Secret Writing and Secret Histories

Shaftesbury blamed secret writing – the fact that 'the natural free spirits of ingenious men' resorted to 'burlesque, mimicry or buffoonery' (34) and that 'the most celebrated authors [had become] the greatest masters of burlesque' (30) – on the fact that writers were 'imprisoned' and 'controlled' by 'the strictness of the laws' and by 'the prevailing pedantry and bigotry of those who reign in them and assume themselves to be dictators in these provinces' (31). The principal persecutors of writers were the laws and agents of state censorship. Shaftesbury's allusions to censors as 'dictators' or 'tyrants' in 1709 make better sense now that we no longer assume that censorship disappeared in 1695 with lapse of the Licensing Act. We now acknowledge that after 1695, *pre-publication* censorship through licensing was replaced (except in the theatre) by forms of *post-publication* censorship that included savage laws punishing transgressors with 'fetters and halters'; successive laws of Seditious Libel, Treason, Blasphemy and Obscene Libel; and, during the repressive 1790s, Gagging laws, and Traitorous Correspondence Acts.

The persistence from Burghley to Pitt of potentially lethal exercises of state censorship helps to explain the persistence of secret writing. A good deal of important work on secret writing has now been done in connection with it.[14] But modern scholars differ in their assessments of how censorship worked. Some argue, following Annabel Patterson, that although much literature was 'conceived in part as the way round censorship', there was collusion between writers and censors, as well as 'conventions that both sides accepted as to how far writers could go in explicit address to the contentious issue of the day'.[15] Others argue in more Foucaldian vein that censorship sought to discipline and punish writers, while they attacked or subverted the system by taking advantage of its 'gaps and loopholes' and using 'art to divide and conquer their adversaries'.[16] Shaftesbury reconciles these two modern views, and in such a way as to suggest one reason for secret history's emergence from the shadows at the turn of the eighteenth century.

Shaftesbury described the operation of censorship as mutable and contradictory: on the one hand, 'whichever [party] chanced to have the power failed not of putting all means in execution to make their private sense the public one' (38); but on the other hand, 'that which was according to the sense of one part of mankind was against the sense of another' and 'would change as often as men changed' (37). The interplay of these two factors infinitely complicates the picture. For as recent scholars have confirmed, the fact that government and religion underwent such frequent, rapid and dramatic changes between the Renaissance and 1800 meant that the authorities failed to present a united front either during licensing or thereafter. What was agreeable to one censor, to the purists of one political or religious party, or to one kind of republican or monarchical regime, was treated as dangerous or seditious by another, with the result that writers might fall victim to the 'sense' of 'one part of mankind' as often as the 'men who chanced to have the power changed'. The careers of Prynne, Milton, Dryden and Bolingbroke are notorious cases in point. At the same time, modern studies of particular cases show that prosecutions deriving from changes in the political or religious landscape were often entwined with issues of collusion and/or with infringements of the accepted conventions for how far writers could go. During the early eighteenth century, when many were writing as party hacks, there was often collusion – in the form of active encouragement, tacit toleration, or useful help – from some of those who had the power to censure and censor publications. But this only made publishing under censorship like playing Russian roulette.

As Paul Hyland showed, Defoe, Steele, and George Ridpath, were all prosecuted by the Tory ministry for authoring secret writings – texts 'encased in cryptics' – about the Hanoverian succession in 1713, the year before Queen Anne's death. This was a moment when the Whig Opposition was already allied with the future George I, and the Tories were divided between a pro-Hanover group who made common cause with the Whigs, and Tories in the Ministry and Parliament who were negotiating with James Stuart in France. A pro-Hanoverian Lord Chief Justice, Thomas Parker, helped George Ridpath to escape punishment for insinuating that Queen Anne sought to put her half-brother, James, on the throne. Defoe was in the pay of Tory Prime Minister Harley, who favoured another Stuart restoration; but Parker had Defoe arrested for 'what were recognised as ironical productions' against the Hanover succession. Meanwhile, Harley-led Parliamentary Tories voted Steele guilty of seditious libel and expelled him from the Commons for his Whig-supported publications in favour of Hanover.[17] Because the authorities did not all speak with one voice, collusion with one group which 'put all means in execution to make their private sense the public one', could get writers in trouble with another group – and sometimes, out of trouble again. However, infringing shared conventions about how far writers could go when addressing topical issues could put it out of the power of those who colluded with them to extricate writers from their difficulties. Randt Robertson has argued, for instance, that Swift's career in the English Church was blighted because he stepped over that line. *The Tale of a Tub* brilliantly made the Tory case against 'mercenary scribblers, critics, freethinkers, papists and Puritan preachers'; but Swift's scatological and irreverent satire, together with some reflections on the Queen, gave his antagonists, and Archbishop Sharp, a handle for arguing that the *Tale* was 'licensed blasphemy' – and thus contravened norms that Swift's powerful friends and enemies shared about what government could publicly countenance.[18] In Britain's face-to-face society, moreover, the structural and historically shifting ideological complexities of censorship were compounded by the effects of personal friendships, enmities and jealousies. Radical printer and bookseller, John Almon, was forced to flee to France to escape his 'persecutors' in England; but as John Nichols tells us, when complaints were lodged against William Bowyer II for printing some radical texts,

Speaker Onslow – who knew Bowyer personally and was well disposed towards him – determined that he posed no threat.

The ways in which individuals negotiated censorship and the extent to which they 'mystified' their meaning varied. But in the literary marketplace overall, few dared to openly declare their work a 'Secret History' on its title page. Most of the self-proclaimed 'Secret Histories' that flourished between the Glorious Revolution and the 1720s were Procopian exposés of the concealed sexual scandals, secret treaties, and corrupt political intrigues of absolutist English or European, Catholic or Papal, courts. Given censorship, it is hard to see how so much thinly veiled *scandalum magnatum* and *arcana imperii* could have been published across three different reigns and multiple changes of Whig and Tory ministries without the encouragement, or at least tacit approval, of the authorities. But if, as Rebecca Bullard has argued, its 'primary political function' was 'opposing arbitrary government', secret history was useful to much of the political elite.[19] By publicising the evils of court-centred personal rule by monarchs and their chosen ministers in widely accessible narrative forms, scandalous secret histories of court intrigues served the interests of a broad spectrum of the elite who were committed to mixed government and the Protestant succession and wished to see Parliament strengthened over the Throne.[20] This did not preclude individual writers from being charged with libel if they went too far. But it did mean that self-proclaimed secret historians found, as Shaftesbury said the 'Roman satirists' had before them, that 'it was no such deep satire to question whether ['humanity or sense of public good'] was properly the spirit of a Court' (48–9). It is instructive to compare this to what generally happened during these decades to expressions of Jacobite sentiment, which the same broad political elite – committed to ensuring that the Stuarts did not return – ruthlessly suppressed. As Toni Bowers discovered, Jacobite writers concealed in Romances the dilemmas of passive obedience, conspiracy, complicity and consent facing subjects loyal to the 'Pretender' under William, Anne and George – using seduction plots, and scattered, multiplied or incomplete parallels, to 'redouble their disguise, involve themselves in mysteriousness, and talk so as hardly to be understood … by those who [were] disposed to do them mischief'.[21]

Masks, Manners and Novels

If for Shaftesbury censorship was one cause of secret writing, polite manners were another. As he observed, 'the standard of politeness and good sense' together with the pervasiveness of informers and domestic spies (48,

58), ensured that men were held 'accountable' not only for 'their actions and behaviour' but for 'their opinions too' (39). And as 'agreement' spread from the Court to the Town, and from courtiers to the gentry, professionals and middling sort 'that there was only one certain and true dress, one single peculiar air, to which it was necessary all people should conform' (39–40), 'counterfeit vizards' were everywhere put upon 'the face of truth' (40). Polite society began to resemble 'a Carnival' where 'every creature wore a mask', and only the naively barefaced looked ridiculous (39). In the political realm, the secrecy with which rulers conducted their business was mirrored by the secrecy of conspirators. However, in the social realm, secrecy pervaded the culture and the everyday through manners. Jon Snyder has shown that in the courtly and diplomatic culture of sixteenth- and seventeenth-century elites, where 'a common metaphor for dissimulation ... was the mask' and 'the art of good manners amount[ed] to nothing other than the skilful practice of dissimulation', courtiers concealed self-interest and ambition, as well as their real thoughts, desires and designs, under 'a pleasing and sincere countenance'. They practised *sprezzatura*, the art of concealing art under an appearance of natural ease, in the knowledge that any sign of 'affectation' (simulation) would give them away.[22] When the courtesy of courts was translated into the politeness of assemblies, coffee houses, and tea-tables, this feature was carried over, to the point where, as Jenny Davidson discovered, hypocritical dissimulation came to be regarded as an essential component of good manners; it was telling the truth to a person's face that became uncivil.[23] Consequently, looking at the society around him at mid-century, Henry Fielding, could only echo Shaftesbury: 'while the crafty and designing part of mankind, consulting only their own separate advantage, endeavour to maintain one constant imposition on others, the whole world becomes a vast masquerade, where the greatest part appear disguised under false visors and habits', and the 'very few only showing their own faces become, by doing so, the astonishment and ridicule of all the rest'.[24] Irony – saying one thing and meaning another – was sardonically homologous to the manners of the polite, who said what was agreeable to others while concealing what they really thought, and controlled the betraying motions of their bodies to conform to 'one single particular air'. As Fielding's principal novels demonstrated, in a masquerading world such as this, it was those who gave themselves away by 'affectation' and 'those who showed their own faces' who made themselves ridiculous.

Since, as Shaftesbury stressed, 'the chief theme and subject' of 'the fabulous author' (i.e. author of fables) was 'purely manners and the moral part' (63), fictions throughout the century were shaped, even defined, by issues of secrecy and dissimulation. When Eliza Haywood turned her attention from the Court to the Town, she called her amatory fictions 'secret histories' because she was doing for the Town what she had done for the Court: 'pluck[ing] off the mask of hypocrisy' to penetrate into 'the secrets of families and characters of persons' and reveal 'the Secret Springs which gave rise to Actions' that publicly appeared.[25] Whether in Town or Court, she was displaying the vicious intrigues and scandalous sexual conduct masked by outward proprieties, and revealing the passions, cunning and self-interest dissembled by the language of courtship and compliment, in order to 'prepare' the bare-faced, credulous and unwary for what Shaftesbury called 'a right practice of the world or a just knowledge of men and things' (57). As some modern critics have argued (but in Shaftesbury's words), she 'led' her women readers 'through the labyrinth of the affections' and 'render[ed] this music of the passions more powerful and enchanting' (63) to show them that 'the only poison to reason is passion' and that 'false reasoning is soon redressed where passion is removed' (43). Haywood's secret histories of Court and Town were thus equally 'scandal chronicles': they revealed shameful passions and disgraceful acts, injurious to reputation, that the respectable were careful to keep secret from the world.

Under their own masks of exemplary propriety and moral didacticism, the 'familiar histories' we call courtship, seduction and domestic novels, did the same. They told what Samuel Jackson Pratt called *Family Secrets* (1797). Acting as an intelligencer or informer to 'all [her] friends without doors' about what was hidden from them within the Harlowe household, Richardson's virtuous Clarissa regaled readers with her family's scandalous secrets: Machiavellian schemes to gain property or power; sensational excesses of sadistic cruelty; clandestine intercourse between illicit lovers; irregular sex in the form of rape and prostitution.[26] Later didactic and sentimental women-authored novels exposed family secrets to attack the 'hazards' to which good women were exposed in their domestic lives and 'the snares which are laid by Treachery for Innocence'.[27] They told of wily seducers and incestuous guardians; of arbitrary, absolutist exercises of parental or husbandly power; of forced, bigamous and clandestine marriages and cunning thefts of women's fortunes. They told of betrayals, abandonment, abductions, rapes and prostitution; and described marital violence, adulteries, illegitimate births and cruel persecutions. In Gothic Romance, where patriarchal domiciles sheltered only dungeons and terrified innocents were haunted by spectres of their past victims, a scandalous family secret and its discovery became the core of the plot. The scandalous, sensational secret was central to the familiar novel in all its forms.[28]

Such novels depended on what Shaftesbury called 'the spirit of curiosity which would force a discovery of more truth than can conveniently be told' (30) in two interconnected ways. First, the explicit and/or generic promise of 'Histories of Private Life' to discover what others kept private – in the contemporary sense of 'secret' and 'removed from public view' (OED) – attracted curiosity about what could not be 'conveniently told'; by arousing curiosity, it attracted readers. Characterised by Hobbes and Locke as an 'Appetite after Knowledge' and 'Lust of the Mind', curiosity was viewed for two centuries both as the appetite that drove the young or ignorant to learn new things and as everyone's primary motive for reading. Curiosity was a passion that could be commercially exploited to promote the consumption of news, pamphlets, (hi)stories and books – and consistently was.[29] During the 1640s, George Wither casually observed that woodcuts were placed on cheap print because 'when levity or a childish delight in trifling subjects have allured [the public] to look on pictures, curiosity may urge them to peep further, that they may seek out their meanings'.[30] This was also how the initials and fictitious names that secret histories substituted for those of real people, operated on contemporary readers. A century later, Haywood's *Female Spectator* observed equally casually: 'From my Observations of human Nature, I found that Curiosity had, more or less, a Share in every Deed; and my business was to hit this reigning Humour in such a Manner, as that the Gratification it should receive from being made acquainted with other People's Affairs, should at the same Time teach everyone to regulate their own.'[31] Prefaces to novels promised to 'gratify this Curiosity which is so natural to a Reader' almost as often as they promised moral instruction.[32] One might say that commercial interests did for 'familiar histories' what political interests had done for 'secret histories' – prompt proclamation to all and sundry that they had secrets to reveal.

But many novels also used the obvious revelation of family secrets that marketed and popularised them, as what Shaftesbury called a 'kind of defensive raillery' (30) – a screen to conceal the fact that they were arguing something more or other than immediately appeared, and relying on the reader's 'spirit of curiosity' to 'force a discovery of more truth than can conveniently be told'. As several scholars have pointed out, contemporary readers could discover that novels were not as politically, religiously or morally correct as they pretended, and that the obvious secrets of private life that they recounted masked insidious ideas, from the criticism or public controversies they provoked – 'anti-Jacobin' critics and writers, for instance, trumpeted the concealed meanings and hidden agendas in 'Jacobin' novels. But as Shaftesbury observed, readers who pursued a fable's 'foils and contrarieties' (63) could also discover for themselves whatever truths novels found it inconvenient to tell. They could observe where carefully scattered observations or contradictory scenes profiled the ostensibly exemplary narrative as 'maintain[ing] what is commonly believ'd, or profess[ing] what is publicly injoin'd', rather than what the author 'really thinks', or where fantastically improbable causalities discredited conventionally happy endings. Applying the long-standing analogy between the family and the state, they could consider how a novel's portrayal of fictional families dissembled insinuations about the state or unobtrusively included parallels to real persons and topical events. The didactic, sentimental and gothic novel's standard practice of representing 'the beauties of a [virtuous] human soul' against 'proper foils and contrarieties' (63) was eminently suited to insertion of an unimposing subtext whose tracery, once reconstructed, contradicted narrative reaffirmation of the proper *sensus communis*. Fanny Burney's *Evelina*, for instance, presented itself as an amusing narrative about a young lady's 'entry into life' and discovery of society's rules and customs by inadvertently transgressing them and making a fool of herself. But readers with the curiosity to pursue the novel's 'foils and contrarieties' could uncover a far more radical text: here the violence, cruelty and humiliation to which Evelina's grandmother is 'comically' subject at Captain Mirvan's hands is analogical to the violence, cruelty and humiliation 'tragically' suffered by Evelina's mother at Lord Beaumont's hands, and to what Evelina herself suffers in society whenever she too lacks an effective male protector. Read against Lady Howard's deference to Captain Mirvan, her social inferior and 'masculine' Mrs Selden's appeal to Lord Beaumont, Evelina's fear of losing Orville's and Villiers' good opinion further illustrates the abject dependence of all ladies on men's protection, money and goodwill. Clearly, there is more to be said about what this novel may insinuate. And that is precisely the point.

During the eighteenth century, as Shaftesbury indicates, there were still good political, legal, social and commercial reasons both for trumpeting fiction's revelations of political, social and/or domestic secrets, and for using the novel's obvious revelations of sensational family secrets to mask its more secretive communications of transgressive or seditious political, social and domestic 'truths'. But because readers could never be sure that they had plumbed all that a fiction might be insinuating by what he called irony – or even that a particular novelist's 'true design' had been 'ironical' – this 'elliptical' or 'enigmatical' manner of writing made each fable what Shaftesbury called 'a kind of Vocal Looking-Glass' for its readers, a Rorschach test reflecting readers' construction of meaning according to their 'wit and humour' and the 'freedom' with which they read.[33] Such dependence on readerly 'making' was not novel: practices of 'shared authorship' between writers and 'active readers' which prised texts open for completion, selection, alteration and revision by reader-(re)writers, and anticipated that textual meanings would be as various as 'the great Variety of Readers', had been current since the Renaissance.[34] In this regard – like censorship, manners, irony and secret writing – the novel was not new.

Notes

1. Anthony Ashley Cooper, Third Earl of Shaftesbury, *Characteristics of Men, Manners, Opinions, Times*, ed. Lawrence E. Klein (Cambridge: Cambridge University Press, 1999), 31.
2. Robert Darnton, *Censors at Work: How States Shaped Literature* (New York: Norton, 2014), 86, 83.
3. Philip Skelton, *Ophiomaches: Or, Deism Revealed*, 2 vols. (London, 1749) 2: 326, quoted in Roger D. Lund, *Ridicule, Religion and the Politics of Wit in Augustan England* (Farnham: Ashgate, 2012), 119; Michael McKeon, *The Secret History of Domesticity* (Baltimore: Johns Hopkins University Press, 2005), 745, n147.
4. I rely here and in what follows on Norman Knox, *The Word Irony and its Context, 1500–1755* (Durham: Duke University Press, 1961) and on the *OED*.
5. Shaftesbury described this elsewhere as 'a Gravity not abhorrent from the use of ... Mirth', and himself as assuming a 'Middle Character' who combined 'Jest' and 'Ernest'. See Lawrence Klein, *Shaftesbury and the Culture of Politeness* (Cambridge: Cambridge University Press, 1994), 96.
6. Knox, *Word Irony*, 181 and 193ff.
7. Knox, *Word Irony*, 211.
8. Quoted in Paula Backscheider, *Spectacular Politics: Theatrical Culture and Mass Power in Early Modern England* (Baltimore: Johns Hopkins University Press, 1993), 113.
9. *The British Journal*, No. 6, 27 Oct. 1722; *The Craftsman*, No. 228, 14 Nov. 1730.
10. Perez Zagorin, *Ways of Lying: Dissimulation, Persecution and Conformity in Early Modern Europe* (Cambridge: Harvard University Press, 1990), 11.
11. Quoted in Annabel Patterson, *Censorship and Interpretation* (Madison: University of Wisconsin Press, 1984), 14.
12. Thomas Gibbons, *Rhetoric: Or a View of its Principal Tropes and Figures* (London, 1767), 77–8. See also, John Ward, *A System of Oratory*, 2 vols. (London, 1759).
13. John Toland, *Clidophorus* (1720), 94, quoted in Annabel Patterson, *Reading Between the Lines* (Madison: University of Wisconsin Press, 1993), 8.

14 See, for instance, in addition to works cited below: Robin Myers and Michael Kerns (ed.), *Censorship and the Control of Print in England and France 1600–1910* (Winchester: St. Paul's Bibliographies, 1992); Sarah Ellenzweig, *The Fringes of Belief* (Stanford: Stanford University Press, 2008); Chris Evans, *Debating the Revolution: Britain in the 1790s* (London: I. B. Tauris, 2006); Annabel Patterson, *Reading Between the Lines* (Madison: University of Wisconsin Press, 1993); David Worrall, *Theatric Revolution: Drama, Censorship and Romantic Period Subcultures 1773–1832* (Oxford: Oxford University Press, 2006); Mogens Laerke (ed.), *The Use of Censorship in the Enlightenment* (Leiden: Brill, 2009).

15 Patterson, *Censorship*, 63, 11.

16 Rand Robertson, *Censorship and Conflict in Eighteenth-Century England* (University Park: Pennsylvania State University Press, 2009), 198, 1.

17 Paul Hyland, 'Richard Steele: Scandal and Sedition,' in *Writing and Censorship in Britain*, eds. Hyland and Neil Sammells (London: Routledge, 1992), 60 ff. For other examples, see Nigel Smith (ed.), *Literature and Censorship* (Cambridge: D. S. Brewer, 1993) and Jason McElligott, *Royalism, Print and Censorship in Revolutionary England* (Woodbridge: Boydell Press, 2007).

18 Roberston, *Censorship and Conflict*, 176, 187.

19 Rebecca Bullard, *The Politics of Disclosure 1674–1725: Secret History Narratives* (London: Pickering & Chatto, 2009), 6; see also Eve Tavor Bannet, '"Secret History": Talebearing Inside and Outside the Secretorie', *Huntington Library Quarterly*, 68:1–2 (2005), 375–96.

20 Here scandalous secret histories of 'king-and-court' become a useful step on the path to 'the King-in-Parliament'.

21 Toni Bowers, *Force or Fraud: British Seduction Stories and the Problem of Resistance, 1660–1760* (Oxford: Oxford University Press, 2011), 34.

22 John R. Snyder, *Dissimulation and the Culture of Secrecy in Early Modern Europe* (Berkeley: University of California Press, 2009), 6, quoted 30, 99.

23 Jenny Davidson, *Hypocrisy and the Politics of Politeness* (New York: Cambridge University Press, 2004). For the transition from court to town, see Anna Bryson, *From Courtesy to Civility* (Oxford: Clarendon, 1998).

24 Henry Fielding, 'An Essay on the Knowledge and Characters of Men', in *English Literature in the Age of Disguise*, ed. Maximillian Novak (Berkeley: University of California Press, 1977), 7, 1. See also Terry Castle, *Masquerade and Civilization: The Carnivalesque in Eighteenth-Century English Culture and Fiction* (Stanford: Stanford University Press, 1986).

25 Eliza Haywood, *The Invisible Spy*, 4 vols. (London, 1755), 1: 23 and *The Female Spectator*, 4 vols. (London, 1745), 1: 3.

26 Samuel Richardson, *Clarissa*, 7 vols. (London, 1748) 1:3

27 Samuel Johnson, *Rambler* no. 4, *The Rambler* (London, 1752), 32.

28 See April London, *The Cambridge Introduction to the Eighteenth-Century Novel* (Cambridge: Cambridge University Press, 2012).

29 For conservative and clerical rejections of curiosity, see Barbara Benedict, *Curiosity* (Chicago: University of Chicago Press, 2001).

30 Quoted by Dagmar Friest, *Governed by Opinion* (London: Tauris, 1997), 131.
31 *Female Spectator*, 1: 4.
32 *The Spectator*, No. 1.
33 Klein, *Politeness*, 112.
34 Stephen B. Dobranski, *Readers and Authorship in Early Modern England* (New York: Cambridge University Press, 2005), 6ff. See also Kevin Sharpe and Steven N. Zwicker (eds.), *Reading, Society and Politics in Early Modern England* (Cambridge: Cambridge University Press, 2003); Eugene Kintgen, *Reading in Tudor England* (Pittsburgh: University of Pittsburgh Press, 1996); William Sherman, *John Dee: The Politics of Reading and Writing in the English Renaissance* (Amherst: University of Massachusetts Press, 1995).

12

Secret History and Anecdote
April London

Tristram Shandy famously opens with the hero's interrupted conception. The corroborating evidence – the source of the secret history of his parents' bedchamber – is provided two brief chapters later:

> To my uncle Mr. *Toby Shandy* do I stand indebted for the preceding anecdote, to whom my father, who was an excellent natural philosopher, and much given to close reasoning upon the smallest matters, had oft, and heavily, complain'd of the injury; but once more particularly, as my uncle *Toby* well remember'd, upon his observing a most unaccountable obliquity, (as he call'd it) in my manner of setting up my top, and justifying the principles upon which I had done it, – the old gentleman shook his head, and in a tone more expressive by half of sorrow than reproach, – he said his heart all along foreboded, and he saw it verified in this, and from a thousand other observations he had made upon me, That I should neither think nor act like any other man's child: – *But alas*! continued he, shaking his head a second time, and wiping away a tear which was trickling down his cheeks, *My Tristram's misfortunes began nine months before ever he came into the world*.
> – My mother, who was sitting by, look'd up, – but she knew no more than her backside what my father meant, – but my uncle, Mr. *Toby Shandy*, who had been informed of the affair – understood him very well.[1]

Why does Tristram choose to classify this episode of his origins as an 'anecdote'? Why does Sterne assign it such narrative prominence? And why, more generally, does the long eighteenth-century novel continue to build on the stylistic norms and conditions of anecdote and its cognate, secret history? The questions are worth pursuing because our own anodyne definition of anecdote as a 'short amusing story about a real incident or person' provides few interpretative clues to the practice of Sterne and his contemporaries. To grasp the genre's significance, we need to recover its period connotations, both formal and conceptual. I want to argue that if we understand anecdote as the *epitome* of secret history – the irreducible essence of a mode often regarded as in decline post-1740 – then the evolution of secret history takes interestingly diverse directions that extend its reach well into the Romantic period.[2] My bracketing texts – Sterne's *Tristram Shandy* and Austen's *Mansfield Park* – suggest that fundamental to this longevity was a gradual re-purposing of anecdote which saw Sterne's use of it to probe fiction's borders with historiography and biography give way to Austen's adapting it to advance the novel's unique claims to representational authenticity.

Tristram Shandy

The tropes of Procopius' *Anekdota* (first translated into English in 1674) remained central to political secret histories over the period. By the mid-eighteenth century, anecdote's foregrounding of revelatory particulars at the expense of generalized public explanation had become equally attractive to new-modelled and emergent genres, including biographies like Boswell's *Life of Johnson* and the increasingly popular modes of antiquarianism, natural history, and travel writing. The embedding of anecdote in late eighteenth-century and Romantic fiction furthered the vitality of secret history in yet another and distinctively self-conscious vein. For contemporary novel readers, anecdote's highly codified literary conventions had effects disproportionate to their actual narrative presence. What begin as Procopian historiographical tropes – the secret knowledge emanating from bedchamber or closet, the sometimes questionable authenticity of first-hand witnesses, the sexual manoeuvring, the telling of truth to power – acquire in their century-long migration from court to commons, from public to domestic, and from history to novel, distinctive formal attributes of concentration, exemplarity, and an ironic closing twist that cues readers to expect surprising disclosures.

The rich expressive possibilities of historiographical anecdote helped to advance its subsequent cross-generic appeal. For Joel Fineman, anecdote serves as 'the literary form that uniquely *lets history happen* by virtue of the way it introduces an opening into the teleological, and therefore timeless, narration of beginning, middle, and end. The anecdote produces the effect of the real, the occurrence of contingency, by establishing an event as an event within and yet without the framing context of historical successivity'.[3] Regarded in the light of period fiction, Fineman's insight suggests that the very compression and coherence of anecdote throws into relief the 'unaccountable obliquity' of experience, conveying both the urge to order – everywhere evident in *Tristram Shandy* – and the recognition that novels can only produce a simulacrum, 'the effect of the real'. Anecdote conceived in these terms anticipates the 'Romantic self-consciousness' that, 'pushed to its limits', Paul Hamilton argues, 'seeks to shatter the reflection or image of plenitude it has created'.[4] Or, perhaps, less grandly, Sterne's reliance on anecdote might be seen as the characteristic reflex of an 'inveterate index reader' who, Melvyn New asserts, 'liberally sprinkle[s *Tristram Shandy*] with the names of authors he never read, books he knew little or nothing about, and technical details (from history and science in particular) that are not the indications of a universal genius'.[5] Yet if Sterne's habits of mind, reading, and composition appear eccentrically personal, his use of anecdote is not: many of his immediate contemporaries similarly adapt its most striking attribute – the capacity both to stimulate and to disrupt the story-making impulse – as counterpoint to their scrutiny of the apparent certainties of history and biography. Anecdotal writing proves particularly suited to such sceptical articulations: even as it homes in on the revelatory detail, telling gesture or exceptional subject, it invites further contemplation of the institutional structures it seemingly rejects.

Sterne is unusual, however, in the range of his allusions to anecdote from neighbouring genres, a noteworthy feat given its recent spread into novels, jest books, pornography, journalism, biography and autobiography, travel narratives, historiography, children's fiction, medical writing, pedagogy, sermons, case law, and conduct literature.[6] Its diffusion through an expanding print culture had been matched from mid-century by a steady widening of its terms. In 1728, Ephraim Chambers' *Cyclopaedia*, a work closely consulted by Sterne, describes '*Anecdotes, anecdota*' as 'used by some authors, for the titles of Secret Histories; that is, of such as relate the secret affairs and transactions of princes; speaking with too much freedom, or too much sincerity, of the manner and conduct of persons in authority, to allow of their being made public'.[7] Samuel Johnson's 1755 *Dictionary* retains this classical understanding in its primary designation of anecdote as indivisible from secret history: 'something yet unpublished; secret history'; the 1777 edition then adds a second meaning that testifies to the growing importance of quotidian experience: 'It is now used, after the French, for a biographical incident; a minute passage of private life.'[8] Numbers of critics have explored secret history's links to novels before Richardson's, developing the two genres' shared fascination with sexuality, matters of supposed fact, the domains of the intimate and domestic, and the contested border between history and invention.[9] Anecdote carries forward these defining expressive and thematic traits well beyond the point at which the Whig ascendancy had diminished the sway of secret history as a discrete novelistic mode. By the time of Austen, in fact, these distinguishing markers serve close to shorthand functions, prompting readers in advance of plot revelations to respond with suspicion to certain characters and situations.

Tristram Shandy occupies an important medial position in this evolution of secret history from court culture propaganda to realist fiction by virtue of its pushing beyond the early eighteenth-century focus 'on amatory and political intrigue' to advance through anecdote a critical assessment of history and biography.[10] Most obviously, anecdote operates in the novel as a framing device, used by Sterne to mark the onset of his hero's account of his life and opinions at the March 1718 convening of the '*beds of justice*' (2: 524) and then its closing with what Tristram considers the 'choicest morsel of what I had to offer to the world'(2: 779), 'that part of my work, towards which, I have all the way, looked forwards, with so much earnest desire' (1: 400), the final 'anecdotes of my uncle *Toby*'s amours with widow *Wadman*' (1: 244). The opening scene of conception, the ongoing allusions to aunt Dinah and the 'tale of family disgrace' (1: 77), and the terminal thwarting of the Widow Wadman's schemes engage – with considerable irony – the standard period coupling of anecdote with sexual scandal. More innovatively, the clustering of anecdotes around the figures of Toby and Yorick implicates the mode in the sceptical treatment of the two genres with which those characters are most closely associated, history and biography.

The depiction of the fall of Strasbourg through the tale of Slawkenburgius is a case in point of Sterne's comic extension of the tropes of secret history: 'It is the lot of few', we are told, 'to trace out the true springs of this and such like revolutions – The Vulgar look too high for them – Statesmen look too low – Truth (for once) lies in the middle'. That middle is here the anecdote of the nose, with its summary revelation that

> 'twas not the *French* – 'twas CURIOSITY pushed [the gates of Strasbourg] open – the *French* indeed, who are ever upon the catch, when they saw the *Strasburgers* … all marched out to follow the stranger's nose – each man followed his own, and marched in.
>
> Trade and manufactures have decayed and gradually grown down ever since – but not from any cause which commercial heads have assigned; for it is owing to this only, the Noses have ever so run in their heads, that the *Strasburgers* could not follow their business (1: 323–4).

The epigrammatic turn of the conclusion effects a genre shift from mock secret history to polished anecdote, summoning a wittily pointed coherence to reconfigure the preoccupation of earlier scandal chronicles with the origins and exercise of power. Turn-of-the-century secret histories had depicted sexual intrigue between *individuals* as the force driving court politics. Sterne's anecdote substitutes *collective* prurience for clandestine sexuality as the impetus to change and, in the process, satirizes both standard public history (with its emphasis on the 'great man') and its renegade alternative, the secret history of the closet (with its emphasis on conniving women). As the nose euphemisms suggest, the satire touches on issues of reception as well as genre through sardonic references to those 'readers in the world, as well as many other good people in it, who are no readers at all, – who find themselves ill at ease, unless they are let into the whole secret from first to last, of every thing which concerns you' (1: 4–5). Typically, Sterne here engages new audiences whose interest in fame was nourished by an expanding periodical culture, even as he simultaneously derides that fascination in the depiction of Slawkenburgius's celebrity and its consequences.

Directing attention away from the acts of errant individuals and towards collective defamation also works to foreground the operations of 'opinion', an increasingly significant aspect of mid-century conjectural and philosophical histories. Sterne's titular reference to 'Life and Opinions' flags its role in the unfolding of *Tristram Shandy*. While Scottish Enlightenment historians tend to evoke opinion as a positive complement to narrowly political explication, Sterne arraigns it as negative and insular. This departure from historiographical practice, coupled with a novelistic use of opinion as a submerged thematic link between otherwise discrete anecdotes, has important consequences. In narrative terms, the tactical connection between opinion and anecdotal form allows Sterne to probe the boundary between the real and the fabricated. By this means, the tale of Slawkenburgius, grounded in the *actual* military and religious contexts of Louis XIV's surprising seizure of Strasbourg, can be shown to share important features with the network of *invented* anecdotes centred on Yorick. The latter include the linked anecdotes of his 'broken-winded horse' (1:20) and his subsidizing of the midwife (both of which are coloured, as with Slawkenburgius, by the unsavoury influence of rumour) and the episode with Phutatorius and the burning chestnut when Yorick, Walter, and Toby meet over dinner with 'the beards of so many commissaries, officials, advocates, proctors, registers … school divines, and others' (1:361) to debate the possibility of un-naming Tristram. Reminding us of the connections between these two anecdotes, the narrator comments that Yorick felt 'as in the affair of the lean horse' that 'his spirit was above' (1:385) explaining that he did not in fact drop a hot chestnut down

Phutatoris' breeches as 'a sarcastical fling' (1:384) at his treatise on the keeping of concubines: 'he ever looked upon the inventor, the propagator and believer of an illiberal report alike so injurious to him, – he could not stoop to tell his story to them – and so trusted to time and truth to do it for him' (1:385).

According to William Hazlitt, Sterne's prose 'is at times the most rapid, the most happy, the most idiomatic of any that is to be found. It is the pure essence of English conversational style'.[11] As so often, Hazlitt's praise more accurately reflects the preoccupations of his own generation than the preceding ones – in this instance, the Romantic-era relish for sociable exchange, fed in part by printed guides to the telling of anecdotes.[12] As Richardson's *Clarissa* indicates, the revelatory individualism of the speaking voice was for an earlier age more likely to be aligned with misconstruction and abuse of power. In Sterne's novel, conversational immediacy is similarly linked to problems of reception. As the 'story-teller' who performs posthumous acts of restitution, Tristram refers in the Phutatoris episode to a number of contemporary discourses that make extended use of anecdote to foreground such problems: most overtly and satirically, case law and religious controversy, more slyly, medical reportage – the debate over the possible curative effects of applying strips of text to Phutatoris' burn – and Table Talk, as the running title of Selden's popular late seventeenth-century work indicates, a mode concerned with 'various Matters of Weight and high Consequence; relating especially to religion and State', but by the mid-eighteenth century tending towards the more casual topicality that marks Piozzi's *Thraliana*. Both the Phutatoris and Slawkenburgius episodes demonstrate Sterne's novelistic adjustment of the scandal chronicle's overt sexuality to suit the complex characterization of Tristram and his alter ego, Yorick.

Representations of uncle Toby tend in turn to draw on the political, historical, and evidential aspects of mid-century anecdote. As we have seen, Toby is the conduit through which the two anecdotes of conception and paternal despair over his son's 'most unaccountable obliquity' reach Tristram. Toby is also directly implicated in what Walter Shandy regards as the critical events of his son's early life: his birthplace and his accidental circumcision, the latter of which is closely tied to Toby's martial exploits.

The anecdotes relating to Tristram's birth at Shandy Hall are verbally differentiated on a scale of formality – extending from conversation, through the conventions of genre, to official, institutional documents – with each expressive mode assigned evaluative connotations. Early in the novel, Tristram patterns himself on the 'historiographer' who is unable to 'drive on his history, as a muleteer drives on his mule, – straight forward', because he has 'fifty deviations from a straight line to make with this or that party as he goes along' (1:41). Immediately, we're provided with a typographical rendering of such deviations when an unadorned list beginning with 'Accounts to reconcile: Anecdotes to pick up' (1:41) is succeeded by the marriage settlement of the Shandys with its stipulation of entitlement to a London birth. Included in the verbatim legal document is the countervailing measure inserted at Toby's direction 'in security of my father' that in the event of a phantom pregnancy, Mrs. Shandy's subsequent confinement must take place in the country, a measure designed 'to put a stop to the practice of any unfair play on the part of my mother, which a marriage article of this nature too manifestly opened a door to, and which indeed had never been thought of at all, but for my uncle *Toby Shandy*' (1:45–6).

At the end of September 1717, there is just such a false journey and, as a result, when his father 'peremptorily insist[s] upon the clause' (1:46), 'the whole weight of the article' falls on Tristram's yet-unborn-self. But the directive is then deferred when Walter decides 'to keep the worst part of the story still to himself … the resolution he had taken of doing himself the justice, which my uncle *Toby*'s clause in the marriage settlement empowered him'. Not until thirteen months later, on 'the very night I was begot', Tristram writes, does Mrs. Shandy have the 'least intimation of [her husband's] design; – when my father, happening, as you remember, to be a little chagrin'd and out of temper, – took occasion as they lay chatting gravely in bed afterwards, talking over what was to come, – to let her know that she must accommodate herself as well as she could to the bargain made between them in their marriage deeds; which was to lye-in of her next child in the country to balance the last year's journey' (1:49). The return in Chapter 17 to the scene of the 'beds of justice' with which the novel began transforms what seemed initially a distinct episode into what now appears (in chronological terms) a *sequence* of events reaching from the marriage settlement through the moment of conception to the actual birth. Here as elsewhere, Toby's machinations provide the connecting – even impelling – link. Trim's removal of the sash weights to aid in the reconstruction of the siege of Namur, the effective cause of Tristram's sash-window circumcision, consolidates Toby's position as the directive figure who makes proximate the bordering realms of the personal and the political, as well as the biographical and the historical.

The relation between these varied contexts is articulated through Sterne's elaboration of anecdote's formal and conceptual aspects. Even the events, times, and places with which Toby is associated share structural features with the mode. The historical moment that defines his adult life, the 1695 recapturing of the citadel of Namur, was itself a 'turning point' in the nine-year King William's War, a momentous incident Toby struggles to convey in an appropriately condensed fashion to those who visit him during his four-year convalescence in London.[13] When he and Trim resolve to leave for the 'neat little country house' adjacent to Shandy Hall, the anecdote describing their departure deploys the customary tropes of secret history (while also simultaneously subverting them). The prurience, the claim to authenticity, the element of sexual intrigue: Tristram deftly evokes each of these aspects of scandal chronicles in his account of his uncle's flight from London:

> Never did lover post down to a belov'd mistress with more heat and expectation, than my uncle *Toby* did, to enjoy this self-same thing in private; – I say in private; – for it was sheltered from the house, as I told you, by a tall yew hedge, and was covered on the other three sides, from mortal sight, by rough holly and thickset flowering shrubs; – so that the idea of not being seen, did not a little contribute to the idea of pleasure preconceived in my uncle *Toby*'s mind (1: 113).

Toby's release in the country from the dilemma of narration – the 'almost insurmountable difficulties … in telling [his] story intelligibly' (1: 94) – is made possible by the topographical equivalent of anecdote, the bowling green on which he and Trim contrive scale re-enactments (with the green functioning as at once a compressed synecdoche of ongoing battles and a much-magnified displacement of Toby's groin injury). What Trim and Toby aspire to create, in short, is a material version of secret history – in the period sense of a history filtered through the subjective consciousness of a participant – that will make the siege he witnessed at once visible *and* covert. In reshaping secret history to express the dual imperatives of biography and history, Tristram relies on the anecdote's characteristic tropes of behavioural eccentricity, sex, and confidential information to signify through uncle Toby the uncertain line separating public and private knowledge.

Over the course of the novel, elaborated anecdotes (including those of the bowling green and the courtship of Widow Wadman) coexist with others of so 'small a compass', as Tristram notes, to be 'rolled up in my mother's hussive' (1: 445–6) and with the gestural and visual equivalents of such anecdotes – Yorick's deathbed grasp of Eugenius' hand, Trim's dropping of the hat to mark Bobby's death. But however privileged anecdote proves as a form to which *Tristram Shandy* recurrently turns, it is itself consistently subject to Sterne's irony. As illustration, we can turn to a highly reflexive episode that begins by disputing the intellectual credibility of anecdotes and closes by replicating – in bathetically undermining terms – their characteristic structure. Walter, convinced that practice with auxiliary verbs will train Tristram's infant mind, supports his argument with a flurry of anecdotes, including that of Piereskius, whose precocity was such that 'if we may give credit to an anecdote concerning him, which we cannot with-hold here, without shaking the authority of all anecdotes whatever – at seven years of age, his father committed entirely to his care the education of his younger brother', to which Yorick adds: 'But you forget the great *Lipsius* … who composed a work the day he was born; – They should have wiped it up, said my uncle *Toby*, and said no more about it' (1: 493).

With this scatological reference in mind, an argument for connections between *Tristram Shandy* and *Mansfield Park* may seem wilfully perverse. In fact, the two novels share a striking number of features: neither of their protagonists anticipates a happy future, both have fraught experiences of familial, individual, and social identities, and for both, the force of memory has the potential to undermine rather than affirm the sense of self. Both authors also assume that their readers are familiar with anecdote's distinctive formal features, with its literary and historical antecedents, and with its associational meanings. Austen, however, scants the biographical and historiographical concerns of Sterne. Her acute literary self-consciousness about anecdote's formal traits and the evaluative charge they carry makes possible ongoing covert allusions to staple features of early eighteenth-century secret histories, including secrecy, betrayal, abuse of power, and the relation of self to social knowledge. By evoking and then deliberately *departing from* anecdotal tropes, Austen gains a purchase on her own era's increasingly complex understanding of narrative representation.

Mansfield Park

While anecdotes are scattered throughout Austen's fiction, *Mansfield Park* is unusual in the prominence it assigns a late-appearing one: the account of Maria Rushworth's elopement with Henry Crawford.[14] The sexual charge attaching to her decampment gains intensity through contrast with earlier, more anodyne anecdotes, most of them centring on sociability and the fulfilment of collective obligations, the very attributes Henry Crawford and Maria Rushworth offend against. A clear example can be seen when Sir Thomas Bertram, newly returned from Antigua, encourages the visiting William Price to recount tales from his sea-faring life because his uncle wishes 'to know the young man by his histories'. With great 'satisfaction', he hears in them evidence of his nephew's 'good principles, professional knowledge, energy, courage and cheerfulness'.[15] Sir Thomas's warm approval hints at his possession of latent traits that will be fully realized at the novel's end when he acknowledges his errors and embraces Fanny as Edmund's wife. To the self-interested Henry Crawford, however, the stories 'gave a different feeling. He longed to have been at sea, and seen and done and suffered as much'. His receptiveness suggests the power of anecdote to alter identity – but also its sometimes-fleeting influence, given that his wish to have 'been a William Price, distinguishing himself and working his way to fortune and consequence with so much self-respect and happy ardour, was … rather eager than lasting' (275). Henry's mercurial nature may make sustained effort impossible. But a later conversation with the now-exiled Fanny suggests that he has at least managed to internalize his attraction to the performative aspect of anecdote and direct its suasive power to courting her (and possibly improving himself).

Henry seeks out Fanny at her father's Portsmouth house after his return from Norfolk, where he had gone to investigate the rumoured 'underhand dealing' of his estate agent. While there, we are told, he

> had begun making acquaintance with cottages whose very existence, though on his own estate, had been hitherto unknown to him. This was aimed, and well aimed, at Fanny. It was pleasing to hear him speak so properly; here, he had been acting as he ought to do. To be the friend of the poor and oppressed! Nothing could be more grateful to her, and she was on the point of giving him an approving look when it was all frightened off, by his adding a something too pointed of his hoping soon to have an assistant, a friend, a guide in every plan of utility or charity for Everingham, a somebody who would make Everingham and all about it, a dearer object than it had ever been yet (469–70).

The passage's tacking between Henry's manipulative appeals, the narrator's sceptical comment on their being 'aimed, and well aimed', and Fanny's openness to his seemingly changed nature will recur in their later meetings as Henry tries to involve her in his plans for the estate. The proximity of these subsequent conversations to his flight with Maria Rushworth might suggest that the elopement is little more than a narrative expedient to save Fanny from his devices; that, in short, she continues to be the passive object of egotistical schemers. Another Portsmouth anecdote, this one focused on a contested knife and limited to the Price family circle, anticipates and supports the alternative course that ultimately rewards Fanny with a central place in the recovered Mansfield order. It is a course that positions Fanny as a self-aware agent, capable of responding forcefully to the chaos surrounding her.

The anecdote of the knife bequeathed to Susan by her dying sister Mary completes the pattern in *Mansfield Park* of re-directed gifts, and is particularly closely related to that of the horse assigned to Fanny by Edmund and then appropriated, with his tacit consent, by Mary Crawford. The two episodes involve analogous relationships: misplaced infatuation (of Mrs Price and of Edmund), helped on by the wilfulness of the substitute beneficiaries (Betsey and Mary Crawford), subverts rightful possession and turns what was initially a gift inspired by affection (for Fanny, and for Susan) into an occasion for resentment or conflict. The intervening account of the two necklaces for the amber cross similarly depends on a contrast between deeply felt personal attachment and received notions of female rivalry. But the structural and thematic parallels between the presents associated with Mary Crawford and the bequeathed knife anecdote underscore a crucial difference: in the latter instance, Fanny considers others' feelings and then acts decisively, spending some of her uncle's leave-taking present of ten pounds to correct what she has identified as a persistent source of dispute in the Portsmouth household. The tact with which she bestows her purchase of a new silver knife is noteworthy: she gives it to Betsey in order indirectly to allow the more deserving Susan 'full possession' (459) of the beloved token of her dead sister. The gift at once eases domestic discord and detaches the two companionate sisters from the Price family dynamic, itself a replication of Mansfield's in its neglect of those shaped by the 'natural light of the mind' (458). The sting of their mother's preferential treatment of Betsey and the father's of his sons gives way to Susan's grateful compliance with her older sister's regulation. Not only does the episode look back to Fanny's childhood deference to Edmund, but also forward to Susan's later assumption of her place at Mansfield and, in a final reorientation, to Edmund's acknowledgement of Fanny's 'mental superiority' (545).

This long-deferred triumph follows a swerve in the novel's plot initiated by yet another anecdote. Fanny receives advance notice of its subject in a cryptic letter from Mary Crawford that hints at an unfolding scandal, but advises that she 'hear nothing, surmise nothing, whisper nothing … I am sure it will be all hushed up' (506). Next day, however, Mr Price asks his daughter to supply the names of her cousins in town so that he can decode a newspaper snippet of gossip (as with early scandal chronicles, the column identifies its targets by their initials). His response to the reported adultery, a clichéd mix of prurience and sanctimonious bluster, offers an appraisal 'from below' of the aristocratic mores he assumes generated Maria's recklessness: Sir Thomas 'may be too much of the courtier and fine gentleman to like his daughter the less. But by G – if she belonged to *me*, I'd give her the rope's end as long as I could stand over her ... so many fine ladies were going to the devil now-a-days that way, that there was no answering for anybody' (509–10). While in the short term his posturing authenticates Fanny's inward 'horror', Austen subsequently relies on anecdotal conventions to develop the class assumptions behind his bombast. The effect is to bring into proximity the 'low' mass readership of newspapers and the putative 'courtly' reader (and subjects) of period secret histories. The middle course between these two unpalatable extremes, as embodied in the ending of *Mansfield Park*, is the novel's representation of a renovated family order that stands as alternative to both Portsmouth vulgarity and Crawford dissoluteness.

The newspaper report has the galvanizing effect of recalling Fanny to Mansfield. Once there, the history of her cousin is particularized in ways that layer on to the bare-bones gossip column a number of familiar tropes, adjusted to anticipate Austen's turn from scandal chronicle to domestic fiction. These include the 'insider' account 'sent express' by an 'old and most particular friend in London', Mr Harding, who 'hearing and witnessing a good deal to alarm him ... wrote to recommend Sir Thomas's coming to London himself and using his influence with his daughter to put an end to an intimacy which was already exposing her to unpleasant remarks', his subsequent report of additional 'very flagrant indiscretion' and the information that the 'maid-servant of Mrs Rushworth, senior, threatened alarmingly'. But despite Harding's 'doing all in his power to quiet every thing', the affair quickly becomes 'public beyond a hope', through the leaguing of Maria's mother-in-law with a servant who 'had exposure in her power, and, supported by her mistress, was not to be silenced' (520–1). The compression of these standard features within a single narrative – female rivalries and confederacies, divided loyalties, grasping servants, public scandal and sexual indiscretion – aligns Maria and Crawford's illicit history with those described in early eighteenth-century secret histories. Here, the negative resonances are balanced by the more positive, if inadvertent, repercussions of the dynamism inherent to the form. The exposure of the miscreants unseats the court favourites and their acolytes – Henry and Mary Crawford, Maria, the Rushworths and Mrs Norris – clearing the way for the purposive and settled rural space of the novel's ending. Edmund and Sir Thomas, eyes opened by the elopement anecdote, at last recognize their earlier misapprehensions; Susan, witness to and beneficiary of Fanny's Portsmouth gift, moves smoothly into her sister's former place at Mansfield; Fanny, whose capacity for acting authoritatively to establish order was first displayed in that knife anecdote will, we are encouraged to believe, continue on that course at Mansfield.

In telling contrast, *Tristram Shandy* shuts down abruptly with the Cock and Bull anecdote of foiled expectations that prompts Mrs Shandy's uncomprehending cry, 'L – d! … what is all this story about?' (2: 809). Readers of *Mansfield Park* have no such doubts about how to answer that question. While Sterne plays on the tension between anecdote's pithiness and its self-perpetuating vitality with the intent of deflecting summary comprehension, Austen's ending deliberately courts the latter. At the close of *Mansfield Park*, those characters affiliated through anecdotal narrative with secret history conventions have been exiled from the circle of distributed rewards. In the final paragraph, we are invited to regard through Fanny's eyes the world that remains and to register the happy visual and affective coordination of 'everything' that strikes her 'within the view and patronage of Mansfield Park' (548). Like Sterne, Austen 'lets history happen' by releasing anecdote's capacity to unsettle; unlike him, she does so in order finally to channel that aggressive energy and hence confirm her own novelistic power to 'quit such odious subjects as soon as I can, impatient to restore every body, not greatly in fault themselves, to tolerable comfort' (533).

Notes

1. Laurence Sterne, *The Life and Opinions of Tristram Shandy, Gentleman*, ed. Melvyn New and Joan New, vols. 1–2 of ed. Melvyn New, Joan New and Peter de Voogd, *The Florida Edition of the Works of Laurence Sterne*, 8 vols. (Gainesville, FL: The University Presses of Florida, 1978–2008), 1: 4.
2. For analysis of works written at the height of secret history's popularity, see Rebecca Bullard, *The Politics of Disclosure, 1674–1725: Secret History Narratives* (London: Pickering & Chatto, 2009).
3. Joel Fineman, 'The History of the Anecdote: Fiction and Fiction' in *The New Historicism*, ed. H. Aram Veeser (New York and London: Routledge, 1989), 61.
4. Paul Hamilton, *Metaromanticism Aesthetics, Literature, Theory* (Chicago: University of Chicago Press, 2003), 3.
5. Melvyn New with Richard A. Davies and W.G. Day, 'Introduction', ed. Melvyn New and Joan New, *The Life and Opinions of Tristram Shandy, Gentleman: The Notes* (vol. 3 of *The Florida Edition of the Works of Laurence Sterne*), 3: 24.

6 Prominent examples include the framing of anecdotes in the context of theology in Yorick's sermon, of medicine in those relating to Walter's favouring of Caesarean sections and of historiography in the recounting of Francis I's war with Switzerland.
7 Cited by Annabel Patterson, *Early Modern Liberalism* (Cambridge: Cambridge University Press, 1997), 159. Ian Campbell Ross's *Laurence Sterne A Life* (Oxford: Oxford University Press, 2001) links the *Cyclopaedia* with Burton's *Anatomy of Melancholy* as the two works of 'encyclopaedic learning' of which Sterne was 'particularly fond' (108).
8 Samuel Johnson, *A Dictionary of the English Language* (London, 1777).
9 See, in addition to Bullard, *Politics*: Robert Mayer, *History and the Early English Novel: Matters of Fact from Bacon to Defoe* (Cambridge: Cambridge University Press, 1997), Michael McKeon, *The Origins of the English Novel, 1660–1740* (Baltimore: Johns Hopkins University Press, 1987), and Eve Tavor Bannet, '"Secret History": Or, Talebearing Inside and Outside the Secretorie' in *The Uses of History in Early Modern England* (San Marino: Huntington Library, 2006), 367–88.
10 Bannet, '"Secret History"', 370–1.
11 William Hazlitt, *The Complete Works of William Hazlitt* ed. P.P. Howe; after A.R. Waller and Arnold Glover, 21 vols. (London and Toronto: J.M. Dent and Sons, [1930–34]), 4:121.
12 See Jon Mee, *Conversable Worlds: Literature, Contention, and Community, 1762 to 1830* (Oxford: Oxford University Press, 2011).
13 *Tristram Shandy*, 3:129 note to 93.6.
14 *Persuasion* is the other Austen novel in which a late-appearing anecdote (the story about Walter Elliot recounted by Mrs Smith to Anne Elliot) is assigned a pivotal role in the resolution of the plot.
15 Jane Austen, *Mansfield Park*, ed. John Wiltshire (Cambridge: Cambridge University Press, 2005), 275.

13

Secret History in the Romantic Period

Miranda Burgess

Open Secrets, 1790s–1810s

British ideas of secrecy in the early years of the Romantic period were shaped by an epistemic contradiction. On the one hand were the acts and prosecutions of the mid-1790s, which produced what John Bugg calls a 'politics of troubled utterance'.[1] At a time when the government of William Pitt was consumed with what it conceived as the secret plots of Britons ranging from Lakeland poets to Belfast printers and members of the London Corresponding Society, writers experienced a practical need not just for secrecy, but actually for political silence. On the other hand was the Foucauldian fact that the self-censoring paranoia of the period was shaped by, and mirrored, the public chatter about secrecy in which government and its agents engaged.[2] John Barrell shows how the treason trials of 1794–1795 brought into ubiquitous public view what Pitt's judicial apparatus claimed were the secret thoughts of individuals and groups. In bringing these prosecutions, meanwhile, the government laid bare its own hidden imaginings, which had led, in their turn, to the open secret of its employment of spies and the cooperation between surveillance and judicial apparatus.[3] There was a further irony: the evidence of treason frequently took printed, and widely circulated, form. For example, among the 10,000 documents concerning British and Irish republican politics the Lord Lieutenant's informers assembled at Dublin Castle between 1796 and 1798 are notebooks seized from the business agent for the radical Belfast newspaper *Northern Star*. These revealed the mechanisms of the *Star*'s circulation – including the Royal Mail.[4]

The Romantic period opened, then, on a culture of secrecy very different from the early-Georgian conditions Eve Bannet describes in her anatomy of the secret history. Secret histories exposed problems resulting from government secretiveness and censorship.[5] The British government of the 1790s, in contrast, paraded its own secrets, which concentrated, in turn, on obsessive investigation of the secrecy of others. It is unsurprising, in this context, that works bearing the genre label 'secret history' persisted into the Romantic period, their authors seeking to capitalize on the widespread association of government with secrecy. It is equally unsurprising, given the repressiveness accompanying the government's open secrets, that such works had come to comprise an attenuated genre saying little about contemporary British political life.

The period from the 1790s to 1820s saw the publication of 'secret histories' of the theatre, French court and French Revolution.[6] The few secret histories of Britain, such as Walter Scott's *Secret History of the Court of James the First* (1811), tended to focus on monarchies from the distant past, anthologizing archival documents rather than describing scenes or imagining dialogue. It was not until the end of the period, during the pro-Reform ministry of Charles Grey, that an avowed secret history of contemporary British government appeared.[7] Even then, the government secrets it claimed to expose were anachronistic: the nefarious private acts of the Liverpool administration of the 1810s, a regime understood, by 1832, to have committed a great many nefarious public ones.

This account, in which the name 'secret history' takes flight from the political present, associating itself with the minor, the past, and the foreign, might suggest that the *genre* is equally marginal to Romantic-period political critique. This essay argues, instead, that the conventions and, to some extent, the aims of secret history remain essential to the literature and politics of the period. In its repressions of the 1790s, the Pittite government portrayed writers and printers as conspirators and paraded the effectiveness of its own secret networks in exposing reformist programs that had often already been made public in print. I shall suggest that the government's public claims about secrecy, and the secrecy government attributed to the print cultures of reform, encouraged a corresponding sense, among writers and printers, of the potency of writing and, especially, of print in mediating between the reading public and the ostensibly secretive political aims of the powerful and disenfranchised alike.

Traces of such an understanding can be glimpsed throughout the period, from Wordsworth's warnings about the 'savage torpor' of readers vulnerable to 'the rapid communication of intelligence' to Hazlitt's assertion that the French Revolution was the 'remote but inevitable result of the invention of the art of printing'.[8] From the 1790s to 1810s, political broadsides tended to concentrate attention, self-reflexively and defensively, on their own agency, and to represent it, in ironic riposte to government's claims about secrecy, as embodied in their appearance in print. Rachel Carnell points out the rapid shifts in narrative mode and the quasi-editorial apparatus that often characterized secret history, emphasizing that these features helped deflect responsibility for political position-taking.[9] Other readers of secret history consider these formal features chiefly as claims to historicity; Srinivas Aravamudan suggests that they both emphasized and undercut the genre's truth claims, creating epistemological uncertainty for readers.[10] Similar shifts and apparatuses appear in Romantic-period print culture, albeit often in debased fashion. Here, however, they emphasize, more than the historicity of content, the medial and agential character of print itself. This chapter examines the United Irishman periodicals of the 1790s as the instantiation of such a self-ironizing appeal to the efficacy of the printed word.

This chapter explores a further legacy of the government's preoccupation with print as the medium of secrecy and the motor of reformist sentiment in what Jon Klancher identifies as the programmes of 'genre reform' undertaken in ideologically various ways from the 1790s to 1810s.[11] Like the secret historians of the early eighteenth century, a subset of genre reformers concentrated on the limits and failings of historiography, which they sought to supplement or correct. Their efforts received added impetus from contemporary debates about the political agency of print. Among these genre-reforming works, the essays of Isaac D'Israeli were especially prominent, as we will see. This chapter will show how D'Israeli's efforts to provide a 'private' or 'secret' supplement to the official narratives of national history shaped the major fictional genres of the second half of the Romantic period: the historical novels of Walter Scott and the domestic novels of Jane Austen.

United Irishman Periodicals: The 'Secret' Agency of Print

In mid-March 1798, a militia guard descended on the Dublin printing office where the newspaper *The Press* was produced. Although proprietor John Stockdale had already been imprisoned for sedition, the militiamen 'destroy[ed] every thing in the office, alledging [*sic*] they had orders from Government not to leave a penny-worth standing (they brought sledges for the purpose)'.[12] There was precedent for such orders: Francis Rawdon-Hastings, Earl of Moira, remarked that a similar attack that wrecked the operations of the *Northern Star* on 19 May 1797 had occurred at 'the secret direction of government'.[13] But smashing Stockdale's presses was, in the event, insufficient inoculation against his newspaper's political force.

Authorized by warrants from Dublin Castle, the militiamen also 'carried off' the fragments.[14]

Founded in September 1797, following the *Northern Star*'s demise, *The Press* was a United Irishmen paper.[15] As such it participated in what Margaret Jacob calls the 'international republican conversation' of the 1790s.[16] Jacob's phrase aptly captures official perceptions of radical networks as simultaneously secret and noisy, 'all vigilance, all activity', their 'address, in eluding detection, … only exceeded by the daring profligacy displayed in the pursuit of [their]… object', as John Gifford argued in the *Anti-Jacobin Review* in 1798.[17] The phrase takes equal note of officialdom's response to these networks: the use of mixed apparatuses of surveillance and publicity to capture what Gifford called the 'authentic … true … communications' of the network and recirculate them in printed form.[18] This radical conversation was as likely to be conducted in newspapers and broadsides as in secret letters; it was at least as much a product of official public whisperings about conspiracy as it was conspiratorial in itself. The reformers engaged, in their turn, in pamphleteering and journalism about the pamphleteering and journalism that was publicizing their affairs. Indeed, the immediate occasion of militia intervention in Stockdale's offices may have been an issue of *The Press* that included an 'Address of the London Corresponding Society to the Irish Nation' declaring, 'if to UNITE in the cause of Reform upon the broadest basis, be treason, we with you are traitors'.[19]

The London Corresponding Society was intimately familiar with the agency of the press, not least in association with secrecy. In 1794 Thomas Hardy, shoemaker and founder, had been tried for high treason on grounds of having 'imagined the death' of George III – if true, an intimately personal act, but one that had been repeatedly made public as having become, in the eyes of government, tantamount to violence. Barrell describes Pitt's government as 'determined to keep up the alarm for the king's safety by inviting the nation to imagine that someone was imagining his death' (46). Even as government and judiciary laboured to expose what they represented as the secret lives of the LCS membership, revealing their own surveillance apparatus in the process, they were aided by the fact that the activities that had brought the LCS to government attention amounted mainly to public meetings – advertised by handbill, with minutes published in the form of pamphlets, petitions and, eventually, periodicals.[20] The secrecy of the LCS was, then, from the outset, doubly exposed: put into circulation by the acts of government (and their publicists in the conservative periodicals, who took up the cries of 'conspiracy' and 'pretence' against the LCS) and by the printed works of LCS members themselves.[21]

It is in this larger context of open secrets and print conspiracies that the Lord Lieutenant's security apparatus demanded the smashing of the Dublin presses. Their nominal owner, Peter Finnerty, had already been pilloried on 30 December 1797 for seditious libel; issues of *The Press* had carried reports of armed attempts to rob deliverymen of copies for sale and of violent intimidation of the paper's advertisers.[22] In becoming subject to the open secret of governmental surveillance and intervention while purveying the ostensible secrets of its United Irishman owners, *The Press* – and the presses its title self-reflexively named – had become the embodiment of political agency.

It is also in this context that the self-conscious parade of such an understanding of print must be read amid the Irish political debates of the 1790s. A pamphlet titled *Report of the Trial of the King Versus Hurdy Gurdy, Alias Barrel Organ, alias Grinder, alias the Seditious Organ, for publishing and causing and procuring to be published a certain false, wicked, malicious and scandalous noise, clamour[,] sound, uproar, vibration, cussion, concussion, percussion or repercussion of the Air, which came on to be tried at the Bar of the King's Bench on the day of 1794, with the Arguments of Council and the Charge of the Judge, taken in Short-hand*, first published serially in the *Northern Star*, provides an excellent example.[23] The pamphlet satirized the 1794 trial of the *Star*'s proprietors for printing 'a certain false[,] wicked, malicious, scandalous and seditious libel'.[24] It draws on the conventions of secret history, alternating rapidly among different points of view: the impersonality of officialdom, including learned citations of statute law; the sententious first-person plural of contemporary reportage; the omniscience of 'editors'; and the informal first-person testimony of witnesses, rendered sometimes in dialogue form and sometimes as indirect speech resembling the free indirect style that would later come to characterize Austen's novels (4, 17–20, 21–23, 23–25). The pamphlet also follows convention in substituting blanks for the names of the speakers whose words it claims to compile. Thus the authors pantomime, as in secret history, the defensive deferral of origins and the preservation of secrecy and document the role of secrecy in the trial the pamphlet depicts.

The agency of radical print is represented in *The Trial of Hurdy Gurdy* as 'noise, clamour[,] sound, uproar, vibration … or aerial pulse', a representation emphasized by the title (5). Noise, it turns out, is an apt figure for the political point being made in the pamphlet: it is as secretive in its inarticulacy (the trial includes debates about the political significance of scales) as it is publicly insistent (38–41). Thus the emphasis on the noisiness of radical politics turns out to be consistent with an emphasis on secrecy.

Among the pamphlet's satiric enactments of secrecy are several directed at the nexus of sound and print. When they withhold 'the musical notes which constitute the air of "CA IRA"' for fear of becoming 'chargeable with insidiously propagating the very thing which it was intended should be suppressed, which has happened in all the late trials of this kind', the authors not only mock the government's insistence on secrecy but also imply that the imperatives of governmental secrecy have become in themselves a source of political publicity, not least for the periodical press (5–6).

The effect of these shifts and inclusions is to emphasize the mediations of radical print, confirming 'that every mischief in the world has been occasioned by the NORTHERN STAR' (25).[25] This assertion heralds the militia attack on the *Northern Star* in 1797 as well as the destruction of *The Press* in 1798. At the same time, and in keeping with these attacks, it is, in the imagination of the writers, the 'Seditious Organ' itself that is on trial, under a series of aliases, rather than its proprietors. The pamphlet substitutes 'Hurdy Gurdy', the real name the newspaper is satirically charged with hiding behind layers of aliases, for the names of its owners and printers. The newspaper is thus represented as a substitute for the secrecy of its producers even as it is credited with political agency.

Secret History of the Historical Novel: Scott's Genre Reform

The press, wrote a correspondent in the *Anti-Jacobin Review* for July 1798, has 'been carrying on an attack, more or less concealed, on the principals of all constitutional authority in church and state'.[26] Broadsides, pamphlets and newspapers – their writers 'either unknown or in contempt' – have 'attack[ed] the bulwarks of our constitution' (58–59). While the moderate reforming press has been 'framing platforms for the artillery, and making mantelets to cover the workmen in the trenches, from the view and fire of the defenders', the popular radical periodicals have 'taken the spade and pickaxe, and wrought diligently at the sap themselves; and when others have been battering the walls, have pushed on the mines under them' (59). Its public output figuratively understood as an underground, subversive activity, the press becomes a war machine. In part, the correspondent argues, the efficacy of its 'concealed' underminings results from 'a change … taking place in society during more than the last half century: literary topics have been much more frequently the matter of conversation' (57). According to the writer, this change makes British and Irish readers susceptible to what he calls, quoting Edmund Burke, 'the French spirit of proselytism' (58).

In his genre-reforming comments on the print culture of the earlier 1790s, Burke had used a similar rhetoric of war. His posthumous *Thoughts on French Affairs* (1797) laments that the circulation of English radical newspapers makes them 'infinitely more efficacious and extensive' than French papers, having become 'part of the reading of all' and 'the whole of the reading of the far greater number'.[27] In this way the periodicals function 'like a battery in which the stroke of any one ball produces no great effect, but the amount of continual repetition is decisive' (348). The result, Burke argued in his better-known *Reflections on the Revolution in France* (1790), is the loss of human nature, cultural particularity and the triumph of abstraction and system. Yet, he suggests, British readers 'have not yet been completely emboweled of our natural entrails [and] … drawn and trussed, in order that we may be filled … with chaff and rags, and paltry, blurred shreds of paper about the rights of man'.[28] The claims of Burke and his conservative contemporaries about the efficacy of 'literature', taken together with the emphasis on the moral weight of the private lives of political actors and readers, and the sense that these privacies have been undermined by corruption, suggest the legacy of secret history.

In the essays of the antiquarian Isaac D'Israeli in particular, the relationship of secret history to the moral significance of literature and private character is explicit. In his second series of *Curiosities of Literature* (1823), D'Israeli published several small pieces that he designated secret histories and provided something like a definition of the genre as he understood its contemporary character. 'Secret history is the supplement of history itself', D'Israeli wrote and is, therefore, 'its great corrector'.[29] Secret history worked at the limits of what D'Israeli called 'public history', its view of particularities and intimacies complementing the generalities of historiography:

> The combination of secret with public history has in itself a perfection, which each taken separately has not. The popular historian composes a plausible rather than an accurate tale; … and facts, presented as they occurred, would not adapt themselves to those theoretical writers of history who arrange events not in a natural, but in a systematic order. But in secret history we are more busied in observing what passes than in being told of it … [I]t is by this more intimate acquaintance with persons and circumstances that we are enabled to correct the less distinct, and sometimes the fallacious appearances in the page of the popular historian.[30]

April London argues that D'Israeli's pursuit of a literary historical alternative to the 'conventional modes of history writing' constitutes a critique of the abstractions of Enlightenment conjectural history from the standpoint of the "psychological" rendering of secret history'.[31] Her argument lends D'Israeli and, by extension, the secret history genre a crucial place amid a broader narrative of historical critique, a practice of genre reform described by, among others, Ina Ferris, Katie Trumpener, Yoon Sun Lee and Ian Duncan.

In this strain of revisionist historicism, 'the antiquarian episteme', as Lee calls it, characterized by 'scattered material and discursive fragments', opposes itself to theories of the nation propounded by conjectural historians, especially those of the Scottish Enlightenment, as continuous and inevitable.[32] A frequent medium of antiquarian historical critique, as Ferris and Trumpener show, was the 'national tale', a narrative genre characterized by 'alternation between the formulaic and formal experimentation', an emphasis on the local and on uneven development and an essentially pragmatic purpose: *address about* as much as *representation of* its subject.[33] To this list of formal features James Mulvihill has recently added 'elaborate narrative apparatus', which, he argues, identifies the national tale as a subset of secret history.[34] Taken together, these features, common though not universal among national tales, emphasize the authenticity claims of these works and identify the history they recount as 'at once common and privileged', intended to be kept hidden but now made broadly accessible.[35]

The narratologically complex historical novels of Walter Scott, with their layered prefaces and competing claims of origin and authorship, have been understood, formally, as a 'sublation of the antiquarian episteme'.[36] The connection with D'Israeli's secret-historical project, and its contexts in the genre-reforming scene of Romantic-period print culture, suggests that the novels should also be read as incorporating and redeploying the features of secret history, and as doing so for ends that resemble those of the earlier genre. Such a reading allows us to identify not only such features of the novels as Edward Waverley's participation in the 1745 Jacobite rebellion, in which he gets caught up because he is motivated by the adventurous spirit of 'romance', but also those such as Jeanie Deans's visit to an incognito Caroline of Ansbach, consort of George II, in an attempt to win clemency for her sister, condemned for a child-murder of which she is innocent, as aspects of Scott's project of genre reform: key features in his historiographic critique.[37]

The petition to the queen in *The Heart of Midlothian* (1818) is rarely considered in scholarship addressing Scott's antiquarian ethos. Yet, to the extent that its aesthetic and ethical force are inherited from secret history, the scene of Jeanie's visit to London, under the guidance of the Duke of Argyle, her landlord and patron, constitutes a more obvious critique of public or standard history. Scott tells his readers, in the omniscient, truth-telling third-person yet as if confidentially, about the private character and the secret (and open secret) career of Argyle, with whom the queen has 'taken care not to break entirely', even as she schemes with his enemies:

> the great services which he had rendered the house of Brunswick in 1715, placed him high in that rank of persons who were not to be rashly neglected. He had, almost by his single and unassisted talents, stopped the irruption of the banded force of all the Highland chiefs; there was little doubt, that, with the slightest encouragement, he could put them all in motion, and renew the civil war; and it was well known that the most flattering overtures had been transmitted to the Duke from the court of St Germains.[38]

Scott also describes the 'private correspondences' and secret motives of Caroline herself (12: 379). We learn that her 'real possession of power, rather than the show of it' depends on her representing her brokerage of 'many a political intrigue' as the 'mere intercourse of society' (12: 379). We learn that she has

> contrived that one of her principal attendants, Lady Suffolk, should unite in her own person the two apparently inconsistent characters, of her husband's mistress, and her own very obsequious and complaisant confidante. By this dexterous management the Queen secured her power against the danger which might most have threatened it.[39]

We learn that she desires Argyle 'to use her personal intercession in making his peace with the administration', with which he is at odds, thereby increasing her own power (12: 384–385). And we watch as Jeanie unwittingly offends her by responding to her assessment of Scotland as 'barbarous' with the observation that 'there are many places besides Scotland where mothers are unkind to their own flesh and blood', a remark that Caroline, well-known to be at odds with her eldest son, takes to herself as the open secret of public opinion; and by innocently referring to Scottish punishments for adultery as the causes of child-murder, affronting both Suffolk and the queen herself (12: 390–391).

That the queen is disguised and anonymous, identifying herself only at the end of the encounter, when she gives Jeanie a needle-case as a remembrance, draws Scott's scene especially close to the secret history, with its narratives of pseudonymous sexual and political intrigue, not least among the women of the court. If, as Lee and others have suggested, Scott's genre-reforming engagement with history focuses on the need to temper abstractions with local detail, capturing aspects of the uneven development of different polities and spaces, it also emphasizes another, partisan and more generally political, corrective. The scenes of court secrecy underline the indispensable role of aristocracy and monarchy – even at their most sexually perverse and politically corrupt – in secretly guaranteeing the wellbeing of ordinary Britons and, indeed, the justice of governance in Britain.

Austen's Politics: Secret History in *Emma* and *Mansfield Park*

Carnell argues that 'by the mid-eighteenth century many novelists had borrowed narratological tropes of secret history', while the 'more obviously politicized genre' of secret history itself became 'less recognizable to scholars as a strand of literary history' (5–6). By the Romantic period, as I have suggested, the contemporary relevance of the genre, at least to British and Irish politics, was also in evident decline. If the novelization of secret history made its conventions newly available to 'literary' interpretation, by extension this process may have contributed to obscure the persistent political implications the conventions brought with them into novels. Conversely, however, considering novelization – the process that, Clifford Siskin suggests, made print culture 'safe' in the eyes of an uneasy British establishment in the 1810s and after – might also help identify, in novels borrowing from secret history, a political agency otherwise difficult to discern.[40]

When Harriet Smith displays her '*Most precious treasures*' to her patron in *Emma* (1816), it is difficult, on the face of it, to imagine a political reading:

> Harriet unfolded the parcel ... Within abundance of silver paper was a pretty little Tunbridge-ware box, which Harriet opened: it was well lined with the softest cotton; but, excepting the cotton, Emma saw only a small piece of court plaister [and] ... the end of an old pencil, – the part without any lead.[41]

Like many antiquarian artefacts, the objects touched by Mr Elton that comprise Harriet's museum are trivial and valueless. Yet their enclosure in layers of paper and cotton satirically mirrors the print apparatuses surrounding secrets in national tales and historical novels, as well as in secret histories. Read in the light of secret history, the banality of Harriet's secrets suggests a displacement of further truths revealed by the scene: the inaccessibility, to Emma as well as Harriet, of politically meaningful details; the blindness of both to the motives of those around them, especially men who, like Mr Knightley and Frank Churchill, live lives beyond the narrator's representational compass.[42] What *Emma* discloses, in its scalar play with privacy and triviality, is the hidden truth of an uneven development that plays out, in classed and gendered ways, across the domestic landscape.

Considering the formal legacy of secret history sheds a more ambitious geopolitical light on Fanny Price's contemplation of the artefacts of her childhood in *Mansfield Park* (1814):

> Every thing was a friend, or bore her thoughts to a friend; and though there had been sometimes much of suffering to her – though her motives had been often misunderstood, her feelings disregarded, and her comprehension under-valued; though she had known the pains of tyranny, of ridicule, and neglect … the whole was now so blended together, so harmonized by distance, that every former affliction had its charm.[43]

Aravamudan terms secret history 'a genre of Enlightenment Orientalism, involving parallel systems of reference … allowing for invective and disavowal' (207). He is thinking of 'eastern' scenes that become 'the screen of projection' for western ideals and fears (204). The 'East Room' of Fanny Price's private retreat becomes, however, the object of explicitly comparative historiographical reflection. Fanny considers questions of scale ('every thing' versus 'harmonized by distance'), aligning one with the experience of 'tyranny … and neglect', the other with a 'charm' unlocked by the abstractions of retrospect. Recent criticism explicates the interventions of *Mansfield Park* in the history of slavery in colonial Antigua, on which the income of Mansfield depends. As the legacy of secret history, however, the shifting scales and historicized details of Fanny's East Room place the novel's gestures to plantation slavery, and the antiquarian tropes that couch them, in a wider context: the ironic genre-reforming critique of British imperial history.

According to Siskin, Jane Austen is the 'safest', most tactically 'depolemicized' of novelists (193, 200). Her novels, Michael McKeon argues, normalize the privatization of national-historical concerns 'within the bounds of family life', so that 'themes of tyranny and the liberties of the subject have been decisively, and all but invisibly, woven into the fabric of the private'.[44] When the conventions of Austen's novels are read as the ironic inheritance of secret history, however, their politics leaps into relief.

Indeed, her works suggest that critical focus on 'realism' in the nineteenth-century novel can be achieved only from a distance that overlooks the legacies of seventeenth-century historiography to Romantic fiction.

Notes

1. John Bugg, *Five Long Winters: The Trials of British Romanticism* (Stanford: Stanford University Press, 2014), 144.
2. Michel Foucault, *The History of Sexuality*, vol. 1, trans. Robert Hurley (New York: Pantheon, 1978), 69–70.
3. John Barrell, *Imagining the King's Death: Figurative Treason, Fantasies of Regicide, 1790–1796* (Oxford: Oxford University Press, 2000), 85.
4. Rebellion Papers 620/15/8, National Archives of Ireland; see Kevin Whelan, *The Tree of Liberty: Radicalism, Catholicism, and the Construction of Irish Identity, 1760–1830* (Cork: Cork University Press, 1996), 67–71.
5. Eve Tavor Bannet, '"Secret History": Or, Talebearing Inside and Outside the Secretorie', *Huntington Library Quarterly* 68:1–2 (2005), 375.
6. *Secret History of the Green Room* (London, 1792); *Secret History of Lewis XI* (London, 1823) and Lewis Goldsmith, *Secret History of the Cabinet of Bonaparte* (London, 1810); *Secret History of the French Revolution* (London, 1797).
7. Anne Hamilton, *Secret History of the Court of England, from the Accession of George the Third to the Death of George the Fourth*, 2 vols. (London, 1832). A narrative rather than documentary compendium, this partisan but relatively low-risk work compared Viscount Castlereagh, Tory Leader of the Commons in the 1810s, to King John and purported to reveal the 'murder' of Charlotte, daughter of George IV, who died in childbirth in 1817 (1: 273, 291).
8. William Wordsworth, Preface (1800) to *Lyrical Ballads*, in *Prose Works*, ed. W. J. B. Owen and Jane Worthington Smyser (Oxford: Clarendon, 1974), 1: 28; William Hazlitt, *Life of Napoleon Buonaparte*, vols. 13–14 of *Complete Works*, ed. P. P. Howe, 21 vols. (London: Dent, 1931), 13: 38.
9. Rachel Carnell, 'Slipping from Secret History to Novel', *Eighteenth-Century Fiction* 28:1 (2015), 7.
10. Srinivas Aravamudan, *Enlightenment Orientalism: Resisting the Rise of the Novel* (Chicago: University of Chicago Press, 2012), 58, 62.
11. Jon Klancher, 'Godwin and the Genre Reformers: On Necessity and Contingency in Romantic Narrative Theory', in *Romanticism, History, and the Possibilities of Genre: Re-forming Literature 1789–1837*, eds. Tilottama Rajan and Julia M. Wright (Cambridge: Cambridge University Press, 1998), 22.
12. William Dowdall, *The Press* (Dublin, 1798), 2.
13. Francis Rawdon-Hastings, Letter to General Lake, 2 Feb. 1798, quoted in Gillian O'Brien, '"Spirit, Impartiality and Independence": *The Northern Star*, 1792–1797', *Eighteenth-Century Ireland/Iris an dá chultúr* 13 (1998), 21.
14. Dowdall, 2. See Nancy Curtin, *The United Irishmen: Popular Politics in Ulster and Dublin, 1791–1798* (Oxford: Oxford University Press, 1994), 223.

15 See Mary Helen Thuente, *The Harp Re-strung: The United Irishmen and the Rise of Irish Literary Nationalism* (Syracuse: Syracuse University Press, 1994), 108.
16 Margaret Jacob, 'Sociability and the International Republican Conversation', in *Romantic Sociability: Social Networks and Literary Culture in Britain, 1770–1840*, eds. Gillian Russell and Clara Tuite (Cambridge: Cambridge University Press, 2002), 25.
17 Review of John Gifford, *A Short Address to the Members of the Loyal Associations*, Anti-Jacobin Review and Magazine 1.2 (August 1798), 184.
18 Review of Gifford, 184–5.
19 *The Press* 69 (17 March 1798), 1.
20 Kevin Gilmartin, *Print Politics: The Press and Radical Opposition in Early Nineteenth-Century England* (Cambridge: Cambridge University Press, 1996), 76, 115.
21 For example, Gifford, Review of Robert Bisset, *History of the Reign of George III*, Anti-Jacobin Review and Magazine 18.73 (July 1804), 246.
22 *Trial of Mr. Peter Fin[n]erty, Late Printer of The Press, for a Libel against His Excellency Earl Camden, Lord Lieutenant of Ireland* (Dublin, 1798); *The Press* 17 (4 November 1797), 2; *The Press* 33 (12 December 1797), 3.
23 *Report of the Trial of the King Versus Hurdy Gurdy* (Dublin, 1794), likely written by United Irishmen William Sampson and Thomas Russell.
24 Quoted in O'Brien, 19; only the printer was convicted. For further background, see O'Brien, 7–23 and Thuente, '"The Belfast Laugh": The Context and Significance of United Irish Satires', in *Revolution, Counter-Revolution, and Union: Ireland in the 1790s*, ed. Jim Smyth (Cambridge: Cambridge University Press, 2000), 67–82.
25 See O'Brien, 13.
26 Letter to the editor, *Anti-Jacobin Review and Magazine* 1 (1798), 58.
27 Edmund Burke, *Thoughts on French Affairs Written in the Years 1791, 1792 and 1793*, in *The French Revolution, 1790–1794*, ed. L. G. Mitchell, vol. 8 of *Writings and Speeches*, gen. ed. Paul Langford, 9 vols. (Oxford: Clarendon Press, 1990), 348.
28 Burke, *Reflections on the Revolution in France*, in *The French Revolution*, 137.
29 Isaac D'Israeli, 'True Sources of Secret History', *Curiosities of Literature*, ed. Benjamin Disraeli, 3 vols. (London: Warne, [n.d.]), 380.
30 'True Sources', 380.
31 April London, *Literary History Writing, 1770–1820* (Basingstoke and New York: Palgrave, 2010), 98, 109.
32 Yoon Sun Lee, 'A Divided Inheritance: Scott's Antiquarian Novel and the British Nation', *ELH* 64:2 (1997), 538–9.
33 Katie Trumpener, 'National Character, Nationalist Plots: National Tale and Historical Novel in the Age of *Waverley*, 1806–1830', *ELH* 60:3 (1993): 690, 693; Ina Ferris, *The Romantic National Tale and the Question of Ireland* (Cambridge: Cambridge University Press, 2002), 11. See also Ian Duncan,

Scott's Shadow: The Novel in Romantic Edinburgh (Princeton: Princeton University Press, 2007), 96–8.

34 James Mulvihill, 'Edgeworth's *Castle Rackrent* as Secret History', *Papers on Language and Literature* 49:4 (2013), 339.
35 Mulvihill, 'Edgeworth's *Castle Rackrent*', 345.
36 Lee, 'A Divided Inheritance', 538.
37 Walter Scott, *Waverley; or, 'Tis Sixty Years Since*, 3 vols. (Edinburgh: Ballantyne, 1814), 2: 260, 302.
38 Scott, *The Heart of Midlothian*, vols. 11–13 of *The Waverley Novels*, 48 vols. (London: Cadell, 1830), 12: 380.
39 Scott, *Midlothian*, 12: 380–1.
40 Clifford Siskin, *The Work of Writing: Literature and Social Change in Britain, 1700–1830* (Baltimore: Johns Hopkins University Press, 1998), 193, 201–2.
41 Jane Austen, *Emma*, ed. James Kinsley (Oxford: Oxford University Press, 2003), 265–6, emphasis in original.
42 See William Galperin, *The Historical Austen* (Philadelphia: University of Pennsylvania Press, 2005), 180–213.
43 Austen, *Mansfield Park*, ed. James Kinsley (Oxford: Oxford University Press, 2003), 119–20.
44 Michael McKeon, *The Secret History of Domesticity: Public, Private, and the Division of Knowledge* (Baltimore: Johns Hopkins University Press, 2005), 693.

PART III
France and America

14

Secret History in Pre-Revolutionary France

Allison Stedman

Although history had been a popular subject of French novelistic production throughout the sixteenth and seventeenth centuries, the first work to bear the name 'histoire secrète' in its title was published in Paris in 1669 by the bookseller Guillaume de Luynes. This work, entitled *Histoire secrète de Procope de Césarée* was not an original work, but rather a translation (by Leonor de Mauger, who wrote under the initials 'L. de M'.) of the *Anekdota* or *Apokrypha historia* originally published by the Byzantine historian Procopius around 550 AD. As Peter Burke describes, when Procopius' account of the scandalous private life of the empress Theodora first appeared in print in 1623, its revelation of previously undivulged events intrigued readers all over the European continent and sparked a veritable vogue as authors scrambled to capitalize on the *Anekdota*'s popularity.[1] Between 1658 and 1725 more than seventy texts announcing themselves as 'secret histories' were published in Latin, Italian, French, German, English and Dutch. In France, during the 1690s and early 1700s, multiple secret histories were being printed every year and when the genre experienced a slight decline during the late 1720s, a monthly journal entitled *Anecdotes ou lettres secrètes sur divers sujets de littérature et de politique* [*Anecdotes or Secret Letters about Various Literary and Political Subjects*] picked up the slack, publishing, as the anonymous editor claims in the 'Avertissement' to the February 1734 inaugural volume: 'une foule de faits propres à réjouir et à instruire' [a proliferation of facts suitable for enjoyment and instruction], thus giving the general public the ability to 'découvrir mille circonstances piquantes, sans lesquelles les faits sont presque toujours peu intéressants' [discover a thousand scintillating circumstances without which the facts are almost always of little interest].[2]

Literary historians have long been intrigued by the rise in production of historical novels, memoirs and pseudo-memoirs during the second part of the seventeenth century. As Faith E. Beasley describes in her seminal study *Revising Memory: Women's Fiction and Memoirs in Seventeenth-Century*

France, women writers in particular turned to these genres as a way to uncover what official historical accounts left out, complementing and supplementing the 'general history' that had been generated by official historiography throughout centuries with a more 'particular' type of history.[3] Instead of seeking to lay out a broad view of the treaties, wars, acts of sovereignty and other events occurring uniquely in the public sector, authors of 'particular history' brought to light the motives and passions behind such officially recorded events, exploring the details and reasoning that underlay the public matters of general history and including actions and individuals that were otherwise excluded from the general record.[4] As Beasley points out, although general histories had long been restricted to the revelation of military campaigns, royal decrees and other public events, Louis XIV's desire to achieve a monopoly over general history during the early decades of his reign made it so that anyone who sought to dabble in particular history offered at least an inadvertent challenge to Louis XIV's absolutism by providing a competing narrative to the official history generated by the crown.[5]

Like the other historically motivated genres that rose in popularity during the French seventeenth century, secret histories challenged the official historical narrative by infusing official relations of public events with details and perspectives related to the 'particular'. However 'secret histories' emerged nearly three decades after historical novels and memoirs had dominated the French literary landscape. While the latter genres had risen to prominence primarily in the wake of the mid-century aristocratic rebellion known as *The Fronde* (1648–1653), secret history took over as a dominant mode of historical fiction during the 1690s, following the centralization of the royal court at Versailles (1682), the decline of the Parisian salon and the increase in the state supervision of individuals following the Colbert administration (1665–1683). As such, the increasing scepticism characteristic of the literary elite during the final decades of Louis XIV's reign can be seen in the way that secret histories position themselves with respect to the absolute nature of royal authority. Although memoirs and historical fiction had suggested that multiple interpretations of public events might be possible – viewing official history from an individualized perspective in the case of memoirs or encouraging readers to imagine alternative perspectives on historical events in the case of pseudo-memoirs and historical novels – none of these narratives asserted that general history's version of the past may in fact be intentionally contrived, obscuring historical truth more so than actually revealing it. Whereas Louis XIV's model of historical discourse had implied that, as Beasley describes, the king was the only historical subject capable of providing the public with access both to 'great events' and to 'general truths', secret history maintained the opposite perspective, calling into question the fundamental truth of any great event whose narrative authority rested on the observation of outward appearances.[6] As such, secret historians not only challenged the details of officially sanctioned historical narratives, but also the hierarchy implicit in the construction of such texts, taking knowledge and power out of the hands of the crown and placing it in the hands of individual citizens who in turn disseminated such knowledge throughout the Republic of Letters.

The exposure of state secrets to the general public had a particular resonance in late seventeenth-century France, since the proper functioning of the absolutist political machine was dependent on the ability of such information to be kept between the king and a few key members of his trusted inner circle. As Jacob Soll describes in *The Information Master: Jean-Baptiste Colbert's Secret State Intelligence System*, although the king's prime minister may have fallen short of his plan to institute a complete absolute government, between 1661 and 1683, 'Colbert [nonetheless] showed Louis how he could dominate and use the world of learning not only as a source of public propaganda, but also as a tool of secret government'.[7] With Louis XIV's benediction, Colbert spent his entire career as prime minister constructing a secret information system designed to assure the monarch's absolute control over all matters related to his kingdom, amassing a state archive that contained some 36,000 printed books and 10,500 manuscripts by the time of his death. He complemented these works with an elaborate reference system that paired book catalogues with textual extracts and glossaries designed to make them accessible for daily, practical political use.[8] As Soll describes, since Colbert's manuscripts were the source of the king's absolutist political power, it was imperative that 'they were to remain secret'.[9] Colbert had no time for the 'formalities of the Republic of Letters', which included openness and commitment to the free exchange of information; his refusal to participate in the commerce of ideas extended to the creation of the official historical narrative devoted to commemorating the glorious moments of Louis XIV's reign. As Beasley explains, the group of historiographers assigned to help Louis XIV create an official memoir of his reign were forbidden from including any information alluding to the interior realms of personality traits and state secrets, to the point that when one of Louis XIV's historiographers

(Charpentier) asked for secret documents to help him in his historiographical undertaking, Colbert rejected the request and Charpentier was forced to resign.[10]

By the time Colbert passed away in 1683, Louis XIV's reliance on secrecy as a tool for maintaining social and political stability was so well known among his subjects that access to secrecy and access to political power had become almost synonymous. In the 1683 hybrid literary compilation entitled *Le Secret, nouvelles historiques avec le Compliment des Vertus au Roy sur la Naissance de Monseigneur le Duc de Bourgogne* [*The Secret, Historical Novels with the Virtues' Compliment to the King on the Birth of Monsieur the Duke de Bourgogne*], for example, the disfavoured aristocrat and rococo novelist Jean de Préchac not only compared Louis XIV's use of secret government to that of other powerful statesmen throughout history, but he also presented the general reader with a model for how secrecy could be used to achieve personal ends, a strategy of particular importance if those ends involved the subversion of the reigning political system.[11] For Préchac, the key to funnelling secret information into the Republic of Letters without opening oneself up to censorship lay in the ability to manipulate the potential of generic heterogeneity and multiplicity to one's own advantage. Rather than presenting the reader with an isolated narrative or a single perspective, which could easily make its author the victim of censorship, Préchac strung together sequences of seemingly unrelated anecdotes, which the reader must read linearly and diachronically to perceive the true meaning of the whole. In *Le Secret*, for example, Préchac does not attack Louis XIV's system of government overtly; he does so secretly by relativizing short stories about the king's use of secrecy to promote social stability with a plethora of other anecdotes in which the relationship between secrecy and absolute authority is called into question. The result is the creation of a literary work that not only subverts Louis XIV's absolutist policies on the level of content, but also on the level of form, encouraging his readers to perpetuate the secret circulation of subversive ideas by making use of a literary technique that ran counter to the standards of generic purity espoused and enforced by the monarchically sanctioned French Academy.[12] This technique would be employed to great effect by secret historians. As Peter Burke describes: 'The method is generally to tell a succession of anecdotes, in the modern sense of the term. Secret history was anecdotal in its methods as well as in its definition'.[13]

With the exception of some anonymous Mazarinades published at the turn of the 1650s and of a small number of classical 'secret histories' set in Antiquity that had originally been published in Latin or Ancient Greek, the first secret history appeared in French in 1685 when Antoine Varillas published *Les Anecdotes de Florence, ou l'Histoire secrète de la maison de Médicis* [*Florentine Anecdotes, or the Secret History of the House of Medici*].[14] His text was followed half a decade later by several anonymous translations of secret histories originally published in English, including the *Histoire secrète des règnes des rois Charles II et Jacques II. Traduit de l'Anglais* [*Secret History of the Reigns of King Charles II and James II. Translated from English*] (1690), which was published in Cologne by the publisher Pierre Marteau; and the *Histoire secrète de la duchesse de Portsmouth* [*Secret History of the Duchess of Portsmouth*], which was published successively in 1690 and 1691 in Holland and London. During the mid 1690s, a small group of authors who were also involved in the creation and dissemination of the French literary fairy tale vogue also published secret histories, to the delight of the worldly public.[15] Charlotte-Rose Caumont de la Force's *Histoire secrète de Marie de Bourgogne* [*Secret History of Mary of Burgundy*] (1694), for example, was reprinted at least three times in 12 months by presses in Paris, Lyon and The Hague; and her 1695 *Histoire secrète de Henri IV, roi de Castille* [*Secret History of Henry IV, King of Castillo*] was met with similar enthusiasm, with at least three additional editions appearing in France and Holland in 1695 alone. By 1699, Jean de Mailly (also known as Louis de Mailly), Eustache Le Noble and Nicholas Beaudot de Juilly, together with La Force and a small number of anonymous authors, had contributed to the publication of nearly a dozen new examples of the genre, causing the moralist critic Abbé Pierre de Villiers to decry the practice in the *Entretiens sur les contes de fées et sur quelques autres ouvrages du temps* [*Inquiry on Fairy Tales and on Some Other Recently Published Works*], a lengthy diatribe written in the form of a dialogue and submitted to the French Academy in 1699. As Villiers' explains in the treatise's third inquiry, although it had been bad enough when a large number of unknowledgeable and uneducated authors were flooding the French literary market with novels and short stories, the situation had recently become far worse now that these same authors were attempting to pose as historians:

> [le problème avec] tant d'auteurs c'est qu'ils croient qu'on peut faire certains Livres sans avoir ni science, ni érudition; ils mettent les Romans au nombre de ces Livres-là; ils veulent être auteurs, il n'ont point envie d'étudier, et [de pire] la plupart se croient capable de faire autre chose, et [ainsi] l'on en a vu entreprendre d'écrire l'Histoire, sans avoir d'autre habilité que d'avoir fait quelques Romans.[16]
>
> [the problem with so many authors is that they think that they certain books can be written without having either knowledge or erudition; they

place novels among the books in this category; they want to be authors (but) they have no desire to study. And even worse, the majority of these think themselves capable of doing other things as well, and some have even been seen to undertake the writing of History without having any other credentials apart from having written some novels.]

As Villiers' concerns reveal, it was one thing to publish history and frame it as a novel or a memoir, but quite another to announce such material as actual 'History'.

The consequences for dabbling in secret history were potentially so steep that no French author ventured to publish an overt secret history of the French court during Louis XIV's reign.[17] Instead, these authors either focused on marginal courts and historical figures from past centuries, or turned to the central players and politics of foreign courts, exposing the secret inner-workings of the Medicis in the case of Varillas' *Anecdotes de Florence*, or of the late medieval Spanish court in the case of La Force's *Histoire secrète de Henri IV*. In most cases, however, these distant courts and obscure figures served as covers for the exposure of beliefs about the current political system that would not have been acceptable if articulated directly. In La Force's *Histoire secrète de Marie de Bourgogne* for example, the fifteenth-century Burgundian Duke Charles the Bold is presented in language that in the context of seventeenth-century France would have been reserved exclusively for Louis XIV, a strategy that subtly relativizes the unique exceptionality of the current monarch without ever mentioning the king's name or reign directly:

> Charles le Guerrier ou le Téméraire était le plus puissant Prince de son temps; grand par l'étendue de ses Etats; et par ses richesses, chéri de ses Alliés, redouté de ses Ennemis; Il était issu du plus beau Sang de l'Univers, puisqu'il se florissait de tirer son origine de l'Auguste maison de France.[18] [Charles the Warrior or the Fearless was the most powerful Prince of his time; great for his far-reaching estates and for his wealth, cherished by his allies, dreaded by his enemies; he was a descendant of the finest bloodline in the universe because he had the favour of drawing his origins from the noble house of France.]

In using the superlative to glorify a previous French ruler whose aristocratic lineage comes from a different bloodline than that of Louis XIV, La Force implicitly undermines the notion that the current king is the greatest monarch who ever lived: a concept that Louis XIV and his administration put forth a great deal of effort to perpetuate.[19]

The relativization of Louis XIV's exceptionality does not stop with the description of the Duke, however. As La Force reveals, the court of

Charles the Bold is not only the most gallant, superb and flourishing in all of Europe, an honour currently reserved for Louis XIV, but more importantly the origin of the court's superiority is its commitment to a set of values that are completely antithetical to the foundational values of Louis XIV's court at Versailles. While Louis XIV relied on centralization, amplification and exclusivity to ensure the pre-eminence of his own court, it was Charles the Bold's commitment to promoting diversity, variety and inclusivity that made his court the most spectacular in all the universe: 'Sa cour était la plus galante, la plus superbe, et la plus florissante de l'Europe. Elle servait d'asile à tous les malheureux, et il était ordinaire d'y voir des Rois détrônés ou persecutés.'[20] [His court was the most gallant, the most superb, and the most flourishing in Europe. It served as an asylum for all the misfortunate, and it was commonplace to find kings there who were dethroned or persecuted.] By featuring a court in which the inclusion of the marginalized is the source of its superiority and acclaim, La Force effectively reverses the absolutist power dynamic put forward by Louis XIV, a reversal that the literary public of the late seventeenth century would have implicitly understood.

Strategies for circumventing the heightened censorship reserved for any text purporting to announce itself as 'history' included publishing a text resembling a secret history but calling it by a different name, or publishing the work anonymously.[21] The fact that 'secret historians' were so reluctant to associate their names with the texts they created means that the majority of secret histories published in French are either unattributed or misattributed, a problem that confounded literary historians in the seventeenth century and still contributes to confusion around the development of the genre today. Although the 1696 *Mémoires secrètes de plusieurs grands princes de la cour* [*Secret memoirs of the Court's Greatest Princes*] is often attributed to the prolific novelist and fairy-tale writer Marie-Catherine le Jumel de Barneville, comtesse d'Aulnoy, she expressly denies having written, along with a number of other texts resembling secret histories that were falsely attributed to her in the signed preface to the last of her historical novels, *Le Comte de Warwick* [*The Earl of Warwick*] (1703).[22] Similarly, as Philippe Hourcade points out in *Entre pic et rétif: Eustache Le Noble, 1643–1711*, although Eustache Le Noble can be credited with authoring the 1696 *Mylord Courtenay, ou Histoire secrète des premières amours d'Elisabeth d'Angleterre* [*Mylord Courtenay, or the Secret History of the First Loves of Elizabeth of England*], there is no evidence that he authored any of the other secret histories that are generally attributed to him in the catalogue of the French National Library and in Burke's chronology of secret histories published in Europe between 1658 and 1725.²³

During the French Enlightenment, as mistrust of monarchical authority increased so did the popularity of secret histories; these continued to be either composed in French or translated into French on a regular basis from the death of Louis XIV (1715) until the eve of the French Revolution (1789). While such authors as George Lockhart (1681–1731) and Jean Rousset de Missy (1686–1762) intrigued early eighteenth-century readers with secret information about the courts of France, England and Spain, other texts claimed to expose cover-ups by political and religious authorities, as in the 1717 edition of the *Lettres du cardinal de Santa Croce* which professed to reveal previously unknown details on how Protestantism had infiltrated France in the decades leading up to the Edict of Nantes (1598).²⁴ During the mid-eighteenth century, as during the final decades of Louis XIV's reign, a revival of the literary fairy-tale vogue drew in several authors already famous for their secret histories, including Madeleine-Angélique Poisson de Gomez, whose *Histoire secrète de la conquête de Grenade* [*Secret History of the Conquest of Grenada*] (1719) and *Anecdotes ou histoire secrète de la maison ottomane* [*Anecdotes or Secret History of the House of Ottoman*] (1724) remained among the most popular and widely circulated secret histories of the early to mid-eighteenth century. Secret histories were also published alongside literary fairy tales and other genres in multi-volume literary anthologies such as the *Bibliothèque de campagne*;²⁵ and some authors even went so far as to combine secret histories with fairy tales and short stories in a single work, as in Charles de Fieux, chevalier de Mouhy's *L'amante anonyme, ou l'histoire secrète de la volupté. Avec des contes nouveaux de fées* [*The Anonymous Lover of the Secret History of Sensuality. With Some New Fairy Tales*] (1755–1756). As Vivian R. Gruder describes in *The Notables and the Nation: The Political Schooling of the French, 1787–1788*, the licentious nature of secret histories already apparent in works such as Mouhy's only increased in the decades leading up to the French Revolution with the circulation of handwritten and printed newsletters that combined secret histories with information from a variety of sources, including news reports, letters, publications, prohibited manuscripts, police reports and rumours.²⁶ These newsletters were often reprinted in series such as the multi-volume *Correspondance littéraire secrète* [*Secret Literary Correspondance*], which appeared regularly in France throughout the 1770s and 1780s.²⁷

Although the historical credibility of these types of texts became increasingly suspect and the reputations of their authors in many cases became increasingly questionable, secret histories nonetheless helped the creation of the publicly critical culture of the French Enlightenment by suffusing the print marketplace with an atmosphere of suspicion and by helping to create a cultural climate in which it was not unheard of to question the official versions of things, even when these versions had been generated by official channels and passed down as history for decades if not centuries.[28] In implying that the official narrative of history was open to other possibilities, secret histories modelled a relationship to the past that ran counter not only to the transfer of historical truth, but also to the transfer of monarchical power from one generation to the next. As such, the genre not only infused the lofty genre of history with the more lowly genres of anecdote and gossip, but more importantly it reduced the lofty and untouchable individuals whose decisions determined the fortunes of the state into average individuals whose passions and emotions were as capable of influencing their decisions as was the rational advice of their ministers. It was this new relationship both to authority and to the past that would make the French Revolution possible.

Notes

1 Peter Burke, 'The Rise of "Secret History"', in *Changing Perceptions of the Public Sphere*, eds. Christian J. Emden and David Midgley (New York and Oxford: Berghahn Books, 2012), 60.
2 'Avertissement', *Anecdotes ou lettres secrètes sur divers sujets de littérature et de politique* (February 1734), i–ii. Although both the publisher and place of publication are anonymous, the journal, which appeared monthly from February of 1734 to June of 1736, is generally attributed to Antoine-Augustin Bruzen de La Martinière, who also edited the ten-volume *Grand dictionnaire géographique et critique* between 1726 and 1739. If La Martinière is, in fact, the editor, the journal would likely have been published in Amsterdam.
3 Faith E. Beasley, *Revising Memory: Women's Fiction and Memoirs in Seventeenth-Century France* (Rutgers: Rutgers University Press, 1990), 20–9. As Beasley explains, particular history: 'is not synonymous with what modern historians call "private history" because … the content of this account is not severed completely from that of general history or from the public sphere – a severance connoted by the term "private" ' (29).
4 Beasley, *Revising Memory*, 12–13, 29.
5 Beasley, *Revising Memory*, 1–2.
6 Beasley, *Revising Memory*, 19.
7 Jacob Soll, *The Information Master: Jean-Baptiste Colbert's Secret State Intelligence System* (Ann Arbor, MI: University of Michigan Press, 2009), 6–7.
8 Soll, *The Information Master*, 7.
9 Soll, *The Information Master*, 102.

10 Beasley, *Revising Memory*, 15.
11 Jean de Préchac, *Le Secret, nouvelles historiques. Avec le Compliment de Vertus au Roy sur la Naissance de Monseigneur le Duc de Bourgogne* (Paris, 1683). The privilege for Préchac's work was issued on 24 November 1682.
12 For an in-depth analysis of how Préchac's 'public-secret' literary technique operates in this text, see Allison Stedman, *Rococo Fiction in France, 1600–1715: Seditious Frivolity* (Lewisburg: Bucknell University Press, 2013), 114–25.
13 Burke, 'The Rise of "Secret History"', 61.
14 Supporters of the *Fronde* occasionally published 'Anti-Mazarin' pamphlets that claimed to reveal secret information about the inner workings of the royal government in the hope that the cultivation of public mistrust and suspicion would garner support for the rebel cause. See, for example, the 39-page pamphlet entitled, 'La conférence secrète du cardinal Mazarin avec le gazetier, envoyée de Bruxelles le septième May dernier' (Paris, 1649).
15 This took place between 1690 and 1715. For more on the literary fairy tale vogue, to which Préchac was also an influential contributor, see Lewis Seifert, *Fairy Tales, Sexuality and Gender in France (1690–1715): Nostalgic Utopias* (Cambridge: Cambridge University Press, 1996) and Raymonde Robert, *Le conte de fées littéraire en France de la fin du XVIIe à la fin du XVIIIe siècle* (Paris: Honoré Champion, 2002). Other practitioners who also published secret histories in the early eighteenth century include Le Noble, Mailly, La Force and Catherine Durand, also known as Catherine Bédacier (1670–1736). Almost all of the authors who published literary fairy tales at the turn of the eighteenth century, including Marie-Catherine d'Aulnoy, also published memoirs or works of historical fiction that resembled secret histories without actually mentioning the words in their titles. For the slippery nature of the term, see Rachel Carnell, 'Slipping from Secret History to Novel', *Eighteenth-Century Fiction* 28:1 (Fall 2015), 1–24.
16 Abbé Pierre de Villiers, *Entretiens sur les contes de fées, et sur quelques autres ouvrages du temps: Pour servir de préservatif contre le mauvais goût* (Paris, 1699), 117–18.
17 There is no evidence, for example, that Eustache Le Noble ever wrote the English text entitled *The Cabinet Open'd, or, The Secret History of the Amours of Madam de Maintenon* (London, 1690), although the text is often attributed to him. See also, note 22.
18 Charlotte-Rose Caumont de la Force, *Histoire secrète de Marie de Bourgogne, divisée en deux volumes* (Lyon, 1694), 1.
19 Charles the Bold was from the house of Valois, while Louis XIV was of Bourbon lineage.
20 La Force, *Histoire secrète de Marie de Bourgogne*, 2.
21 For this reason it is often argued that texts which do not explicitly announce themselves as secret histories could nonetheless be included in this category, particularly those texts published prior to the mid-1680s. See, for example, Anna Arzoumanov's work on Bussy-Rabutin's *Histoire amoureuse des Gaules*, or John D. Lyon's interpretation of Lafayette's *La Comtesse de Tende*. Anna

Arzoumanov, '*L'Histoire amoureuse des Gaules*, entre chronique scandaleuse et divertissement galant', *Littératures Classiques* 54 (2005), 141–51. John D. Lyons, 'La Présence d'esprit et l'Histoire Secrète: Une Lecture de la Comtesse de Tende', *XVIIe Siècle* 45:181 (1993), 717–32.

22 For a list of the books that d'Aulnoy claims as properly attributed to her, see Allison Stedman, 'Marie-Catherine 'Marie-Catherine Le Jumel de Barneville, Comtesse d'Aulnoy', in *Dictionary of Literary Biography: Seventeenth-Century French Literature*, ed. Françoise Jaoüen (Detroit: Thompson Gale, 2003), 12–18.

23 These include: *The Cabinet Opened, or The Secret History of the Amours of Madam de Maintenon* (London, 1690), *Histoire secrète de la conjuration des Pazzi* (Genève [Geneva], 1697) and *Epicaris, suite des histoires secrètes des plus fameuses conspirations* (Paris, 1698). For a chronology of secret histories published in Europe between 1658 and 1725, see Burke, 'The Rise of "Secret History"', 67–9. For Le Noble's specific contributions see also, Philippe Hourcade, *Entre pic et rétif: Eustache Le Noble (1643–1711)* (Paris: Amateurs de livres, 1988).

24 Prospero Santa Croce, *Lettres du cardinal di Santa Croce, écrites pendant son nonciature en France, au cardinal Boromée neveu du pape Pie IV. Et tirées des manuscrits originaux de la Bibliothèque du Vatican. Contenant l'histoire secrète de la naissance et des progrès de la religion reformée en France* (La Haye [The Hague], 1717).

25 *Bibliothèque de campagne ou Amusements de l'esprit et du cœur*, 12 vols. (La Haye [The Hague], 1735–52).

26 Vivian R. Gruder, *The Notables and the Nation: The Political Schooling of the French, 1787–1788* (Cambridge MA: Harvard University Press: 2007), 136.

27 For the attribution of the *Correspondance* and for more on this type of literary production, see Gruder, *The Notables and the Nation*, 136–66.

28 See further, Kathryn Hoffman, 'Reality and Power in the *Secret Histories*', *Cahiers-du-Dix-septieme siècle: An Interdisciplinary Journal* 1:1 (1987), 149–58. For the parallel of this phenomenon in England, see Melinda Alliker Rabb, *Satire and Secrecy in English Literature from 1650 to 1750* (Basingstoke and New York: Palgrave MacMillan, 2007), especially 2–8.

15

Secret History in Late Eighteenth- and Early Nineteenth-Century France

Antoinette Sol

The chain of events put in motion in July 1789 changed not only the course of history in France, but also the very notion of history itself. Norbert Elias tells us that different societies conceive of time differently: as cyclical, exemplary, and/or linear. The Revolution disrupted the cyclical or dynastic vision of history by imposing a radical, epistemic break between past and present and introduced the linear model based on progress in which tradition is rejected and the uniqueness of each moment is emphasized. Robert Darnton, in his work on Revolutionary pamphlets, *The Devil in the Holy Water*, explains that, to the French, the social 'order they had destroyed only a few months earlier [seemed] as if it belonged to another era, what they called the '*ancien régime*'.[1] The attempt to interpret contemporary events, to put them in perspective in combination with a newly deregulated press, created the conditions for the explosion of publications in all genres: eyewitness accounts, anecdotes, polemical attacks, memoirs, biographies, slanderous pamphlets, broad sheets announcing rapidly changing official government regulations, laws and policy among others.[2] Along with the changing views of what was considered history came questions on how to write it. During the Revolution, the distinction blurs between reputable and disreputable forms of historical writing. Secret revelations become a weapon in the arsenal of opposing factions published to correct 'history', and they take on a deadly seriousness. Scandalous publications, using familiar forms, took on a new importance in the political firmament during the Revolution. They broke with the past and were integral to emerging modern genres such as journalism, historiography, and the modern biography by circulating breaking news, making use of newly 'liberated' state documents, and through revolutionary and counter-revolutionary *vie privées* [private lives].[3]

The eighteenth century's growing literate population was an avid consumer of both authorized histories and unauthorized, scandalous, and revelatory 'secret' histories. The types of history written in the eighteenth century, both official and secret, included memoirs, *histoires de vie* [life stories], historical anecdotes, along with annals and chronicles. Secret histories mimicked these but also drew upon other genres. *Roman-mémoires* [fictional memoirs], apocryphal memoirs, *libelles* [libels] or pamphlets, private lives, secret histories, *romans à clef*, and anecdotes illuminated recent past events and famous contemporary figures. These texts purported to be based on personal experience, eyewitness accounts, and 'authentic' documents, both real and invented. Their goal was to scandalize the reader with revelations about the private life of a distinguished personality in power and dishonour them. Official history was classical, erudite, didactic, and a function of the state, while contemporary history or counter history came in the form of *libelles*, a term used to refer to scandalous histories and to all sorts of cheap, inexpensively printed, mostly short, satirical, slanderous, and often pornographic pamphlets.[4]

The sheer number of published collections and pamphlets of defamatory discourse is impressive: from 312 in the period 1774–1786, to over 12,000 from 1789–1792.[5] In the years preceding 1789, *libelles*, although increasingly virulent, were read with prurient interest and often with amusement (less so by their targets). They were a quick and dirty way for authors to make money and soil the reputation of an adversary.[6] A lucrative sideline was to be had by offering the manuscript to the party or parties concerned before publication for a sum of money; in effect, the authors blackmailed their targets.[7] The overthrow of the monarchy made all sorts of secret official documents available.[8] Publications such as *La Police de Paris dévoilée* [*The Paris Police Unveiled*] (1790) and *La Bastille dévoilée* [*The Bastille Unveiled*] (1789) by Louis-Pierre Manuel or *Histoire des prisons de Paris* by J. B. Nougaret, were based on documents taken from the Bastille. Other types of secrets unveiled, such as *La Chasteté du clergé dévoilée* [*The Clergy's Chastity Unveiled*] (1790), were very popular. Hidden truths now revealed would figure in new types of secret histories, 'le dépôt encore vierge des Secrets', [the still virgin depot of secrets] such as *Mémoires politiques et militaires, pour server à l'histoire secrète de la revolution française* [*Political and Military Memoires to Serve as a Secret History of the French Revolution*] (1799) by Antoine Sérieys.[9]

The imaginary of the *libelles*, consisting of the accumulation of stereotypes and clichés used and re-circulated, created archetypes rather than portraits of real people. These same archetypes figured in the stories that authors borrowed one from another and readers recognized them easily. In fact, recognition and comparison between versions that either countered a previous *libelle* or confirmed one, constituted, in great part, the pleasure the reader found in the genre.[10] The permanence of the characters described and the recycling of anecdotes contrast with the contemporaneousness of the genre. Woven out of current rumours and into a loose intertextual network, these 'half-humorous, half-damaging' works were taken as *divertissements*; if there were some grains of truth to be found, these were incidental.[11] Chartier points out that the value of this body of ephemera is related to its timeliness: to its quality of 'breaking news'.[12] These *libelles*, then, are at the nexus of two contradictory movements: an unchanging mythological or symbolic imaginary that also partakes of current time, and of accelerated events that characterize Revolutionary times.

The Revolution effectively ends not only History as it is known up until then, but also changes the register and sharpens the purpose of *libelles*. If the pamphlets remain obscene and pornographic, as Antoine de Baecque points out, a new virile hero, patriotic and healthy, with regular and hygeinic sexual practices counterbalances *ancien régime* corruption, represented by the debauched, morally corrupt, and syphilitic aristocrat.[13] The role of pornography in these pamphlets served to signal the division between the old order and the new, emphasizing the idea of regeneration.[14] Metaphors of degeneracy and rebirth abound in an attempt to define the *sans-culotte*, the re-born Frenchman, the taker of the Bastille.[15] Michael Winston proposes that this 'new man' of the Revolution participates in Condorcet's and Volney's vision of progress to 'regenerate humanity through reform and hygiene' and play its part 'in the creation of a new political mythology'.[16] This new regenerated, healthy and heterosexual revolutionary body represents the promise of a new society and partakes of the political Manichaeism of the early years of the Revolution, 1789–1791.[17] The noble's 'aristocratic excess saps the very strength of the body politic'; his sexuality is plagued by impotence. In contrast, the energetic patriot is characterized by his vigour and productive sexual practices manifest in his *régénération foutative* or 'fuckative regeneration'.[18] In one pamphlet, *L'Echo foutromane* [*Erotomaniacal Echo*] (1792), the Revolutionary takes on the aspect of a demi-god. The author, tongue firmly in cheek, describes a wedding night in which the young bride 'conceived of the man who was to come to her bed from the storming of the Bastille, and to take possession of her after overthrowing a tyranny – for it is certain that a regenerated man is a demi-god coiled to spring'.[19] He is the incarnation of Hercules.

The patriot's amorous attention is vigorous and hygienic and sexual congress found itself under the surveillance of the new government. One such publication proposed detailed moral and hygienic rules for a new society.²⁰ *Requête et décret en faveur des putains, des fouteuses, des macquerelles et des branleuses: contre les bougres, les bardaches et les brûleurs de paillasses* [*Petition and Decree in Favour of Prostitutes, Whores, Madams and Masturbatrixes: Against Pederasts, Fags, and Johns Who Refuse to Pay*] (1793) proposes certain regulations to promote healthy sex and to keep the participants disease free. The *Catéchisme libertin à l'usage des filles de joie et des jeunes demoiselles qui se destinent à embrasser cette profession* [*The Libertine's Catechism for the Use of Ladies Pleasure and Young Ladies Who Choose This Profession*] (1791) attributed to Théroigne de Mericourt, participates in this movement by couching healthy guidelines for prostitutes in religious terms. However, as Winston reminds us, there is not a univocal reading of this literature. He points out that while some Revolutionary political figures in the text behaved according to the new principles, Marat in particular 'was singled out for attack and ridicule' and his potency and virility were questioned.²¹ Thierry Pastorello points to the break with former Revolutionary pamphlets: 'The clear and articulate opposition of unnatural and exclusive sexual behaviour of homosexuality to healthy and socially productive "conjugal" behaviour, along with demographical allusions, appears to be innovative.'²² Above all, the pamphleteers relished putting the patriot or the democratic pimp or madam front and centre. The topic of sodomy appeared as a leitmotif in libertine literature; however, there is a distinct change in the signification of the trope. Lynn Hunt describes a shift in the readership of *libelles*: 'The libertine literature of the *ancien régime*, destined exclusively for upper-class men, now becomes a partly, perhaps even a predominantly, popular genre' with the abrupt shift from a book-orientated written culture to one orientated towards journalists.²³

Some of the most virulent language in secret histories was reserved for Marie-Antoinette. In the mid-1770s, Queen Marie-Antoinette supplants the King's mistresses and ministers and becomes, along with the Royal family and its entourage, the focal point for a literature of character assassination and hate. She figured in innumerable secret histories and *libelles*, revealing her putative corruption, debauchery, unnatural sexual proclivities, and prolificacy. The register of these writings were, as Chantal Thomas points out, hyperbolic and their motto was excess.²⁴ Their cultural work was de-sacralization.²⁵ Texts with titles such as *La Messaline francaise* [*The French Messalina*] (1789), targeting a royal favourite such as Jule de Polignac, or the queen herself in *Les amours de Charlot et Toinette* [*The Loves of Charlot and Toinette*] (1789), *Le Godmiché royal* [*The Royal Dildo*] (1789), *L'Autrichienne en goguettes, ou l'orgie royale* [*The Austrian Woman* on the Loose, or the Royal Orgy](1791) and, in reference to nymphomania, *Fureurs uterines de Marie-Antoinette* [*Marie-Antoinette's Uterine furies*] (1791), were popular, saw multiple editions, and denounced the moral corruption of Marie-Antoinette. One work, published in multiple parts, was particularly effective in defaming the queen. The first part, *Essais historiques sur la vie de Marie-Antoinette d'Autriche, reine de France, pour server à l'histoire de cette princesse* [*Historical Essays on Marie-Antoinette, Queen of France's life, to Serve as a History of this Princess*], was published anonymously in 1789 and carries the imprint of London. The second part, *Essais historique sur la vie de Marie-Antoinette, reine de France et de Navarre* [*Historical Essays on Marie-Antoinette, Queen of France and Navarre*] carries the imprint of Versailles, 1789. The two were combined into *Vie de Marie-Antoinette d'Autriche, reine de France* [*The Life of Marie-Antoinette of Austria, Queen of France*] to which a third volume, *Vie privée, libertine et scandaleuse de Marie-Antoinette d'Autriche, ci-devant reine de France* [*The Private, Libertine and Scandalous Life of Marie-Antoinette of Austria, Former Queen of France*] was added in 1793.[26] Each builds on the other and requires the reader to suspend his or her incredulity and critical faculties.[27] Through the merger of the fictional, political and pornographic, the queen was, as Lynn Hunt states, 'not only lampooned and demeaned in an increasingly ferocious pornographic out pouring, but she was also tried and executed'.[28]

The authors of *libelles* such as these acknowledge that the events recounted are both exaggerated and difficult to believe, but insist that there is truth in them.[29] However, the author of the first of the *Essais* takes pains to differentiate them from the old type of slanderous and defamatory *libelle*, by claiming that his text prepares the way to escape 'dangerous influence' and is a weapon in the fight against tyranny.[30] The author then makes a case for finding an 'illustre victim', a scapegoat, on which to place blame. Marie-Antoinette, the author writes, 'owes the nation an illustrious victim … and this voluntary victim will be her' (iii). The author then suggest it is plausible ('il est vraisemblable') that the *essais* are really the *Passe-temps d'Antoinette* [*Antoinette's Past-times*], another notorious manuscript found at the Bastille (i) and published under the new title. This manuscript was one that the king made great efforts to procure in order to prevent its publication. Although the author, posing as the editor, describes the work's faults – it lacks method, detail, nerve, and nuance – he praises its many anecdotes which will fire the reader's imagination; it will be up to the reader, he explains to fill in the portrait that is merely sketched out in the text (vi). To read this work well, then, requires the reader's active participation and relies on previous knowledge of *libelles* to fill in the gaps.

Political pornography tapers off somewhat with the execution of the queen. However, secret histories and revelations do not. The targets of *vie privées* become the Revolutionaries themselves in waves of internal fighting, referred to by Antoine de Baecque as 'une guerre des petites brochures' [a pamphlet war].[31] These short biographies were a political tool used to control how key Revolutionary participants and the body politic were represented during the Terror. They were used both positively and negatively to eulogize or to justify political ousters. Virtue as the sign of an absolute rejection of corrupt *ancien régime* practices was the order of the day from 1789 to 1794.[32] Dissimulation was a crime against virtue; the duty of the patriot was to reveal a once-respected politician's true secret nature as royalist, corrupt, and debauched. Virtuous indignation at the hypocrisy and the hidden venality of the targeted personality was the mode of these texts. Linton calls this period of trials of Jacobin and former Jacobin politicians 'the politicians' Terror'.[33] The ideology of political virtue, based on devotion to the public good and abnegation of self-interest, left politicians open to accusations of inauthenticity and ambition. Political opponents wielded the club of virtue and anti-republicanism to great effect. The symbolic violence of the pamphlets justified the physical violence enacted on the body of the person.[34]

Succeeding waves of attacks through the press announced a change both in political power and in controlling interests. The Jacobins, according to Linton, were the first political leaders to adopt terror as 'an official and legalized policy to sustain the republic' whose professed ideology was 'humanitarian and liberal'.[35] With the Terror being, according to Annie Jourdan, a civil, counter-revolutionary and external intimidation tactic in a time of war, pamphlet campaigns were waged, in turn, against the Girondins or Brissotins, the Hébertists, the Dantonists and the Robespierreists. It was a Terror turned inwards and the waves of accusations of secret conspiracies 'pointed to an inner anxiety about other people's motives' and the impossibility of true transparency.[36]

Robert Darnton considers these short, quickly produced, cheap hostile biographies (*vies privées* or *vies secrètes*) so different in tone – despite their structural and generic resemblance with their *ancien régime* antecedents – as to form a new genre 'the Jacobin libel'.[37] Lacking the Rabelaisian lewd humour of *ancien régime* libels, the denunciations and revelations of revolutionary libels were typical of Jacobin propaganda as irony gave way to indignation and outrage, sexual deprivation to economic corruption.

Darnton identified forty-two of these types of *vie privée* or *vie secrète* published between 1789 and 1800: some were written to denounce, others to defend.[38] The tone of *Vie privée de Marat* [*The Private Life of Marat*] (1793), for example, was countered by the highly critical *Vie criminelle et politique de J. P. Marat* [*J.P. Marat's Criminal and Private Life*] (1795). Others, such as *Vie privée des cinq membres du Directoire* [*The Private Lives of Five Members of the Directory*] (1795) were flattering informational biographies, similar to those crafted by today's political candidates, or celebrations of heroic military figures as in *Vie privée du general Buonaparte* [*The Private Life of General Buonaparte*] (1798). Quite a few were published to justify an execution or in an attempt to put a particular spin on events.[39] An indication that these *vie privées* were issued as part of a defamatory campaign is found in a series targeting Pierre Manuel, Jérôme Pétion, Jacques Pierre Brissot and Louis-Philippe d'Orléans issued, unusually, by the same printer, the Imprimerie de Franklin, rue de Cléry.[40]

The *vie secrète* and *privée* are most often structured in a similar manner. They open with an introduction or some sort of preface in the first person giving reasons for the publication. Almost half of these biographies include an engraved medallion portrait. The *Vie politique de Jérôme Pétion, ci-devant maire de Paris, ex-député à la Convention-nationale, et traître à la République française* [*The Political Life of Jérôme Pétion, Former Mayor of Paris, Ex National Convention Deputy, and Traitor to the French Republic*] (1793) is a good example. The narrator addresses the reader, 'ami lecteur' [reader friend], and explains that he will reveal the traitor who camouflaged 'ses perfidies avec le talent de se faire aimer' [his perfidiousness with a talent to be liked] (8) and his hidden anti-republican activities. The narrator, like the reader, insists that he was taken in by the target's appearance of virtue which masked an appetite for money or power. He then exhorts his readers not to fall into this trap again. There is a physical and moral portrait of the person followed by a biography starting with his childhood, illustrating that the talent for dissimulation was apparent at an early stage. The life story of the subject is illustrated through anecdotes up to the present time. The private and political sides of the subject's life merge. When the accusations are egotism, greed, royalism, and ambition, the lexical field used is one of dissimulation: *feindre, affecter, appas, ruse, masque, traitrise*, [to pretend, to affect, to ruse, to mask, and betrayal], etc. Appealing to the reader's sentiment, the narrator laments 'Oh! How this monster is clever, dangerous and barbarous behind this façade of the most worthy qualities of sensibility, compassion, humanity, generosity, sweetness and good will. Is it possible that crime can be clothed in the colours of virtue?' (29). The list of qualities for which Pétion was admired makes his perfidy and betrayal of his colleagues and the people all the worse.

As the wheel turned, Robespierre, who warned his colleagues against the power of calumny in 1792, was subjected to character assassination after his arrest and execution in July 1794.[41] He was not only vilified in pamphlets such as *Portraits exécrables, du traître Robespierre et ses complices* [Execrable Portraits of the Traitor Robespierre and His Accomplices] (1794) or *Vie secrette, politique et curieuse de M.J. Maximilien Robespierre* [Secret, Political and Curious Life of M.J. Maximilien Robespierre] (1794), but was also made into a monster. Mette Harder describes the 'posthumous sustained assault on his character' during the Thermidorian Reaction (1794–1795) and explains that the vilification of Robespierre was not only necessary to explain the abrupt turn in events, but also to cast him as a scapegoat for the Terror.[42] It was an effective strategy: *députés* could blame everything on Robespierre and his coterie, distance themselves from the Terror, and deflect attention away from the fact that they all participated in voting on the same laws and policies. While Thermidorians were attempting to put the Terror behind them, counter-revolutionaries called attention to the plight of its victims by publishing lists of their names together with the charges and dates of their execution.[43] Political use of slanderous pamphlets and *vies privées* continued throughout the Reaction into the Directory, until Napoleon put a stop to the hard-earned right of the freedom of the press.[44]

A different example of *vie privées* at the turn of the eighteenth century can be found in those concerning the revolutionary figure of Toussaint Louverture (1742–1803). He was the subject of controversy and figured in a mythology created around the Saint-Domingue rebellion and the creation of an independent Haiti in a series of attacks and responses in the early 1800s. The *Vie privée, politique et militaire de Toussaint-Louverture, par un homme de sa couleur* [*The Private, Political and Military Life of Toussaint-Louverture, by a Man of His Colour*] (*an* X [year X in the Republican calendar, or 1801]), was a response to *La vie de Toussaint-Louverture, chef des noirs insurgés de Saint-Domingue* [*The Life of Toussaint-Louverture, Leader of Black Insurgents of Saint-Domingue*] (*an* X) by Dubroca, or to a similar one. It follows the standard formula set out in the Jacobin libel in which the veil is lifted and hypocrisy revealed, betrayal, tyranny and atrocities exposed. In the preface, the author gives his reasons for this rebuttal after making it clear that his politics lie with France and Bonaparte, 'le réparateur de tous les maux' (8), is the answer to Saint-Domingue's problems. In response to a 'virulent diatribe composed by Santonax[45] or his henchmen' that consists of 'a web of lies and invented facts' (10), he writes that the colony only has to accept the peace that Bonaparte offers (9). He explains that one should not consign to oblivion all the good that Toussaint Louverture did (despite his errors) and one should preserve his honour and reputation, counting him among humanity's benefactors (11).

Secret histories, political and private biographies were still published in the new century but Napoleon, starting in 1800, kept a tight control over the press by devising an elaborate 'system competent to curb the unbridled individualism that the Revolution had evoked'.[46] He suppressed fifty out of sixty-three newspapers and required that works be approved by a Commission of Revision before publication.[47] Unacceptable content included anything that could be seen to challenge his authority. Authors' works were routinely censored and seized. However traces of *libelles*' rhetoric and images made their way into the growing number of memoirs, both real and fictional and into 'sentimental' novels whose popularity soared at the turn of the century. Elisabeth Brossin de Méré wrote a series of *vie privées* in an effort to earn money. She cites 'témoins oculaires' [eye witnesses] and includes anecdotes circulated in pamphlets. Following the tradition of *libelles*, in her *Historical Memoires of Jeanne Gomart de Vaubernier, Countess Du Barry* (1803), she includes letters, newspaper articles, secret archive documents and made public juridical transcripts. When Du Barry is arrested during the Revolution, Brossin de Méré, without comment, footnotes the date Dubarry's interrogators, or accusers, are guillotined in a reversal of the lists of revolutionary victims made public. Guénard includes letters and texts from other reference works and songs and romances circulated at the time. The Thermidorian creation of a monstrous Robespierre as evil incarnate also finds its way into her novels. One of the best sellers of the turn of the century was her daring counter-revolutionary novel, *Irma* (1801), a thinly disguised fictional history of the royal family during the Revolution in which the author incorporated Thermidorian propaganda such as Robespierre's intention to marry Louis XVI's daughter and his installation on the throne.[48]

In 1815, with the second exile of Napoleon and the restoration of the Monarchy, we find publications such as *Mémoires secrets sur Lucien Buonaparte, Prince de Canino* [*Secret Memoires about Lucien Buonaparte, Prince of Canino*] (1818) with its claim that they 'respirent la vérité' and are not like the wave of similar less authentic titles (ix), or *Histoire secrète des amours de la famille de N. Bonaparte* [*The Secret History of the Love Life of N. Bonaparte's Family*] (1815). If the first presents its claim to historiography, the second title surely belongs to the latter category. It is structured by a series of nine *soirées*, beginning with the matriarch of the Bonaparte family, Laetitia Bonaparte. Each of the eight Bonaparte siblings and their mother gather to recount their love lives. It paints a portrait of a rather stupid promiscuous and adulterous family. In a series of anecdotes, venereal disease, incest, and murder by poison are acts and conditions shared by family members. A bawdy and lewd text, coming full circle in imitation of the political situation's reversion to monarchy, it harks back to the style of *ancien régime* secret histories.

Throughout the nineteenth century, the government struggled to control subversive publications that undermine its authority: the *ancien régime* and the French Revolution demonstrate that while states may not fall due to secret histories and slanderous publications, they can be damaged by them.[49] Indeed rumours, scandal and anecdotes are still potent political weapons in partisan politics: one only has to think of the persistent belief in some quarters that Barack Obama is Muslim or that he was not born in the United States, despite factual evidence to the contrary. For a certain public, these types of secrets carry more weight than fact, appeal to their worst fears, and shore up their unreasonable politics and prejudices at a visceral level. Unauthorized biographies, ideologically orientated blogs, other types of social media publications the persistence of the tabloid press – online and in print – all speak to the enduring lure of the secret revealed, the unmasking of the powerful and the rich.

Notes

1 Darnton, Robert, *The Devil in the Holy Water, or the Art of Slander from Louis XIV to Napoleon*, 1st edn (Philadelphia: University of Pennsylvania Press, 2009), 343.
2 Antoine de Baecque writes, 'Treatises on finance, proposals for new systems of government organization, and scholarly reflections all figure prominently; but so do such less respectable varieties as pornographic pamphlets, political denunciations, eulogies, or 'Les Cris de Paris' … bespeaking the pamphleteers attempt to adapt traditional forms to the evolving realities of revolutionary politics'. See 'Pamphlets: Libel and Political Mythology', in *Revolution in Print: The Press in France, 1775–1800*, ed. Robert Darnton and Daniel Roche (Berkeley: University of California Press, 1989), 166.
3 For a discussion on the evolution of pamphlets and the literary market see Chantal Thomas, 'The Heroine of the Crime: Marie-Antoinette in Pamphlets', in *Marie Antoinette: Writings on the Body of a Queen*, ed. & trans. by Dena Goodman (New York: Routledge, 2003), 99–116; Jean-Luc Chappey, 'Usages politiques et sociaux de la biographie entre la convention et le directoire (1794–1799)' in Olivier Ferret, Anne-Marie Mercier-Faivre (dir.), *Biographie*

et politique. Vie publique, vie privée, de l'Ancien Régime à la Restauration (Lyon: Presses universitaires de Lyon, coll. 'Littérature et idéologies', 2014); and Andries Lise's study, 'Récits de survie: les mémoires d'autodéfense pendant l'an II et l'an III' in *La Carmagnole des muses: l'homme de lettres et l'artiste pendant la Révolution*, Jean-Claude Bonnet (dir.) (Paris: Armand Colin, 1988), 261–74 as well as Jeremy Popkin, 'Pamphlet Journalism at the End of the Old Regime', *Eighteenth-Century Studies* 22:3 (1989), 351–67.

4 Sophie-Anne Leterrier, 'Histoire en revolution', *Annales historiques de la Révolution française* 320 (2000), 65–75. For a discussion on the relationship between history and pamphlets, also see Marc Angenot, *La Parole pamphlétaire. Typologie des discours modernes* (Paris: Payot, 1982).
5 de Baecque, 'Pamphlets: Libel and Political Mythology', 165.
6 See Robert Darnton, *The Forbidden Bestsellers of Pre-Revolutionary France* (W.W. Norton, 1995).
7 There was a concerted attempt by the King to suppress these embarrassing *libelles*. The targets of the pre-revolutionary revelatory texts would often pay to purchase the entire run if they could not pay off the author before publication. See Robert Darnton, *The Literary Underground of the Old Regime* (Cambridge MA: Harvard University Press, 1982) and *The Devil in the Holy Water*.
8 Darnton, *Devil in the Holy Water*, 54.
9 Antoine Sérieys, *Mémoires politiques et militaires, pour servir à l'histoire secrète de la révolution française*, 2 vols. (Paris, an VII [1799]), 1: i.
10 Fiona McIntosh-Vajabédian, *Écriture de l'histoire et regard rétrospectif: Clio et Épiméthée* (Paris: Honoré Champion, 2010), 11.
11 See Mette Harder, 'Odious and Vile Names: Political Character Assassination and Purging in the French Revolution', in *Character Assassination Throughout the Ages*, ed. Martijn Icks and Eric Shiraev (Basingstoke and New York: Palgrave Macmillan, 2014), 173–90.
12 Chartier, *Roger, Lectures et lecteurs dans la France d'Ancien Régime* (Paris: Seuil, 1987), 246.
13 Antoine de Baecque, 'Dégénérescence et régénération: le livre licencieux juge la Révolution française', in *Mélanges de la Bibliothèque de la Sorbonne, no. 9: Livre et Révolution*, eds. Frédéric Barbier, Sabine Juratic and Dominique Varry (Paris: Aux Amateurs de Livres, 1989), 125.
14 Thierry Pastorello, 'La sodomie masculine dans les pamphlets révolutionnaires', *Annales Historiques de la Révolution Française*, 361 (2010), 91–108.
15 de Baecque, 'Pamphlets: Libel and Political Mythology', 167.
16 Michael E. Winston, *From Perfectibility to Perversion: Meliorism in Eighteenth-Century France*, The Age of Revolution and Romanticism: Interdisciplinary Studies (Book 34) (New York: Peter Lang, 2005), 159 and de Baecque, 'Pamphlets', 168.
17 Winston, *From Perfectibility to Perversion*, 124.
18 de Baecque cited in Winston, *From Perfectibility to Perversion*, 159–60.
19 Cited in de Baecque, 'Pamphlets: Libel and Political Mythology', 175.

20 de Baecque in 'Pamphlets: Libel and Political Mythology' cites Sade's *La Philosophie dans le boudoir ou les instituteurs immoraux* (1795) launched by Rétif de la Bretonne's series on the subject beginning with *Le Pornographe* (1769).
21 Winston, *From Perfectibility to Perversion*, 162.
22 Pastorello, 'La sodomie masculine', 107.
23 Lynn Hunt, 'Pornography and the French Revolution' in *The Invention of Pornography: Obscenity and the Origins of Modernity, 1500–1800*, ed. Lynn Hunt (New York: Zone Books, 1993), 321.
24 Chantal Thomas, *The Wicked Queen: The Origins of the Myth of Marie-Antoinette* (New York: Zone Books, 1999), 10.
25 de Baecque, Dégénérescence et régénération', 123.
26 Mette Harder writes that there were sixteen reprints and multiple versions of the *Essais* between 1789 and 1790, along with six 'forgeries' from 1791 to 1793 ('Odious and Vile Names', 176). See Darnton for a description of the publication history of these pamphlets (*The Devil in the Holy Water*, 415–21).
27 Philip Robinson, 'Le phenomène de la pseudo-histoire dans le tournant des Lumières', in *Le Tournant des Lumières. Mélanges en l'honneur de Malcolm Cook*, eds. Katherine Astbury and Catriona Seth (Paris: Classiques Garnier, 2012), 204.
28 Hunt, 'Pornography and the French Revolution', 108.
29 'Les choses incroyables que l'on va lire ne sont pas inventées à plaisir, fussent-elles un peu exagérées, au moins le fonds est-il vrai'. See *Essais historiques sur la vie de Marie-Antoinette d'Autriche, reine de France* (Londres [London], 1789), iii.
30 'la libelle est l'ouvrage qui diffame, qui calomnie, qui outrage, qui flétrit; mais l'ouvrage qui raconte, qui prémunit, qui conduit à la façon d'échapper à la tyrannie, n'est rien moins qu'un libelle' (Ibid. ii).
31 See Antoine de Baecque, *Les Eclats du rire: La culture des rieurs au XVIIIe siècle* (Paris: Calmann-Lévy, 2000).
32 Marisa Linton, *Choosing Terror: Virtue, Friendship, and Authenticity in the French Revolution* (Oxford: Oxford University Press, 2015), 7.
33 Linton, *Choosing Terror*, 2.
34 Ourida Mostefai, 'La violence pamphlétaire et ses stratégies en France a l'époque des lumières' La Violence pamphlétaire et ses stratégies en France à l'époque des lumières' in *Progrès et violence au XVIIIe siècle*, eds. Valérie Cossy and Deidre Dawson (Paris: Honoré Champion, 2001), 281.
35 Linton, *Choosing Terror*, 11.
36 For a discussion on the violence directed at specific groups see Linton, *Choosing Terror*, 11–13.
37 Darnton *Devil in the Holy Water*, 56. Darnton reports that a skilled worker made between 40 and 50 sous a day. A *vie privée* generally cost 30 sous, thus was not outside the purchasing power of the common man (*Devil in the Holy Water*, 75).
38 Darnton, *Devil in the Holy Water*, 424. See Mette Harder for an account of attacks and counter-attacks between warring political factions ('Odious and Vile Names', 177–79, in particular). See also Linton, *Choosing Terror*.

39 See Darnton, 'Orleans, Manuel, Brissot and Hébert lives appeared after executions and to justify them' (*Devil in the Holy Water*, 422).
40 Darnton concludes that the issue of these *vie privées* from the same printer were part of a propaganda campaign waged against current political targets in an effort to consolidate power (*Devil in the Holy Water*, 56).
41 Harder, 'Odious and Vile Names', 177.
42 See Harder, 'Odious and Vile Names', 174, Antoine de Baecque, 'Robespierre, monstre-cadavre du discours thermidorien', *Eighteenth-Century Life*, 21:2 (1997), 203–21, and Julia V. Douthwaite, *The Frankenstein of 1790 and Other Lost Chapters from Revolutionary France* (Chicago: University Of Chicago Press, 2012), for a discussion on Robespierre's constructed monstrosity.
43 Chappey, 'Usages Politiques', 155.
44 Harder, 'Odious and Vile Names', 183.
45 In the wake of slave rebellions in 1791, Léger-Félicité Sonthonax was sent to Saint-Domingue from 1792–1795 by the Assembly with thousands of troops to maintain order.
46 Victor Coffin, 'Censorship and Literature under Napoleon I', *The American Historical Review*, 22, no. 2 (1917), 288.
47 J. Holland Rose, 'The Censorship under Napoleon I', *Journal of Comparative Legislation and International Law, New Series*, 18, no. 1 (1918), 58–65.
48 *Irma, ou les Malheurs d'une jeune orpheline. Histoire indienne, avec des romances, publiée par la citoyenne Guénard*, 4 vols. (Delphy; Paris, an VIII [1799]).
49 Sandy Petrey, 'Pears in History', *Representations* 35. Special Issue: Monumental Histories (1991), 52–71.

16

Secret History in British North America and the Early Republic

Kevin Joel Berland

The development of secret history in North America is best approached from the perspective of the transatlantic book trade. London printers continually reissued seventeenth-century secret histories to meet the demand for revelations of covert political forces threatening to impose arbitrary power on free subjects. Colonial booksellers imported the major secret histories from London; the extent of this commerce is apparent in numerous colonial newspaper advertisements and news stories related to secret history. Books focusing on British and European matters concerned colonial subjects who considered themselves British and were just as wary of threats to individual liberty and commerce as metropolitan readers. During the eighteenth century, then, secret history was a marketable export commodity for the London book trade.

The first work written and published in North America bearing *secret history* in its title did not appear until 1808. Nonetheless, the operative principles of secret history penetrated colonial discourse, first as an idiomatic phrase indicating an approach to making obscure matters public – especially regarding arbitrary government – and then as a mode of exposing political corruption, scandal, and political moves to curtail individual liberty in the interest of private benefits. Although no full-length secret histories emerged from the movement toward independence in the second half of the century, revelations of the clandestine machinations of absolutism were essential in public discourse.

The most significant secret histories of the period, William Byrd's two Dividing Line histories, remained unpublished for over one hundred years. Written between 1728 and 1745, they combine a narrative of the expedition charting the Virginia-North Carolina boundary with remarkable secrets about British colonial history and scandal concerning public figures.

Secret History in Colonial Newspapers and the Book Trade

Colonial newspapers created value for their readers by publishing items borrowed from London papers. A few instances will serve to illustrate the importance of the transatlantic commerce in secret history. In 1732, Philadelphia's *American Weekly Mercury* noted the publication of Eustace Budgell's pamphlet exposing the persecution Robert Walpole and his spies were allegedly carrying out against him. Budgell did not himself call his pamphlet a secret history, but the full title indicates it fit the genre's criteria: *Liberty and Property: A Pamphlet Highly necessary to be read by every Englishman, who has the least Regard for those Two Invaluable Blessings. Containing Several Curious Stories and Matters of Fact, with Original Letters and other Papers.*[1] For colonial newspapers it was clearly a secret history, as the *American Weekly Mercury* explained:

> Last Week a very remarkable Pamphlet was published under the Title of *Liberty and Property*, wrote by *Eustace Budgell*, Esq; This Pamphlet contains a great deal of Secret History, and some most surprising Stories, for the Truth of which the Author nevertheless seems to produce undeniable Vouchers. He declares that though his Papers have been twice seized, and taken from him; yet that he has still something to lay before the Parliament at their next Meeting; so that perhaps we shall at last know the Contents of that Memorial against a certain great Man which Mr. *Budgell* delivered into his Majesty's own Hand at St. James's. The first Edition of this Pamphlet was bought up in 5 days.[2]

Budgell contended that Walpole had defaulted on a promise of political advancement, and afterwards directed his associates to foment trouble for Budgell, causing great suffering.

Why, if Budgell did not name his pamphlet a secret history, did the *American Weekly Mercury* describe the contents of *Liberty and Property* as such? Possibly the newspaper had Opposition sympathies, or the editors were catering to the public appetite for peeking behind the scenes of political affairs. Be this as it may, Budgell offers ostensibly informed, revelatory history, attractive to readers already suspicious about the arcane, unprincipled machinations of those in power – and colonial readers were fully prepared to be suspicious.

Suspicion of metropolitan authorities governing the political and commercial lives of colonial subjects fuelled the North American market for secret histories. Imports remained steady throughout the eighteenth century, even after the revolution. In 1751 New York's New Printing House offered David Jones's *Secret History of White-Hall*; in 1785 Isaiah Thomas's

Worcester, Massachusetts bookstore advertised *The Secret History of Queen Elizabeth and the Earl of Essex*; in 1790 Samuel Campbell announced a shipment from London of an 'extensive supply of Books. In various departments of Literature', including 'Mirabeau's *Secret History of Berlin*'.[3] In 1794 Isaac Beers imported *The Secret History of the arm'd Neutrality*, and in 1795, the Salem Bookstore and Circulating-Library advertised the arrival from London of an 'interesting and useful Collection of Literature', including *Secret History of the Green Room*, and *Secret History of Persons of Quality*.[4] In Philadelphia Robert Campbell and Co. advertised 'A large and extensive assortment of the latest and best London editions' including the 'Secret history of Charles the 2d'.[5] In 1798, Blake's Boston Bookstore advertised the importation of assorted books including 'Dupage's secret history of the French Revolution'.[6]

Another measure of the importation of secret histories is their presence in circulating libraries. Louis Alexis Hocquet de Caritat's annotated library catalogue directs his customers to volumes of secret history:

> Female Favourites, History of. This work will afford a large fund of entertainment for those who are fond of secret history; the anecdotes are in an easy, agreeable style.
> Green-Rooms, secret History of, containing Memoirs of the Actors and Actresses of the three Theatres Royal
> High German Doctor, or Secret History of England, written in the year 1716
> Macpherson's Original Papers, containing the Secret History of Great Britain
> White-Hall, Secret History of, from the Restoration of Charles II, down to the Abdication of the late King James

Caritat also lists fictive secret histories such as Eliza Haywood's 'Secret Histories, Novels and Poems' and Anne Yearsley's *Royal Captives, a Fragment of Secret History*.[7]

Works published in Britain promising revelations concerning conditions in British North America were of compelling interest in the colonies. An important instance is the exposé of the Hudson's Bay Company by former surveyor Joseph Robson. In his *Account of Six Years Residence in Hudson's Bay*, he claims that for eighty uninterrupted years the Company's monopoly of the fur trade hindered other commerce in the region, while the owners enriched themselves. Robson does not himself call his condemnation a secret history, but his approach to the matters that concern him is consistent with the genre. The Company claimed they had settled the region and promoted trade benefitting Britain, but this public stance only masked the venal nature of their actual practice:

> They have … contented themselves with dividing among one hundred persons, a large profit upon a small capital; have not only endeavoured to keep the true state of the trade and country an impenetrable secret, but industriously propagated the worst impressions of them; and rather then enjoy the inconceivable advantages of a general cultivation in common with their fellow subjects, have, even to the hazard of their own separate interest, exposed both country and trade to the incroachments of the French.[8]

There was no mistaking Robson's strategy; *The New-York Gazette* identified the *Account* as secret history:

> We hear that the whole Secret History of the Fur Trade, as well in America as in Europe, with the several Methods practised by our artificial Neighbours to purchase that Commodity, not only for themselves, but for us, with our Manufactures Duty free, will be clearly explained, and a Multitude of other commercial Finesses brought to Light; which may possibly convince all who are open to Conviction, that the Navigation, Trade, and Prosperity of Great-Britain, must, in a great Measure, depend on the Administration of Affairs in the British Colonies, and a due Attention to the salutary Laws made for promoting a good Correspondence between those Settlements and their Mother Country.[9]

The *Gazette* stressed the Company's transformation of colonial trade from a public benefit into enrichment for a select circle. The owners evaded duties on exports of colonial manufactures. Worse, they stood idly by while the French expanded their commercial networks to the south and west. According to the *Gazette*, Robson exposes a long-hidden pattern of connivance by which the Company stole funds that should have gone to colonial administrations and to the crown, a conspiracy exploiting delegated authority for the enrichment of a few.

Not all secret histories were created equal; in the colonies, as in the metropole, a devalued version of the term indicated mere gossip, rumour, or scandal. In *The New-York Weekly Journal*, one 'Hester Decent' complained about a young woman who insisted on talking throughout church services. 'While the Lessons were reading, she whisper'd the Secret History of every Woman within four or six neighbouring Pews: At other Opportunities, she hinted what Gentlemen ogled such a Gentlewoman.'[10] Mock-serious tagging of gossip could deliver shock value. An exposé of female fashion in the *New-York Journal* conveyed hush-hush detail about the source of the stock of human hair milliners sold to construct fashionably elevated hairdos:

> in the Hospitals, whatever Patients died, their Hair became the Perquisite of the Nurses, who carefully sheared them, to supply this great Demand

for Human Hair. That both the *Small* Pox, and a Distemper still more disagreeable, supplied the greatest Part: For a Number of Girls, who had once been very fine Girls, died continually in the Lock Hospital, whose Heads of Hair the Nurses took particular Care to save from the Grave; and that from such Crops the Heads of our *politest Ladies* were furnished. To these Ladies I leave the Consideration of this article of secret History, which appears to be a Matter of Fact; and make no Doubt but they will reconcile themselves to it, so long as suits the prevailing Humour.[11]

The scandal in this case is especially sharp, offering insight into the rich irony of genteel ladies adorning themselves with hair collected from impoverished women and prostitutes who died of smallpox or venereal disease.

It is not always easy to distinguish the boundary between gossip and revelations of consequence. Ostensibly, secret history provides valuable information to which the ordinary person might not be privy. Gossip's allegation and innuendo are not subject to verification, and may prove to be instruments of malice, envy, and detraction, dishonestly used to attack men of excellence:

> The envious whisperer is more dangerous. He easily gains attention by a soft address, and excites curiosity by an air of importance. As secrets are not to be made cheap by promiscuous publication, he calls a select audience about him, and gratifies their vanity with an appearance of trust, by communicating his malicious intelligence in a low voice: And as every one is pleased with imagining that he knows something not yet commonly divulged, secret history easily gains credit; but it is for the most part believed only while it circulates in whispers, and when once it is openly told, is openly confuted.[12]

The circulation of damning anecdotes, even those acknowledged as conjectural, creates a negative impression that can survive correction or confutation, an effect shared by gossip and serious secret history.

These instances demonstrate how popular print media in the colonies engaged with metropolitan traditions of secret history. In the transatlantic book trade and in colonial and early federal newspapers, the steady attraction of unknown or unsuspected insights into economic and political matters remains constant.

William Byrd's Secret Histories

The influence of British secret histories is everywhere apparent in Byrd's two manuscript narratives about the 1728 expedition to survey the

Virginia-North Carolina border. William Byrd II of Westover, Virginia – gentleman planter, amateur naturalist, diarist, government official, and author – submitted his official report to the governor and the Board of Trade in 1728. Afterwards, he added layers of political and personal commentary to fashion two accounts, *The History of the Dividing Line Betwixt Virginia and Carolina*, and *The Secret History of the Line*. Intending the *History of the Dividing Line* for the London literary marketplace, he enriched the work with layers of detail about the colonial history of British North America, its topography, botany, zoology, mineralogy, and other topics of interest. The *Secret History* was circulated privately to select readers; this revealed the personal weaknesses, venality, ill-temper, libertine proclivities, and base motives of members of the expedition. Byrd's library – the largest in British North America at the time – included many of the classic secret histories.[13] Byrd's approach is consistent with John Philips's claim to the lofty principles of Suetonius in *The Secret History of the Reigns of K. Charles II, and K. James II*, 'as well to Vindicate, as to Inform', revealing hidden truths by exposing abuses during the reign of the last Stuart kings.[14] Whether dealing with scandal about historical and contemporary figures or with political intrigue, the secret histories with which Byrd was familiar claim to reveal (or to simulate revelation of) momentous and extraordinary things not known to the general public.

The brief history of the British colonies that opens Byrd's *History of the Dividing Line* is written in this spirit, disclosing the erosion of Virginia's preeminence in spite of its royal pedigree. 'The first Settlement of this fine Country was owing to that great ornament of the British Nation, Sir Walter Raleigh, who obtain'd a Grant thereof from Queen Elizabeth of ever glorious Memory, by Letters Patent dated March the 25th 1584' (65). From Elizabeth's royal favour sprang Byrd's imaginary Virginia: law-abiding, loyal, industrious, devout without enthusiasm, and well-governed by royally-appointed officers and upright men of the colonial patrician elite. Originally Virginia comprised the entire continent: 'All that part of the northern American Continent, now under the Dominion of the King of Great Britain, and stretching quite as far as the Cape of Florida, went at first under the General Name of Virginia.' However, to benefit special interests the territory was broken up: 'The other British Colonies on the main, have one after another, been *carved out* of Virginia, by Grants from his Majesty's Royal Predecessors.' Byrd's powerful slicing metaphor persists – New England 'was *pared off* from Virginia' and subdivided by royal patents. Then 'the next Country *dismember'd* from Virginia, was New

Scotland', and again, '*Another Limb lopt off* from Virginia, was New-York'. Finally, 'what wounded Virginia deepest was *the cutting off Maryland* from it by Charter from King Charles the 1st' (66–72; emphasis added). For Byrd the royal charter endowed Virginia with a fundamental superiority, a position manifested in commentary wholly consistent with the perspectives and techniques of secret history. New England, he declares sarcastically, was populated by fractious dissenters, Presbyterians, Independents, and Puritans who 'thought themselves persecuted at home'. Byrd eyes New England with suspicion because its foundation lay in the disruption of the English social, political, and ecclesiastical order. Hinting that the dissenters who 'flocked' over to New England were essentially the same people who had deposed and executed the Royal Martyr King Charles I, he explicitly links New England with Interregnum leaders: 'And about this time it was, that Messrs. Hampden and Pimm, and (some say) Oliver Cromwell, to shew how little they valued the King's Authority, took a Trip to New-England' – an entirely apocryphal rumour. Again, Byrd's version of the 1681 recall of governor Edmund Andros stresses the colonies' contempt for legitimate authority: they 'laid unhallowed hands' on Andros and sent him back to England a prisoner (69–70).

Byrd represents the Dutch settlement of New Amsterdam as an encroachment on the earlier British title. Supposedly the Dutch West India Company 'tamper'd' with the English ship captains conveying Puritans to the banks of the Hudson River, bribing them to land their passengers far to the north. This 'Finesse' allowed the Dutch to settle along the Hudson themselves (71). When Charles I granted the Maryland charter to Sir George Calvert, Lord Baltimore, 'it begat much Speculation … how it came about, that a good Protestant King should bestow so bountiful a Grant upon a Zealous Roman Catholick'. Perhaps, Byrd adds, it was 'one fatal Instance amongst many others of his Majesty's complaisance to the Queen' (72).

Byrd impugns the character of Pennsylvania's founder William Penn, introduced as 'a Man of much Worldly Wisdom', a phrase conventionally indicating watchfulness for material gain, rather than spiritual values. Penn supposedly took advantage of the charting of New Jersey, noticing 'a narrow Slipe of Land, lying betwixt that Colony, and Maryland'. Byrd here indulges in satirical understatement, for royal grants to Penn included all lands between the 43rd parallel and just north of the 39th parallel westward to the Delaware River – hardly a narrow slip. Affecting puzzlement, Byrd wonders how a Quaker could have had such influence with the 'Popish Prince' Charles II, though it was well known that the grants were meant to repay the king's debt of more than £16,000 owed to Admiral Penn, William's father. Instead, Byrd introduces a scandalous alternate explanation. The young Penn was a handsome rake, a 'Man of Pleasure' who indulged in an 'Amour' with the Duke of Monmouth's mistress: 'But this Amour had like to have brought our Fine Gentleman in Danger of a Duell, had he not discreetly shelter'd himself under this peaceable Perswasion' (74). Byrd's satirical thrust is triple, at the same time lashing Penn's alleged libertinism, his hypocritical conversion, and the Quakers' pacifism. Significantly, Byrd names his explanation a 'piece of Secret History' (73–74). Although this is the only overt use of the term, Byrd's *History of the Dividing Line* is firmly rooted in the historiographical perspective and rhetoric of the genre, evident throughout the narrative in countless revelations.

The title of Byrd's other account, *The Secret History*, overtly signaled its purpose: disclosure of devious politics and shocking personal actions, libertine anecdotes, and buried facts illuminating public and private proceedings. The title promises to provide the real story, no matter how shocking – scandal, banter, mock-serious polemics, satire, lampoon and ridicule. At the same time, Byrd was drawn to the manner in which authors of secret histories claimed the moral high ground, either seriously or satirically, working toward the common good through exposing vice and folly. Several details will demonstrate this orientation.

For many years North Carolina commissioner Edward Moseley had found means to delay the survey while, in his capacity as Surveyor-General, he defied royal commands to profit personally from patenting land in the disputed boundary region. At the outset of the expedition, Moseley was contrary and recalcitrant until Byrd took him aside and showed him some papers, evidently the Board of Trade's scathing report to the Privy Council reproving Moseley's obstructions during an earlier failed survey. The other Carolinian commissioners knew little or nothing of surveying. Nominally in charge of the men who did the actual work, they were interested only in crude merriment and the expectation of promised land grants. In episode after episode, Byrd exposes the crudity, gluttony, profanity, drunkenness, venality, exploitation of women, and other vicious proclivities of his North Carolinian adversaries. Byrd assumes for himself a moderate narrative persona, 'Steddy', to observe the immoderate conduct of the Carolinians. Though members of the North Carolina executive council and of their colony's patrician elite, they were vulgar and greedy, fearful of their governor, unprepared for the work of the expedition, jealous, lazy, grossly abusive of women, eager to profit monetarily from the survey, and half-hearted in supporting the expedition, which they abandoned before the task was completed. Byrd offers them up as satirical character sketches with funny names – Puzzlecause, Jumble, Plausible, Shoebrush – each man demonstrating his own particular vice or folly. The narrative contains equal parts of chronology (the day-to-day business of the expedition), scandal (sloth, drunkenness, and 'gross Freedoms' with vulnerable women), and disclosure of the undercurrents of politics (363). Two of the commissioners travelled to their capital 'to recover the great Fatigue of doing nothing & to pick up new Scandal against their Governour' (370).

One of the Virginia commissioners, a customs officer Byrd names Firebrand, constantly opposed Byrd, siding with the Carolina commissioners and even abandoning the expedition with them. In a knowing aside, Byrd explains Firebrand's 'prudent Consideration' as an attempt to cash in on 'the Lucre of his Attendance during the Genl. Court' and claiming at the same time full compensation for attending the survey he left early (399).

Without multiplying instances of such revelations, it is safe to say that Byrd was both consumer and composer of secret history, implicitly claiming the moral high ground for serious and satirical purposes alike. Eager to represent himself as canny and in control, he adapted metropolitan and continental models to his colonial narrative, inventing a transatlantic version of the genre. His *Secret History* focuses on personality, employing satirically exaggerated character sketches and revealing the hidden springs of action, the motivations, political and economic agendas, flawed character, and scandalous behaviour of his Carolinian opponents. Byrd grounds his *Secret History* on the ideology of the Virginia patrician elite: the laws, customs, economics, culture, polity, and religion (stoutly Anglican) form a standard by which individuals of other colonies are judged and found wanting.

Secret History and Independence

Colonial mistrust of metropolitan authority increased in the years leading up to the American Revolution. North American booksellers and publishers promoted certain works as particularly applicable to the times. The preface to the 1770 Philadelphia edition of Marmontel's *Belisarius* positions it as a cautionary tale about corrupt politicians overpowering a weak monarch – not coincidentally how some writers explained contemporary colonial troubles. A new subtitle pointedly addresses colonial readers:

> The history of Belisarius, the heroick and humane Roman General. A Man who possessed the most immoveable Fidelity, and practised the most disinterested Patriotism, in the Court of a weak Emperor, surrounded by a Junto of as

> *corrupt and abandoned Ministers, as ever enslaved and disgraced Humanity; whose Malice and Envy remained unsatiated, till by misrepresentation and perjury they accomplished the Downfal of this greatest and most excellent of all human Beings, in whose amiable and exalted Character every Virtue exists that is admirable or desirable, in the Sage Lawgiver, Brave Hero, Noble Patriot, Profound Politician, Exploring Philosopher, Sober Citizen, Industrious Farmer, Honest Lawyer, or in the most humble, and most perfect Divine.*[15]

With this subtitle, Marmontel's *Belisarius*, long a favourite of British opponents of absolutism, becomes an ancient template for understanding modern ills. Colonial readers may extrapolate from the secret history of the Byzantine Junto how corrupt ministers turn every occasion to their own profit.

Misgivings about the continued liberty of colonial subjects took on a special force in the Hutchison Letters affair of 1773. Benjamin Franklin, Massachusetts's agent in London, obtained letters from Governor Thomas Hutchison and Lieutenant-Governor Andrew Oliver to Thomas Whately, prime minister George Grenville's secretary for colonial policy. Franklin sent the letters confidentially to the speaker of the Massachusetts assembly to alert them to Hutchinson's misrepresentation of the colonial situation. While a special committee considered the letters in detail, the assembly's clerk, Samuel Adams, leaked extracts to the press framed in a manner designed to inflame the public. The assembly moved to demand Hutchinson's recall on grounds that he sought to establish arbitrary power in the governor's office and to deprive colonial subjects of their constitutional liberties. Hutchinson protested he had never recommended such measures; what he actually said was that no individual or branch of colonial government could choose whether or not to submit to royal authority. Published extracts of the letters exaggerated the absolutism of his position, targeting him as an agent of 'the Injustice and Oppression, so long and so loudly complained of, by the King's American Subjects'.[16] The extracts already appeared to reveal surreptitious dealings when an additional secret history factor emerged. The *Boston Evening Post* charged that Hutchinson's private opinion was the reverse of his public view. The governor's public authoritarianism

> must sound extremely harsh in the Ears of every true Friend to his Country; and must fill his Mind with the most disagreeable Ideas, especially, when considered as coming from the Governor, who, if secret History may be credited, repeatedly said, among his intimate Friends, that the Parliament of Great-Britain have no more Right to make Laws for us, than for the Inhabitants of China; but that we have a good Right to resist them, whenever it shall be in our Power.[17]

The author offers a tepid qualifier – 'If he did say so, or Words of the same Import, which I don't affirm' – followed by an avowal of the truth of what Hutchinson *might* have said: 'I believe there is not an honest sensible Man upon the Continent, who is not of his Opinion.' Here the peculiar force of secret history works through a bifurcated statement. Hutchinson says one thing emphatically in public, but holds quite another opinion in private. Backing away from certifying the truth of the secret history does not remove the original smear; indeed, negative allegations persist in public discourse regardless of denial or doubt. The affective rhetoric here has two points: first, it establishes Hutchinson's hypocrisy in the reader's mind, for his secret opinions were so remarkable that it would require 'a profound Casuist … to reconcile them with his publick Declarations'. The second point is to emphasise that the liberty of the colonial subject is so self-evident that even an agent of monarchic authority must concur.[18] Widespread belief in disjuncture between private belief and public policy thus supports a propaganda war. The public's suspicions were confirmed when the *Boston Gazette* published the full Hutchinson-Oliver correspondence, in which it was easy to discover the positions attributed to Hutchinson in the extracts; the newspapers redoubled their attacks. No evidence, however, has emerged to corroborate the *Boston Evening Post*'s assertion that Hutchinson was secretly on the side of the colonists.[19]

North America produced no full-length secret histories in the colonial period, the lead-up to the American Revolution, or in the early years of the republic. Still, what Rebecca Bullard has called the 'discourse of disclosure' was an instrument of political rhetoric, employed to disable an opponent with charges of secret motives.[20] For instance, in a 1785 Pennsylvania controversy over legislation to combat piracy, charges were made – as 'a piece of secret history' – that 'the *fabricator* of the new legislation 'had more in view, than what the *plausible* preamble sets forth'. Because the effective clauses of the law went beyond the preamble, it was imputed that interested parties had fashioned the preamble's vague language to speed its passage in the assembly for the benefit of private interests. However, the *Pennsylvania Packet*'s columnist 'Veritas' labelled these charges groundless, for the new act was fully consistent with extant statues, required no skullduggery to pass in the assembly, and benefitted no discernible private interests.[21]

Secret history was invoked in early federal politics, as in the controversy over the 1795 treaty with Great Britain. The Jay Treaty, as it was known, provided for the British army's withdrawal from the Northwest Territory and subjected wartime debts and the border with Canada to arbitration. The Jeffersonian faction opposed the treaty, insisting that the secret negotiations had included undisclosed (and implicitly disgraceful) terms. In the *Daily Advertiser*, one commentator railed:

> If we attend to the measures of Congress, we shall see one system in them all. A system of peace. To make the chance of peace the best possible, they have made preparation for war. These few words explain the history of the last session. Those who like secret history will find abundant materials for their curiosity. The great aim of the party and the insid[i]ous measures they took to carry their point, will be known and understood.
>
> The steady citizens who feel an interest in good order will see the extreme hazard of our peace and honour, and will rejoice in the termination of the session.[22]

Such machinations should be seen as a dangerous precedent leading to arbitrary rule by those in power in congress.

By the end of the eighteenth century, secret history had become fully embedded in civic discourse, to the extent that the term was proverbial in social and political commentary. Otherwise, the adaptation of the discourse of discovery to other literary forms may be traced through Ann Yearsley's novel, *The Royal Captives: A Fragment of Secret History* (London, 1795) to Leonora Sansay's *Secret History; or the Horrors of St. Domingo* (Philadelphia, 1808). Sansay's epistolary novel claims to reveal what really went on during the Haitian Revolution. Sansay displays the hidden motives of colonial and imperial actors, and adds novelistic sensibility by focusing on two American sisters entangled in events. As Gretchen Woertendyke has observed, the novel furnishes 'intimate secrets for the benefit of public history'. Dressing up her own Caribbean experience as historical fiction, Sansay transforms the secret history into a double revelation: 'the more visible history of violence in the Haitian Revolution' and the criminal 'exploitation of women'.[23] This progression in North American secret history, finally, marks an evolution from satire and political discourse to the communication of important ethical issues through the reactions of sensible characters (and readers) to the discovery of great wrongs and injustice.

Notes

1 *Liberty and Property: A Pamphlet* (London, 1732); five editions appeared in 1732, and two of a second part. On Budgell and Walpole, see 'Eustace Budgell', *The Lives of the Poets of Great Britain and Ireland*, vol. 5 (London, 1753), 10–12; Bertrand Goldgar, *Walpole and the Wits: The Relation of Politics to Literature, 1722–1742* (Lincoln: University of Nebraska Press, 1970); and Tone Sundt

Urstad, *Sir Robert Walpole's Poets: The Use of Literature as Pro-Government Propaganda, 1721–1742* (Newark: University of Delaware Press, 1999).
2 *American Weekly Mercury* 673 (16–23 November 1732); the August dateline matches the first London advertisements of Budgell's pamphlet in the *Daily Journal* 3612 (1 August 1732).
3 *New-York Gazette* 453 (23 September 1751); *Thomas's Massachusetts Spy: Or, The Worcester Gazette* 15, 740 (9 May 1785); *Daily Advertiser* 1671 (28 June 1790).
4 *Columbian Centinel* 22, 51 (4 March 1795).
5 *Philadelphia Gazette & Universal Daily Advertiser* 13, 2452 (3 August 1796).
6 *Massachusetts Mercury* 11, 40 (18 May 1798).
7 *The Feast of Reason and the Flow of Soul. A New Explanatory Catalogue of H. Caritat's General & Increasing Circulating Library* (New York, 1799), 35, 41, 43, 64, 100, 165, 197.
8 Joseph Robson, *An Account of Six Years Residence in Hudson's-Bay, from 1733 to 1736, and 1744 to 1747* (London, 1752), 66.
9 *New-York Gazette Revived in the Weekly Post-Boy* 489 (1 June 1752).
10 *New-York Weekly Journal* 294 (23 July 1739).
11 *New-York Journal; or, the General Advertiser* 1299 (11 November 1767).
12 *The Pennsylvania Chronicle, and Universal Advertiser* 3, 24 (3–10 July 1769), 200.
13 On Byrd's collection of secret histories, see Kevin J. Hayes, *The Library of William Byrd of Westover* (Madison: Madison House and the Library Company of Philadelphia, 1997), 64; and Kevin J. Berland, ed., *The Dividing Line Histories of William Byrd II of Westover* (Chapel Hill: University of North Carolina Press for the Omohundro Institute for Early American History and Culture, 2013), 243–44. Further references given in the text.
14 [John Philips], *The Secret History of the Reigns of K. Charles II, and K. James II* ([London], 1690), A2r-v.
15 *The History of Belisarius* (America [i.e., Philadelphia], 1770).
16 *Boston Evening Post* 1965 (24 May 1773).
17 *Boston Evening Post* 1965 (24 May 1773).
18 *Boston Evening Post* 1965 (24 May 1773).
19 On the affair of the Hutchinson letters, see Bernard Bailyn, *The Ordeal of Thomas Hutchinson* (Cambridge MA: Harvard University Press, 1974).
20 Rebecca Bullard, *The Politics of Disclosure, 1674–1725: Secret History Narratives* (London: Pickering & Chatto, 2009), 7.
21 *The Pennsylvania Packet, and Daily Advertiser* 2148 (23 December 1785).
22 *Daily Advertiser* 10, 2909 (12 June 1795).
23 Gretchen Woertendyke, 'Romance to Novel: A Secret History', *Narrative* 17: 3 (2009), 255, 266.

17

Secret History in the Early Nineteenth-Century Americas

Gretchen J. Woertendyke

In the United States, the secret history was veiled behind, or embedded within, other generic markers: travel narratives, romances, tales, and serialized novels all participate in discourses of revelation and concealment, especially as geopolitics across the region attempted to consolidate the nation. In the half century since independence and in the departure from a constitutional monarchy, writers in the United States worked to establish a comprehensive historical narrative, one integral to the expansiveness of the territories and the ingenuity of its people. The uncertainty about the role of fiction further complicated the creation of histories, the sort that could adequately represent the belief in the nation's providential design. Critics and readers abroad often dismissed the possibility of American art, thwarting calls for a national literature. Sydney Smith, editor of the *Edinburgh Review* at the time, infamously asked who, 'in the four corners of the globe … reads an American book?' (1820). Such mocking helped to create some of the most critically canonical works and early manifestos by writers such as Ralph Waldo Emerson and Walt Whitman. But the focus on writing a great 'American book' and the literary criticism reinforcing its ultimate emergence has long obscured other fictional forms, and especially the popular fiction of the period. It is in these other forms of fiction, or the 'little histories', where secret histories get embedded.[1]

A private memoir and an allegory of state secrets, the secret history, in whatever guise, cannot be understood apart from its specific sociopolitical and historical context. As sectional, class, and racial crises over the institution of slavery became central to public discourse, slave narratives, confessions, urban crime mysteries, and exposés were staples of literary production, serialized in periodicals and as stand-alone forms. Popular, occasional, and otherwise outside of the mainstream, this literature invited readers into the private histories of unfamiliar characters and behind the veil of cultural taboos. It offered glimpses into criminality, sexual deviance, and the secret lives of slaves from a safe distance, making readers voyeurs of policed and prohibited experience. Joined by the already popular police gazettes, such as John Cleeve's *Weekly Police Gazette* (1834–1836) and *The National Police Gazette* (1845), sensational fiction, and stories of 'true crimes' catered to, indeed created the market for, secret histories as an amalgamation of genres that are, both in character and content, regional, hemispheric, and transatlantic.

Fiction, History, and the Novel

In the transformative period between 1790 and 1860 the proliferation of print brought working class, urban readers to newspapers in unprecedented numbers, where fiction and the 'news' intermingled freely, often muddling the distinction.[2] The suspicions of colonial readers shifted in focus from arbitrary government and the obstruction of individual liberties, to myriad perceived threats, domestic and foreign, to governance in the nineteenth century. The Alien and Sedition Acts put into effect in 1798 under President John Adams made public opposition to the government illegal, fostered anti-immigration policies, and made 'any false, scandalous and malicious writing against the government' a crime.[3] Fears of French revolutionary terror and Haitian refugees led to many sympathetic newspaper editors' imprisonment and the overall obstruction of democracy. In this context, secrecy operates as a legalized armament *against* the people and helped establish the grounds for the secret history.

Leonora Sansay's *Secret History; or the Horrors of St. Domingo* (1808) is striking because it identifies *as* a secret history, but much of the fiction produced in the period adopts the genre's narrative strategies and orientation towards its readers. In the quasi-fictional narrative about her fraught marriage to Louis Sansay and travels to Saint-Domingue at the height of the revolutionary struggle against France, images of French creoles, the luxurious life of Pauline Bonaparte, and slave violence form the backdrop to domestic cruelty. Though little is known of Sansay's early life, her relationship with Aaron Burr, which began in 1796, was instrumental in shaping both her private and public life.

Encouraged by Burr to marry a refugee from Saint Domingue in 1800, Sansay's sense of betrayal by Burr and her desire for public notice helped to produce *A Secret History; or the Horrors of St. Domingo*. Written as a series of letters to 'Colonel Burr, Late Vice-President of the United States', the *Secret History* relies on violent, erotic, and macabre images to reveal the private horrors of her marriage. Sansay, too, seems to have used the narrative to expose her intimacy with the Vice President. The

Haitian Revolution in Sansay's narrative betrays as much, or more, about the domestic relations between her alter-ego 'Clara' and her husband, St Louis (and by implication, Sansay's relationship with Aaron Burr), for example, than the private lives of the characters do about the revolutionary struggles unfolding in Saint-Domingue.[4]

Sansay's narrative plays with several genres at once: biography, secret history, and the gothic novel. Her use of anecdote as a vehicle through which privacy and publicity, truth and fiction, are often indistinguishable suggests a self-consciousness that invites readers to decode the narrative. As April London suggests, writers in the eighteenth century frequently used the anecdote in their fiction – useful in its 'capacity both to stimulate and to disrupt the story-making impulse – as counterpoint to their scrutiny of the apparent certainties of history and biography. 'Anecdotal writing', London illustrates, 'proves particularly suited to such sceptical articulations: even as it homes in on the revelatory detail, telling gesture, or exceptional subject, it invites further contemplation of the institutional structures it seemingly rejects'.[5] In Sansay's narrative, then, anecdote exploits its ambiguous and contradictory definitions – as something unpublished, or previously unknown – to put the large-scale History of imperial contest and institutional destruction up against the private tales of her secret affairs, with both men and women.

In the intimacy of epistolary novels such as Charles Brockden Brown's *Wieland, or Transformation: An American Tale* (1798), the narrative is structured as a series of private revelations. In Brown's novel, Clara testifies to her family's bizarre secrets; and Hannah Foster's *The Coquette: or, The History of Eliza Wharton; a Novel; Founded on Fact* (1797) is a thinly veiled story of a real-life scandal and mysterious circumstances surrounding the death of Elizabeth Whitman (1752–1788). Whitman was well-born, part of an extended family of ministers and educators, including Jonathan Edwards and the Reverend Aaron Burr, father of the third vice president of the United States and subject of his own scandalous trial for treason. In late spring of 1788, she left her home bound for Boston but instead arrived at a tavern in Danvers, Massachusetts. Registering under an assumed name, she claimed to be waiting for her husband's arrival. She gave birth to a stillborn child, destroyed any letters and documents that might identify her, and died two weeks later from complications from childbirth. In the ten years between her death and Foster's retelling, the newspapers took a keen interest in Whitman's story such that readers understood the news-novel matrix of *The Coquette* as the 'secret history' of Elizabeth Whitman.[6] In their Preface to *The Coquette; or, The History of Eliza Wharton; A Novel;*

Founded on Fact, Jennifer Harris and Bryan Waterman draw on the several existing, heavily annotated editions of the novel as evidence of the 'inestimable number of readers' who conjectured about the circumstances of her death: 'men and women alike wept over [her grave site], and at least one poet, John Patch, wrote an ode to it ... nineteenth-century tour guides advertised it as an attraction.[7] By 1866, *The Coquette* saw more than ten editions in print, including a serialized newspaper edition.

As the example of *The Coquette* illustrates, secret history in the United States may best be understood as what Michael McKeon identifies as an 'association of forms' that mediate the publicity of the seventeenth-century genre into one increasingly preoccupied by privacy. What McKeon calls a 'movement from domestication to domesticity', or 'the assumption by the private realm of tendencies toward thematic and teleological significance that formally had characterized only the public realm', is a development that secret histories are uniquely suited to negotiate.[8] As the public and the private are recognizably separate categories by the nineteenth century, the conventions of earlier secret histories become a transient, if not always seamless, aspect of the genre. Keys give way to explicit anecdotes and where the earlier form structured the private realm in service of the public, nineteenth-century narratives of secrecy tend to reverse this relationship, using the public realm in service of either disclosing or concealing private secrets. Though Foster's narrative has been identified as both a seduction and a conduct novel, generations of readers seem compelled to discover Whitman's secrets. Reading Foster's novel as a secret history provides another means of understanding the passionate response it generated, a response that include regular pilgrimages to Whitman's gravestone throughout the nineteenth century and into the twentieth.

Story-Papers, the Penny-Press, and 'True Crime'

The instability of early magazine culture in the late eighteenth century up through the 1820s hampered the development and circulation of serialized fiction and thus a potential market for secret histories. Restricted by limitations in distribution, itinerant merchants, long distances between central publishing houses, and emergent technologies in printing and transportation, early magazine culture developed unevenly. Charles Brockden Brown's attempt to publish a serialized novel, *The Memoirs of Stephen Calvert* (1799–1800), for example, went unfinished. Ultimately the difficulties of writing, editing, and publishing led to Brown's *Monthly Magazine* folding at the end of 1800. Advances in printing technologies

(1815) and the opening of the Erie Canal (1826) eventually helped bridge regional markets and consolidate antebellum magazine, periodical, and newspaper production.[9] Where early republican newspapers functioned as party platforms for politicians, the conspiratorial tenor and widespread hyperbole of these venues established a practice that conditioned later writers and readers alike. Such conditioning nurtured the development of secret history as writers sought to be published, establish a name, and invite speculation and controversy. Publications such as *Peter Porcupine's Gazette* (1797–1800), written, edited, and published by William Cobbett, rigorously targeted all manner of secret societies, which he deemed the largest threat to U.S. security. Freemasons, French Jacobins, the American Society of United Irishmen, and abolitionists of all kinds were ridiculed mercilessly. Newspapers and later pamphlets such as Cobbett's helped to produce a foundation for conspiratorial rhetoric, panic, and broad cultural paranoia, much of which bled into fictional forms such as the gothic novel, but also more popular forms of fiction like the secret history, found in the pages of nineteenth-century weeklies.

Two early nineteenth-century newspapers became instrumental to serialized fiction and the popularity of secret history by transforming eighteenth-century political dogma into publications that conjoined generic 'impurity' and the 'principle of contamination': Benjamin Day's *New York Sun* (1833) and James Gordon Bennett's New York *Herald* (1835).[10] Here, pirate ships, fugitive slave advertisements, society ladies, and legislative notice featured side-by-side, blending disparate content for readers by virtue of the newspaper's structural form. These papers printed news and stories about daily experiences of living in the city, replete with poverty, crime, mystery, deviance, and reformist outcries. They relied on advertising rather than political subsidies, which increased circulation and readers exponentially. The newspapers sold for a penny, so were newly accessible to most readers and, as such, pitched to a markedly different audience than previous iterations of the form. Such publications thrived on scandal, both political and sexual, two thematic engines of seventeenth and eighteenth-century secret histories. For example, in 1836, Bennett's paper picked up the story of a young prostitute's murder, adapting the conventions of fiction as well as secret histories, and creating a mystery out of material already well known. The panic fostered by Bennett's treatment of Helen Jewetts's murder by a nineteen-year-old clerk, named Richard P. Robinson, was published serially and included various images of Jewett's partially naked corpse lying on the bed, which Robinson had set on fire after the attack, and 'transcripts' of Robinson's trial.

The Jewett-Robinson murder case proved exceptionally sensational and Bennett took every opportunity to insinuate secrecy, confession, and mystery in the pages of the *Herald*. Bennett focused on the most grotesque, scandalous, and macabre details of the crime and its aftermath. He began by entering the crime scene before Jewett's body was removed, depicting her as a 'beautiful female corpse' which 'surpassed the finest statue in antiquity'.[11] He later published a false report that her 'beautiful body' had been dug up from the grave in order to perform a more accurate autopsy. As David Anthony points out in his treatment of Helen Jewett's case, 'even the grave is suspected of secrets'.[12] The media sensation was not limited to the New York *Herald*, in the months following the murder the case was covered zealously. Newspapers printed daily transcripts of Robinson's trial and, in the wake of Jewett's discovery, at least six pamphlets about the crime were published, all of which took up the question of why she would turn to prostitution rather than marriage.[13]

Just as readers responded to Foster's *The Coquette* as the secret history of Elizabeth Whitman, so too did readers seem to understand the tale of Helen Jewett's prostitution and murder as accountable *only* as a secret history. Both tales inspired identification with and sympathy for the female victims: Whitman's faithful protection of her lover until her death was seen as fidelity. As Harris and Waterman note, 'her grave became a site of pilgrimage where courting couples might pledge their love … her gravestone turned into relics, chipped away by romantic pilgrims'.[14] Similarly, one paper published that several women were seen collecting the burnt remains of Jewett's bed from outside the brothel, souvenirs of her tragic fall, and evidence of her secret history.[15] In this way, Bennett's paper offered a 'key' for decoding the mystery of Jewett and Robinson's fall – a mystery not of the murder, but of how these characters came to their tragic ends from otherwise privileged backgrounds.

In the aftermath of the financial crisis, the Panic of 1837, secret histories driven by the protection of – and thus window into – the private lives of mysterious figures, are joined by narratives meant to expose the secret corruption of a state, one that so failed to protect its citizens from economic disaster. No writer generated more controversy, sold more fiction, and exposed the so-called elite of his Philadelphian society more than George Lippard. Averaging over a million words annually, Lippard raged against the establishment and reached an unprecedented number of readers between 1842 and 1852. His career began as a copyeditor and city news reporter for the *Spirit of the Times*, a paper well suited to Lippard's political philosophy, before moving on to write for and edit the *Citizen Solider*.[16] In

1842, Lippard got his start writing the 'City Police' daily column for the *Spirit of the Times*, which required him to spend time at the Mayor's Police Court. Here, he honed what would become his aesthetic, interweaving narratives of true crime, with 'vivid Dickensian caricatures' and his own conviction about the unequal application of justice in Philadelphia.[17] Writing under the pseudonym 'Toney Blink', and then later 'Billy Brier', Lippard sought to make public the invisible, secret, world of respectable members of society: the clergy, bankers, police, lawyers, and the literary elite from which he felt especially excluded. In a series of ten instalments called 'Our Talisman', Lippard claims to have been given a ring that would allow him full access into the private chambers of the privileged. Here, he exposes the 'injunction of secrecy' that allows society's leaders to profit from the unwitting, even as he undermines the 'literati' who, according to Lippard, work tirelessly to discredit the Penny Press and sensational fiction more broadly.

As Christopher Looby demonstrates, in the overlap of literary and journalistic spheres, we can see Lippard 'chafing against the boundaries of fact and the limitations of journalistic form' –conditions out of which his sensational, serialized fiction emerges.[18] The most popular and well known of Lippard's fiction is *The Quaker City; or, The Monks of Monk Hall, A Romance of Philadelphia Life, Mystery, and Crime* (1845), which sold over 60,000 copies in its first year in print. *The Quaker City* was serially published in ten instalments and, like *The Coquette* and the pages of the New York *Herald*, was based on real events both sensational and mysterious. Based on a famous murder case of 1843, a man named Singleton Mercer was acquitted for the murder of Mahlon Heberton. Heberton had allegedly killed Mercer's sister after seducing her into what was either a brothel or a cheap room-for-rent establishment, with his promises of marriage.

As was the case of Jewett's murder, and Elizabeth Whitman's disappearance, the Mercer murder trial and acquittal was widely known. Splashed all over the pages of Philadelphia newspapers, the sensational event became a flashpoint for readers of *The Quaker City*. Lippard also included several subplots, violent, satiric, and with strains of the gothic, all of which fanned the flames of its rapidly growing appeal. Readers were especially keen to learn which of Philadelphia's local elite were targets of Lippard's revelations about hidden secrets, corruption, and criminal deviance. The desire to unmask those in seemingly irreproachable social positions compromises discrete categories of privacy and publicity; the secret history in mid-nineteenth-century America thrives upon exposure, which reinforces a sense of history worthy of public display. In this sense, the nationalist impulse to claim cultural significance seems to underlie the form even as it explicitly depends upon the seediest aspects of that culture for its popularity.

Most fascinatingly, when the first two-thirds of Lippard's novel were bound in 1845, and dedicated to Charles Brockden Brown, it was accompanied by *Key to the Quaker City: or, The Monks of Monk-Hall*. The title page reads, 'Published by the Author, and for Sale by all Booksellers', and it contains separately numbered pages at the back, with a short list of 'ERRATA OF THE QUAKER CITY'.[19] The *Key* is supposed to clarify any aspects of *The Quaker City* that remain mysterious or occluded; it claims to come from the lawyer, 'Old K____' who is mentioned in the original Preface to its first bound publication, 'The Origin and Object of this Book'. Given to Lippard from his deathbed, we hear from the 'good old lawyer' that his papers:

> '[c]ontain a full and terrible development of the Secret Life of Philadelphia. In that pacquet, you will find, records of crimes, that never came to trial, murders that have never been divulged; there you will discover the results of secret examinations, held by official personages, in relation to atrocities too horrible for belief—'.[20]

Here we find the features of secret histories, including a 'key', the omitted name of 'Old K—', and the cagey tension between concealment and disclosure, publicity and privacy, that the construction of 'secret examinations' implies. As Looby identifies the relative rarity of such keys in nineteenth-century U.S. fiction (Harriet Beecher Stowe's *Key to Uncle Tom's Cabin* (1853) is another), in the longue durée of transatlantic literary history, paratextual keys for unlocking the secrets embedded in texts are unremarkable. Lippard draws upon the formal structures – and conceptual affinities – of secret histories by including the publication of a *Key* when the novel is packaged as such. In this way, he retains the mystery and deferral associated with serialized publications (readers are left in an anticipatory state as certain secrets remain concealed until subsequent instalments), in its new, totalizing, and novelistic form. The publication of the *Key to Quaker City* does not, in fact, reveal all of the narrative secrets of its foundational fiction but rather serves to preserve and even intensify what Looby calls the 'antinomy of secrecy and publicity'. In this way, then, serialization, popular fiction, and Lippard's drive to expose all of the corruption and scandal underlying the respectable surface of state apparatus, create a secret history for early nineteenth-century U.S. readers.

In Lippard's novel, secrecy is the circuit that traffics between the private histories of marginal, suspect individuals and the public affairs of a fraudulent state.[21]

Confessions of Violence – Race, Slavery, and the Secret History

In the year following publication of Harriet Beecher Stowe's *Uncle Tom's Cabin* (1852), contemporary reviews and responses were polarizing: praised by some as remarkable for its sympathetic portrayal of a slave's life, her novel also received scathing reviews, especially from her southern interlocutors. Its instantaneous success – it sold 300,000 copies in 1852 – drew understandable ire from southern critics. Stowe transgressed several social boundaries: a northern woman writing about the south, a white woman writing about black experience and slave experience, and a Christian woman undermining the religious arguments for the maintenance of slavery, her novel touched upon the most explosive and controversial aspect of antebellum U.S. culture. John R. Thompson, in his 1852 review published in *The Southern Literary Messenger*, claims that Stowe 'intermeddle[d] with things which concern her not', effectively handing over the 'state to the perilous protection of diaper diplomatists and wet-nurse politicians'.[22] In another review, George Frederick Holmes argues that Stowe 'furnish[es] no evidence – whatever against the propriety or expediency of the slave'.[23] Stowe's response was to 'furnish' a response to her critics, published as *A Key to Uncle Tom's Cabin; Presenting the Original Facts and Documents Upon Which the Story is Founded; Together with Corroborative Statements Verifying the Truth of the Work* (1853). Motivated by a desire to legitimate her claims, disclose the secrets underlying the text, and absolve her of any scurrilous associations (including accusations of her own racist ideology), Stowe's *Key* functions quite differently than Lippard's for *The Quaker City*. Nevertheless, they share belief in the discourse, if not the realization of, revelation and disclosure and, perhaps, an impulse to simply show more about what, and how, each knows their subject(s).

Stowe's sentimental novel, however, touched upon the core conflict of the nineteenth-century Americas: if, and to what extent, the institution of slavery should continue. Slavery and its malignant influence on every facet of existence, from political, economic, geographic, psychological, existential, and much more, was an open secret. Legislation such as the Fugitive Slave Act of 1850 made even the most reluctant participants in the institution tacit supporters. While the violence inflicted upon black bodies and minds persisted as an open secret, the interior, secret, lives of slaves themselves remained concealed. Events such as Gabriel Prosser's conspiracy to revolt in Virginia, 1800; Denmark Vesey's forestalled slave insurrection in Charleston, 1822; and ultimately, Nat Turner's Rebellion in Virginia in 1831, made knowing the secret histories of slaves newly urgent. The increasing waves of violence across the Atlantic world, particularly in the wake of the Haitian Revolution, forced advocates of slavery to contend with black agency – and thus black subjectivity – so long denied and rejected. The acknowledgment of black subjectivity, however, required mediation, one that would not threaten the institution but would instead strengthen the rationale for its expansion throughout the southern hemisphere.

The Confessions of Nat Turner (1831), published by Thomas Gray, was one of the earliest narratives focused on an individual slave, and motivated by public need to know his secrets. After Nat Turner's capture, death sentence, and incarceration for the rebellion, which killed over 200 black and white residents of Southampton, Virginia, an industrious and financially destitute slaver owner, Gray, capitalized on the public desire to understand who Nat Turner was. Variously identified as a 'true account', a 'testimony', and a 'confession', *The Confessions of Nat Turner* offered the only source of insight into the central figure of the most successful U.S. slave revolt up to that time.

Gray secured access to Turner while in jail; claiming he was 'willing to make a full and free confession', Gray maintained that this account was published 'with little or no variation, from his own words … [which] certainly bear one stamp of truth and sincerity'.[24] The heavy editorial hand of Turner's confessions, though, makes very little of his private history visible, much less trustworthy; but it draws upon the sensational violence and the desire to account for it by an increasingly fearful public.[25] For Gray and the readers of *The Confessions of Nat Turner*, his testimony became evidence of a vulnerable system in need of reinforced surveillance, vigilante justice, and most importantly, access into the lives of slaves.[26]

The motivation, audience, and effects of later slave narratives such as Harriet Jacobs' *Incidents in the Life of a Slave Girl. Written By Herself* (1861) and *Narrative of the Life of Frederick Douglass, An American Slave, Written by Himself* (1845) are quite different to those surrounding the publication of Turner's 'Confessions'. Both edited and circulated by a white interlocutor, these secret histories of slavery – canonized as 'slave narratives' – were published to exemplify the 'horrors' of slave existence, and the depredation of the slave, to touch the lives of white readers in the fight for emancipation. Lydia Maria Child (for Jacobs) and William Lloyd Garrison (for Douglass) were both outspoken champions of abolitionism, who understood that the spectacular violence of slavery seemed an abstraction in the absence of an eyewitness account from a former slave.

In Jacobs' *Preface by the Author* she begins: 'Reader, Be Assured This narrative is no fiction. I am aware that some of my adventures may seem incredible; but they are, nevertheless, strictly true.' Stating that she hopes to shed light on the experiences of slavery as a woman, she also claims that she would have preferred 'to have been silent about my own history', painful and shameful as it is to her.[27] As Brown's and Foster's epistolary forms, and Lippard's serial forms, all tantalize readers by deferring knowledge and withholding secrets, Jacobs' heightens the sense of secrecy, disclosure, and concealment by expressing her wish to keep her history hidden from public view. Her performed reluctance also legitimates the 'testimony' readers are invited to read. Child's *Introduction by the Editor* similarly functions to entice readers with anticipatory desire for the spectacle of private experience of very public forms of violence. She writes,

> I am well aware that many will accuse me of indecorum for presenting these pages to the public; for the experiences of this intelligent and much-injured woman belong to a class which some call delicate subjects, and other indelicate. This peculiar phase of Slavery has generally been kept veiled; but the public ought to be made acquainted with its monstrous features, and I willingly take the responsibility of presenting them with the veil withdrawn.[28]

Child's 'indelicate' disclosure of this 'peculiar phase of Slavery' hints at the true secret history at the core of Jacobs' narrative – her sexual compliance with a white man to avoid being raped by her owner. The combination of Jacob's willingness to confess her personal sins for public veneration, and Child's commitment to exposing the 'monstrous features' of female slaves' experience, raises the stakes of secret history considerably and explicitly. Child not only exposes the 'darkness of blackness' that underlies Jacobs' life, but also exposes herself to censure and condemnation.[29]

By the mid-nineteenth century, the nation's ugly secret was on the precipice of comprehensive public account and subsequent destruction. Reformist movements and discourses of democracy fuelled the development and popularity of secret history throughout the nineteenth century. The growth in periodical fiction, cheaper printing and distribution, and increasingly diverse readership all facilitated the forms of secret history, increasing both its supply and demand in a period of far-reaching cultural transformation. Finally, secrecy and its generic forms provided an alibi for a young nation concerned about its shallow past, sometimes shameful present, and uncertain future. These competing valences suggest how and why the secret history remains veiled in U.S. literary histories, but also, the ways in which the secret history found fertile ground in early America.

Notes

1 In the preface to *The Secret History of Queen ZARAH; and the Zarazians*, Joseph Browne writes, in a passage borrowed from Morvan de Bellegarde's 'sur l'Histoire': 'The Little *Histories* of this kind have taken Place of *Romances*, whose Prodigious Number of Volumes were sufficient to tire and satiate such whose heads were most fill'd with those Notions.' See [Joseph Browne], *Queen Zarah and the Zarazians; Being a Looking-Glass for — In the Kingdom of ALBIGION* (*Albigion* [London], 1705), A2r (italics reversed).
2 For publishing statistics in the nineteenth century, see Ronald J. Zboray, *A Fictive People: Antebellum Economic Development and the American Reading Public* (Oxford: Oxford University Press, 1993); for discussions about popular literary forms and working-class readers see Michael Denning, *Mechanic Accents: Dime Novels and Working Class Culture in America* (London: Verso, 1987); for the relationships between writers, newspapers, and publishing see Meredith L. McGill, *American Literature and the Culture of Reprinting, 1834–1853* (Philadelphia: University of Pennsylvania Press, 2003); for sensational literature and its relation to empire see Shelley Streeby's *American Sensations: Class, Empire, and the Production of Popular Culture* (Berkeley: University of California Press, 2002).
3 Published as '*An Act in Addition to the Act, Entitled "An Act for the Punishment of Certain Crimes Against the United States"*', in Section 2 of The Alien and Sedition Acts. This Act was approved on 14 July 1798. See The Avalon Project. Available at: www.avalon.law.yale.edu/18th_century/sedact.asp.
4 See Michael Drexler, Introduction to Sansay's *Secret History; or the Horrors of St. Domingo and Laura* (Peterborough: Broadview Press, 2007), 1–37.
5 See April London, 'Anecdote and Secret History' in this volume; Lionel Gossman describes anecdote as 'a species of historical writing that deliberately eschewed large-scale "narrativization,"' referring to Hayden White's terminology. See 'Anecdote and History', *History and Theory* 42 (May 2003), 150.
6 See Lennard J. Davis, *Factual Fictions: The Origins of the English Novel* (Philadelphia: University of Pennsylvania Press, 1997), 42–70.
7 Jennifer Harris and Bryan Waterman, Preface to Hannah Foster, *The Coquette and The Boarding School*, ed. Jennifer Harris and Bryan Waterman (New York: Norton, 2013), xv–xvi.
8 Michael McKeon, *The Secret History of Domesticity: Public, Private, and the Division of Knowledge* (Baltimore: Johns Hopkins University Press, 2005), xxii–xxiii.

9 See Ronald Zboray, *A Fictive People: Antebellum Economic Development and the American Reading Public* (Oxford: Oxford University Press, 1993), 55–68; Frank Luther Mott, *A History of American Magazines,* 5 vols. (Cambridge: Harvard University Press, 1938–1968); Ralph Leslie Rusk, 'Newspapers and Magazines' in *The Literature of the Middle Western Frontier*, 2 vols. (New York: Columbia University Press, 1925), 131–203.

10 I take my terms, 'impure' and 'contamination' from Jacques Derrida and Avital Ronell's theory of genre in Derrida, Jacques and Avital Ronell, *Critical Inquiry*, vol. 7, no. 1, On Narrative (Autumn, 1980), 55–81.

11 *New York Herald*, April 11, 1836.

12 See David Antony, 'The Helen Jewett Panic: Tabloids, Men, and the Sensational Public Sphere in Antebellum New York', *American Literature* 69:3 (September 1997), 489.

13 See pamphlets such as *The Thomas Street Tragedy: The Murder of Ellen Jewett and Trial of Robinson* (New York, 1836); *An Authentic Biography of the Late Helen Jewett, A Girl of the Town by a Gentleman Fully Acquainted with Her History* (New York, 1836). Her name was often misidentified as 'Ellen'.

14 See Harris and Waterman's preface to Foster's *The Coquette*, xv–xvi.

15 See *The Illuminator*, 5 May 1836, quoted in Anthony, 'The Helen Jewett Panic', 489.

16 The mantra for *The Spirit of the Times* was 'Democratic and Fearless; Devoted to No Clique, and Bound to No Master'.

17 See Christopher Looby, 'Lippard in Part(s): Seriality and Secrecy in The Quaker City', *Nineteenth-Century Literature*, 79:1 (June 2015), 4. My discussion of Lippard is indebted to Looby's essay and to David Reynolds 'Introduction', *The Quaker City: Or, The Monks of Monk Hall, A Romance of Philadelphia Life, Mystery, and Crime* (Amherst: University of Massachusetts Press, 1995), vii–xli.

18 Looby, 'Lippard in Part(s)', 9.

19 Looby, 'Lippard in Part(s)', 30.

20 Lippard, *The Quaker City: Or, The Monks of Monk Hall, A Romance of Philadelphia Life, Mystery, and Crime*, ed. David S. Reynolds (Amherst: University of Massachusetts, 1995), 3.

21 Lippard joined his brand of socialist politics to his sense of social conspiracy when he established *The Brotherhood of the Union*, a secret society made up of 'a quasi-religious and patriotic ritual that would remind workers that they were members of a larger Brotherhood of Toil founded by Jesus and fought for by George Washington' (David Reynolds, cited in Matt Cohen and Edlie L. Wong, 'Introduction', in Lippard's *The Killers: A Narrative of Real Life in Philadelphia*, ed. Cohen and Wong (Philadelphia: University of Pennsylvania Press, 2014), 6).

22 See *Southern Literary Messenger*, October (1852):1, 630–640 [page 1]).

23 *Southern Literary Messenger*, December (1852).

24 See *The Confessions of Nat Turner and Related Documents*, ed. Kenneth S. Greenberg (Boston: Bedford/St. Martin's, 1996), 40.

25 For a fuller discussion of *The Confessions of Nat Turner* in relation to the confession, see Woertendyke, 'Trials and Confessions of Fugitive Slave Narratives', in *Journeys of the Slave Narrative in the Early Americas*, ed. Nicole Aljoe and Ian Finesth (Charlottesville: University of Virginia Press, 2014), 47–73.
26 See Dwight McBride, *Impossible Witnesses: Truth, Abolitionism, and Slave Testimony* (New York: New York University Press, 2001); Jeannine Marie DeLombard, *Slavery on Trial: Law, Abolitionism, and Print Culture* (Chapel Hill: University of North Carolina Press, 2007); and Saidiya Hartman, *Scenes of Subjection: Terror, Slavery, and Self-Making in Nineteenth-Century America* (Oxford: Oxford University Press, 1997).
27 Harriet Jacobs, *Incidents in the Life of a Slave Girl. Written By Herself*, ed. Nell Irvin Painter (New York: Penguin, 2000), 3.
28 Jacobs, *Incidents in the Life of a Slave Girl*, 5–6.
29 See Herman Melville, 'Hawthorne and His Mosses', where he refers to the 'blackness of darkness'. Available at: www.eldritchpress.org/nh/hahm.html.

Epilogue
Secret History at the Start of the Twenty-First Century
Rachel Carnell

As the essays in this collection demonstrate, secret history has been influential in the political public sphere in Britain, France, and the United States since the late seventeenth century. Despite its prominence in the rough and tumble of partisan politics in England and revolutionary politics in France, the form slipped away from mainstream literary circles as the novel became a dominant literary genre in many Western cultures. By the early nineteenth century, Isaac D'Israeli would refer to the genre as 'often a treasure under ground'.[1] Even as some of its complex narratological features were adopted by novelists, secret histories became lost to literary history, visible to mid twentieth-century scholars, including Ian Watt, merely as flawed romance novels.[2] However, secret history has never disappeared from the political public sphere; its presence, in the form of creative nonfiction and political anecdotes is still evident in the public sphere today, in both print and electronic media.

While in the eighteenth century, secret history was certainly not considered high literature (as Alexander Pope's facetious remark in 1714 about the sustained popularity of *The New Atalantis* suggests), secret histories nevertheless were widely read by those in the corridors of power.[3] In 1709 everyone who was anyone in English court circles had read Delarivier Manley's *New Atalantis*, even those, like Alexander Pope and Lady Mary Pierrepont who were unimpressed by Manley's skill as a writer.[4] The Earl of Sunderland took Manley's writing seriously enough to arrest her for libel. By contrast, it is hard to tell who in the Washington corridors of power actually read *The Secret Life of Bill Clinton: the Unreported Stories* when it appeared in 1997. The *New York Times* never deigned to review it but merely maligned its author in an article about the 'Clinton crazies ... of conservative and sometimes conspiratorial bent'.[5] In other words, the tell-all anecdotal secret history has never disappeared, even if it was relegated, as Eve Tavor Bannet observes, to 'the wrong side of opposition between truth and scandal, fact and fiction'.[6]

This, in any case, is the narrative of secret history now familiar to many of us in academia, in part through the influence of twentieth-century New Criticism that disdained the connection between 'high' literature and politics. In 1953, Robert Penn Warren wrote an introduction for the Modern Library edition of his 1946 novel *All the King's Men*, insisting that it 'was never intended to be a book about politics'.[7] Nevertheless, for many readers, the work must have felt like a secret history of Hugh P. Long, or Warren would not have felt compelled to defend his novel so staunchly as a work of literature, not politics. The complex narrative voicing, in which Warren establishes his narrator as an outsider, echoes the tradition of secret historians writing against the dominant narratives of history. Yet Warren, in his preface, insists that he was alluding to works of high literature, such as *The Faerie Queene*, rather than the quotidian details of twentieth-century politics (conveniently ignoring the possibility of reading Spencer's epic as a secret history of Elizabeth I).

Despite a denigrating attitude towards political secret history in twentieth-century literary circles, examples of secret history are nevertheless everywhere today: in memoirs, biographies, narrative non-fiction, and websites purporting to offer scientific or medical information that undercuts establishment scientific thinking regarding everything from vaccines to climate change. In the early twenty-first century, in which large portions of Western populations receive news and information through television or electronic media, the impulse to divulge secrets or a hidden back-story is as strong as ever. The rhetorical tropes that marked the narratological self-consciousness of the secret historian, however, appear to be diminishing in our increasingly post-print era, signalling a new phase in our post-Enlightenment public sphere in which political anecdotes may be less likely to offer evidence-based challenges to dominant narratives of history and more likely to circulate as unattributed and unsubstantiated rumour.[8]

Our taste for anecdote today is visible in a range of contemporary publications. In acknowledging the innovation of Ruth Scurr's biography of John Aubrey (1626–97) – structured as fragmentary anecdotal entries in an imagined diary – Stuart Kelly suggests that her format is appropriate for a reading public accustomed to reading blogs:

> Imagine a webpage devoted to, let us say, Edward Bulwer-Lytton. Each page would correspond to a day of his life; and any contributor could place there known facts about what he did that day, what he wrote that day, either professionally or personally, what others said or wrote about him on that day, and historic events that happened simultaneously.[9]

For Kelly, 'The centoic, diaristic method' brings Aubrey to life again, 'by reshaping and remoulding, by cutting and pasting'.[10] Through her anecdotal diaristic structure, of course, Scurr also restores to Aubrey the taste for anecdote that marked his own era.

Despite a certain amnesia about the term in academic circles, the phrase 'secret history' still appears to retain a cultural cachet for educated readers today: Donna Tartt used the term two decades ago as the title of a mystery novel, *The Secret History* (1992), highly regarded for its resonant allusions to ancient Greek culture. The Harvard historian Jill Lepore used the term more recently for a work of popular history *The Secret History of Wonder Woman* (2014), in which she teases out the early feminists important in the life of William Moulton Marston, the creator of the comic strip *Wonder Woman*. In her introduction, moreover, Lepore sounds something like Andrew Marvell in *An Account of the Growth of Popery* (1677) announcing that he is uncovering the true events of the behind-the-scenes negotiations for the Secret Treaty of Dover in 1670. In repudiating a previous history of Wonder Woman, she insists that the author 'hasn't really got the history of Wonder Woman. All he's got is her Amazonian legend' (xii). By contrast, Lepore insists that she has done her homework; she went 'to the archives' and found

> thousands of pages of documents, manuscripts and typescripts, photographs and drawing, letters and postcards, criminal court records, notes scribbled in the margins of books, legal briefs, medical records, unpublished memoirs, story drafts, sketches, students transcripts, birth certificates, lectures notes, FBI files, movie scripts, the carefully typed meeting minutes of a sex cult, and tiny diaries written in secret code. (xiii)

Her emphasis on printed evidence places her firmly within the tradition of the coffee-house public sphere, in which printed newspapers and pamphlets were read and discussed. However, Lepore's revision of Moulton's life story will today compete for attention in the public sphere with an anticipated new movie version of the Wonder Woman story, which is likely to re-emphasize the mythic qualities of the heroine rather than the historical backstory of the comic strip's creator.

Lepore's evidence-based approach is typical not only of neoclassical secret history but of our contemporary taste or popular history and investigative journalism. Best-selling titles in this genre – from *The Smartest Guys in the Room: The Amazing Rise and Scandalous Fall of Enron* (2003) to *The Big Short: Inside the Doomsday Machine* (2010) and *Hidden America: From Coal Miners to Cowboys, an Extraordinary Exploration of the Unseen People Who Make this Country Work* (2012) – emphasize both the 'amazing' or 'extraordinary' stories hitherto unknown or 'unseen' by the reading public.

Epilogue: The Start of the Twenty-First Century

In other words, secret history has not entirely disappeared to the wrong side of literary history: its tradition informs high and low literature, and its basic impulse lives on in the increasingly popular genre of creative non-fiction, the 'fastest growing part of the market for books' today.[11]

Many of these modern-day secret histories begin with an author's preface that resembles Procopius's to his *Anekdota*, in their acknowledgment of their personal knowledge of the scandals they were uncovering. Michael Short describes his insider knowledge of the financial industry and its bubbles: 'I'd stumbled into a job a Saloman Brothers in 1985, and stumbled out, richer, in 1988, and even though I wrote a book about the experience, the whole thing still strikes me as totally preposterous – which is one reason the money was so easy to walk away from. I figured the situation was unsustainable'.[12] As a reviewer of the movie adaptation of the book points out, 'Part of the book's appeal – a side-effect of its author's smart, breezy, plain-spoken style – was that it offered readers the illusion of retroactive prescience'.[13] This illusion of prescience, effected by the narrator's confessional tone, is what secret histories have long offered readers. In the film version of Short's book, this prescience is given to viewers by the character of Jared Vennett, 'serving as our guide to the apocalypse unfolding around them', who occasionally 'cast[s] his baby blues toward the camera to tell us that something didn't really happen in quite the way it's being shown – or that, incredibly enough, it actually did'.[14]

One of the forerunners in this tremendously popular style of contemporary nonfiction (often translated into popular film) was Carl Bernstein and Bob Woodward's best-selling work of investigative political journalism, *All the President's Men* (1974), a book that documented the secret history of the fraudulent manoeuvres of government officials covering their actions in a smear campaign against the Democratic contender for President during the presidential election season of 1972. In structuring the book as a detective story about their act of discovery, a decision that may have been shaped by actor and director Robert Redford's early interest in that angle of their story, Woodward and Bernstein also follow in the tradition of certain secret historians, including Delarivier Manley, who thematize the act of revealing secrets.[15]

Nowadays it is possible to learn this rhetorical turn from a course or a video. In Tilar Mazzeo's guide to *Writing Creative Nonfiction*, a guidebook to accompany her video course in *The Great Courses* series, Mazzeo suggests starting a non-fiction narrative with an anecdote that includes a secret. 'Secrets are always tantalizing' (22), she advises. When a story arc is weak, Mazzeo suggests that the author should introduce herself and her act of uncovering this story into the narrative as a 'secondary character' (36). In other words, the rhetorical devices we have inherited from secret histories are now considered standard, teachable, rhetorical skills, appropriate for creative non-fiction. Literary agents, moreover, advise that in the US market, narrative or creative non-fiction often sells better than fiction.[16]

That the rhetorical skills of the secret historian nowadays may need to be taught, however, suggests that there are dynamics at play in our Web-based contemporary public sphere that make it easy to leave out the moments of narratological self-consciousness that so often marked earlier secret history. If searching a given topic online, readers may find an article from a reputable newspaper source; however, the article will be disconnected from the rest of the newspaper, including its op-ed page or other markers indicating the editorial board's political leaning. Recent research about newspaper readership, moreover, demonstrates that there are a greater number of visits to newspaper websites online than there are print readers, but 'the average visit to The New York Times' website and associated apps in January 2015 lasted only 4.6 minutes – and this was the highest of the top 25 [newspapers]'.[17]

While each year fascinating works of investigative journalism and narrative nonfiction are published, many of which include the voice of a narrator who openly states her own subject position, we are also awash with websites giving the appearance of objectivity with no markers of subject position. A student assigned to find evidence on the Internet about the fossil record and evolution from reputable 'institutional' sources will have trouble distinguishing sites offering science-based narratives from those that offer pseudo-scientific refutations of evolution.[18] One facet of our post-modern condition, in other words, is that every one wants to make the claim to having secret insider knowledge – and everyone with a tablet or a smartphone can post something to a website.

At the same time, the border between information that used to be considered secret or private, and information that is now routinely shared in the electronic sphere is becoming blurred. 'Reality' television shows purport that they are revealing the secrets of daily life and yet simultaneously suggest that there may be no secrets behind the screen. We are witnessing a generation of young persons raised to deploy their electronic personae on sites in which 'public' is the default option; this public self is not necessarily framed with nuanced narratological self-awareness. Twenty years ago in *The Secret Life of Bill Clinton*, which *The New York Times* described as a work of conspiracy theory, Ambrose Evans-Pritchard was careful to phrase his theories as *his* beliefs, rather than facts checked scrupulously by multiple cross checking of sources. He sums up his theories: 'It is *my* contention that every salient fact put forward by the Clinton administration about Waco is a lie.'[19] In our current decade, in which electronic media and television increasingly dominate now continuous news cycles, it is not surprising that counter-factual anecdotes proliferate.

During the 2015–2016 U.S. presidential election campaign, the political fact-checker Angie Drobnic Holan observed of a leading Republican presidential candidate: 'Donald J. Trump's record on truth and accuracy is astonishingly poor.' Her team found of seventy Trump statements, 'fully three-quarters' came up as 'Mostly False, False or "Pants on Fire"' (a claim they reserve for statements 'not only inaccurate but ridiculous').[20] Unlike Ambrose Evans-Pritchard, who carefully phrased his account of the Waco Texas events as *his* belief, Donald Trump apparently does not feel obliged to acknowledge the subjectivity (or lack of factuality) of his invented anecdotes.

As Trump now famously claimed at a rally in Birmingham Alabama on 21 November 2015: 'I watched when the World Trade Center came tumbling down … And I watched in Jersey City, N.J., where thousands and thousands of people were cheering as that building was coming down. Thousands of people were cheering.'[21] When George Stephanopoulos pointed out that 'the police say that didn't happen', Trump insisted: 'It was on television. I saw it … It was well covered at the time.' Referring to 'people over in New Jersey [where there is] a heavy Arab population … cheering as the buildings came down', Trump did not bother using any other standard of fact for this invented anecdote than the assertion that he once saw it on television.[22] Instead, Trump relied on a vague (invented) memory of television images for his evidence, presumably appealing to portions of the population whose access to facts may be based on things they might remember once having seen on television. He also cunningly used the interview in which his facts are challenged as a means of reiterating false images and repeating them in such a way as to conjure up images in his viewers' minds (some Arab-looking persons cheering for something somewhere) that might appear to validate his fictional anecdote.

The breadth and persistence of Donald Trump's appeal is certainly alarming to those of us who believe in the liberating possibilities of the evidence-based tradition of the Whig public sphere. At the same time, it is true that even the coffee houses of the mythic public sphere of eighteenth-century Britain self-segregated to some extent into bubbles of Whig, Tory, and Jacobite regulars.[23] Moreover, appealing to a reading public that feels alienated from those in power (and their reliance on the scientific method) is also nothing new. Delarivier Manley understood this in 1709 when she mocked the Whigs in power not only for their personal ambition but for their reliance on scientific evidence. Although an educated, well-read and sceptical thinker herself, Manley nevertheless structured her *Secret Memoirs ... from the New Atalantis* (1709) as a dystopian version of Francis Bacon's empirically forward-thinking and politically progressive *New Atlantis*, implicitly suggesting that the scientific truth and political 'progress' that followed the Revolution of 1688–89 were of most benefit to Whig favourites.

Even while mocking Bacon's evidence-based utopian vision, Manley, however, did not deviate extensively from well-established facts of history and well-known gossip; she merely retold this historical gossip with Tory spin. Moreover, her dedications (to influential Tories) fully disclosed the partisan bent of her satirical response to Bacon. Today, by contrast, anecdotes with no basis in fact are tweeted or posted with no narratological acknowledgement of subjectivity or partisan bias. Moreover, the rise of electronic media has resulted in a decline in sales and advertising revenues in mainstream newspapers, meaning that there are fewer resources to devote to investigative journalism, thus fewer resources to tell the factual back-stories to counter-factual anecdotes or corporate suppression of inconvenient truths, for example, about global warming.[24] Nevertheless, the future of the public sphere, even of humanity itself, may depend on whether factual self-reflective secret history will succeed in balancing out the influence of unattributed counter-factual anecdotes.

Notes

1 [Isaac D'Israeli], *Despotism; Or, The Fall of the Jesuits: A Political Romance, Illustrated by Historical Anecdotes*, 2 vols. (London: Murray, 1811) 2: 317, Archive.org.
2 Rachel Carnell, 'Slipping from Secret History to Novel', *Eighteenth-Century Fiction* 28, 1 (Fall 2015), 4–6.
3 'Let Wreaths of Triumph now my Temples twine,/ ... As long as *Atalantis* shall be read'. Canto III, II. 161, 165, cited from A. Pope, *The Rape of the Lock and Other Poems*, ed. G. Tillotson (New Haven: Yale University Press, 1962), 180–1.
4 In a letter in which she comments on the danger of censoring secret history by prosecuting Manley, Pierrepont expresses her concern that 'better pens' will now be reluctant to write 'more elegant and secret memoirs' than Manley did in her 'faint essay'. Mary Pierrepont to Frances Hewet, 12 November

Epilogue: The Start of the Twenty-First Century 263

[1709], in *The Complete Letters of Lady Mary Wortley Montagu*, ed. Robert Halsband, 3 vols. (Oxford: Clarendon Press, 1965), 1: 18.

5 Philip Weiss, 'Clinton Crazy', *New York Times Magazine*, 23 February 1997. Available at: www.nytimes.com/1997/02/23/magazine/clinton-crazy.html.

6 Eve Tavor Bannet '"Secret history"': Or, Talebearing Inside and Outside the Secretorie' in Paulina Kewes, *The Uses of History in Early Modern England* (San Marino: Huntington Library, 2006), 367.

7 Robert Penn Warren, Introduction, *All the King's Men* (New York: Modern Library, 1953), vi.

8 I am indebted to the lively discussion about secret history that followed a talk I gave to the Alternate Histories Research Cluster at the University of Manitoba's Institute for the Humanities, 12 January 2016: 'The Secret History of Secret History: From Procopius to *Primary Colors*'. I appreciate the generosity of the Institute for the Humanities in hosting this event.

9 Stuart Kelly, 'Enter John Aubrey', *Times Literary Supplement*, 25 February 2015. Available at: www.the-tls.co.uk/tls/public/article1523401.ece.

10 Kelly, 'Enter John Aubrey'.

11 Tilar Mazzeo, *Writing Creative Nonfiction* (Chantilly: The Teaching Company 2012), 7.

12 Michael Lewis, *The Big Short: Inside the Doomsday Machine* (New York: W. W. Norton, 2010), xiii.

13 A. O. Scott, 'In "The Big Short", Economic Collapse for Fun and Profit', *New York Times* 10 December 2015. Available at: www.nytimes.com/2015/12/11/movies/review-in-the-big-short-economic-collapse-for-fun-and-profit.html.

14 A. O. Scott, 'In "The Big Short".

15 The actor Robert Redford suggests in a short documentary about making the film version of *All the Presidents' Men* that he first suggested this structure for a movie before Woodward and Bernstein had written the book, acknowledging that his suggestion may have influenced their decision to structure the book this way. See 'Telling the Truth About Lies: The Making of *All the President's Men*', directed by Gary Leva (2006). Rebecca Bullard points out that as a Tory, Manley was both 'appropriating and attacking' the structure of previous Whig secret histories by her inclusion of several naïve narrators retelling well-known anecdotes about prominent Whig courtiers. See R. Bullard *The Politics of Disclosure 1674–1725: Secret History Narratives* (London: Pickering & Chatto, 2009), 93.

16 Conversation with Marcy Posner of Folio Literary Management, October 2010.

17 Michael Barthel, 'Newspapers: Fact Sheet *State of the News Media 2015*', Pew Research Center. Journalism and Media. Available at: www.journalism.org/2015/04/29/newspapers-fact-sheet.

18 My daughter, an eighth-grade student at the time, was instructed by her science teacher to look for websites ending in 'org' or 'edu', an instruction intended to locate sites representing genuine scientific information. This

technique did not work, however, given the proliferation of organizations devoted to posting counter-factual scientific 'facts' on websites ending in 'org'.
19 Ambrose Evans-Pritchard, *The Secret Life of Bill Clinton: The Unreported Stories* (Washington: Regnery Publishing, 1997), xv, emphasis added.
20 Angie Drobnic Holan, 'All Politicians Lie. Some Lie More Than Others, *The New York Times*, 11 December 2015.
21 Cited in Lauren Carroll, 'Fact-checking Trump's claim that thousands in New Jersey cheered when World Trade Center tumbled', 22 November 2015. Available at: www.politifact.com/truth-o-meter/statements/2015/nov/22/donald-trump/fact-checking-trumps-claim-thousands-new-jersey-ch/.
22 Cited in Caroll, 'Fact-checking Trump's claim'.
23 As Thomas Macaulay notes, 'every rank and profession, and every shade of religious and political opinion, had its own headquarters'. *The History of England From the Accession of James II*, 6 vols. (New York: Harper and Brothers, 1856), 1: 276.
24 Newspaper revenues continue to fall, as does the number of journalists employed by newspapers. See Barthel, 'Newspapers: Fact Sheet'.

Select Bibliography

PRIMARY SOURCES

Amhurst, Nicholas, *Terræ Filius: The Secret History of the University of Oxford,* ed. William E. Rivers (Cranbury: University of Delaware Press, 2004).
Austen, Jane, *Emma,* ed. James Kinsley (Oxford: Oxford University Press, 2003).
— *Mansfield Park,* ed. John Wiltshire (Cambridge: Cambridge University Press, 2005).
An Authentic Biography of the Late Helen Jewett, A Girl of the Town by a Gentleman Fully Acquainted with Her History (New York, 1836).
Bampfield, Joseph, *Colonel Joseph Bampfield's Apology,* ed. John Loftis and Paul H. Hardacre (Lewisburg: Bucknell University Press, 1993).
Behn, Aphra, *Love-Letters Between a Nobleman and his Sister,* ed. Janet Todd (Harmondsworth: Penguin, 1996).
Blackwell, Mark, Liz Bellamy, Christina Lupton, and Heather Keenleyside (eds.), *British It-Narratives, 1750–1830* (London: Pickering and Chatto, 2012).
Burke, Edmund, *The French Revolution, 1790–1794,* ed. L. G. Mitchell, vol. 8 of *Writings and Speeches,* gen. ed. Paul Langford, 9 vols. (Oxford: Clarendon Press, 1990).
Burnet, Gilbert, *Bishop Burnet's History of His Own Time,* 6 vols. (London, 1724–34).
Byrd, William. *The Dividing Line Histories of William Byrd II of Westover,* ed. Kevin Joel Berland (Chapel Hill: University of North Carolina Press for the Omohundro Institute for Early American History and Culture, 2013).
Cabala, Mysteries of State (London, 1654).
The Cabinet Opened, or Secret History of Mme de Maintenon (London, 1690).
'The Caravan, and the Dog Carlo', *The Sporting Magazine,* 23.135 (1803), 148–9.
Care, Henry, *History of the Damnable Popish Plot* (London, 1680).
CARLO, The Roscius of Drury-Lane Theatre (London, 1804).
Cato, or Interesting Adventures of a Dog of Sentiment (London, 1816).
Coventry, Francis, *The History of Pompey the Little; or, the Life and Adventures of a Lap-Dog* (London, 1751).
Defoe, Daniel, *The Secret History of the October Club; from its Original to this Time,* 3 parts (London, 1711).
— *The Secret History of the White-Staff,* 3 parts (London, 1714–15).

The Secret History of the Secret History of the White-Staff, Purse, and Mitre (London, 1715).

D'Israeli, Isaac, *Despotism; Or, The Fall of the Jesuits: A Political Romance, Illustrated by Historical Anecdotes*, 2 vols. (London, 1811).

'True Sources of Secret History', *Curiosities of Literature,* ed. Benjamin Disraeli, 3 vols. (London, [n.d.]).

Dryden, John, *Absalom and Achitophel. A Poem* (London, [1708(?)]).

Poems, 1681–1684, ed. H. T. Swedenberg, Jr., vol. 2 (1972) of *The Works of John Dryden*, 20 vols. (Berkeley: University of California Press, 1972–1990).

Of Dramatic Poesy and Other Critical Essays, ed. George Watson, 2 vols. (London and New York: Dent; Dutton, 1962).

Dunton, John, *The Art of Living Incognito*, 2 Parts (London, 1700).

The Athenian Spy: Discovering the Secret Letters Which Were Sent to the Athenian Society by the Most Ingenious Ladies of the Three Kingdoms (London, 1704).

The Life and Errors of John Dunton (London, 1705).

Queen Robin: or The Second Part of Neck or Nothing, Detecting the Secret Reign of the Four Last Years (London, 1714).

Essais historiques sur la vie de Marie-Antoinette d'Autriche, reine de France (Londres [London], 1798).

Fenwick, Elizabeth, *The Life of Carlo, the Famous Dog of Drury-Lane Theatre: With his Portrait, and other Copper Plates* (London, 1804).

The Life of the Famous Dog Carlo: with his portrait, and other copper plates (London, 1809).

Force, Charlotte-Rose Caumont de la, *Anecdote galante et secrète de la duchesse de Bar* (Amsterdam, 1709).

Histoire secrète de Marie de Bourgogne, 2 vols. (Lyon, 1694).

Foster, Hannah, *The Coquette and The Boarding School*, ed. Jennifer Harris and Bryan Waterman (New York: Norton, 2013).

Gavin, Antonio, *A Master-Key to Popery. Containing a Discovery of the most Secret Practices of the Secular and Regular Romish Priests in the Auricular Confessions, etc.* (Dublin, 1724).

Gibbon, Edward, *The History of the Decline and Fall of the Roman Empire*, ed. David Womersley, 3 vols. (New York: Allen Lane, 1994).

Gibbons, Thomas, *Rhetoric: Or a View of its Principal Tropes and Figures* (London, 1767).

Gillray, James, *The Theatrical Bubble* (London, 1805).

Goldsmith, Lewis, *Secret History of the Cabinet of Bonaparte* (London, 1810).

Guénard, Madame, *Irma, ou les Malheurs d'une jeune orpheline. Histoire indienne, avec des Romances*, 4 vols. (Delphy and Paris, an VIII [1799]).

Hamilton, Anne, *Secret History of the Court of England, from the Accession of George the Third to the Death of George the Fourth*, 2 vols. (Boston, 1901).

Hawkesworth, John, *Almoran and Hamet*, in *Oriental Tales*, ed. Robert Mack (Oxford: Oxford University Press, 1992).

Haywood, Eliza, *The Adventures of Eovaai, Princess of Ijaveo*, ed. Earla Wilputte (Peterborough, Ontario: Broadview Press, 1999).
The Invisible Spy, 2 vols., 2nd edn (London, 1759).
Hazlitt, William, *Life of Napoleon Buonaparte*, vols. 13–14 of *Complete Works*, ed. P. P. Howe, 21 vols. (London: Dent, 1931).
Hearne, Thomas, *Ductor Historicus* (London, 1698).
Histoire secrète de la conjuration des Pazzi (Paris, 1697).
The History of Belisarius (America [i.e., Philadelphia], 1770).
History of the Revolution of the 18th Fructidor (London, 1800).
Hobbes, Thomas, *Behemoth or the Long Parliament*, ed. Ferdinand Tönnies, 2nd edn (London: Cass, 1969).
Hooke, Nathaniel, *The Secret History of Colonel Hooke's Negotiations in Scotland, in Favour of the Pretender; in 1707* (Dublin, 1760).
Jacobs, Harriet, *Incidents in the Life of a Slave Girl. Written By Herself*, ed. Nell Irvin Painter (New York: Penguin, 2000).
Johnstone, Charles, *Chrysal; or the Adventures of a Guinea* (London, 1760).
Jones, David, *The Secret History of White-Hall, from the Restoration of Charles II down to the Abdication of the late K. James* (London, 1697).
Kelly, Michael, *Reminiscences of Michael Kelly, of the King's Theatre, and Theatre Royal Drury Lane* (London, 1826).
Ker, John, *The Memoirs of John Ker of Kersland in North Britain Esq. Containing His Secret Transactions and Negotiations in Scotland, England, the Courts of Vienna, Hanover, and Other Foreign Parts* (London, 1726).
The Kings Cabinet Opened: Or, Certain Packets of Secret Letters & Papers, Written with the Kings own Hand, and taken in his Cabinet at Nasby-Field, June 14. 1645 (London, 1645).
Lee, Sophia, *The Recess; Or, a Tale of Other Times*, Ed. April Alliston (Lexington: The University Press of Kentucky, 2000).
Le Moyne, Pierre, *Of the Art Both of Writing and Judging of History* (London, 1695).
The Life of Ellen Jewett; Illustrative of Her Adventures with Very Important Incidents, from her Seduction to the Period of her Murder (New York, 1836).
Lippard, George, *The Killers: A Narrative of Real Life in Philadelphia*, ed. Matt Cohen and Edlie L. Wong (Philadelphia: University of Pennsylvania Press, 2014).
The Quaker City: Or, The Monks of Monk Hall, A Romance of Philadelphia Life, Mystery, and Crime, ed. David S. Reynolds (Amherst: University of Massachusetts, 1995).
A Loyal Congratulation to the Right Honourable, Anthony, Earl of Shaftesbury: Upon the Disappointment of his, the King and Kingdoms Enemies, by the Loyal Grand Juries Finding the Bill against him Ignoramus (London, 1681).
Macaulay, Thomas, *The History of England From the Accession of James II*, 6 vols. (New York, 1856).
Macky, John, *Memoirs of the Secret Services of John Macky, Esq … Also, The True Secret History of the Rise, Promotions, &c. of the English and Scots Nobility;*

Officers, Civil, Military, Naval, and Other Persons of Distinction, from the Revolution (London, 1733).

Manley, Delarivier, *The New Atalantis*, ed. Ros Ballaster (London: Penguin, 1991; New York: Penguin Classics, 1992).

Marana, Giovanni Palo, *Letters Writ by a Turkish Spy*, Ed. Robert Midgley, 8 vols. (Dublin, 1736).

Milton, John, *Complete Prose Works of John Milton*, 8 vols. (New Haven: Yale University Press, 1953–1982).

Paradise Lost, A Poem in Twelve Books, ed. Thomas Newton, 2 vols. 3rd edn (London, 1754).

la Mothe le Vayer, François de, *Oeuvres*, 2 vols. (Paris, 1662).

N. N., *The Blatant Beast Muzzl'd: or, Reflexions on a Late Libel, entituled, The Secret History of the Reigns of K. Charles II and K. James II* ([London] 1691).

Oldmixon, John, *Arcana Gallica: or, the Secret History of France, for the Last Century* (London, 1714).

The Critical History of England; Ecclesiastical and Civil, 2 vols. (London, 1726).

Pagès, François Xavier, *Secret History of the French Revolution* (London, 1797).

The Player's Tragedy. Or, Fatal Love, A New Novel (London, 1693).

Pope, Alexander, *Epistles to Several Persons*, ed. F. W. Bateson (London: Methuen; New Haven: Yale University Press, 1951).

A Master-Key to Popery, or, A True and Perfect Key to Pope's Epistle to the Earl of Burlington, transcribed by Lady Burlington and reprinted by John Butt in Clifford, James L. and Louis A Landa (eds.), *Pope and His Contemporaries: Essays Presented to George Sherburn* (Oxford: Clarendon Press, 1949).

The Prose Works of Alexander Pope, ed. Norman Ault and Rosemary Cowler, vol. 2 (Hamden: Archon Books, 1986).

The Rape of the Lock and Other Poems, ed. G. Tillotson (New Haven: Yale University Press, 1962).

Préchac, Jean de, *Le Secret, nouvelles historiques. Avec le Compliment de Vertus au Roy sur la Naissance de Monseigneur le Duc de Bourgogne* (Paris, 1683).

Procopius, *Anecdota or Secret History*, trans. H. B. Dewing (London: Heinemann, 1935).

Arcana historia, trans. Nicolò Alemanni (Lyon, 1623).

The Debaucht Court; or, The Lives of the Emperor Justinian and his Empress Theodora the Comedian (London, 1682).

Histoire secrète de Procope de Césarée, trans. Leonor de Mauger (Paris, 1669).

The Secret History of the Court of the Emperor Justinian, (London, 1674).

The Secret History, trans. G. A. Williamson (London: Penguin, 1966).

Rapin, René, *Instructions for History, with a Character of the Most Considerable Historians Ancient and Modern*, trans. J. Davies (London, 1680).

Reynolds, Frederick, *The Life and Times of Frederick Reynolds*, 2 vols. (London, 1827).

Ridley, James, *The Tales of the Genii: or, the Delightful Lessons of Horam, the Son of Asnar*, 2 vols., 3rd edn (London, 1766).

Robson, Joseph, *An Account of Six Years Residence in Hudson's-Bay, from 1733 to 1736, and 1744 to 1747* (London, 1752).

Ryves, Thomas, *Imperatoris Iustiniani defensio aduersus Alemannum* (Londini [London], 1626).
Saint-Hyacinthe, Thémiseul de, *L' Histoire de Prince Titi. A[llegorie].R[oyale]* (Paris, 1726).
Salmon, Thomas, *Impartial Examination of Bishop Burnet's History of His Own Time*, 2 vols. (London, 1724).
Sansay, Leonora, *Secret History; or the Horrors of St. Domingo and Laura*, ed. Michael Drexler (Toronto: Broadview, 2007).
Santa Croce, Prospero, *Lettres du cardinal di Santa Croce, écrites pendant son nonciature en France, au cardinal Boromée neveu du pape Pie IV. Et tirées des manuscrits originaux de la Bibliothèque du Vatican. Contenant l'histoire secrète de la naissance et des progrès de la religion reformée en France* (La Haye [The Hague], 1717).
Scott, Helenus, *The Adventures of a Rupee* (London, 1782).
Scott, Walter, *The Heart of Midlothian*, 4 vols. (Edinburgh, 1814).
 Waverley; or, 'Tis Sixty Years Since, 3 vols. (Edinburgh, 1814).
The Secret History of an Old Shoe (London, 1734).
The Secret History of Lewis XI in *Memoirs of Philip de Comines*, 2 vols. ed. Andrew R. Scuble (London, 1823).
A Secret History of Pandora's Box (London, 1742).
Secret History of the French Revolution (London, 1797).
The Secret History of the Reigns of K. Charles II and K. James II ([London?], 1691).
The Secret History of White-Hall, From the Restoration of Charles II Down to the Abdication of the late K. James (London, 1697).
Shaftesbury, Anthony Ashley Cooper, Third Earl of, *Characteristics of Men, Manners, Opinions, Times*, ed. Lawrence E. Klein (Cambridge: Cambridge University Press, 1999).
Sketch of the Life of Miss Helen Jewett (Boston, 1836).
A Sketch of the Life of Richard P. Robinson, the Alleged Murderer of Helen Jewett (New York, 1836).
Smollett, Tobias, *The History and Adventures of an Atom*, ed. O. M. Brack (Athens: University of Georgia Press, 2008).
Somers, John, *The True Secret History of the Lives and Reigns of All the Kings and Queens of England* ([London], 1702).
Sterne, Laurence, *The Florida Edition of the Works of Laurence Sterne*, ed. Melvyn New, Joan New and Peter de Voogd, 8 vols. (Gainesville: The University Presses of Florida, 1978–2008).
Swift, Jonathan. *A Tale of a Tub and Other Works*, ed. Marcus Walsh (Cambridge: Cambridge University Press, 2010).
The Thomas Street Tragedy: The Murder of Ellen Jewett and Trial of Robinson (New York, 1836).
Turner, Nat, *The Confessions of Nat Turner and Related Documents*, ed. Kenneth S. Greenberg, (Boston: St. Martin's 1996).
Tyrrell, James, *The General History of England*, 5 vols. (London, 1704).

Varillas, Antoine, *Anekdota Heterouiaka. Or, The Secret History of the House of Medicis*, trans. Ferrand Spence (London, 1686).
Ward, Edward, *The London Spy*, 4th edn, 2 vols. (London, 1709).
Williams, Anna, *Miscellanies in Verse and Prose* (London, 1766).

SECONDARY SOURCES

Aravamudan, Srinivas, *Enlightenment Orientalism: Resisting the Rise of the Novel* (Chicago: University of Chicago Press, 2011).
Archer, John Michael, *Sovereignty and Intelligence: Spying and Court Culture in the English Renaissance* (Stanford: Stanford University Press, 1993).
Backscheider, Paula, *Spectacular Politics* (Baltimore: The Johns Hopkins University Press, 1993).
Baecque, Antoine de, 'Dégénérescence et régénération: le livre licencieux juge la Révolution française', in *Mélanges de la Bibliothèque de la Sorbonne, no. 9: Livre et Révolution*, eds. Frédéric Barbier, Sabine Juratic, and Dominique Varry (Paris: Aux Amateurs de Livres, 1989), 123–32.
 Les Eclats du rire: La culture des rieurs au XVIIIe siècle (Paris: Calmann-Lévy, 2000).
 'Pamphlets: Libel and Political Mythology', in *Revolution in Print: The Press in France, 1775–1800*, eds. Robert Darnton and Daniel Roche (Berkeley: University of California Press, 1989), 165–176.
 'Robespierre: Monstre-cadavre du discours thermidorien', *Eighteenth-Century Life*, 21.2 (1997), 203–21.
Ballaster, Ros, *Fabulous Orients: Fictions of the East 1662–1785* (Oxford: Oxford University Press, 2005).
 Seductive Forms: Women's Amatory Fiction from 1684–1740 (Oxford: Clarendon Press, 1992).
Bannet, Eve Tavor, 'The Narrator as Invisible Spy', *Journal for Early Modern Cultural Studies* 14.4 (2014), 143–62.
 '"Secret History": Or, Talebearing Inside and Outside the Secretory', *Huntington Library Quarterly* 68.1/2 (2005), 375–96; reprinted in *The Uses of History in Early Modern England*, ed. Paulina Kewes (San Marino: Huntington Library, 2006), 367–88.
Beasley, Faith E., *Revising Memory: Women's Fiction and Memoirs in Seventeenth-Century France* (New Brunswick: Rutgers University Press, 1990).
Beetham, Margaret, *A Magazine of Her Own? Domesticity and Desire in the Women's Magazine, 1800–1914* (London: Routledge, 1996).
Benedict, Barbara M., *Curiosity: A Cultural History of Modern Inquiry* (Chicago: University of Chicago Press, 2001).
 'The Curious Genre: Female Enquiry in Amatory Fiction', *Studies in the Novel* 30.2 (1998), 194–210.
Blackwell, Mark, ed., *The Secret Life of Things: Animals, Objects, and It-Narratives in Eighteenth-Century England* (Lewisburg: Bucknell University Press, 2007), 9–14.

Bowers, Toni, *Force or Fraud: British Seduction Stories and the Problem of Resistance, 1660–1760* (Oxford: Oxford University Press, 2011).
Brooks, Helen E. M., *Actresses, Gender, and the Eighteenth-Century Stage: Playing Women* (Basingstoke and New York: Palgrave Macmillan, 2015).
Bullard, Rebecca, *The Politics of Disclosure, 1674–1725: Secret History Narratives* (London: Pickering & Chatto, 2009).
Burke, Peter, 'The Rise of "Secret History"', in *Changing Perceptions of the Public Sphere*, eds. Christian J. Emden and David Midgley (New York and Oxford: Berghahn Books, 2012).
Bush-Bailey, Gilli, *Treading the Bawds: Actresses and Playwrights on the Late-Stuart Stage* (Manchester: Manchester University Press, 2006).
Carnell, Rachel, 'Eliza Haywood and the Narratological Tropes of Secret History', *Journal for Early Modern Cultural Studies*, 14 (2014), 101–21.
  Partisan Politics, Narrative Realism and the Rise of the British Novel (Basingstoke and New York: Palgrave Macmillan, 2006).
  'Slipping from Secret History to Novel', *Eighteenth-Century Fiction*, 28.1 (2015), 1–24.
Chartier, Roger, *Lectures et lecteurs dans la France d'Ancien Régime* (Paris: Seuil, 1987).
Cole, Lucinda, '"Human-Animal Studies," Introduction, "Animal, All too Animal,"' Special issue, *The Eighteenth-Century: Theory and Interpretation* 52.1 (2011), 1–11.
Conway, Alison, *The Protestant Whore: Courtesan Narrative and Religious Controversy in England, 1680–1750* (Toronto: University of Toronto Press, 2010).
Cornand, Suzanne, 'Ecriture d'une chronique: l'exemple des *Mémoires secrets dits de Bachaumont*', Carole Dornier and Claudine Poulouin (dirs.), *Elseneur; L'Histoire en miettes. Anecdotes et témoignages dans l'écriture de l'histoire (XVIe – XIXe siècle)*, 19 (October 2004), 255–78.
Curtin, Nancy, *The United Irishmen: Popular Politics in Ulster and Dublin, 1791–1798* (Oxford: Oxford University Press, 1994).
Darnton, Robert, *Censors at Work: How States Shaped Literature* (New York: Norton, 2014).
  The Devil in the Holy Water, or the Art of Slander from Louis XIV to Napoleon, (Philadelphia: University of Pennsylvania Press, 2009).
Darnton, Robert and Daniel Roche (eds.), *Revolution in Print: The Press in France, 1775–1800* (Berkeley: University of California Press, 1989).
Davis, James Herbert Jr., *Fénelon* (Boston: Twayne, 1979).
Davis, Lennard J., *Factual Fictions: The Origins of the English Novel* (Philadelphia: University of Pennsylvania Press, 1997).
DeLombard, Jeannine Marie, *Slavery on Trial: Law, Abolitionism, and Print Culture* (Chapel Hill: University of North Carolina Press, 2007).
Denning, Michael, *Mechanic Accents: Dime Novels and Working-Class Culture in America* (New York and London: Verso, 1987).
Dobranski, Stephen B., *Readers and Authorship in Early Modern England* (New York: Cambridge University Press, 2005).

Ferris, Ina, *The Romantic National Tale and the Question of Ireland* (Cambridge: Cambridge University Press, 2002).
Festa, Lynn, 'The Moral Ends of Eighteenth- and Nineteenth-Century Object Narratives', in *Secret Life of Things: Animals, Objects, and It-Narratives in Eighteenth-Century England*, ed. Mark Blackwell (Lewisburg: Bucknell University Press, 2007), 309–28.
   Sentimental Objects of Empire in Eighteenth-Century Britain and France (Baltimore: The Johns Hopkins University Press, 2006).
Fineman, Joel. 'The History of the Anecdote: Fiction and Fiction', in *The New Historicism*, ed. H. Aram Veeser (New York: Routledge, 1989), 49–76.
Flint, Christopher, 'Speaking Objects: The Circulation of Stories in Eighteenth-Century Prose Fiction', in *Secret Life of Things: Animals, Objects, and It-Narratives in Eighteenth-Century England*, ed. Mark Blackwell (Lewisburg: Bucknell University Press, 2007), 162–86.
Fuchs, Barbara, *Romance* (New York: Routledge, 2004).
Gallagher, Noelle, *Historical Literatures: Writing About the Past in England, 1660–1740* (Manchester: Manchester University Press, 2012).
Galperin, William, *The Historical Austen* (Philadelphia: University of Pennsylvania Press, 2005).
Genette, Gerard, *Figures of Literary Discourse*, trans. Alan Sheridan (New York: Columbia University Press, 1982).
Gerrard, Christine, *The Patriot Opposition to Walpole. Politics, Poetry, and National Myth, 1725–1742* (Oxford: Clarendon Press, 1994).
Gilmartin, Kevin, *Print Politics: The Press and Radical Opposition in Early Nineteenth-Century England* (Cambridge: Cambridge University Press, 1996).
Goldgar, Bertrand, *Walpole and the Wits: The Relation of Politics to Literature, 1722–1742* (Lincoln: University of Nebraska Press, 1970).
Gruder, Vivian R., *The Notables and the Nation: The Political Schooling of the French, 1787–1788* (Cambridge: Harvard University Press, 2007).
Hamilton, Paul, *Metaromanticism: Aesthetics, Literature, Theory* (Chicago: University of Chicago Press, 2003).
Harder, Mette, 'Odious and Vile Names: Political Character Assassination and Purging in the French', in *Character Assassination Throughout the Ages*, eds. Martijn Icks and Eric Shiraev (Basingstoke and New York: Palgrave Macmillan, 2014).
Hartman, Saidiya, *Scenes of Subjection: Terror, Slavery, and Self-Making in Nineteenth-Century America* (Oxford: Oxford University Press, 1997).
Heyd, Uriel, *Reading Newspapers: Press and Public in Eighteenth-Century Britain and America* (Oxford: Voltaire Foundation, 2012).
Hoffman, Kathryn, 'Reality and Power in the *Secret Histories*', *Cahiers-du-Dix-septieme siècle: An Interdisciplinary Journal* 1.1 (1987), 149–58.
Holland, Rose, J. 'The Censorship under Napoleon I', *Journal of Comparative Legislation and International Law, New Series*, 18.1 (1918), 58–65.
Hourcade, Philippe, *Entre pic et rétif: Eustache Le Noble (1643–1711)* (Paris: Amateurs de Livres, 1988).

Hunt, Lynn (ed.), *The Invention of Pornography: Obscenity and the Origins of Modernity, 1500–1800* (New York: Zone Books, 1993), 301–40.
Hyland, Paul, 'Richard Steele: Scandal and Sedition', in *Writing and Censorship in Britain*, ed. Neil Sammells (London: Routledge, 1992).
Jackson, Rosemary, *Fantasy: The Literature of Subversion* (London: Methuen, 1981).
Keating, Erin, 'In the Bedroom of the King: Affective Politics in the Restoration Secret History', *Journal for Early Modern Cultural Studies*, 15.1 (2015), 58–82.
Kintgen, Eugene, *Reading in Tudor England* (Pittsburgh: University of Pittsburgh Press, 1996).
Klancher, Jon, 'Godwin and the Genre Reformers: On Necessity and Contingency in Romantic Narrative Theory', in *Romanticism, History, and the Possibilities of Genre: Re-forming Literature 1789–1837*, eds. Tilottama Rajan and Julia M. Wright (Cambridge: Cambridge University Press, 1998), 21–38.
Knights, Mark, *Representation and Misrepresentation in Later Stuart Britain: Partisanship and Political Culture* (Oxford: Oxford University Press, 2005).
Knox, Norman, *The Word Irony and its Context, 1500–1755* (Durham: Duke University Press, 1961).
Kramnick, Jonathan, *Actions and Objects from Hobbes to Richardson* (Stanford: Stanford University Press, 2010).
Laerke, Moegens (ed.), *The Use of Censorship in the Enlightenment* (Leiden: Brill, 2009).
Leterrier, Sophie-Anne, 'Histoire en revolution', *Annales historiques de la Révolution française* 320 (2000), 65–75.
Loar, Christopher, *Political Magic: British Fictions of Savagery and Sovereignty, 1650–1750* (New York: Fordham University Press, 2014).
Looby, Christopher, 'Lippard in Part(s): Seriality and Secrecy in the Quaker City', *Nineteenth-Century Literature*, 79.1 (June 2015), 1–35.
London, April, *The Cambridge Introduction to the Eighteenth-Century Novel* (Cambridge: Cambridge University Press, 2012).
  Literary History Writing, 1770–1820 (Basingstoke and New York: Palgrave Macmillan, 2010).
Loveman, Kate, *Reading Fictions, 1660–1740: Deception in English Literary and Political Culture* (Aldershot: Ashgate, 2008).
Lund, Roger, D., *Ridicule, Religion and the Politics of Wit in Augustan England* (Farnham: Ashgate, 2012).
Lynch, Deidre Shauna, *The Economy of Character: Novels, Market Culture, and the Business of Inner Meaning* (Chicago: University of Chicago Press, 2007).
Lyons, John D., 'La Présence d'esprit et l'Histoire Secrète: Une Lecture de la Comtesse de Tende', *XVIIe Siècle* 45.181 (1993), 717–32.
Marshall, Alan, *Intelligence and Espionage in the Reign of Charles II, 1660–1685* (Cambridge: Cambridge University Press, 1994).
Mayer, Robert, *History and the Early English Novel: Matters of Fact from Bacon to Defoe* (Cambridge: Cambridge University Press, 1997).
McBride, Dwight, *Impossible Witnesses: Truth, Abolitionism, and Slave Testimony* (New York: New York University Press, 2001).

McElligott, Jason, *Royalism, Print and Censorship in Revolutionary England* (Woodbridge: Boydell Press, 2007).
McGill, Meredith L., *American Literature and the Culture of Reprinting, 1834–1853* (Philadelphia: University of Pennsylvania Press, 2003).
McKeon, Michael, *The Origins of the English Novel, 1660–1740* (Baltimore: The Johns Hopkins University Press, 1987).
  '*Paradise Lost* in the Long Restoration, 1660–1742: The Parody of Form', in *Milton in the Long Restoration*, eds. Blair Hoxby and Ann Baynes Coiro (Oxford: Oxford University Press, 2016), 503–30.
  The Secret History of Domesticity: Public, Private, and the Division of Knowledge (Baltimore: The Johns Hopkins University Press, 2005).
Mee, Jon, *Conversable Worlds: Literature, Contention, and Community, 1762 to 1830* (Oxford: Oxford University Press, 2011).
Mulvihill, James, 'Edgeworth's *Castle Rackrent* as Secret History', *Papers on Language and Literature* 49.4 (2013), 339–63.
Nussbaum, Felicity, *Rival Queens: Actresses, Performance, and the Eighteenth-Century British Theatre* (Philadelphia: University of Pennsylvania Press, 2010).
Parsons, Nicola, 'The Miscellaneous *New Atalantis*', in *New Perspectives on Delariver Manley*, eds. Aleksondra Hultquist and Elizabeth Matthew (New York: Routledge, 2017), 201–13.
  Reading Gossip in Early Eighteenth-Century England (Basingstoke and New York: Palgrave Macmillan, 2009).
Patterson, Annabel, *Censorship and Interpretation* (Madison: University of Wisconsin Press, 1984).
  Early Modern Liberalism (Cambridge: Cambridge University Press, 1997).
  Reading Between the Lines (Madison: University of Wisconsin Press, 1993).
Popkin, Jeremy, 'Pamphlet Journalism at the End of the Old Regime', *Eighteenth-Century Studies* 22.3 (1989), 351–67.
Potter, Lois, *Secret Rites and Secret Writing: Royalist Literature, 1641–1660* (Cambridge: Cambridge University Press, 1989).
Powell, Manushag N., *Performing Authorship in Eighteenth-Century Periodicals* (Lewisburg: Bucknell University Press, 2012).
Rabb, Melinda Alliker, *Satire and Secrecy in English Literature from 1650 to 1750* (Basingstoke and New York: Palgrave Macmillan, 2007).
Rivero, Albert J., '"Hieroglifick'd" History in Aphra Behn's *Love-Letters between a Nobleman and his Sister*', *Studies in the Novel* 30.2 (1998), 126–38.
Roach, Joseph, *It* (Ann Arbor: University of Michigan Press, 2007).
Robert, Raymonde, *Le conte de fées littéraire en France de la fin du XVIIe à la fin du XVIIIe siècle* (Paris: Honoré Champion, 2002).
Robertson, Randy, *Censorship and Conflict in Seventeenth-Century England* (University Park: Pennsylvania State University Press, 2009).
Roper, Alan, 'Absalom's Issue: Parallel Poems in the Restoration', *Studies in Philology* 99.3 (2002), 268–94.
  'Who's Who in *Absalom and Achitophel*?', *Huntington Library Quarterly* 63.1 (2000), 98–138.

Rose, Margaret A., *Parody: Ancient, Modern, and Post-Modern* (Cambridge: Cambridge University Press, 1993).
Shklovsky, Victor, 'Sterne's *Tristram Shandy*: Stylistic Commentary', in *Russian Formalist Criticism: Four Essays*, eds. Lee T. Lemon and Marion J. Reis (Lincoln, 1965), 25–57.
  Theory of Prose, trans. Benjamin Sher (Chicago: University of Chicago Press, 1990).
Siskin, Clifford, *The Work of Writing: Literature and Social Change in Britain, 1700–1830* (Baltimore: The Johns Hopkins University Press, 1998).
Smith, Chloe Wigston, *Women, Work, and Clothes in the Eighteenth-Century Novel* (Cambridge: Cambridge University Press, 2013).
Smith, Geoffrey, *Royalist Agents, Conspirators, and Spies: Their Role in the British Civil Wars, 1640–1660* (Farnham: Ashgate, 2011).
Smith, Nigel (ed.), *Literature and Censorship* (Cambridge: D. S. Brewer, 1993).
Snyder, John R., *Dissimulation and the Culture of Secrecy in early Modern Europe* (Berkeley: University of California Press, 2009).
  'From Infamy to Intimacy: Anne Bracegirdle's Mad Songs', *Restoration*, 35 (2011), 1–20.
Solomon, Diana, *Prologues and Epilogues of the Restoration Theater: Gender and Comedy, Performance and Print* (Newark: University of Delaware Press, 2013).
Stedman, Allison, 'Marie-Catherine Le Jumel de Barneville, Comtesse d'Aulnoy', in *Dictionary of Literary Biography: Seventeenth-Century French Literature*, ed. Françoise Jaoüen (Detroit: Thompson Gale, 2003).
  Rococo Fiction in France, 1600–1715: Seditious Frivolity (Lewisburg: Bucknell University Press, 2012).
Straub, Kristina, *Sexual Suspects: Eighteenth-Century Players and Sexual Ideology* (Princeton: Princeton University Press, 1992).
Streeby, Shelley, *American Sensations: Class, Empire, and the Production of Popular Culture* (Berkeley: University of California Press, 2002).
Swenson, Rivka, *Essential Scots and the Idea of Unionism, 1603–1832* (Lewisburg: Bucknell University Press, 2016).
  'History', in *The Cambridge Companion to Women's Writing in Britain, 1660–1789*, ed. Catherine Ingrassia (Cambridge: Cambridge University Press, 2015), 135–46.
  'Optics, Gender, and the Eighteenth-Century Gaze: Looking at Eliza Haywood's *Anti-Pamela*', *The Eighteenth-Century: Theory and Interpretation* 51.1–2 (2010), 27–43.
  'The Poet as Man of Feeling,' in *The Oxford Handbook of British Poetry, 1660–1800*, ed. Jack Lynch (Oxford: Oxford University Press, 2016), 195–209.
Thomas, Chantal, 'The Heroine of the Crime: Marie-Antoinette in Pamphlets', in *Marie Antoinette: Writings on the Body of a Queen*, ed. & trans. Dena Goodman (New York: Routledge, 2003).
Thompson, Helen, *Fictional Matter: Empiricism, Corpuscles, and the Novel* (Philadelphia: University of Pennsylvania Press, 2016).
Thuente, Mary Helen, '"The Belfast Laugh": The Context and Significance of United Irish Satires', in *Revolution, Counter-Revolution, and Union: Ireland*

in the 1790s, ed. Jim Smyth (Cambridge: Cambridge University Press, 2000).

The Harp Re-strung: The United Irishmen and the Rise of Irish Literary Nationalism (Syracuse: Syracuse University Press, 1994).

Urstad, Tone Sundt, *Sir Robert Walpole's Poets: The Use of Literature as Pro-Government Propaganda, 1721–1742* (Newark: University of Delaware Press, 1999).

Wall, Cynthia, *The Prose of Things: Transformations of Description in the Eighteenth Century* (Chicago: University of Chicago Press, 2006).

Warner, William, *Licensing Entertainment: The Elevation of Novel Reading in Britain, 1684–1750* (Berkeley: University of California Press, 1998).

Weber, Harold, *Paper Bullets: Print and Kingship under Charles II* (Lexington: The University Press of Kentucky, 1996).

Weil, Rachel, *A Plague of Informers: Conspiracy and Political Trust in William III's England* (New Haven: Yale University Press, 2013).

Wiseman, Susan, *Conspiracy and Virtue: Women, Writing, and Politics in Seventeenth-Century England* (Oxford: Oxford University Press, 2006).

Woertendyke, Gretchen, 'Romance to Novel: A Secret History', *Narrative* 17.3 (October 2009), 255–73.

'Trials and Confessions of Fugitive Slave Narratives', in *Journeys of the Slave Narrative in the Early Americas*, eds. Nicole Aljoe and Ian Finesth (Charlottesville: University of Virginia Press, 2014), 47–73.

Woolf, D. W., *The Idea of History in Early Stuart England* (Toronto: University of Toronto Press, 1990).

Reading History in Early Modern England (Cambridge: Cambridge University Press, 2000).

Zboray, Ronald J., *A Fictive People: Antebellum Economic Development and the American Reading Public* (Oxford: Oxford University Press, 1993).

Žižek, Slavoj, 'Fantasy as a Political Category: A Lacanian Approach', *Journal for the Psychoanalysis of Culture and Society* 1.2 (Fall 1996), 77–85.

For they know not what they do: Enjoyment as a Political Factor, 2nd edn (New York and London: Verso, 1991).

Zook, Melinda, 'Contextualizing Aphra Behn: Plays, Politics, and Party, 1679–1689', in *Women Writers and the Early Modern British Political Tradition*, ed. Hilda L. Smith (Cambridge: Cambridge University Press, 1998).

Radical Whig and Conspiratorial Politics in Late Stuart England (University Park: Pennsylvania State University Press, 1999).

'Turncoats and Double Agents in Restoration and Revolutionary England': The Case of Robert Ferguson, the Plotter', *Eighteenth-Century Studies* 42.3 (Spring, 2009), 363–78.

Zwicker, Steven N., *Lines of Authority: Politics and English Literary Culture, 1649–1689* (Ithaca: Cornell University Press, 1993).

Index

absolutism, 207, 208, 211, *See also* arbitrary government
Académie Française, 208, 209
Acts of Union (1707), 92
Adams, John, 243
Adams, Samuel, 238
Adams, William, 141
Adcock, Rachel, 75
Addison, Joseph and Richard Steele
    Spectator, The, 94, 147, 148
    Tatler, The, 147, 152
Aesop, 161
Alemanni, Nicolò, 1, 3
Alien and Sedition Acts (1798), 243
allegory, 18, 27, 28, 47, 60–73, 147, 151, 242, *See also roman à clef*
Almon, John, 165
Amyot, Jacques, 37
Anderson, Benedict, 148
Andros, Edmund, 235
Anne, Queen, 93, 106, 108, 165
Anthony, David, 247
Anti-Jacobin Review, The, 191, 193
Antonina, wife of General Belisarius, 3
Aravamudan, Srinivas, 6, 90, 190
arbitrary government, 4, 5, 30, 68, 83, 87, 103, 111, 134, 135, 137, 166, 168, 229, 238, 240, 243, *See also* absolutism
Aretino, Pietro, 155
Atterbury, Francis, 62
Aubrey, John, 257, 258
Austen, Jane, 190, 192, 198
    Emma, 197, 198
    Mansfield Park, 175, 182–86, 198
automata, 122

Bacon, Francis, 33, 34, 162, 262
Baecque, Antoine de, 218
Baker, Richard, 39
Bakhtin, Mikhail, 105, 106
Ballaster, Ros, 10, 11, 90, 91, 151

Bampfield, Joseph, 89, 91–92, 95
Bannet, Eve Tavor, 7, 10, 88, 148, 188, 256
Barry, Elizabeth, 52
Beasley, Faith E., 205, 206, 207
Bécu, Jeanne, comtesse du Barry, 224
Beers, Isaac, 231
Behn, Aphra, 2, 17, 48
    Emperor of the Moon, 82
    Love-letters between a Nobleman and his Sister, 5, 9, 18–19, 23, 24, 26, 27, 28, 74–85
Belisarius, General, 3, 237, 238
Benedict, Barbara, 94, 151
Bennett, James Gordon, 246, 247
Berkeley, Henrietta, 74
Bernstein, Carl, 259
Bethel, Slingsby, 66
Betterton, Thomas, 52
Birmingham, Alabama, 261
Black Box affair, the, 68, 83
Blackwell, Mark, 117
Bonaparte, Laetitia, 225
Bonaparte, Napoleon, 223, 224, 225
Bonaparte, Pauline, 243
Boston, Mass., 231, 238, 239, 244
Boswell, James, 175
Bowers, Toni, 76, 79, 166
Bowyer, William, 165, 166
Boyer, Abel, 37
Bracegirdle, Anne, 46, 50, 52, 53, 54, 55, 56
Brady, Nicholas, 56
Braithwaite, Richard, 37
Brémond, Sébastien, 49
Brissot, Jacques Pierre, 222
British Journal, The, 162
Brooke, Henry, 138
Brossin de Méré, Elisabeth, 224
Brown, Charles Brockden, 244, 245, 249, 252
Browne, Joseph. *See Secret History of Queen Zarah and the Zarazians, The*
Budgell, Eustace, 230
Bugg, John, 188

277

Bullard, Rebecca, 41, 47, 52, 53, 68, 75, 81, 84, 87, 95, 117, 134, 135, 166, 239
Bulwer Lytton, Edward, 257
Burke, Edmund, 194
Burke, Peter, 7, 205, 208, 212
Burnet, Gilbert, 93
Burney, Fanny, 170
Burr, Aaron, 243, 244
Butler, James, 2nd Duke of Ormond, 108
Byrd, William, 229, 233–37

Cabala, Mysteries of State, 4
Calvert, George, First Baron Baltimore, 235
Camden, William, 37
Campbell, Robert, 231
Campbell, Samuel, 231
Care, Henry, 39
Caritat, Louis Alexis Hocquet de, 231
Carnell, Rachel, 11, 47, 84, 88, 89, 94, 134, 190, 197
Carson, James P., 125
Caryll, John, 50
Catherine of Braganza, 65, 66
Cavendish, William, First Duke of Newcastle, 48
Chambers, Ephraim, 148, 176
Charles I, 91, 235
Charles II, 4, 6, 41, 46, 48, 49, 51, 52, 60, 65, 92, 106, 107, 209, 231, 234, 235
Charles the Bold, Duke of Burgundy, 210
Charleston, South Carolina, 251
Charlotte, Princess, of Mecklenburg-Strelitz, 139
Chartier, Roger, 218
Chassebœuf, Constantin François de, comte de Volney, 218
Churchill, John, First Duke of Marlborough, 106
Churchill, Sarah, Duchess of Marlborough, 108
Cicero, 36
Cleeve, John, 243
Clinton, Bill, 256, 260, 261
Cobbett, William, 246
Cockburn, John, 38
Colbert, Jean-Baptiste, 206, 207, 208
College, Stephen, 60
Condon, Thomas, 80
Condorcet, Nicholas de, 218
Cooper, Anthony Ashley, First Earl of Shaftesbury, 48, 60, 62, 67, 69, 72, 78, 107
Cooper, Anthony Ashley, Third Earl of Shaftesbury, 160–64, 166
Coventry, Francis, 127
Coventry, William, 48, 49

Craftsman, The, 162
Cromwell, Oliver, 66, 91, 235
Curll, Edmund, 107

D'Urfey, Thomas, 46
D'Israeli, Isaac, 190, 194, 195, 256
Danchin, Pierre, 52
Daniel, Samuel, 37
Danvers, Mass., 244
Darnton, Robert, 160, 216, 221, 222
Day, Benjamin, 246
Defoe, Daniel, 2, 105, 149, 162, 165
   The *Review*, 148–51
Democritus, 117
Douglass, Frederick, 251, 252
Dover, 49, 51, 52, 108, 258
Downes, John, 51
Drury Lane (Theatre Royal), 52, 123, 124, 127, 139
Dryden, John, 17, 26, 48, 104, 164
   Absalom and Achitophel, 18, 60–72, 106
   All for Love, 23
   Conquest of Granada, The, 51
Dugdale, William, 36
Duke of York. *See* James II
Duncan, Ian, 195
Duncombe, John, 139
Dunton, John, 89, 94, 152, 153, 156
Dutch West India Company, The, 235

Edinburgh, 124
Edinburgh Review, The, 242
Edwards, Jonathan, 244
Elias, Norbert, 216
Elizabeth I, 37, 234, 257
Emerson, Ralph Waldo, 242
epic, 17–23, 26, 27, 43, 103, 107, 257
Epicurus, 117
Eugene, Prince of Savoy, 108
Evans-Pritchard, Ambrose, 261
Eveling, Stanley, 62
Exclusion Crisis, 19, 34, 48, 60, 61

Fénelon, François de Salignac, 135, 138, 140, 142
Fenwick, Eliza, 117, 122–29
Ferguson, Robert, 78, 83
Fermor, Arabella, 107
Ferris, Ina, 195
Festa, Lynn, 118
Fieux, Charles de, chevalier de Mouhy, 212
Filmer, Robert, 110
Fineman, Joel, 175
Finnerty, Peter, 192

Flint, Christopher, 118
Force, Charlotte-Rose Caumont de la, 209, 210, 211
Foster, Hannah, 244, 245, 247, 252
France, 2, 4, 7, 9, 11, 149, 150, 165, 194, *See also* Revolution, French
Franklin, Benjamin, 238
Reynolds, Frederick, 123, 127
Frederick, Prince of Wales, 93, 136, 137, 139
Freemasonry, 246
Fronde, The, 206
Fuchs, Barbara, 95
Fugitive Statesman, The, 61

Gallagher, Catherine, 60
Garrick, David, 128, 139
Garth, Samuel, 106
Gavin, Antonio, 109
Genette, Gérard, 35
George I, 165
George II, 92, 93, 136, 137, 138, 195
George III, 136, 139, 141, 191
Gerrard, Christine, 137
Gibbon, Edward, 41
Gifford, John, 191
Glorious Revolution. *See* Revolution of 1688–89
Gomez, Madeleine-Angélique Poisson de, 212
Gray, Thomas, 251
Grey, Charles, Second Earl Grey, 189
Grey, Ford, Earl of Tankerville, 19, 67, 74
Gruder, Vivian R., 212
Gwyn, Nell, 50, 51, 52, 67

Habermas, Jürgen, 148
Haiti. *See* Revolution, Haitian
Hamilton, Anthony, 106
Hamilton, Paul, 176
Hampden, John, 235
Hanoverian dynasty, 92, 93, 165
Hardy, Thomas, 191
Harley, Robert, First Earl of Oxford, 149, 165
Harris, Jennifer, 245, 247
Harris's List of Covent Garden Ladies, 153–56
Hawkesworth, John, 136, 139, 140
Hayward, John, 34
Haywood, Eliza, 2, 75, 84, 95, 231
  Adventures of Eovaai, 95, 136, 138–39
  Female Spectator, The, 169
  Invisible Spy, The, 88, 94, 95
  Secret History of the Present Intrigues of the Court of Caramania, 106
Hazlitt, William, 179, 189
Hearne, Thomas, 42
Heberton, Mahlon, 248

Henrietta Maria, Queen, 41
Henriette Anne, Princess, Duchess of Orléans, 41
heroic poetry. *See* epic
Hill, Richard, 46, 54
Hobbes, Thomas, 34, 36, 169
Holan, Angie Drobnic, 261
Holmes, George Frederick, 250
Homaïs, ou La Reine de Tunis, 49
Hooke, Nathaniel, 92
Hourcade, Philippe, 211
Howard, Robert, 47, 51
Hudson's Bay Company, The, 231, 232
Hume, Robert D., 47, 48
Hunt, Lynn, 220
Hutchinson, Thomas, 238, 239
Hyland, Paul, 165

Jacob, Margaret, 191
Jacobinism, 170, 221, 223, 246
Jacobitism, 89, 92, 93, 108, 165, 166, 195, 261
Jacobs, Harriet, 251, 252
James II, 4, 6, 12n. 14, 12n. 2, 13n. 18, 13n. 26, 45n. 38, 45n. 42, 45n. 43, 67, 69, 82, 83, 93, 209, 234, 241n. 14, 264n. 23
Jermyn, Henry, 41
Jersey City, N.J., 261
Jewett, Helen, 246, 247, 248
Johnson, Samuel, 61, 176
  The *Fountain*, 143
  Rasselas, 136
Johnstone, Charles, 117, 118–22
Jones, David, 5, 6, 230
Jourdan, Annie, 221
Juilly, Nicholas Beaudot de, 209
Justinian, Emperor, 1, 3, 23, 41, 103, 106, 113, 118, 147, 151

Keating, Erin, 9, 11, 81
Kelly, Michael, 124
Kelly, Stuart, 257, 258
Ker, John, 88, 89, 92, 93, 95
Kéroualle, Louise Renée de Penancoët de, Duchess of Portsmouth, 49, 67, 68, 110, 112, 209
keys. *See* roman à clef
King, Rachel Scarborough, 152
Kings Cabinet Opened, The, 4
Klancher, Jon, 190
Knox, Norman, 161
Kramnick, Jonathan, 117
Kynaston, Edward, 48

Lacan, Jacques, 134
Le Clerc, Jean, 38

le Jumel de Barneville, Marie-Catherine, comtesse d'Aulnoy, 211
Le Moyne, Pierre, 37, 43
Le Noble, Eustache, 209, 211
Lee, Nathaniel, 48
Lee, Sophia, 89, 90
Lee, Yoon Sun, 195
Leibniz, Gottfried Wilhelm, 92
Lennox, Charlotte, 111–14
Lepore, Jill, 258
Lincoln's Inn Fields, 50, 52
Linton, Marisa, 221
Lippard, George, 247–50, 252
Loar, Christopher, 95
Locke, John, 117, 169
Lockhart, George, 212
London, 231, 234, 238
London Corresponding Society, The, 188, 191, 192
London, April, 195, 244
Long, Hugh P., 257
Looby, Christopher, 248, 249
Louis XIV, 4, 91, 135, 178, 206, 207, 208, 210, 211, 212
Louis XVI, 224
Louis-Philippe II, Duke of Orléans, 222
Louverture, Toussaint, 223, 224
Love, Harold, 48
Loveman, Kate, 11, 49, 84
Lowther, John, Viscount Lonsdale, 38
Lucretius, 117
Luttrell, Narcissus, 69
Lynch, Deidre, 123

Macky, John, 93, 94
Mailly, Jean de, 209
Mallet, David, 138
Mancini, Hortense, Duchess of Mazarin, 67
Manley, Delarivier, 2, 75, 84, 105, 106, 107, 108, 111, 112, 113, 161, 162, 256, 259, 262
  New Atalantis, The, 104, 105, 108, 109, 110, 111, 113, 148, 151, 256, 262
  Secret History of Queen Zarah and the Zarazians, The. See *Secret History of Queen Zarah and the Zarazians, The*
Manuel, Pierre, 217, 222
Marana, Giovanni Paolo, 89, 90, 91
Marat, Jean-Paul, 219
Marie-Antoinette, 219, 220
Marlborough, Duke and Duchess of, *See* Churchill
Marmontel, Jean-François, 237, 238
Marston, William Moulton, 258
Marteau, Pierre, 209
Marvell, Andrew, 258

Mary II, 4
Maryland, 235
Masham, Abigail, 106, 108
Massachusetts, 238, 244
Mauger, Leonor de, 1, 205
Mayer, Robert, 93
Mazzeo, Tilar, 259
McKeon, Michael, 7, 8, 10, 33, 47, 49, 68, 160, 198, 245
Mercer, Singleton, 248
Mericourt, Théroigne de, 219
Milton, John, 103, 110, 164
  Paradise Lost, 17–31
Missy, Jean Rousset de, 212
Mohun, Charles, 4th Baron Mohun, 46
Montagu, Charles, Earl of Halifax, 67
Moseley, Edward, 236
Mountfort, William, 46, 54
Mulvihill, James, 195

Nalson, John, 42
Ness, Christopher, 64, 65, 106
New Amsterdam, 235
New Jersey, 235, 261
New York, 230, 246, 247, 248, 256, 260, 261
New, Melvyn, 176
Newton, Isaac, 117
Nichols, John, 165
Nicolson, William, 38
Nokes, James, 51
North Carolina, 229, 234, 236
North, Thomas, 37
Nougaret, J. B., 217
Nussbaum, Felicity, 46, 50

Obama, Barack, 225
Oldmixon, John, 39, 41
Onslow, Arthur, 166
Otway, Thomas, 48
Ovid, 107

Palmer, Barbara, Countess of Castlemaine and Duchess of Cleveland, 41, 49, 67, 68
Panic of 1837, The, 247
Parker, Thomas, 165
Parsons, Nicola, 9, 11
Pastorello, Thierry, 219
Patterson, Annabel, 164
Penn, William, 235, 236
Pennsylvania, 235, 239
Pepys, Samuel, 51
Pétion, Jérôme, 222
Philadelphia, 231, 237, 247, 248
Philidor, Paul, 122
Pierrepont, Mary, 256

Piozzi, Hester Thrale, 179
Pitt, William, 164, 188, 189, 191
Player's Tragedy, The, 46, 53, 54, 55, 56
du Plessis, Armand Jean, Cardinal-Duke of Richelieu, 89
Plutarch, 4, 37, 62
Polignac, Jules de, 219
Polybius, 34
Pope, Alexander, 108, 256, *See also* Scriblerus Club, The
   Dunciad, The, 106
   'Epistle to Burlington', 107
   Key to the Lock, A, 107, 108
   Master Key to Popery, A, 108–10
   Rape of the Lock, The, 107, 256
Popish Plot, The, 24, 39, 65, 68, 83
Pratt, Samuel Jackson, 168
Préchac, Jean de, 208
Pretender, The. *See* Stuart, James Francis Edward
Procopius, 1–5, 7–9, 103, 113–4, 118–19, 147–9, 175, 205, 259
Prosser, Gabriel, 251
Prynne, William, 162, 164
Pym, John, 235

Quintilian, 162

Rabb, Melinda Alliker, 88
Ralegh, Walter, 35, 234
Ralph, James, 136, 137, 140
Rapin, René, 38, 43
Rawdon-Hastings, Francis, Earl of Moira, 190
Redford, Robert, 259
Revolution of 1688-89, 4, 34, 52, 53, 62, 69, 83, 89, 103, 166, 262
Revolution, American, 230, 237, 239
Revolution, French, 11, 89, 189, 194, 212, 213, 216–25, 231, 243, 256
Revlution, Haitian, 251
Reynolds, Frederick, 123, 127
Richardson, Samuel, 168, 176, 179
Richelieu, Cardinal of, *See* Plessis
Ridley, Elizabeth, 141
Ridley, Gloseter, 141
Ridley, James, 136, 140, 141
Ridpath, George, 165
Rivero, Albert J., 81, 82, 83, 84
Roach, Joseph, 46
Robertson, Randy, 165
Robespierre, Maximilien, 223, 224
Robinson, Richard P., 246, 247
Robson, Joseph, 231, 232
roman à clef, 3, 5, 84, 88, 112, 217, 247–9, *See also* allegory
Roman Catholicism, 68, 108, 109, 110, 166

romance, 2, 5, 7, 8, 11, 17, 18, 19, 20, 23, 24, 26, 27, 43, 47, 77, 81, 84, 94, 95, 111, 112, 136, 139, 154, 155, 156, 160, 161, 166, 168, 195, 224, 242, 256
Romulus and Hersilia, or, the Sabine War, 48
Roper, Alan, 60, 61, 66, 67
Rose, Margaret, 103
Rushworth, John, 38, 42
Rye House Plot, 74, 83, 92

Sacheverell, Henry, 108
Saint-Hyacinthe, Thémiseul de, 136, 137
Salem, Mass., 231
Salmon, Thomas, 43
Scott, Helenus, 121
Scott, James, 1st Duke of Monmouth, 18, 19, 23, 24, 26, 48, 51, 60, 61, 66, 67, 68, 69, 74, 76, 77, 81, 82, 83, 106, 107, 236
Scott, Walter, 189, 190, 195–97
Scriblerus Club, The, 105
Scudéry, Madeleine de, 111
Scurr, Ruth, 257, 258
Secret History of Queen Zarah and the Zarazians, The, 5
Sedley, Charles, 48
Sérieys, Antoine, 217
Settle, Elkanah, 65, 67
Shadwell, Thomas
   The Lancashire Witches, 48
   The Sullen Lovers, 51
Shafesbury, Earls of, *See* Cooper
Shakespeare, William, 107
   Anthony and Cleopatra, 23
Sheridan, Richard Brinsley, 124
Short, Michael, 259
Sidney, Algernon, 162
Siskin, Clifford, 197, 198
Skelton, Philip, 160
Slingsby, Mary, 48
Smith, Chloe Wigston, 118
Smith, Sydney, 242
Smollett, Tobias, 121
Society of United Irishmen, 190–93, 246
Socrates, 161
Solomon, Diana, 46, 53
Somers, John, Baron, 6, 104
Sophia, Electress of Hanover, 92, 93
Spectator, The. *See* Addison, Joseph and Richard Steele
Spence, Ferrand, 6
Spence, Joseph, 141
Spencer, Charles, 3rd Earl of Sunderland, 256
St John, Henry, Viscount Bolingbroke, 164, *See also Craftsman*, The
Stanley, Eliza, 136, 137

Staves, Susan, 48
Steele, Richard, 165, *See also* Addison, Joseph and Richard Steele
Steen, Francis F., 76
Stephanopoulos, George, 261
Sterne, Laurence, 174, 175–82, 186
Stowe, Harriet Beecher, 249, 250
Straub, Kristina, 56
Stuart, James Francis Edward, 92, 165
Stuart, John, 3rd Earl of Bute, 139, 140
Suetonius, 4, 234
Swift, Jonathan, 105, 108, 110, 111, 165, *See also* Scriblerus Club, The
  Gulliver's Travels, 105, 106
  Tale of a Tub, A, 106, 107, 165

Tacitus, 34
Tartt, Donna, 258
Tate, Nahum, 47
Tatler, The. *See* Addison, Joseph and Richard Steele
Tea-Table, The, 147
Theodora, Empress, 3, 23, 119, 205
Thomas, Chantal, 219
Thomas, Isaiah, 230
Thompson, Helen, 117
Thompson, John R., 250
Thucydides, 34
Tory party, 7, 75, 78, 79, 80, 84, 104, 105, 107, 108, 140, 165, 166, 261, 262
Trump, Donald J., 261
Trumpener, Katie, 195
Turner, Nat, 251
Tyrrell, James, 39

United Company, The, 50, 52
United States of America, 2, 9, 11, 229–40, *See also* Revolution, American

Varillas, Antoine, 1, 4, 6, 209, 210
Vesey, Denmark, 251
Villiers, Abbé Pierre de, 209, 210
Villiers, George, 2nd Duke of Buckingham, 47, 48, 49, 64, 65, 69
Virgil, 107
Virginia, 229, 234, 235, 237, 251

Waco, Texas, 261
Walpole, Robert, 136, 137, 138, 230
Walters, Lucy. *See* Black Box Affair, The
Wandering Whore, The, 155
Ward, Edward, 87, 91, 94, 147
Warner, William B., 76
Warren, Robert Penn, 257
Waterman, Bryan, 245, 247
Wentworth, Henrietta, 24, 81
Whig party, 4, 7, 19, 53, 66, 67, 68, 69, 74, 75, 77, 78, 79, 80, 81, 82, 83, 84, 90, 103, 104, 108, 110, 148, 165, 166, 176, 261, 262
Whitman, Elizabeth, 244, 245, 247, 248
Whitman, Walt, 242
William III, 4, 8, 93, 166, 181
William, Prince, Duke of Cumberland, 137
Williams, Anna, 143
Winston, Michael, 218
Wither, George, 169
Woodward, Bob, 259
Worcester, Mass., 231
Wordsworth, William, 189
Wortley Montagu, Mary. *See* Pierrepont

Yearsley, Ann, 231, 240

Zagorin, Perez, 162
Žižek, Slavoj, 134, 135, 143
Zook, Melinda, 75, 79, 83